'page

rich
dense

CONVERSABLE WORLDS

CONVERSABLE WORLDS

Literature, Contention, and Community 1762 to 1830

JON MEE

OXFORD
UNIVERSITY PRESS

OXFORD
UNIVERSITY PRESS

Great Clarendon Street, Oxford ox2 6DP

Oxford University Press is a department of the University of Oxford.
It furthers the University's objective of excellence in research, scholarship,
and education by publishing worldwide in

Oxford New York

Auckland Cape Town Dar es Salaam Hong Kong Karachi
Kuala Lumpur Madrid Melbourne Mexico City Nairobi
New Delhi Shanghai Taipei Toronto

With offices in

Argentina Austria Brazil Chile Czech Republic France Greece
Guatemala Hungary Italy Japan Poland Portugal Singapore
South Korea Switzerland Thailand Turkey Ukraine Vietnam

Oxford is a registered trade mark of Oxford University Press
in the UK and in certain other countries

Published in the United States
by Oxford University Press Inc., New York

British Library Cataloguing in Publication Data
Data available

Library of Congress Cataloging in Publication Data
Data available

Typeset by SPI Publisher Services, Pondicherry, India
Printed in Great Britain
on acid-free paper by
MPG Books Group, Bodmin and King's Lynn

ISBN 978–0–19–959174–9

1 3 5 7 9 10 8 6 4 2

for Jane 'sweet converse'

Acknowledgements

Like every other book, this one is the product of conversations, including many that took place before it was even conceived of as a project. The award of a Philip J. Leverhulme Major Research Fellowship guaranteed freedom to talk and think once the project had begun, so I will begin by acknowledging the generosity of the Leverhulme Trust. The Master and Fellows of University College, Oxford, and the English Faculty of the University of Oxford allowed me to take up the award in the first place. After I moved to the Department of English and Comparative Literatures at the University of Warwick, my colleagues there patiently put up with my absence. I thank my colleagues at all three institutions.

The conversations that fed into this book took place across three continents. Although I had left the Australian National University long before I began writing it, conversations there with Dipesh Chakrabarty, Ranajit Guha, Iain McCalman, and Gillian Russell played a part in shaping many of the key ideas. I was lucky enough to return to the Humanities Research Centre at the ANU for three months at the end of 2009 to finish my first draft. I am extremely grateful to the Director, Debjani Ganguly, for granting me the fellowship, and to Leena Messina for endless amounts of help sweetened with great good humour. Alex Cook, Ned Curthoys, Ian Higgins, Kate Fullagar, Iain McCalman, Kate Mitchell, and Gino Moliterno made sure that conviviality and ideas were constantly flowing. Gillian was great support and inspiration on this trip as always. Thanks also to Ben and Tom. Clara Tuite has guided me with Austen more than once. I also thank Susan Conley and Deirdre Coleman in Melbourne. John and Mary-Ann Hughes have made Sydney a second home. 'Barzura' and 'Missing Bean' are neck and neck as my favourite coffee shops in the world.

I benefited greatly from two fellowships in North America: the Schaffner Visiting Professorship at the University of Chicago and a visiting scholarship at the Yale Centre for British Art. Jim Chandler was a generous host and wonderfully encouraging in Chicago. I also thank Bill Brown and Leela Gandhi. The graduate class I taught there helped flesh out many of the basic ideas in this book: I thank Anahid Nersessian, John Havard, Darrel Chia, and Daniel Harris for their contributions. I also thank the Director, Amy Meyers, for the award of the fellowship at the Yale Center for British Art and Cassandra Albinson, Lisa Ford, Matthew Hargraves, and Maria Singer for their help and advice. I'm also grateful to the Center for providing so many of the illustrations for this book. While they were at the Center, Stacey Sloboda and Julius Bryant both kindly shared their knowledge of English interiors with me. I am grateful to Elizabeth Denlinger for help with the Hays letters in the Pforzheimer Collection of the New York Public Library. Blair Worden and Steve Pincus invited me to speak at the 'Civil and Religious Liberty' conference at Yale University in July 2008. I also gained a great deal from the chance to talk about my ideas on Godwin in the Middle Modernity Lecture Series at the University of Wisconsin. Thanks very much to Theresa Kelley for the invitation. Some of the materials in Chapter 3 were fleshed out in a talk at the Clark Library in February 2009. I'm grateful to Saree Makdisi and Michael Meranze for the opportunity to speak there. Thanks to Saree, Christina, and the kids for the hospitality. Helen Deutsch has helped me a lot with Johnson. I'm also very grateful to Felicity Nussbaum for the invitation to the USC-Huntington Early Modern Studies Seminar and for sharing her thoughts on Piozzi. Whether in his American or British circumstance, Kevin Gilmartin has been a constant source of support, and generous in giving up his time to read my work and in allowing me access to his own. I hope to see the conversable world of Lucky Baldwin's Bar again some time soon.

John Barrell and Harriet Guest are a continuing source of inspiration to me. Much of what is good in this book is indebted to them. The Centre for Eighteenth-Century Studies at the University of York has never failed to provide a convivial environment for talking about ideas. Emma Major generously let me see her work on Barbauld and Montagu. Elizabeth Eger has also helped me a great deal with Bluestocking sociability. Graham Snell, Secretary of Brooks's Club London, provided Elizabeth and I with the opportunity to view the paintings by Knapton and Reynolds discussed in Chapter 2. Josephine McDonagh and Luisa Calè have also been a constant source of encouragement and ideas. Thanks to Jo for setting up that early symposium on the idea of conversation. Tone Brekke has profoundly shaped my understanding of Wollstonecraft. Larry Klein and Phil Connell generously invited me to speak at Cambridge on Hazlitt. I'm also indebted to Corinna Wagner for the chance to speak in Exeter on some of the topics covered in Chapter 2 and to the Restoration and Reform seminar in Oxford for the chance to try out my ideas on Austen there. Tea-table conversation with Kathryn Sutherland helped me think about Austen's conversable style early on in the project. While towards the end, Mike Suarez provided a stimulating and encouraging lunch at Campion Hall. Susan Matthews and Ian Haywood gave me a chance to work out an overview for myself by inviting me to deliver a plenary lecture at the British Association of Romantic Studies conference at Roehampton in

2009. Scotland figures regularly in this book, and visits there have been sustained by the conviviality of Glasgow, especially with my old friend David Goldie. If only he did not walk so far in front of me up those hills, we could probably have talked about the book more! Thanks anyway to David and Debbie for all the years of warmth and welcome. Alex Benchimol, Gerry Carruthers, Nigel Leask, and Murray Pittock have shown me the spirit of Scottish sociability continues in rude health across their great city. I thank Patricia Boyd of the Edinburgh Special Collections Department for providing me with a copy of the George Drummond essay. Quotations from Katherine Plymley's diaries are by kind permission of the owners of the Corbett of Longnor collection currently held at the Shropshire Archives. I am extremely grateful to Liz Young and the archivists in Shrewsbury for their help. Reading Kathryn Gleadle's work introduced me to Plymley. Coffee-shop conversation with Kathryn helped me understand even more about it. Librarians at the John Rylands Library, the Huntington Library, and the Central Library at Reading have also been extremely helpful with manuscript materials.

Much of the writing and research for this book took place in Oxford. Peter McDonald's influence is a pervasive one. Marilyn Butler's tutored me from very early on in the sociable idea of the academic life. The Bodleian Library remains a wonderful place to work. I particularly thank Vera Ryhaljo for many years of support (and a choice selection of barbed comments). While I was still at the University, I was lucky enough to supervise a convivial cohort of graduate students, whom I'm glad still to see often. Mark Crosby, David Fallon, James Grande, and David O'Shaughnessy will be familiar with lots of things in this book, not least because they generously read sections. Conversations with Georgina Green about the 1790s have always been illuminating. Corin Thorsby helped me think about Byron's conversational style, although his lordship's appearances are somewhat fleeting in the book. Pamela Clemit and Mark Philp have been extremely generous in sharing their knowledge of Godwin's letters and diaries with me. I was fortunate to be around in Oxford when their editing work was in progress. Mark's influence played a part in shaping my ideas from very early on. While we were at University College together, Sarah Haggarty helped me think about some of the key concepts. Pablo Mukherjee has reintroduced me to convivial coffee-shop *adda* as part of everyday life. Despite not being a resident of the People's Republic of East Oxford, I salute its values and hope to have met Eliza Hilton's standards of creativity. I am sorry to have played a part in the dispersal of that particular conversable world, although it seems capable of constant renovation. This book has been written with a faith in the productive power of conversation of all kinds. Throughout its gestation, the Hudson-Huyg collective has been incredibly supportive. My parents, Bob and Sandra, and my siblings, Chris and Bec, continue to remind me that the best conversation is funny, warm, and sometimes fractious. Jane Huyg and Sharmila Jordan-Mee have shown me there's more to life than conversation and Nottingham Forest. Errors and omissions, of course, remain the fault of the author, but perhaps, unknown reader, we can talk about those at some future date.

Contents

List of Abbreviations

BLJ	*Boswell's Life of Johnson*
CL	*The Collected Letters of Samuel Taylor Coleridge*
E	*The Examiner*
MP	Jane Austen, *Mansfield Park*
KPN	Katherine Plymley's notebooks
LCS	London Corresponding Society
NA	Jane Austen, *Northanger Abbey*
P	Jane Austen, *Persuasion*
P&P	Jane Austen, *Pride and Prejudice*
S&S	Jane Austen, *Sense and Sensibility*
PPW	*Political and Philosophical Writings of William Godwin*
SCI	Society of Constitutional Information
S	*The Spectator*
T	*The Tatler*

Relevant details are given in the Bibliography.

List of Illustrations

Introduction: Opening Gambit

What to use for my opening gambit? How to begin communicating with you, dear reader, as you sit in your office or at home, in the library or coffee shop? I wonder what your responses to this book will be, just as you must wonder what designs I have on you. Would it be easier if I were there to chat with you? Perhaps we would be able to recreate the 'sweet converse' so many eighteenth-century poets wrote about. But our problem would not disappear. As the phrase 'opening gambit' suggests, there is always hazard and uncertainty when interaction begins. The co-presence of interlocutors doesn't make them transparent each to the other, for bodies can get in the way of conversation. In the eighteenth century, there was a common interdiction against dwelling on bodily disorders in conversation, as if the company were unwilling to be reminded of the potential for gross obstruction to the smooth and agreeable circulation of thoughts and feelings.[1] Opening words are a gamble in any conversation, not least because of their potential to generate unintended consequences, including the possibility that dialogue may be aborted even before it begins, perhaps with a smack in the mouth or some other form of verbal or non-verbal violence. And when discussion does begin, the participants may still misunderstand each other, although imperfect understanding is by no means necessarily unproductive.[2]

---

[1] See, for one example, 'An Essay on Conversation', *Ladies Magazine*, 2 (November 2, 1751), 405.

[2] For the classic account of 'conversational implicature', see H. P. Grice, 'Logic and Conversation', in Peter Cole and Jerry L. Morgan (eds), *Speech Acts, Syntax and Semantics* (New York/London: Academic Press, 1975), 41–58. Various of Grice's 'maxims' of the 'co-operative principle', for instance, on avoiding redundancy, sound very like those set out in eighteenth-century handbooks and essays on conversation. From my perspective, Grice's account tends to downplay the diversity of conversational practices that the eighteenth-century handbooks were designed to regulate, not least by ignoring the combative aspects of social talk. There are similarities in this regard with Jürgen Habermas's theory of communicative action, but he differentiates the 'telos of reaching understanding…inherent in language' from the intentionalist semantics of Grice. See Habermas, *On the Pragmatics of Communication*, ed. Maeve Cooke (Cambridge: Polity Press, 1999), esp. 227–9.

Where communication is understood in terms of the authentic matching of minds *en rapport*, rather than the mundane business of making meanings together in language, then conversation is likely to be a perpetual disappointment. But the word 'conversation' does not imply a tendency towards telepathy.[3] It might be better understood as a kind of 'barter', a material practice, based on the singularity of experience.[4] The word 'conversation' in English originally brought with it a sense of the broader social experience of *making* lives in conjunction with others. OED gives 'living or having one's being *in* a place or *among* persons' and 'consorting or having dealings with others; living together; commerce, intercourse, society, intimacy' as the earliest meanings of the word. Conversation always takes place somewhere between located subjects who are in the business of making some kind of sense—for whatever purposes and however obscurely even to themselves—of each other and their situations.[5] It involves mediation rather than 'contact between interiorities', even if the participants sometimes aim to overcome the materiality of what they are about.[6] The importance of opening one's self to the other in some modern thinking about conversation, such as Theodore Zeldin's, puts its priorities on the abeyance of conflict, as did many eighteenth-century theorists of conversation.[7] 'Freedom' has been a

---

[3] For a fuller discussion of this point, see John Durham Peters, *Speaking into the Air: A History of the Idea of Communication* (Chicago/London: University of Chicago Press, 2000). Jean-Luc Nancy's writing has also influenced my thinking, especially *The Inoperative Community*, ed. Peter Connor, trans. Peter Connor, Lisa Garbus, Michael Holland, and Simona Sawhney (Minneapolis/London: University of Minnesota Press, 1991). For Nancy, 'being in common' has nothing to do with 'communion' or 'fusion' into any ultimate identity. Communication and communion are fundamentally opposed in his writing. Instead Nancy looks to an idea of community built out of relations between dispersed and fragmented identities. Such communities of 'articulation' throw into relief 'the play of a juncture: what takes place where different pieces touch each other without fusing together, where they slide, pivot, or tumble over one another, one at the limit of the other' (*The Inoperative Community*, 76). For an obvious influence on the critique of 'fusion' in both Nancy and Peters, see Emmanuel Levinas, 'The Other in Proust' (1947), in *The Levinas Reader*, ed. Séan Hand (Oxford: Blackwell, 1989), 161–5.

[4] I take this idea of 'barter' from Dipesh Chakrabarty's description of translations between life worlds that do not invoke 'the mediation of a universalizing, homogenizing middle term'. See his *Provincializing Europe: Postcolonial Thought and Historical Difference* (Princeton/Oxford: Princeton University Press, 2000), 85. Eighteenth-century uses of 'polite' and 'rational' in relation to conversation often make them a 'middle term' in this way. Appeals to forms of sympathetic identification beyond mediation discussed later in this Introduction are the apotheosis of this universalizing tendency.

[5] See the discussion of the word's signification in Peter Burke, *The Art of Conversation* (Cambridge: Polity Press, 1993), 89–122.

[6] Peters, *Speaking into the Air*, 9.

[7] See Theodore Zeldin, *Conversation: How Talk Can Change Your Life* (London: Harvill Press, 1998). Zeldin's idea of authentic conversation acknowledges the risk of opening the self to the other, but assumes the goal is a kind of communion with 'a partner,...a lover,...a

recurrent word in writing about conversation, but never far away is the paradox that wishes to ensure liberty by stabilizing, universalizing, or even imposing the terms of exchange *a priori* in an effort to ensure that misunderstanding and contention are avoided. Quite apart from anything else, this perspective overlooks a combative tradition that has always found pleasure and utility in a more contentious idea of conversation.[8] For Richard Lovell Edgeworth the pleasures of 'the free communication of ideas' required a willingness to be 'attacked, [and] exposed to argument and ridicule'.[9] Exploring these tensions within the idea of the conversable world is at the heart of this book.

SELECT COMPANY

In one of very many eighteenth-century essays on conversation, John Hill recognized the value of 'the mixed conversation' of coffee houses: 'How instructive must it be, to hear the observations of a number of different people on a variety of objects.' The question was whether such mixed and inclusive talk could be 'restrained within any bounds of order and regularity'. Hill particularly worried that those who were disingenuous in conversation talked 'at the expence of some person for whom they must profess to respect and esteem'. For Hill ingenuousness, followed by 'affability and modesty', was to be prized above all other virtues in conversation, but this desire for reciprocity could flatten difference out in the name of consensus.[10] Eighteenth-century writing on conversation often assumed it flourished best with 'a well chosen friend'.[11] Contemporaries took this condition to promote 'the mutual communication of thoughts' and properly 'reciprocal commerce', but it also meant pre-selecting interlocutors with whom one shared values and a verbal code.[12]

Dialogue may not always be 'dialogic' in M. M. Bakhtin's sense, at least not when it attempts to transcend rather than work through the

---

guru,...God' (4), that is, a species of fusion at odds with the mundane work of making sense in language.

[8] See Burke, *Art of Conversation*, 92–3.

[9] R. L. Edgeworth (and Maria Edgeworth), *Memoirs of Richard Lovell Edgeworth*, 2 vols (London, 1820), I: 189.

[10] John Hill, 'The Inspector. No. 4', in *The Inspector*, 2 vols (1753), I: 15–18.

[11] Joseph Addison believed 'the Mind never unbends it self so agreeably as in the Conversation of a well chosen Friend' (*S* 93, I: 395). All references to *The Spectator* are to Donald F. Bond's edition, 5 vols (Oxford: Clarendon Press, 1987) as *S* followed by original issue number and then volume and page number. See also Britannicus, 'Essay on Conversation', *Sentimental Magazine* (April 1775), 149–51 (149).

[12] These phrases are used by Britannicus, 'Essay on Conversation', 149.

heteroglossia of language. 'Dialogism' for Bakhtin always registers the structuring presence of the variety of different kinds of language circulating in and around any given speech situation.[13] An emergent eighteenth-century critique of the philosophical dialogue as a genre was that its 'abstract and idealizing modes of representation', as Michael Prince describes them, could not meet the growing taste for the 'wholly mundane process of conversational exchange'.[14] Genres like the novel responded formally to the idea of values emerging from intersubjective exchanges by developing an idiom that drew its paradoxical authority from their proximity to the everyday world of conversation. Robin Valenza claims that 'more so than the essay, the novel comes to define the kind of writing that stood at the opposite pole of polite letters from learned discourse because it not only affects a conversable style, but also attempts to model conversibility.'[15] My only reservation about this judgment is it may be too quick to give priority to the novel over the periodical essay. The heteroglossia typical of eighteenth-century reviews was not stilled by the more coherent voices of the nineteenth-century quarterlies. If the *Edinburgh Review*, for instance, presented itself as sifting through a diffused literature in order to provide its readers with 'the more liberal talk of generalizing into principles', then its pretensions to a more equal and wide survey could not disguise its dependence upon a host of less famous publications, which it drew upon and used to disseminate its values. Nor did it ever entirely homogenize the proliferation of different voices in its own pages.[16]

The narrowing of the definition of 'conversation' onto verbal communication was a development that took place during the period covered by this book, but the tightening of focus only intensified the concern with intersubjective communication as a key terrain for working out the

---

[13] See M. M. Bakhtin, *The Dialogic Imagination: Four Essays*, ed. Michael Holquist, trans. Caryl Emerson and Michael Holquist (Austin: University of Texas Press, 1981). 'Heteroglossia' is conceived by Bakhtin in terms of the discursive diversity at work in any speech situation: 'The living utterance, having taken meaning and shape at a particular historical moment in a socially specific environment, cannot fail to brush up against thousands of living dialogic threads, woven by socio-ideological consciousness around the given object in utterance' (276). Bakhtin sees the novel's great achievement as the creation of a 'zone of contact with an inconclusive present' (37), but these qualities could just as easily be identified with the periodical essay.

[14] See Michael Prince, *Philosophical Dialogue in the British Enlightenment: Theology, Aesthetics and the Novel* (Cambridge: Cambridge University Press, 1996), 194, 244.

[15] See Robin Valenza, *Literature, Language, and the Rise of the Intellectual Disciplines in Britain, 1680–1820* (Cambridge: Cambridge University Press, 2009), 46.

[16] For a reading of the literary periodicals of the early nineteenth century in terms of heteroglossia, see Mark Schoenfield, *British Periodicals and Romantic Identity: The 'Literary Lower Empire'* (Basingstoke: Palgrave Macmillan, 2009), esp. 24–7. Schoenfield's book provides an astute commentary on the tensions in the *Edinburgh* between the drive towards coherence and the heteroglossic tendencies mentioned above.

community's values. Conversation may have been promoted as an arena for settling differences without conflict, a perceived advance over the seventeenth century's 'wars of Truth', but it proved a battleground for all kinds of anxieties about the nature of communication with the other. This question was itself caught up in tensions between ideas of select company and the promise of a broadening participation.[17] The situation was complicated further by conflicting understandings of what constituted conversation as opposed to other forms of speech, including some that saw a role for combative talk as pleasurable and productive. These tensions shaped and were shaped by cultural practices as a new and self-consciously commercial society came into being. The social historian Peter Burke has noted the flourishing of handbooks for conversation in sixteenth-century Italy, seventeenth-century France, and eighteenth-century England. In the first half of the eighteenth century, more than fifty works on conversation were published in Britain alone. What had been a 'trickle became a stream', as Burke puts it, using a metaphor of cultural 'flow' everywhere present in eighteenth-century discussions of conversation.[18] Roughly speaking, we might map Burke's three ages of conversation onto a revival of classical humanism in the Italian Renaissance, the courtliness of Louis XIV, and the aspiration to politeness and participation in the commercial society taking shape in eighteenth-century Britain. Although they often translated continental treatises, where the British handbooks and essays on conversation differ most from their Italian and French antecedents is in their aversion to 'ceremony and compliment'.[19] Outside the medium of print, the importance of the paradigm is indicated by the emergence in the 1720s and 1730s of the 'conversation piece' as an important genre in the visual arts. Usually centred on the family, as refined by William Hogarth, and then in the 1760s by a second generation including, for instance, Johann Zoffany, the genre stressed domestic life rather than the grandeur of official portraiture, showing sociable groups in

[17] I take the phrase 'wars of Truth' from John Milton's *Areopagitica*. See *Selected Prose*, ed. C. A. Patrides (Harmondsworth: Penguin, 1974), 243. One thread followed by this book is that this Miltonic notion of discourse remained more active in eighteenth-century paradigms of conversation than often allowed, especially by those historians and critics who collapse conversation into politeness.

[18] Burke, *Art of Conversation*, 109. On ideas of conversation as a form of combat, see 92 and 112. See also Warren E. Leland, 'Turning Reality Round Together: Guides to Conversation in Eighteenth-Century England', *Eighteenth-Century Life*, 8 (1983), 65–87. Among the most influential continental books were Giovanni della Casa's *Galateo*, published in English as early as 1576, and Guazzo's *The Art of Conversation*. See Burke's discussion, 98–102.

[19] Burke, *The Art of Conversation*, 111. See also Lawrence E. Klein, 'The Figure of France: The Politics of Sociability in England, 1660–1715', *Yale French Studies*, 92 (1997), 30–45.

or near their homes, often engaged together in some occupation.[20] Definitions of British conversation in terms of its plain and even egalitarian quality were ubiquitous in the period covered by this book and central to the uneven and long drawn out transition from a culture of tradition, where identities and values were taken to be intrinsic or bestowed by external authorities, to one where they were taken to be constructed by exchanges between participants, whether within the family or out in the world.

The attraction of conversation was precisely that it was the form of speech identified with the ordinary life of citizens. Part of the 'daily murmur', the investment in this zone of 'practical, ever unstable compromises' meant that it increasingly drew the attention of regulatory ambitions that could never quite contain or define it.[21] Conversation didn't just happen in eighteenth-century Britain. It was scrutinized, policed, promoted, written about, discussed, and practised. In 1740, George Drummond, a young Scotsman studying at Edinburgh College, wrote an essay on 'Rules for Conversation' guided by a concern with 'comfortable success in almost every scene of life'.[22] Produced from within the same clubbable Edinburgh world that incubated David Hume, Drummond's essay begins by emphasizing the human need for sympathetic contact with others. If Drummond saw a curative aspect to this predisposition, it also served the principle of getting on in the world. In this regard, 'hints thrown out in Conversation', thought Drummond, 'have much more powerful charms, than those of Eloquence.' The informality of conversation contrasts with the 'publick character' of the 'Orator'. Implicitly, Drummond's contrast is between classical republican values and the emergent sociability of the commercial world celebrated in Hume's essays. To thrive in this world, Drummond insists on the Addisonian imperative 'to render our selves agreeable'. Often the essay quotes more or less directly from *The Spectator*, illustrating its importance for Scottish culture's investment in polite sociability: 'The Conversation of our friends serves to fill up in a manner no less agreeable, than advantageous, the vacant & detachd

---

[20] See Mario Praz, *Conversation Pieces: A Survey of the Informal Group Portrait in Europe and America* (University Park: Penn. State University Press, 1971); Ronald Paulson, *Emblem and Expression: Meaning in English Art of the Eighteenth Century* (London: Thames and Hudson, 1975), esp. 121–36; David H. Solkin, *Painting for Money: The Visual Arts and the Public Sphere in Eighteenth-Century England* (New Haven/London: Yale University Press, 1993), esp. 48–77; Kate Retford, *The Art of Domestic Life: Family Portraiture in Eighteenth-Century England* (New Haven/London: Yale University Press, 2006).

[21] See Michel de Certeau, *The Capture of Speech and Other Political Writings* (Minneapolis: University of Minnesota Press, 1997), 96, 94.

[22] George Drummond, 'Rules of Conversation', Edinburgh University Library, Special Collections Department, Dc.4.54/17.

parts of time, that we gain from the necessary duties of life, & which otherwise would ly heavy on our hands.'[23]

POLITE CONVERSATION

The numerous examples of handbooks and other kinds of advice should correct any idea that Joseph Addison and Sir Richard Steele somehow invented the discourse of politeness, but *The Tatler* and *The Spectator* did have an enormous impact on later eighteenth- and early-nineteenth-century ideas of conversation throughout Britain.[24] From early on various clubs and societies subscribed, including the Gentleman's Club at Spalding, Lincolnshire, formed at a coffee house in 1709 to discuss the essays in *The Tatler*.[25] Cheap editions later on meant both *The Tatler* and *The Spectator* had an increasingly wide circulation.[26] Anthologies like Anna Laetitia Barbauld's 1804 edition helped further the dissemination of their ideas on conversation.[27] 'There is scarcely an individual', wrote Vicesimus Knox in 1779, 'not only of those who profess learning, but of those who devote any of their time to reading, who has not digested the Spectators.'[28] James Boswell came to London in 1762 intent on imitating Addison to the point of visiting many of the places he knew from *The Spectator*. Well into the nineteenth century, various ventures, like Leigh Hunt's *Examiner*, figured themselves as conforming to an Addisonian pattern of literature

---

[23] Compare Joseph Addison on the question of how to innocently 'fill up our Time' in the 'empty spaces of Life' (*S* 93, I: 395).

[24] See Brean Hammond, *Professional Imaginative Writing in England 1670–1740: 'Hackney for Bread'* (Oxford: Oxford University Press, 1997), 153, on the tendency to regard Addison and Steele 'as arising *ex nihilo* and as engrossing the polite entirely in and of themselves'.

[25] For details of this club, see Lawrence E. Klein, 'Politeness and the Interpretation of the British Eighteenth Century', *Historical Journal*, 45 (2002), 869–98 (893) and Peter Clark, *British Clubs and Societies, 1580–1800: The Origins of an Associational World* (Oxford: Oxford University Press, 2000), 78–9.

[26] William St Clair places *The Spectator* in the 'old canon' that became widely available after the 1774 change in the intellectual property regime (*The Reading Nation in the Romantic Period* (Cambridge: Cambridge University Press, 2004), 131). The decisive importance of 1774 has been disputed by various scholars; see, for instance, Richard B. Sher, *The Enlightenment and the Book: Scottish Authors and Their Publishers in Eighteenth-Century Britain, Ireland, and America* (Chicago/London: University of Chicago Press, 2006), 313, and Thomas F. Bonnell, 'When Book History Neglects Bibliography: Trouble with the "Old Canon" in the Reading Nation', *Studies in Bibliography*, 57 (2005–6), 243–61, but the more general point about the dissemination of *The Spectator* holds true.

[27] See *Selections from the Spectator, Tatler, Guardian, and Freeholder, with a preliminary essay by Anna Laetitia Barbauld* (London, 1804).

[28] Quoted in John Brewer, *The Pleasures of the Imagination: English Culture in the Eighteenth Century* (London: Harper Collins, 1997), 101.

and conversation. John Bell believed he was following Addison's aim of
bringing philosophy out of the cloisters and 'into the daily commerce of
life' by creating the portable pocket edition, including editions of *The
Tatler* and *The Spectator*.[29] Whether Addison and Steele would have
agreed is a question that many commentators asked when they viewed
the expansion of the reading public fuelled by Bell and other publishers
of cheap editions. The pressure put on the conversational paradigm
associated with *The Spectator* by a dissemination it both encouraged and
feared is a theme that runs through this book.

Addison and Steele's project has remained beguiling to most accounts
of eighteenth-century culture, although often to differing ends. Within
the historiography of eighteenth-century Britain, *The Spectator* is often
identified with the development of the nation's identity as 'a polite and
commercial people'.[30] From this perspective, the tectonics of the conversable world ran from the domesticity of the dinner table through to clubs
and on to more open spaces, such as the coffee houses and theatres, not to
mention places of business such as the Royal Exchange, where the rules of
civility were thought to guarantee a relatively easy interaction between
strangers. As this summary mapping suggests, polite conversation was not
just a practice, but also an influence on the physical forms taken by the
eighteenth-century urban renaissance. Peter Borsay's work shows that a
great deal of civic investment took place with the aim of propelling
company 'into contact with each other to gossip and flirt, to see and be
seen'. Usually this encouragement was governed by the regulation of the
passions enjoined by the code of politeness.[31] Like many other historians
of eighteenth-century British society, Borsay understands the larger aim as
the reunification of a divided elite around a discourse that downplayed
conflict, especially the religious and political differences associated with
the Civil War and Restoration. Politeness promoted a culture of 'smooth
emollience', its architecture and its ideas of conversation invested in the
easy circulation of bodies and talk.[32] Conversation provided a crucial
paradigm for the early-eighteenth-century national imaginary in this
regard, understood as a comforting sign of a complex social machinery

---

[29] Handbill for 'Bell's Edition of Blackstone's Commentaries' (John Johnson Collection, Bodleian Library).
[30] See Paul Langford, *A Polite and Commercial People: England 1727–1783* (Oxford:
Oxford University Press, 1992). Langford takes his title from William Blackstone's *Commentaries on the Laws of England* (1765–9).
[31] See Peter Borsay, *The English Urban Renaissance: Culture and Society in the Provincial
Town 1660–1770* (Oxford: Clarendon Press, 1989), 150.
[32] Brewer, *Pleasures of the Imagination*, 103.

in action, but also viewed as a perpetual engine in itself, spreading improvement in its wake.

Despite all the capital and imaginative investment in it, the politeness project was not necessarily completed in practice. Millions were unable to participate through poverty and illiteracy. Contrary to the assumptions of the elite, many in the middling and lower ranks interacted in conversable worlds of their own making, although often with their own codes of behaviour and language. Their social superiors often deemed even those who shared an aspiration to 'improvement' incapable of being polite.[33] For all the rhetoric to the contrary, politeness did not open its arms to the populace at large. Commentators were constantly on the lookout for signs that pretensions to politeness were not undermining social hierarchy or traditional forms of knowledge. Even within the elite, the public world was still torn by strife and controversy, sometimes even over the idea of conversation itself. Quite apart from riots and other forms of public disorder, the press was full of invective, and pamphleteers could use violent language to encourage violent acts. Intolerance and exclusion—supported by the coercive power of the law and the military—were part of the day-to-day life of this modern commercial society. Against this turbulent background, Lawrence E. Klein, whose work has done more than anyone else's to extend our understanding of the category, thinks of politeness as an attempt to establish 'a norm in a world of often wild and incoherent sociabilities'.[34] For 'Britannicus' in the *Sentimental Magazine*, 'politeness' was 'the primum mobile of society and conversation'. Not the affectation of 'the beau', his essay goes on to insist, but 'an easy, unaffected, and well-bred carriage'. By softening differences, politeness 'makes us beloved, and our company courted by all ranks of people'.[35] In Klein's account of the politeness paradigm, its key values of 'moderation, mutual tolerance, and social comity' were 'concretized in the high esteem for conversation and conversability'. For David Hume and many others, conversation was the place where politeness had to be practised by skilful management, but also where rough edges were worn off through the experience of interacting with others in a process of polishing.[36] What

---

[33] For some early examples of such aspirations, see Lawrence E. Klein, 'Politeness for Plebes: Consumption and Social Identity in Early Eighteenth-Century England', in Ann Bermingham and John Brewer (eds), *The Consumption of Culture 1600–1800: Image, Object, Text* (London/New York: Routledge, 1995), 362–82, and for others from later in the century, Trevor Fawcett, 'Self-Improvement Societies: The Early "Lit. and Phils."', in *Life in the Georgian Town: Papers Given at the Georgian Group Symposium* (London: The Georgian Group, 1985), 15–25.

[34] Klein, 'The Figure of France', 34.

[35] Britannicus, 'Essay on Conversation', 150.

[36] Klein, 'Politeness and the Interpretation of the British Eighteenth Century', 874–5.

Hume's version of the politeness paradigm implicitly acknowledged was that conversation out in the world was frequently bumpy. Many other writers on politeness set out to moderate those who 'love disputing in Conversation' before they even opened their mouths, but the ubiquity of warnings against invective and raillery only suggests the continuing pleasure taken in contention and dispute.[37]

Hester Piozzi thought the word 'polite' implied 'from its very derivation freedom from all asperity, an equable smoothness over which we roll, and never are stopped or impeded in our course'.[38] Included in the development of ideas of polite conversation was an emphasis on 'the feminization of culture' that understood the presence and to a degree participation of women to soften interaction and dispute. Feminized domestic virtues were an important part of the configuration of conversation in *The Tatler* and *Spectator*. For Hume, 'Women of Sense and Education' might aspire to be 'the Sovereigns of the Empire of Conversation'.[39] Their presence was an index of the progress of civility. For many others, the cultural visibility of women was a sign not of progress, but of a decline into effeminacy and luxury wrought by commercial society. Their conversation was identified with gossip and chatter rather than what were deemed to be proper standards of talk underpinned by a classical education.[40] Even among those committed to the eighteenth century as a world of clubs, like William Hutton of Birmingham, a properly regulated female sociability was almost a contradiction in terms:

If I mention a society, composed of many people without a leader, every one speaking at the same time, and striving who shall speak loudest; not one knowing how to write their name, scarcely to sign a cross, or with which hand to sign it; it may fairly be supposed, I am introducing a *female club*.[41]

Against such attitudes, women like Elizabeth Montagu and Hester Lynch Piozzi increasingly exploited the idea that women naturally took a lead in the conversable world. Bolstered by her role as a proprietor of Samuel

[37] Jean Baptiste Morvan, *Reflexions upon the Politeness of Manners; with Maxims for Civil Society* (London, 1707), 138. Morvan's book was translated from the French more than once.

[38] Hester Lynch Piozzi, *British Synonymy; or, An Attempt at Regulating the Choice of Words in Familiar Conversation*, 2 vols (London, 1794), I: 262.

[39] See 'Of Essay-Writing', in David Hume, *Essays, Moral and Political*, 2 vols (Edinburgh, 1741–2), II: 5. This essay only appeared in the first edition of *Essays*.

[40] For a general introduction to these issues, see E. J. Clery, *The Feminization Debate in Eighteenth-Century England: Literature, Commerce and Luxury* (Basingstoke: Palgrave Macmillan, 2004).

[41] William Hutton, *Courts of Requests: Their Nature, Utility, and Powers Described* (Birmingham, 1787), 263.

Johnson's conversation, Piozzi used the assumption that conversation was a feminized domain to justify her 'Attempt at Regulating the Choice of Words in Familiar Conversation'. 'While men teach to write with propriety', she claimed, 'a woman may at worst be qualified—through long practice—to direct the choice of phrases in familiar talk.' Touching on a long-standing theme in writing about conversation, she distances her labours from the scholarly study of grammar, and describes her book as 'intended chiefly for the parlour window, and acknowledging itself unworthy of a place upon a library shelf'. Polite conversation was construed as a modest virtue, but the dissemination of domestic ideology, however unevenly through the eighteenth century, meant those virtues were increasingly seen as intrinsic to the welfare of the public at large. For all her professions of humility, Piozzi was convinced 'private virtues are PUBLIC benefits': 'Let not princes flatter themselves therefore: they will be watched in private as much as in public life; and those who cannot pierce further, will judge of them by the appearances they shall exhibit in both.' She believed 'the domestic purity' of 'our own court, ministry, nobles, and clergy' had saved Britain from Revolution. Her policing of conversation was intended to make sure this remained the case.[42]

Conversation may have been a species of 'small change', circulating around the everyday world of the tea table, but the currency of such domestic virtue was increasingly, if variously, regarded as a public benefit.[43] As Henry Mackenzie put it, discussing the usefulness of 'cultivated sentiment' in *The Mirror* in response to a series of readers' letters about quarrels in domestic life:

the lesser virtues must be attended to as well as the greater: the manners as well as the duties of life. They form a sort of *Pocket Coin*, which, though it does not enter into great and important transactions, is absolutely necessary for common and ordinary intercourse.

For Mackenzie and many other Scottish writers, the familiar pages of the periodical press were the cultural medium best suited to 'consult[ing] the feelings of those with whom we live'. Out of this 'common and ordinary intercourse', it was imagined, would arise a wider society free from conflict and able to carry forward the grander business of improvement.[44] The ethos of polite conversation was widely understood to exclude disagreeable and divisive subjects—most obviously religious and political differences—

---

[42] Piozzi, *British Synonymy*, I: ii, 151; II: 170.
[43] See Harriet Guest, *Small Change: Women, Learning, Patriotism, 1750–1810* (Chicago: University of Chicago Press, 2000).
[44] *The Mirror*, no. 33 (18 May 1779), 262, 270.

from social talk and from belles-lettres. Consequently, Piozzi's policing of conversation was aimed against what she perceived to be 'our QUERU-LOUS temper'. Acknowledging a delight in combative talk as a national characteristic, *British Synonymy* reiterates the constant eighteenth-century objection to 'those UNEASY conversers, who set every thing in the most unfavourable light'. For Piozzi the pleasure taken in conversing on contentious public affairs had reached their nadir in the radical culture of the 1790s: 'Twas thus the sophistry of Priestley, the calculations of Price, and the insolence of Paine, obtained attention, only by that certain charm, that strange pleasure our people take in hearing that they are undone.'[45] The delight querulous spirits took in debating public affairs gained more attention because of the perverse enjoyment people found in discussing their woes.

CONTENTIOUS CLAIMS

The British tendency to debate public affairs Piozzi wanted to quash may sound something like the account of eighteenth-century social talk associated with Jürgen Habermas's concept of the bourgeois public sphere. *The Spectator* is a foundational text in his analysis, but unlike historians working within the politeness paradigm 'rational-critical' debate is the privileged form of talk in Habermas's version of eighteenth-century culture.[46] For Habermas, citizens interacting in their private capacities produced a new idea of public opinion beyond the official sites of publicity in the Court or Church. The transformation took place in the home, the 'intimate' sphere in Habermas's bifurcated model of the private, but carried across into the new places of commercial leisure: assembly rooms, exhibition spaces, and (most famously of all) coffee houses. Habermas's account of the formation of the classical public sphere implicitly makes conversation an almost magical technology that transmuted coffee into public opinion. Supposedly anyone was allowed into the coffee shop, regardless of class and, once inside, or so it seemed to many foreign visitors at the time, rank was less important than what was said. This egalitarian ethic may be something of a myth, but it was one many believed late into the century. Francis Grose, for instance, in a 'Sketch of the Times' published in 1792, claimed that 'provided a man has a clean shirt and

---

[45] Piozzi, *British Synonymy*, II: 179–80.

[46] See Jürgen Habermas, *The Structural Transformation of the Public Sphere: An Inquiry into a Category of Bourgeois Society*, trans. Thomas Burger with the assistance of Frederick Lawrence (Cambridge, MA: MIT Press, 1989), 51.

three pence in his pocket, he may talk as loud in a coffee house as the 'squire of ten thousand pounds a-year'.[47] Of course, not everyone could come by three pence or a clean shirt easily, but Grose obviously saw coffee shop conversation as a distinctly democratic forum. Only two decades later, writers like Leigh Hunt were looking back on the open commerce of the coffee shop as a lost golden age.[48]

Many of the essays in *The Spectator* do represent themselves as originating in coffee house conversations and feeding back into them. Perhaps taking their self-representations too much at face value, Habermas notes that 'the periodical articles were not only made the object of discussion by the public of the coffee houses but were viewed as integral parts of this discussion.'[49] This account of Addison and Steele's project must be balanced against more recent emphasis on its attempts to regulate the 'barren Superfluity of Words' (*S* 476, IV: 187).[50] Even at the time of *The Spectator*, London possessed an array of different kinds of coffee houses, inhabited by different classes of readers and talkers, as Lewis Theobald, for instance, acknowledged in *The Censor*. The original target of Pope's attacks on Grub Street hacks in *The Dunciad*, Theobald claimed to find topics to supply his printer by frequenting coffee houses. Turning away from the places where business is transacted and from the fashionable resorts of 'brocaded *Narcissi*', he acknowledged more down-market venues had their role. In these spaces, 'Neighbouring Mechanicks meet to learn a little News. He seeks from their Politicks, to procure an Opinion of their Wisdom.' If Theobald seems relatively tolerant of the proliferation of conversable worlds, he is not without his own sense of the absurdity of the pretensions of '*Declaimers* in politics'. 'I must confess', writes Theobald, 'at the same time, it is provokingly ridiculous to hear a *Haberdasher* descant on a *General's* Misconduct.' 'Declamation' implies the failure to accommodate one's self to the other intrinsic to polite turn taking.[51] *The Spectator* has several essays examining the degradation of conversation in

[47] Francis Grose, *The Olio, A Collection of Essays, Dialogue etc* (London, 1792), 207.
[48] See Markman Ellis, *The Coffee-House: A Cultural History* (Phoenix: London, 2005), 220–4.
[49] Habermas, *Structural Transformation*, 42.
[50] See Brian Cowan, 'Mr. Spectator and the Coffeehouse Public Sphere'. *Eighteenth-Century Studies*, 37 (2004), 345–66. Revisionist accounts are now legion, but include Geoff Eley, 'Nations, Publics, and Political Cultures: Placing Habermas in the Nineteenth Century', in Craig Calhoun (ed.), *Habermas and the Public Sphere* (Cambridge, MA: MIT Press, 1996), 289–339 and Nancy Fraser's 'Politics, Culture, and the Public Sphere: Towards a Postmodern Conception', in Linda Nicholson and Steven Seidman (eds), *Social Postmodernism: Beyond Identity Politics* (Cambridge: Cambridge University Press, 1995), 287–312.
[51] *The Censor*, 2 (61), 213–16.

such venues, making plain the distinction between what went on there and its idea of polite conversation, providing its own accounts of the ridiculous pretensions of tradesmen who set themselves up as 'coffee house politicians', an extremely durable trope for the idea conversation degenerated when those outside the political elites took it upon themselves to talk politics.

Geoff Eley has noted the omission from Habermas's original discussion of any account of the emergent 'plebeian public sphere' associated with the popular radical movement of the 1790s. The question of whether the press of 'the crowd' could be included within polite culture (or were capable of creating conversable worlds of their own) was at issue from very early on in the century. It was a question Godwin wrestled with in his thinking about conversation as a political modality in the 1790s. Sometimes he sounds rather like Habermas in his emphasis on rational deliberation, as I suggest in Chapter 3, but with perhaps more freedom allowed for the 'collision of mind with mind'. Critics like Nancy Fraser have argued *The Structural Transformation of the Public Sphere* 'treats deliberation as the privileged mode of public-sphere interaction' to the exclusion, for instance, of more 'contestatory' forms of address.[52] The version of open discourse imagined by Habermas as 'rational-critical' has little room for the distortions of the passions. More recently, Habermas has insisted his theory of communicative action is grounded in the practical coordination of life worlds, acknowledging the materiality of the processes of conversation, but there is still a drive towards a scenario of rationalized transparency between speakers in his thinking. To my mind, Eley's critique of Habermas tends to perpetuate this idea of communication, extending 'rational' competency to popular counter-publics without much consideration of whether there were more diverse kinds of verbal codes in play there. In one sense at least, neither departs too widely from the politeness paradigm in their tendency to downplay those combative or heated forms of conversation ('wrangling', 'raillery', 'enthusiasm', etc) that troubled so much of the conduct literature on conversation.[53]

Although frequently collocated with each other and with 'conversation' in the eighteenth century, neither 'polite' nor 'rational' were uncontested terms. 'Rational' could imply an urge towards heated disagreement with

---

[52] Fraser, 'Politics, Culture, and the Public Sphere', 292.
[53] See the 'free-and-easy' sociability described in Iain McCalman's *Radical Underworld: Prophets, Revolutionaries, and Pornographers in London, 1795–1840* (Cambridge, Cambridge University Press, 1988). For an excellent discussion of some of these issues, see Philip Connell and Nigel Leask, 'What is the People?', in *eidem* (eds), *Romanticism and Popular Culture in Britain and Ireland* (Cambridge: Cambridge University Press, 2009), 3–48, esp. 8–23.

polite consensus. Those who appeal to the politeness paradigm often invoke the idea that it was intended to transcend the religious divisions of the previous century. Klein, for instance, invokes a characterization of Anglican churchmen after the Restoration as 'just as susceptible as their congregations to the new fashions and fads, just as anxious to be thought "rational", just as eager to partake in the new culture of the polite, with its values of sociability, benevolence and good conversation, and just as suspicious of anything that smacked of "enthusiasm"'.[54] Not all church people felt this way. For some, ideas of 'polite' and 'rational' conversation threatened to sacrifice too much to the smooth flow of opinion. Hume and his Edinburgh friends were attacked by the Popular Party in the Church of Scotland for using politeness to exclude 'all the high flights of evangelical enthusiasm, and the mysteries of grace, which the common people are so fond of'.[55] By the time Lord Chesterfield's letters to his son were published in 1774–5, the politeness paradigm was increasingly vulnerable to criticism as a form of dissimulation. English evangelical circles associated with the Clapham Sect worried about the worldliness of politeness if that meant quietening their urgent sense of the immanence of God's word. So, in Cowper's 'Table Talk', discussed in Chapter 4, politeness may be 'a mask we wear' and a spirit of contradiction necessary to 'brush the surface and make it flow'. William Wilberforce spent evenings writing up lists of 'launchers' or topics that would enable him to turn the conversation to godly subjects.[56] Godly conversation often imagined itself firing missiles at complacency rather than oiling the wheels of politeness, although there was plenty of tension around the distinction. In his 'Essay on Conversation' published in the *Wesleyan-Methodist Magazine* of 1825, the Revd James Wood tried to negotiate his own way through the thicket. 'The necessities and the sympathies of our nature lead to intercourse,' he accepted. He acknowledged also the maxim that talk had to take account of 'the company we are in.' However, he was adamant that 'no principle of truth should be sacrificed in order to gain favour; no disposition ought to be seen or felt, to compromise matters with the men of the world.'[57] Nearly fifty years earlier, Hannah More had

[54] Klein, 'Politeness and the Interpretation of the British Eighteenth Century', 890, quoting from John Spurr, *The Restoration Church of England, 1646–1689* (New Haven, CT/London, 1991), 383–4.

[55] John Witherspoon, *Ecclesiastical Characteristics: or, The Arcana of the Church Policy. Being an Humble Attempt to Open up the Mystery of Moderation*, 5th edn (Edinburgh, 1763), 27.

[56] See Robert Wilberforce and Samuel Wilberforce, *The Life of William Wilberforce*, 5 vols (London, 1838), II: 101, 104, 210.

[57] James Wood, 'Essay on Conversation', *Wesleyan-Methodist Magazine*, 4 (1825), 820–3.

complained that advice on conversation to the young women of her time meant 'her piety is to be anxiously concealed, and her knowledge affectedly disavowed, lest the former should draw on her the appellation of an enthusiast, or the latter that of a pedant.'[58] Witty and easy men of letters like Sydney Smith, significantly educated in Edinburgh, the home of sentimental easiness, found it easy to ridicule such opinions, mocking Hannah More as the kind of person happy to chat about the Pelagian heresy at the tea table.[59]

The trade-off between polite ease and the vigorous pursuit of knowledge, godly or secular, remained a concern for many of those who identified 'rational' conversation not with a polite conformity to custom but a more emphatic desire for reform and improvement. From this perspective combat in conversation could be perceived as part of a necessary winnowing process, although often enjoyed as a pleasure in itself. Groups like the Club of Honest Whigs, discussed in Chapter 2, who frequented the Chapter Coffee House in the 1760s, revelled in a culture of vigorous scientific, political, and theological disagreement. At around the same time, Richard Lovell Edgeworth's society of literary men at Slaughter's coffee house revelled in 'the first hints of discoveries, the current observations, and the mutual collision of ideas'.[60] Politeness was not a priority in an environment where 'the argument was always ingenious, and the ridicule sometimes coarse'. Edgeworth contrasted the advantages of its conversational mode with more formal societies where 'men give the result of their serious researches, and detail their deliberate thoughts.' Neither the politeness paradigm nor the rational-critical account of eighteenth-century conversation properly accounts for this congested and contested terrain, although both describe tendencies that contemporaries recognized and fought over within it. Part of this book's method is to trace the logic of the various metaphorical clusters that formed themselves around the idea of conversation in the long eighteenth century. What this method reveals is that such clusters unpack themselves in different ways in different circumstances. Not the least of these tropes, already encountered several times in this Introduction, is the opposition between the 'conversable world' that provides my title and the 'cloistered' domain of 'learning' found, for example, in Addison, Shaftesbury, Hume, and a host of other often nameless contributors to eighteenth-century periodical literature.[61]

---

[58] Hannah More, 'Thoughts on Conversation', in *Essays on Various Subjects, Principally Designed for Young Ladies* (London, 1777), 38.

[59] For Smith's mockery of More, see *Edinburgh Review*, 14 (April 1809) 145–51 (150).

[60] Edgeworth, *Memoirs*, 88–9.

[61] See the discussion in Valenza, *Literature, Language, and the Rise of the Intellectual Disciplines*, esp. 37–53.

Often what is going on in these tropes is a redefinition of literary culture away from (Catholic) scholarship and classical language and towards the vernacular culture of Protestantism and the world of goods. In this context of orienting knowledge towards the interactions of the everyday world, conversation starts to be defined as an intrinsic, sometimes even the primary characteristic of being human. Henry Fielding's 'An Essay on Conversation', for instance, which first appeared in his *Miscellanies* (1743), takes the chief difference between man and 'Brutes' to be not the social instinct as such, but 'Conversation' in the sense of 'the reciprocal Interchange of Ideas, by which Truth is examined, Things are, in a manner, *turned round*, and sifted, and all our Knowledge communicated to each other.'[62] Fielding's essay soon shifts from simply talking about social speech to the question of how to live together more generally, but it is worth noting how far he equivocates between the issue of making things together in language and the question of creating the conditions for forms of communication without friction. If 'reciprocal Interchange' suggests a participatory ethos of making culture in language, 'sifting' opens up a more regulatory perspective concerned with the refinement of raw materials. For Sir Richard Steele the 'conversable world' was never identical with the 'busy world' it drew upon.[63] Often set into play as a way of critiquing traditional institutions of knowledge and power, there was a constant anxiety about just how far the everyday world of conversation could be allowed to extend.

A CULTURE OF CONVERSATION

Fielding's ideas on conversation were formed more by civic humanist traditions in general and Cicero in particular than any idea of the public as constituted by the interactions of the coffee shop and popular press, but for many others 'conversation' and 'commerce' were coming to be used interchangeably.[64] Drummond's 1740 essay is explicit in seeing skills in conversation as a stock one can trade off to rise in the world: 'Conversation

---

[62] Henry Fielding, 'An Essay on Conversation', in *Miscellanies*, ed. Henry Knight Miller, 3 vols (Oxford: Clarendon Press, 1972), I: 120.

[63] Valenza, *Literature, Language, and the Rise of the Intellectual Disciplines*, 45.

[64] Fielding's modern editors take him to occupy a middle ground between the newer ideas of politeness and 'the traditional assumptions of a hierarchical society and the polite "ceremony" (as opposed to mere "civility") that could only be learned in the best company' (I: xxxv). On the importance of Cicero for eighteenth-century handbooks on conversation more generally, see Burke, *Art of Conversation*, 94, 96, and 99–100. Stephen Copley notes that the *New General English Dictionary* (1737) defined 'commerce' as 'Trade, Dealing, Traffick, Conversation by Word or Letter. Correspondence of any Kind' (Stephen Copley,

is a sort of commerce, towards which every one should furnish his Quota, that is should hear & speak in his turn.'[65] From this kind of perspective, conversation and belles-lettres were perceived as part of the same world of improvement and information. Print culture was being disseminated and dispersed into sociable forms of reading like book clubs and literary and philosophical societies. David Hume was only one among several writers who took it to be the case that conversation could only flourish in a modern commercial society where there was a new diversity of things to talk about, many of them provided by the circulation of books facilitated by improvements in transportation, newspapers, and eventually the postal service. It was a connection widely parodied by the suggestion that books were being read only as fodder for conversation and social display. By the 1790s, Coleridge's friend William Jackson of Exeter complained that learning was being debased into 'the shuttle cock of conversation'. Analogies drawn between reading and conversation were blurring a fundamental difference for Jackson:

The object of conversation is entertainment—the object of reading is instruction. No doubt, conversation may instruct, and reading may entertain; but this occasional assumption of each other's characteristic, only varies the principle, without destroying it.

The consistency of humanistic learning that writers like Fielding and Swift had feared would be undermined by commercial culture now seemed seriously threatened by a tide of conversation presumptuously assuming it could furnish the materials of culture:

A conversation is furnished from the impulse of the moment, books consist of digested thoughts, which are selected from many others.[66]

People like Coleridge and Jackson may have articulated such anxieties with a new intensity towards the end of the century, but more generally the periodical press, especially, remained committed to an idea of literature as a culture of conversation. From this perspective, the republic of letters was engaged in a process of sifting 'digested thoughts' by linking together dispersed communities of readers.

Essays on conversation kept coming from the periodical press right through the period covered by this book, reiterating the role of the

<hr/>

'Commerce, Conversation and Politeness in the Early Eighteenth-Century Periodical', *British Journal for Eighteenth-Century Studies*, 18 (1995), 63–77 (66–7)).

[65] Drummond, 'Rules of Conversation', 105.

[66] William Jackson, *The Four Ages; Together with Essays on Various Subjects* (London, 1798), 142–4.

periodicals as the veins and arteries of a culture committed to circulation as the life force of the body politic. 'An Essay on Conversation' published in the *Weekly Miscellany; or, Instructive Entertainer* for 6 December 1779 positioned conversation in a middle space between the sensuous enjoyments of the table and 'more serious and interested pursuits'.[67] Typically, the space of relative free play is defined in terms of the liberties of British civil society: 'the free and personal communication of our opinions and sentiments on domestic, political, or literary subjects'. Freedom is always strongly associated with conversation in the eighteenth century, not least because of its opposition to ceremony and incorporation within itself of multiple other forms (anecdote, punning, raillery, dialogue, complaint, etc). The authority for the *Weekly*'s definition soon turns out to be Cicero again, although it transpires conversation flourishes best, so the essay claims, under the free conditions of a modern commercial society, affiliated to the forms of the Roman republic, but—as Hume also suggested— bettering it in terms of the politeness of its manners.[68] 'Only in civilized countries, and among the learned and polished part of mankind' continues the essayist in the *Weekly*, can anything 'subsist deserving the name of conversation'. 'Savage' societies are limited to details of hunting and fighting. Nor are tyrannies encouraging of conversation. In societies where individuals and the community are 'estranged from public affairs, one pities the langour and littleness of social and private entertainments.' Only commercial modernity, it seems, can provide those 'easy and social meetings, in which are freely and calmly discussed domestic, political, and literary subjects'.

The essay in the *Weekly* was published at a troubled time for those who put their faith in conversational exchange as the motor of improvement. By 1779, heading towards defeat in the American War, not everyone in Britain was as confident about improvement. Free and calm discussion, particularly of politics, seemed a rare commodity. Even the *Weekly*, so invested in the privileges of being a modern European, gets on to the business of how conversation needs to be improved. The ethos of circulation and participation turns out to have threatened as much as encouraged polish and ease. 'Insulting dissertations and harangues' are reprobated, as are 'noisy vociferous mirth and laughter, the empty boast of unimitated birth and merit': 'Our great progress and improvement in arts and letters have enlarged the sphere of modern conversation to a boundless extent.'

---

[67] See 'An Essay on Conversation', *Weekly Miscellany*, 13 (6 December 1779), 221–6.
[68] For a contrast between Cicero on conversation and theories of deliberative democracy derived from Habermas, see Gary Remer's 'Political Oratory and Conversation: Cicero versus Deliberative Democracy', *Political Theory*, 27 (1999), 39–64.

What exercises the essay as it exercised a great deal of writing about conversation in the period is the question of how to regulate the flow. Cicero is important in essays like this one precisely because he provides an affiliation with a tradition of classical conversation, but the analogy often felt strained. As William Young, the Whig MP, put it looking back from 1777 at the conversational ethos of classical Athens: 'Then individuals formed a community, now, more properly, it may be said that a community consists of individuals.'[69]

This book will discuss periodical essays like the *Weekly*'s quite often, perhaps more than many books concerned with the literary culture of the late eighteenth and early nineteenth centuries.[70] Its attention in this regard ranges from well-known exponents like Addison and Steele, much reprinted and increasingly available in the Romantic period, through to Hazlitt and Hunt, both of whom, if with different kinds of affiliation, were very much aware of their conversational inheritance. These essayists were only the best known of the hundreds of anonymous writers who practised and extolled the virtues of conversation in the form of the familiar essay, a form that became strongly identified with the ease of conversation. One early defence of Montaigne's essays vindicated their digressive manner as the 'Liberty' assumed 'in common Conversations'.[71] Essays after the manner of Montaigne, according to Scott Black, 'foreground their own work in interweaving and assimilating other texts, and they invite the same of their readers'.[72] Hazlitt believed it was an invitation sustained much better in Montaigne than what he perceived as the sermonizing of Addison, but his judgment was still predicated on the general understanding of the conversational ambitions of the form. Essayists were frequently perceived as the water carriers of culture, developing connections between different knowledge networks, ensuring the circulation of ideas and information, allowing their readers into their personal and informal reflections. The genre presented itself as attuned to the diversity of experience in everyday life, written in a manner of easy address to its reader, often developing an idiomatic and personal style designed to give the impression of the writer as a friend or acquaintance of his or her

---

[69] William Young, *The Spirit of Athens, Being a Political and Philosophical Investigation of the History of that Republic* (London, 1777), 9.

[70] However, see Mark Parker, *Literary Magazines and British Romanticism* (Cambridge: Cambridge University Press, 2000); Kim Wheatley (ed.), *Romantic Periodicals and Print Culture* (London/Portland, Or: Frank Cass, 2003); and Schoenfield, *British Periodicals and Romantic Identity*.

[71] 'Vindication of Montaigne' (1700), quoted in Scott Black, *Of Essays and Reading in Early Modern Britain* (Basingstoke: Palgrave Macmillan, 2006), 93.

[72] Black, *Of Essays*, 2.

readers. The many essays *on* conversation were only reiterating the more general aspiration to an interactive and participatory idea of culture that was implicit in the genre.

There was more to this than just a rhetorical pose, although it was obviously exploited to gain a kind of paradoxical authority-in-ordinariness for the writer.[73] Terry Eagleton has understood this process in places like *The Spectator* as a form of 'masking' working to disguise a class 'consolidation' around the values of the new commercial society. My own approach is in broad agreement with this judgment, but such accounts must be careful not to represent complex and uneven historical processes as the teleological fulfillment of some prior ideological intention.[74] The idea of the conversation of culture certainly played a part in the navigation away from traditional forms of aristocratic authority and towards new forms of cultural identity, but it was an anxious process, often at odds with itself, never completed as such. Within it were ideas of liberation never entirely regulated into stable forms of commercial modernity, still unfulfilled in our own versions of democratic participation. The essays in *The Spectator* and other periodicals of the time were not just manifestations of some ideological script, but made their own contribution to the idea that culture was the product of processes of exchange between participants rather than the fulfillment of prior identities. They also reveal a complex relationship to a proliferating world of conversation that seems to have often been far from polite or equable. *The Spectator* both claims its authority in part from knowledge of this new urban culture and at the same time seeks to regulate it into smoother forms of exchange.

The idea of a culture of participation was not entirely a textual mask, but emerged out of and fed into reading practices. Relations in the marketplace for books were not straightforwardly anonymous for most of the eighteenth century, but part of a relatively 'knowable community of discourse'.[75] Eighteenth-century and early-nineteenth-century periodicals, especially, were a mainstay of book clubs and reading groups, and often emerged out of particular groups, then inviting other readers to

[73] See Clifford Siskin, *The Work of Writing: Literature and Social Change in Britain 1700–1830* (Baltimore/London: Johns Hopkins University Press, 1998), 164.
[74] See, for instance, Terry Eagleton, *The Function of Criticism from the* Spectator *to Post-Structuralism* (London: Verso, 1984), 10. A similar critique is to be found in Copley's 'Commerce, Conversation and Politeness', and, more broadly, David Simpson's *The Academic Postmodern and the Rule of Literature: A Report on Half-Knowledge* (Chicago: University of Chicago Press, 1995). Hammond, *Professional Writing*, 153, takes issue with the reading of spectatorial ease as a form of mask. See also Black's comments, *Of Essays*, 86–7.
[75] See Jon P. Klancher, *The Making of English Reading Audiences, 1790–1832* (Madison: University of Wisconsin Press, 1987), 20.

bring their conversation into their pages. The *Gentleman's Magazine* founded in the 1730s is an obvious example of the periodical that opened its pages to its readers. As late as 1796 the *Monthly Magazine*, formed out of the networks of Rational Dissent, projected itself as a 'budget' to which its readers could contribute and draw upon.[76] Perhaps more obviously priding itself on the professional brilliance of its writers, even Hunt's *Examiner* recruited readers to become writers themselves.[77] If periodicals were not always the products of social authorship, they were frequently at least consumed as part of a sociable setting that reinforced ideas of culture as a form of conversation. I do not simply mean that they were read out loud, although they often were, inside and outside the home, but also that their contents were deliberately oriented towards facilitating discussion. In 1821, the *Monthly Magazine* published a letter of 'Facts relative to the State of Reading Societies and Literary Institutions in the United Kingdom'. The writer addressed the *Monthly* because it had been 'always attentive to the formations of Book societies, and Literary Institutions of every description'.[78] The letter claims a group in Leicester, which included John Aikin Sr. and Joseph Priestley, formed the first of these reading societies in 1740. No doubt identifying this point of origin was flattering to the Dissenting associations of the *Monthly*, but it serves to indicate that eighteenth-century clubs and societies had always existed in a reciprocal relationship with newspapers and periodicals.

John Feltham's *Picture of London* (1802) described 'the best of the periodical works (the reviews, magazines, and annual registers)' lying on the tables of coffee houses for general use, facilitating the continuing use of these venues 'as lounging places for political and literary conversation'. Booksellers could also serve as 'lounging shops', providing newspapers and periodicals to stimulate further the flow of talk.[79] Bookshop sociability

---

[76] See Jon P. Klancher, *The Making of English Reading Audiences, 1790–1832* (Madison: University of Wisconsin Press, 1987), 22–3. For more on the ethos of the *Monthly*, see Felicity James, *Charles Lamb, Coleridge and Wordsworth: Reading Friendship in the 1790s* (Basingstoke: Palgrave Macmillan, 2008), 75–8, and Adriana Craciun, 'Mary Robinson, the Monthly Magazine, and the Free Press', in Wheatley (ed.), *Romantic Periodicals and Print Culture*, 19–40.

[77] The sociability of the Hunt group is discussed in my final chapter, but see the accounts of the emergence of Keats's first book of poetry from the 'buzz of...mixed conversation' in John Barnard, 'First Fruits or "First Blights": A New Account of the Publishing History of Keats's *Poems* (1817)', *Romanticism*, 12 (2006), 71–101, and 'Charles Cowden Clarke and the Leigh Hunt Circle 1812–1818', *Romanticism*, 3 (1997), 66–90.

[78] See 'Facts relative to the State of Reading Societies and Literary Institutions in the United Kingdom', *Monthly Magazine*, 51 (June 1, 1821), [mispaginated].

[79] John Feltham, *A Picture of London; being A Correct Guide* (London, 1802), 26–7 and 249–50.

was a feature of literary culture throughout the period covered by this book, which did not in any meaningful sense witness the advent of a 'mass' reading public, more properly a phenomenon of the 1840s and 1850s, despite the alarms of writers like Coleridge and Jackson. What data we have suggest a remarkable expansion in the number of imprints from 1763, but the result was not a sudden jolt in relations between readers and writers.[80] Although early-nineteenth-century publishers like Archibald Constable have been understood as converting 'the eighteen-century bookseller into the modern entrepreneurial publisher', the trade was still far from industrialized, print runs were still relatively small, and relations between readers and writers were not the purely alienated kind sometimes assumed to come into being once steam-driven presses appeared in the 1810s.[81] Booksellers, of course, had their commercial interests at heart in encouraging conversation on their premises. Edinburgh publishers like William Creech presided over a relatively porous world of writers and readers as 'a means of cultivating relationships with authors and potential authors'. In the associational world of the Scottish Enlightenment, 'books were revised for publication on the basis of comments and criticisms by members of these societies who heard oral renditions of earlier drafts or read them privately, the social aspect of Scottish club life takes on a high degree of importance for book culture.'[82] Large-scale, long-running firms did emerge during this period, but even the more professionalized busi-nesses remained places of conviviality, news, and gossip. Most remained small scale and dominated by the manual press until well into the 1820s and beyond.[83] London publishers like Taylor and Hessey, for instance, who published Keats's poetry and ran the *London Magazine*, still inter-acted with authors and readers in ways at least recognizable from the sociability of Joseph Johnson's bookshop in the 1790s. These circles were part of a world where reading and interpretation were not concluded by an encounter between solitary reader and singular text, but were often experienced as part of an ongoing process of conversation with others. One might well read in one's closet, but come to an understanding of what one had read alone in much more conversational circumstances, circum-

---

[80] See Michael F. Suarez, S. J., 'Towards a Bibliometric Analysis of the Surviving Record, 1701–1800', in Michael F. Suarez, S. J., and Michael L. Turner (eds), *The Cambridge History of the Book*, Vol. 5: *1695–1830* (Cambridge: Cambridge University Press, 2009), 39–65.

[81] Ian Duncan, *Scott's Shadow: The Novel in Romantic Edinburgh* (Princeton, NJ: Princeton University Press, 2007), 21.

[82] Sher, *Enlightenment and the Book*, 108 and 440.

[83] See James Raven, *The Business of Books: Booksellers and the English Book Trade 1450–1850* (New Haven, CT/London: Yale University Press, 2007), esp. 220–7.

stances that might conceive understanding not as a completion of the text in the mind of the reader, but as an open-ended conversation akin to what Elizabeth Vesey imagined when her literary gatherings pushed back the furniture to allow 'a zig-zag path of communication free from impediment'.[84] What was taken to constitute 'conversation' in these different contexts of reading and discussion, of course, varied wildly. There also remained the related question, increasingly fraught by the early decades of the nineteenth century, as to how far these different groups could be said to cohere into a 'public' in any meaningful sense.

The valorization of conversation in relation to the idea of the public was part of the much longer process Roger Chartier has described as 'desacralized reading'. Among the characteristics Chartier identified with 'the new style of reading' in eighteenth-century France were 'the reader's increased mobility before more numerous and less durable texts; the individualization of reading, when, in essence it became a silent and individual act taking place in privacy; the religious disinvestment of reading, which lost its charge of sacrality'.[85] 'Individualization of reading' is a dubious term given how much of the proliferation of reading took place in the new sociability of eighteenth-century society. In some regards, the phrase speaks more to developments in early-nineteenth-century Britain to which I'll return later in this Introduction. More often the emphasis on conversation in eighteenth-century cultural commentary was part of a drive to value 'learning' only in so far as it is put out into circulation. Part of this formation conceived of reading as a productive form of conversation between the living and the distant or the dead, effectively bringing back to life what otherwise might have lain hidden in musty libraries.[86] So in weighing against each other the *'eminent Means or Methods* whereby the Mind is improved in the Knowledge of Things', Isaac Watts judged the great advantage of reading to be the fact it allowed readers to partake in 'the Sentiments, Observations, Reasonings and Improvements of all the learned World, in the most remote Nations, and in former Ages, almost from the Beginning of Mankind'. Where

[84] See Madame D'Arblay [Frances Burney], *Memoirs of Doctor Burney*, 2 vols (London, 1832), II: 264.

[85] See Roger Chartier, *The Cultural Origins of the French Revolution*, trans. Lydia G. Cochrane (Durham, NC: Duke University Press, 1991), 89–91.

[86] Compare Hans-Georg Gadamer's *Truth and Method*, 2nd edn, trans. rev. Joel Weinsheimer and Donald G. Marshall (London/New York: Continuum, 2004), where 'conversation' as *'the fusion of horizons'* (370) recurs as a trope for reading. For a critique of this tendency to identify conversation with access to a psychology beyond the text, see Peters, *Speaking into the Air*, 148–9, and Tilottama Rajan, *The Supplement of Reading: Figures of Understanding in Romantic Theory and Practice* (Ithaca/London: Cornell University Press, 1990).

conversation gains for Watts is in the elucidatory possibilities of presence: 'When we *converse* familiarly with a learned Friend, *we have his own Help at hand to explain his every Word and Sentiment* that seems obscure in his Discourse.' The idea of friendship as a form of pre-selection in conversation that ensured relatively smooth processes of exchange was common enough, but Watts is particularly committed to a Protestant inflection of the idea that conversation brings things into circulation that might otherwise been lost outside of any productive economy of knowledge:

> *CONVERSATION calls out in to Light what has been lodged in all the Recesses and secret Chambers of the Soul:* By occasional Hints and Incidents it brings old useful notions into Remembrance; it unfolds and displays the hidden Treasures of Knowledge which *Reading, Observation, and Study* had before furnished the Mind. By mutual Discourse the Soul is awakend and allured to bring forth its Hoards of Knowledge, and it learns how to render them useful to Mankind. A Man of vast Reading without Conversation is like a *Miser* who lives only to himself.

Here conversation is a necessary supplement giving value to reading, bringing it out into the open world of discussion. For Watts, unlike many other 'polite' commentators, this included a more tolerant attitude to combative talk: 'Under this Head of *Conversation* we may also rank *Disputes* of various kinds.'[87] The implication is that reading is not a passive activity, but to flourish requires vigorous social interaction. For Watts, being with another in conversation was not the same thing as transparency. Although his discussion begins by contrasting them as roads to improvement, conversation and reading are understood as part of a process oriented towards the discovery of truth. It may prosper best if open to disagreement and even conflict.

Milton's wars of truth are at least to be glimpsed in Watts, perpetuating an idea of conversation as a zone of collision into the eighteenth century. More often the century's conversational turn has been understood—both in its eighteenth-century moment and a post-modern nostalgia for it—as a form of regulation designed to exclude contention and politics in the name of 'civilized' values.[88] The 'rules of conversation' did often operate so as to exclude those who it was thought might introduce too much of the irrationality of the crowd into the public sphere. William Godwin was one of many writers at the end of the century who critiqued this tendency in the discourse of politeness:

---

[87] Isaac Watts, *The Improvement of the Mind: or, a Supplement to the Art of Logick* (London, 1741), 30, 32, 40, 42, and 33. See the detailed discussion in Chapter 1.

[88] See the discussion in Simpson, *Academic Postmodern*, esp. 43–58.

By politeness many persons understand artificial manners, the very purpose of which is to stand between the feelings of the heart and the external behaviour. The word immediately conjures up to their mind a corrupt and vicious mode of society, and they conceive it to mean a set of rules, founded in no just reason, and ostentatiously practised by those who are familiar with them, for no purpose more expressly, than to confound and keep at a distance those who, by the accident of their birth or fortune, are ignorant of them. (*PPW*, V: 221)

No doubt polite conversation was frequently oriented towards this smooth flow of 'improvement' across commercial society. One of the features of eighteenth-century recreations of urban space described by Peter Borsay 'was their open plan, with a minimum of obstacles to interfere with the vision of those using them, and few nooks and crannies for the shy to hide in'. The aim was what Borsay calls 'free flow'.[89] 'Flow' is another trope that is everywhere collocated with conversation in eighteenth-century discourse, most frequently invoked by quoting from Pope's 'First Satire on the Second Book of Horace' on 'the Feast of Reason and the Flow of Soul' (l. 128).[90] Part of a long civic-minded tradition that understood conversation as a political modality, Godwin was one of many writers— many, including Watts, associated with Dissent—reluctant to sacrifice the productive potential of 'collision' to smoothing the flow of improvement. The more commonly articulated fear of many eighteenth-century promoters of conversation was that too much collision would impede the smooth flow of improvement, creating blockages in the system, overflowing the banks of properly regulated currents of exchange, and inundating the land with forms of false knowledge. Godwin had anxieties of his own as to how far collision should be allowed to go, but in *Political Justice* (1793) at least he kept alive a notion of conversation as productively combative that can be traced back to Watts.

RETRENCHMENT

Part I of this book is primarily concerned with the emergence of the conversational paradigm and its variants, including the attempts to refine and restrict it in print and in practice. The first chapter focuses on three influential but various iterations of the conversational paradigm found in earlier eighteenth-century writers, including Addison, Hume, and Watts. The overlaps and tensions between their ideas illustrate the ubiquitous, persistent, and contentious nature of the eighteenth century's conversational

---

[89] See Borsay, *The English Urban Renaissance*, 273.
[90] *The poems of Alexander Pope*, ed. John Butt (London: Routledge, 1989).

turn. The second chapter turns to the complex of conversable worlds that competed and interacted in forms of sociable practice and via representations in print and other media after 1762. The year corresponds to the beginning of Boswell's descriptions of his imitations of Addison in his 'London Journal', and his visits to places such as the Beefsteak Club. In the years that followed, swimming around figures like Samuel Johnson, Elizabeth Montagu, and Hester Piozzi, Boswell immersed himself in the full flow of London talk that fertilized and was fertilized by books, periodicals, pamphlets, and newspapers, but it was a fraught landscape through which conversation shaped an often uncertain course. Circulation remained a hegemonic value across cultural forms, but anxieties about inundation and blockage seem to intensify in comparison with the relative optimism of the earlier eighteenth century. Part II of this book is concerned with a series of case histories from the period after 1790, identified with Romanticism by traditional literary histories. No 'strong' version of the familiar periodization between the eighteenth century and Romanticism is intended by my bipartite structure, especially not one that simply condones an idea of the aesthetic transcending what Kant called 'having to grope about by means of experience among the judgments of others'.[91] This narrative appears in rather travestied form in Stephen Miller's belief that 'the conversable world contracted insofar as an increasing number of Englishmen—and probably Scotsmen as well—spent less time conversing in clubs and coffeehouses and more time enjoying the pleasures of the imagination by viewing lovely prospects.'[92]

Various more subtle narratives of withdrawal have depicted the early years of the nineteenth century as a watershed in British sociability. Peter Burke suggests that by 1800, 'in most parts of Europe, the clergy, the nobility, the merchants, the professional men—and their wives— had abandoned popular culture to the lower classes, from whom they

---

[91] Immanuel Kant, *A Critique of the Power of Aesthetic Judgment*, ed. Paul Guyer, trans. Guyer and Eric Matthews (Cambridge: Cambridge University Press, 2000), 163.

[92] Stephen Miller, *Conversation: A History of a Declining Art* (New Haven, CT/London: Yale University Press, 2006), 174. Miller's book is organized around an opposition between conversation (rooted in an eighteenth-century golden age) and a modern world where 'unrelenting contention' displaces the 'art of conversation'. The loss of the art of conversation for Miller is primarily the fault of a 'counter-culture' that values anger as self-expression (xiii). The idea of a fall from a golden age of flowing conversation, free from contention and dispute, is a recurrent feature of the discourse on the topic. Even Addison and Steele present themselves as attempting to restore something that has been lost. Most eighteenth-century commentators figure the art of conversation as battling against the kind of ideological debate Miller mourns as a product of 1968! See also Jenny Davidson's *Hypocrisy and the Politics of Politeness: Manners and Morals from Locke to Austen* (Cambridge: Cambridge University Press, 2004) on the complex negotiations between ideas of sympathy, hypocrisy, and politeness in the period.

were now separated, as never before, by profound differences in world view.'[93] Dror Wahrman's work has suggested that around the same time the middling sort increasingly distinguished themselves from the lower orders, who were abandoned to an impoverished category of 'the people'.[94] The growing taste for private theatricals at the end of the century has been linked to the withdrawal of the elite from the playhouses and 'the discomforting proximity of the lower orders'.[95] Hazlitt certainly complained at the loss of the social mix he associated with the London theatres. Others shared Matthew Bramble's feeling that urban developments in places like Bath were producing too much confusion of rank: 'a very inconsiderable proportion of genteel people are lost in the mob of impudent plebeians'.[96] Perhaps in an attempt to remove the bottlenecks and collisions that threatened the smooth flow of Georgian urban life, social space in general seems to have become more segregated by the end of the century. Peter Clark notes the increased regulation of clubs. Some began to purchase their own purpose-built premises rather than frequenting rooms in taverns and coffee houses. The rise of the disciplines meant scientists, for instance, may have increasingly divided into professionalized groups against the more open sociability associated with the eighteenth century.[97] Plenty of British writers in the early nineteenth century also noted the decline of the 'golden age' of the coffee houses. Isaac D'Israeli, for instance, believed it 'a custom which has declined within our recollection, since institutions of a higher character, and society itself, has improved so much of late'.[98] D'Israeli saw as improvement what those like Hazlitt, nostalgic for a culture of vigorous debate he identified with the 1790s, saw as retrenchment and retreat. These developments may have been the products of a society increasingly being formed into constellations of individual consumers, the world of self-enclosed nineteenth-century city dwellers described by Georg Simmel and Walter Benjamin, turned in upon themselves against the proximity of an unknown crowd, rather than subjects who constituted themselves out of conversations with

[93] See Peter Burke, *Popular Culture in Early Modern Europe* (London: Temple Smith, 1978), 270, and see the discussion in Connell and Leask, 'What is the People?', 10.

[94] See Dror Wahrman, *Imagining the Middle Class: The Political Representation of Class in Britain, c. 1780–1840* (Cambridge: Cambridge University Press, 1995).

[95] Gillian Russell, *The Theatres of War: Performance, Politics and Society 1793–1815* (Oxford: Clarendon Press, 1995), 122–3. Russell notes the parallel withdrawal of the elite into private concerts described in Simon McVeigh, *Concert Life from Mozart to Haydn* (Cambridge: Cambridge University Press, 1989), 299.

[96] Tobias Smollett, *The Expedition of Humphry Clinker*, ed. and intro. Lewis M. Knapp, rev. Paul-Gabriel Boucé (Oxford: Oxford University Press, 1984), 37.

[97] Clark, *British Clubs and Societies*, 247–54.

[98] Isaac D'Israeli, *Curiosities of Literature*, 3 vols (London, 1817), III: 378.

others.[99] The result, as Richard Sennett understands it, was 'a public realm filled with moving and spectating individuals', made up of spaces 'of the gaze rather than scenes of discourse'.[100]

Confirmation of Sennett's narrative of the disappearance of a mixed social world where 'people expected to talk and be talked to' might be found in the accounts of travelers like the German visitor Christian Augustus Goede.[101] Searching London, he looked in vain for the 'small familiar clubs' of the previous century, frequented, he believed, by the likes of Addison and Steele. Goede laid the blame (somewhat anticipating Habermas) on the commercial spirit that he thought permeated every aspect of British culture.[102] He accepted that learned societies were numerous, but found in them 'few instances of active co-operation'. Goede discovered a London dominated by what Sennett calls the 'ethics of indifference'.[103] Perceptions of conversation as a squeezed middle term between chaotic crowds and isolated individuals was echoed in Hannah More's *Coelebs in Search of a Wife*, where the hero is told: 'In London man is every day becoming less of a social, and more of a gregarious animal. Crouds are as little favourable to conversation as to reflection' (II: 186).[104] The preference in More's novel for conversation to seek the safe haven of domestic life finds an unexpected echo in Leigh Hunt's essay 'Coffee-Houses and Smoking'.[105] Writing in the guise of Harry Honeycomb, an obvious reference to Will Honeycomb from the cast of *The Spectator*, Hunt begins by mourning the passing 'of all the old coffee-houses and the wits'. He offers his own version of the withdrawal narrative: 'People confine themselves too much to their pews and boxes. In former times there was a more humane openness of intercourse.' The complication comes with the valorization of a comfortable domesticity that is a feature of much of his essay writing: 'I confess, if I were a wit, I would rather have a room to myself and friends. I should like to be public only in my books.' It emerges that Addison and Steele have been the architects of their own

---

[99] See Walter Benjamin on Simmel in *Charles Baudelaire: A Lyric Poet in the Era of High Capitalism*, trans. Harry Zohn (London: New Left Books, 1973), 37.
[100] See Richard Sennett's *Flesh and Stone: The Body and the City in Western Civilization* (New York/London: Norton, 1994), 347 and 358.
[101] Ibid. 344.
[102] C. A. G. Goede, *The Stranger in England; or Travels in Great Britain, containing Remarks on the Politics—Laws—Manners—Customs—and Distinguished Characters of that Country, translated from the German*, 3 vols (London, 1807), II: 140–1.
[103] Sennett, *Flesh and Stone*, 257.
[104] All references to More's novel are to *Coelebs in Search of a Wife*, 2 vols (London, 1808) and given in the text with volume and page number.
[105] See Leigh Hunt, 'Coffee-Houses and Smoking', *New Monthly Magazine*, 16 (January 1826), 50–4.

downfall, 'ruin[ing] their own pipes and wine' by encouraging 'a greater taste for literature and domesticity'. He finds his needs for a more comfortable form of sociability met by a room at Gliddon's snuff and tobacco shop in King Street. Here, in the kind of self-enclosed commercial venue bemoaned by Goede, 'the conversations were maintained in very quiet and gentlemanly tones.'[106] Comfortable Hunt may be at Gliddon's, but he doesn't close off other possibilities in the expanding metropolis, places like the 'Dog and Coal-hole' and 'Dolly's Beef-steak House' are allowed to have attractions of their own. Far from a straightforward eclipse of coffee house sociability, Hunt sees the conversation of culture as reformulating itself in new and different situations, including the more domesticated spaces that the previous century had played its part in creating.

The ambiguities of Hunt's position hints at some of the caveats I'd want to enter against any generalized picture of retrenchment and retreat in conversation. For a start, Hunt's account of the 'humane openness of intercourse' in eighteenth-century sociability is open to question. The impulse to regulate 'select' company so as to facilitate the smooth flow between like-minded participants was, as we have seen, felt as a pressure militating against open conversation from early in the eighteenth century. Nor did conversation simply disappear as a paradigm of literary culture in the nineteenth century. It was frequently dismissed, as Kant dismissed it, as mere gossip or triviality, part of the world that from the perspectives of Romantic ideology the visionary writer had to transcend in order to find the maturity of (usually 'his') singular voice. This position was qualitatively different even from the most restricted eighteenth-century models of 'select conversation', but it still tended to perpetuate an idea of culture as conversation, even if one where dialogue—tending towards an idealized reciprocal exchange—was privileged over the messiness of social talk. Literature started to imagine itself as a world of sympathies between feeling subjects—including the relations between writers and silent readers—more to be trusted than the world of mutual incomprehension out there. Such ideas were not exclusive to the late eighteenth century. Nor are they simply pitting the oral against the written, but rather an idea of communion is 'preserving', as Rajan puts it, 'the "inspired text" from interpersonal difference'.[107] Critics have often suggested that the figuring of writing as conversation in the period explored by this book offered a compensatory idea of the metaphysics of presence in the world of reading

---

[106] See Leigh Hunt, 'Coffee-Houses and Smoking', *New Monthly Magazine*, 16 (January 1826), 51, 53, and 54.
[107] Rajan, *Supplement of Reading*, 4.

where writers were increasingly unknown to their readers. I'll be returning to this idea quite often, but it needs to be treated carefully so as not cement its own binary between oral speech and print culture. What Samuel Johnson called 'the boundless chaos of a living speech' in many regards came to look as an unpromising ground on which to found an idea of national culture. Even Johnson's conversation, invoked as a monument to the solidity of British culture at times of crisis after his death, was sometimes a dubious ally in this regard, too brutal and uncouth for emulation. Conversation, in this guise, frequently appears in literary contexts as the sign of a fallen world in contrast to the silent communion allowed by reading (or viewing) that gained its authority by analogy to dialogue, but also sometimes defined in terms of its insulation from the chaos of talk in circulation.

Furthermore, whatever its implications for the relationship between literary culture and social life more broadly construed, the desire for a dialogue that transcended the everyday world was often related to an explicitly democratic desire to critique hierarchy. In *Memoirs of Emma Courtney*, part of the response by Mary Hays's heroine to her gendered exclusion from society is to intensify the dream of a language that transcends the mediations of social talk. The problem explored in the novel is that the yearning leads its heroine only into a dialogue with her own projections, a critique that Barbauld and John Thelwall were applying to Coleridge's poetry around the same time. Writers like Godwin, Hays, and Wollstonecraft all sometimes displayed a tendency to think of conversation as a sharing of consciousness at odds with their pleasurable experiences of debate and disagreement in literary London. The atmosphere of paranoia about government surveillance can only have intensified the tendency in the 1790s. Many radicals and reformers feared a system of spies and informers had penetrated not just the coffee house, but also even the sanctity of the home. By 1800 what remained for Godwin and his circle, according to Jon Klancher, was 'a London public sphere that is no longer principally argument against argument, nor confrontation face to face, but is now increasingly experienced as an incremental, unprepared for, astonishing process of erasure and disappearance'.[108] In attending to the displacements of conversation, this book does not narrate a fall into commercial alienation and individualism, much less does it celebrate a retreat into privacy or the recreation of conversation as a primarily private or domestic virtue. In the nineteenth century,

---

[108] See Jon Klancher, 'Discriminations, or Romantic cosmopolitanisms in London', in James Chandler and Kevin Gilmartin (eds), *Romantic Metropolis: The Urban Scene of British Culture, 1780–1840* (Cambridge: Cambridge University Press, 2005), 65–82 (70).

the work of making social life through language continued to feed the understanding of culture as a form of conversation. Hunt's Harry Honeycomb essay offers one version, hinting at ways that private conversation could be imagined as a form of publicity. Any number of recent studies have reiterated the social and group aspects of authorship in the Romantic period, including those that gathered around Hunt and the Cockneys. I've already suggested that bookshop sociability remained an important aspect of literary culture well into the 1820s. Even if one accepts that a bourgeois public sphere retreated to the virtuality of print, coordinated around individual readers consuming newspapers at the breakfast table, then at least the counter-public of popular radicalism after 1815 'remained stubbornly active and physical, never confined to the printed page'. Kevin Gilmartin shows its print culture to be 'saturated with speeches and debates, and with rich evidence of collective reading practices'.[109] Even in terms of individual reading practices, evidence from commonplace books such as Anne Lister's suggests plenty of polite readers 'poached' from the texts they read, often creating miscellanies of extracts to be circulated among friends as part of sociable practices of reading and writing.[110] This point does not imply any utopian free circulation of cultural knowledge. Until her inheritance, Lister's access to books was more or less constrained to circulating libraries, a restriction of female knowledge that played its own part in making conversation such an important medium for women.

When it comes to the larger field of literary production, Clifford Siskin is surely right to insist conversation remained a crucial term 'for describing not just the private individual exchanges, nor the public ones generated out of their multiplicity, but the flow *across* those newly constituted fields.'[111] The conversation of culture remained a domain structured around power and inequality, anxious about incursion and inundation, a place of contention as much as a place of dialogue, where 'collision' might be as much at issue as 'communion'. Two aspects of conversation stand out from the assumptions at work in these ideas: the desire for reciprocal dialogue and the understanding of culture emerging out of the everyday worlds of its participants. Although they were both often at play in the appeal to conversation as culture's medium, they were often in a deeper tension. The privileging of coordinated consciousness

---

[109] See Kevin Gilmartin, *Print Politics: The Press and Radical Opposition in Early Nineteenth-Century England* (Cambridge: Cambridge University Press, 1996), 30.

[110] Stephen Colclough, 'Recovering the Reader: Commonplace Books and Diaries as Sources of Reading Experience', *Publishing History*, 44 (1998), 5–37.

[111] See Siskin, *The Work of Writing*, 164.

and spirit-to-spirit reciprocity could repress the more hazardous idea of working through social practices. If definitions of the field of literary production in terms of visionary genius or professional specialism grew apace and gathered cultural authority, they did not simply erase the understanding or practices of reading and writing as taking place within and between variously situated conversable worlds.

PART I

1

Some Paradigms of Conversability in the Eighteenth Century

This chapter explores the complex and tangled web of ideas and assumptions about conversation that were to be inherited by the late eighteenth century. Taken together these assumptions reinforced a general idea of culture as a form of conversation, even as they struggled to accommodate the multiple contradictions contained in the general idea. Conversation spoke to a sense of the opening out of society in the name of modernizing improvement, for instance, but also appealed to a classical past. These affiliations with the past were frequently provoked by anxieties about proliferation and inundation that produced ongoing attempts to set limits to the idea of improvement. So, to give just one instance, perceptions of conversation as a polite performance aiming to consolidate certain kinds of social behaviour had to struggle with questions about the role of the passions and affections in the sociable world, and whether those passions facilitated or obstructed the creation of community. Hume's writing, I'll be contending, was the product of a culture of intellectual sociability in Edinburgh committed to 'politeness' and 'improvement'. He did all he could to promote conversation as a practice among the Scottish literati, but politeness and improvement could form a tense relationship if a commitment to rational enquiry privileged candour over agreeableness. Hume's own style after his *Treatise* (1738) is usually now understood in terms of his abandoning philosophical prose for polite letters, but his manner often displayed more spiritedness and spark than this summary might imply. His tendency 'upon all occasions to have a fling at the clergy', for instance, was taken to mar his 'very pretty style', at least by the Duchess of Atholl.[1]

Polite forms were not always sufficient for redeeming content considered likely to cause contention. Behind notions of conversation as a form

---

[1] Quoted in Mark R. M. Towsey, ' "Patron of Infidelity": Scottish Readers Respond to David Hume *c.*1750–*c.*1820', *Book History*, 11 (2008), 89–123 (89).

of pleasurable instruction could lurk very different emphases. Some writers, like the Rational Dissenters Isaac Watts and, later, Joseph Priestley, looked to conversation as a form of knowledge production, like a spark struck out between two flints, capable of bringing newness into the world. Neither was uninterested in questions of politeness, but for Priestley, especially, conversation as a conduit of truth had to be wary of conceding too much to civility or taste. The Lunar Society where Priestley met with other luminaries of the provincial enlightenment, men like Matthew Boulton, Erasmus Darwin, and Richard Lovell Edgeworth, used conversation as a medium for transmitting the latest experimental science.[2] Such men often took pleasure from the combative process of testing opinion. The 'rational' in these circles could be construed as a challenge to those received truths perpetuated out of custom or mere fashion. Priestley believed it imperative 'in conversation', as in other forms of discourse, 'to get access to the minds of those who are disposed to think, and…to employ ourselves simply in the propagation of truth'.[3] In this and other regards, 'politeness' and 'rational' conversation did not always make a neat fit. For Hester Lynch Piozzi, as we have already seen, this commitment to truth looked like a querulousness unwilling to adapt itself to the ways of the polite world. This chapter looks at a series of earlier eighteenth-century contexts where conversation was defined, written about, and subjected to influential scrutiny, sometimes controversially. They have been chosen partly because they exerted peculiar and diverse pressures on what we think of as the Romantic period, as later chapters will show, but none of them were absolutely distinct, nor were the trajectories of any of them intrinsically linked to any specific later formation. Addison and Steele's influence on the later period, for instance, was ubiquitous, but the implications were sharply contested between the *Quarterly Review* and *The Examiner* in the 1810s. Each of the earlier eighteenth-century cases discussed in this chapter fed into the general paradigm of conversation still being developed at the end of the century, reinforcing its importance to understanding of culture emerging in eighteenth-century Britain, but tensions within and between each of them meant they could scarcely supply a secure sense of the identity of the conversable world.

---

[2] See Jenny Uglow, *The Lunar Men: The Friends Who Made the Future* (London: Faber and Faber, 2003).

[3] Joseph Priestley, 'The Importance of Free Enquiry in Matters of Religion', in *Sermons by Richard Price and Joseph Priestley* (London, 1791), 103. The sermon was originally preached in 1785.

CONVERSING WITH MR. SPECTATOR

Throughout the eighteenth century and beyond, writers and readers of all kinds looked back to Joseph Addison and Sir Richard Steele's *Spectator* (1711–14) as the key text of the paradigm of conversability. Addison and Steele may not have invented the criteria of polite conversation, but they were regarded as defining figures for those later developing their own versions of conversability. Increasing access to cheap editions and anthologies made sure those outside the elite, including, for instance, Robert Burns in the 1770s, could encounter the world of *The Spectator* as a promise of a diffused republic of letters, whatever the regulatory intentions of its authors.[4] Presenting itself as centred in the urban culture of the coffee house, theatre, and clubs, *The Spectator* reported on and promoted a world where the position of the court as the seat of the nation's authority was being displaced by the day-to-day activities of its citizens. A literature of the ordinary was what it promised, predicated on 'mundane interdependence', written from within the bowels of everyday life.[5] Addison famously described himself as 'ambitious to have it said of me, that I have brought Philosophy out of Closets and Libraries, Schools and Colleges, to dwell in Clubs and Assemblies, at Tea-Tables, and in Coffee-Houses' (*S* 10, I: 44).[6] Addison and Steele situated their discourse in opposition to the unworldly wrangling of scholasticism, the inaccessibility of the court, and the pedantry of the universities, on the one hand, but also against what seemed a potentially limitless proliferation of print culture on the other. The clubbable face-to-face interactions described in many of their essays attempt to create a safety zone within the world of the wild and incoherent sociabilities posited by Klein. One of their watchwords was 'simplicity'. Indeed in Sir Richard Steele's *The Tatler*, the predecessor to the *The Spectator*, the project framed itself in terms of its desire to halt the 'decay of conversation' away from this standard of simplicity. Although this might sound a somewhat nostalgic note for what I have been representing as a modernizing formation, Steele's concerns

---

[4] Burns told Dr. John Moore that 'my knowledge of modern manners, and of literature and criticism, I got from the Spectator': Burns to Dr. John Moore, August 1787, *The Letters of Robert Burns*, ed. G. Ross Roy, vol. I: *1780–1789*, 2nd edn (Oxford: Oxford University Press, 1985), 133–46 (138).

[5] Scott Black, *Of Essays and Reading in Early Modern Britain* (Basingstoke: Palgrave Macmillan, 2006), 99.

[6] All references to *The Spectator* are to Donald F. Bond's edition, 5 vols (Oxford: Clarendon Press, 1987) as *S* followed by original issue number and then volume and page number.

about conversation are set in the context of the expectation that 'we should rise in our Publick Diversions, and Manner of enjoying Life, in proportion to our Advancement in Glory and Power' (*T* 12, I: 104).[7] Steele's 'decay' is a fall from a standard of colloquial simplicity deemed natural to his countrymen and, potentially, about to be fulfilled again in 'the present Grandeur of the *British* Nation'. This British colloquial simplicity—its 'free, brisk, and lively air' as one conduct book put it—is the expression of the national character, continually, as Klein has shown, contrasted with the formality of Frenchified manners and the ceremony of the court of Louis XIV.[8]

In contrast to the hierarchical emulation of French courtly culture, for Addison and Steele conversation was primarily a discourse that took place across a level horizontal plane: 'Equality is the Life of Conversation,' wrote Steele,

and he is as much out who assumes to himself any Part above another, as he who considers himself below the rest of the Society. Familiarity in Inferiors is Sauciness; in Superiors, Condescension; neither of which are to have Being among Companions, the very Word implying that they are to be equal. When therefore we have abstracted the Company from all Considerations of their Quality or Fortune, it will immediately appear, that to make it happy and polite, there must nothing be started which shall discover that our Thoughts run upon any such Distinctions. Hence it will arise, that Benevolence must become the Rule of Society, and he that is most obliging must be most diverting. (*T* 225, III: 174)

Both *The Tatler* and *The Spectator* are much taken up with the question of how to create the egalitarian conditions in which companionable conversation might flourish. In *Spectator* 93, Addison addressed the issue in terms of 'certain Methods for the filling up their empty Spaces of Life' (*S* 93, I: 395). The question pertains primarily to those 'who are not always in a perpetual hurry of affairs, of those only who are not always engaged in Scenes of Action'.

Addison himself was only in this situation because he had lost government office when the Tories came to power under Queen Anne, a period of enforced leisure that gave him time to create an image for himself among the circle of wits at Button's coffee house. *The Spectator* project grew out of the same situation. In both capacities, Addison appeared as the

---

[7] *The Tatler*, ed. by Donald F. Bond, 3 vols (Oxford: Clarendon Press, 1987), III: 174. All references in the text are to this edition, abbreviated to *T*, followed by original issue number and then volume and page number.

[8] [D. A.], *The Whole Art of Conversation* quoted in Lawrence E. Klein, 'The Figure of France: The Politics of Sociability in England, 1660–1715', *Yale French Studies*, 92 (1997), 30–45, esp. 37.

private man outside the world of political expediency and party interest. Valerie Rumbold has shown that when the word 'conversation' appears in book titles from around this time, it still tends to be associated with a religious idea of 'the whole of a life lived in community under God' rather than merely what she calls 'social talk'.[9] Addison's latitudinarian Anglicanism plays a more important part in his thinking about the role and nature of conversation in the latter sense than many later eighteenth-century writers, who, like the novelist Henry Fielding in his essay on the subject, usually pass quickly over the topic of religion to address questions of human sociability. Fielding identifies three kinds of conversation: with God; with ourselves; and with others, but soon leaves aside the first two in order to concentrate on 'the reciprocal Interchange of Ideas'.[10] Addison more definitely acknowledged the virtues of conducting private conversations with God:

There is another kind of Virtue that may find Employment for those Retired Hours in which we are altogether left to our selves, and destitute of Company and Conversation; I mean, that Intercourse and Communication which every reasonable Creature ought to maintain with the great Author of his Being.

Nevertheless, his brand of polite Anglicanism continually leads him back to the conversable world of social talk and the pleasures 'of thinking himself in Company with his dearest and best of Friends'.[11] Awareness of God's presence does not bring any experience of transcendent religious awe, always likely to be associated with the enthusiasm of Dissent by latitudinarian Anglicanism; rather for Addison properly regulated piety points the imagination back to the life of social talk, which providentially offers the fullest experience of human being:[12]

But the Mind never unbends it self so agreeably as in the Conversation of a well chosen Friend. There is indeed no Blessing of Life that is in any way comparable to the

---

[9] See Valerie Rumbold, 'Locating Swift's Parody: The Title of *Polite Conversation*', in H. J. Real (ed.), *Reading Swift: Papers from the Fifth Münster Symposium on Jonathan Swift* (München: Wilhelm Fink, 2008), 255–72 (255 and 257). I am very grateful to Professor Rumbold for providing me with a copy of her essay.

[10] Henry Fielding, 'An Essay on Conversation', in *Miscellanies*, ed. Henry Knight Miller, 3 vols (Oxford: Clarendon Press, 1972), I: 121.

[11] Black's *Of Essays* dismisses critics who relate Addison's development of the familiar essay to traditions of Protestant self-reflection in favour of a resolutely secular and commercial understanding. The idea of Addison as the evangelist of 'mundane interdependence' (99) perhaps underestimates the transitional nature of the project and its often tense negotiations with other versions of sociability in the new urban culture.

[12] Thought of God immediately raises the image of the sociable circle of friends for Addison. Note the contrast with Coleridge's 'This Lime Tree Bower my Prison', discussed in Chapter 4.

Enjoyment of a discreet and virtuous Friend. It eases and unloads the Mind, clears and improves the Understanding, engenders Thoughts and Knowledge, animates Virtue and good Resolutions, sooths and allays the Passions, and finds Employment for most of the vacant Hours of Life. (*S* 93, I: 395–7)

Addison's preference in this essay for 'Intimacy with a particular Person' over 'a more general Conversation' intimates a narcissistic aspect to *The Spectator*'s idea of conversation. If general conversation is a virtuous activity, its attractions are less than the kind of talk that pre-selects its company to ensure a closer form of communion.

Addison may be part of a broad historical process by which the public came to be perceived as created from interactions of private men (and, to a lesser extent, women), as Habermas would have it. Familiarity in Addison's writing may function as a turn away from the ceremonial formality found in courts, but the emphasis is on regulation and consolidation rather than the kind of political enquiry that 'rational-critical debate' implies. What may seem like an egalitarian logic in Addison and Steele's writing actually aims to suppress difference and bring the play of particularities into balance. Even in their more expansive moods, they identify conversation with a freely flowing kind of circulation relatively insulated from any jolting encounter with strangeness.[13] Knowledge is only a subordinate matter here, more the concern of second order or 'general' conversation 'with such as are able to entertain and improve those with whom they converse' (*S* 93, I: 397). The real function of conversation is for it to take a foundational place among 'the practical devices' as John Money puts it, 'by which the moral problems of a commercializing society were negotiated'. Conversation provided a key means by which, to continue using Money's terms, Addison and the rising commercial classes could 'replicate themselves, and their values, as the providential preservers of the health and progress of civil society'.[14] For Addison and Steele conversation has little to do with the *production* of knowledge, unlike another sometime contributor to *The Spectator*, Issac Watts, whose ideas are discussed later in this chapter. Their perspective has more to do with confirming what is already known to the circles of select company for those out-of-doors readers unable to gain access to Mr. Spectator's club itself.

For Steele, the process is imagined as one by which the company is 'abstracted' from questions of 'Quality or Fortune' into the desire to be

---

[13] For a useful discussion of this issue, see Terry Eagleton's *Trouble with Strangers: A Study of Ethics* (Chichester: Wiley-Blackwell, 2009), especially Part 1.

[14] John Money, 'The Masonic Moment: Or, Ritual, Replica, and Credit: John Wilkes, the Macaroni Parson, and the Making of the Middle-Class Mind', *Journal of British Studies* 32 (4) (1993), 358–95 (361).

agreeable and 'pleasing [to] each other when we meet' (*T* 225, III: 173–4). For Addison and Steele, human identity and values are not fixed, but shaped by and towards social interaction. The emphasis is on 'the collective imitation and communication of human example rather than on the obedient mimesis of transcendental order and divine ordinance.'[15] One must comport oneself in a particular sort of way to make conversation possible, and the experience of conversation confirms and deepens the experience of politeness and strengthens the foundations of civil society. By being agreeable, we show ourselves to others as capable of easy exchange, and the pleasurable experience of such exchange deepens our desire to perpetuate it. In this regard, as Klein and others have pointed out, polite conversation is also a performance, concerned above all else with how one behaves towards others, but the experience is commonly advertised as a kind of narcissistic entry into a hall of mirrors, with everyone performing versions of the same self. Sincerity might seem an essential aspect of any idea of conversation based on 'simplicity' and English 'freedom', especially when defined against the servile courtliness identified with the French, but for *The Spectator* such liberty can be overvalued if it leads to a crude speaking of home truths rather than the perpetuation of agreeableness.

Servility, Steele makes clear in *Spectator* 280, is to be abjured in conversation. The servile man, who makes himself abject before his monarch or patron, surrenders 'his very Soul', but civility entails an attention to 'the Art of Pleasing' rather than simply speaking one's mind. What matters is not that one's interlocutors are told the truth, but 'the Opinion they have of your Sincerity'. Recognizing, not without reluctance, that the world in which conversations take place is one where there is constant intercourse with 'either those above you or below you', the arts of politeness are neither magisterial nor craven:

This Servitude to a Patron, in an honest Nature, would be more grievous than that of wearing his Livery; therefore we shall speak of those Methods only which are worthy and ingenuous. (*S* 280, II: 592)

Steele's essay develops this point by taking up the example of a great ruler who is able to enjoy conversation precisely because he lays aside his power. The Emperor Augustus is presented as the kind of monarch who was able to perpetuate a republican civility, although Steele implicitly invokes the commercial context of the early eighteenth century by mention of the idea of making one's fortune:

---

[15] Ibid. 360.

Augustus lived amongst his Friends as if he had his Fortune to make in his own Court: Candour and Affability, accompanied with as much Power as ever Mortal was vested with, were what made him in the utmost Manner agreeable among a Set of admirable Men, who had Thoughts too high for Ambition, and Views too large to be gratified by what he could give them in the Disposal of an Empire, without the Pleasures of their mutual Conversation. A certain Unanimity of Taste and Judgment, which is natural to all of the same Order in the Species, was the Band of this Society; and the Emperour assumed no Figure in it but what he thought was his Due from his private Talents and Qualifications, as they contributed to advance the Pleasures and Sentiments of the Company. (592)

Classical republican virtue is in a tacit negotiation here with the realities of getting on in the eighteenth-century world. Steele's 'rational and select Conversation' (591) is not without anxieties as to where this performative conception leaves the question of virtue, and breaks off by acknowledging that 'I am here prating of what is the Method of Pleasing so as to succeed in the World, when there are Crowds who have, in City, Town, Court, and Country, arrived at considerable Acquisitions, and yet seem incapable of acting in any constant Tenour of Life'. The implication is that the question of succeeding in the world is already at odds with the larger public spiritedness imagined of Augustus's courtiers. Steele's solution is simply to 'shorten this Enquiry after the Method of Pleasing'. The brisk closure presents itself as privileging consideration for others over pursuing the moral question to any logical conclusion. To go to such lengths would be too much like the pedantry of the colleges and cloisters. If Steele grants to himself the freedom to break off his train of thought, what he leaves the reader with scarcely represents a happy resolution of the question of the social virtues in a commercial society: 'so may I to my Reader abridge my Instructions, and finish the Art of Pleasing in a Word, *Be rich*' (593).

The italics used for the phrase '*Be rich*' may indicate something of the irony at work in the injunction, but they scarcely stabilize its uncertain effects. Steele's essay very clearly involves itself in the difficult question of producing communal values in the context of a world of getting and spending. Conversation shapes these values through 'commerce', correlating it with the role of trade in producing the nation's wealth. One of the most striking passages in *The Spectator* in this regard is Addison's tear-filled joy at the scenes before him at the Royal Exchange:

Nature seems to have taken a particular Care to disseminate her Blessings among the different Regions of the World, with an Eye to this mutual Intercourse and Traffick among Mankind, that the Natives of the several Parts of the Globe might have a kind of Dependance upon one another, and be united together by their common Interest. (*S* 69, I: 294–5)

Trade becomes not a means of making personal fortunes, but a form of special providence whereby human beings interacting through conversation come to recognize their mutual interdependence.

Klein's important work on politeness positions *The Spectator* as the popular organ of a Whig project of sociability for which the more philosophical correlate is the writing of Anthony Ashley Cooper, the third Earl of Shaftesbury.[16] Both were explicitly committed to bringing philosophy out of retirement and into the sociable world of clubs and conversation. For Shaftesbury, as for Addison and Steele, conversation was not simply a principle of the social world, but also part of the process through which subjectivity is created. Shaftesbury translates the ancient principle of self-knowledge as 'Divide yourself'.[17] Polish is acquired by staging such a conversation within the self, so that we may 'as in a looking-glass, discover ourselves and see our minutest features.' The process can then be taken out into society to be further polished in the conversable world of 'good company and people of the better sort'.[18] By writing philosophical dialogues, after the manner of Plato, Shaftesbury suggested, one might provide 'a kind of mirror or looking-glass to the age'.[19]

Subjectivity is acquired through entering into conversation with others on what I have called a 'horizontal' plane, but for Shaftesbury this terrain has a more narrowly aristocratic ambit than *The Spectator's*. His version of republican virtue may have been hostile to the culture of the Court, but its 'circle of good company' tends to form most naturally in the environs of the parks of the landowning classes rather than the associational world of the commercial city.[20] Shaftesbury's version of Whig values subscribes much more clearly to a masculine civic humanist ethos than the modernizing *Spectator*. He sees commercial society as corrosively effeminizing through its reliance on 'scrupulous nicety' rather than what he calls those 'masculine helps of learning and sound reason'.[21] From this perspective, Addison and Steele's world looked dangerously close to a feminized discourse of chitchat and gossip.[22] Shaftesbury's principle of 'amicable collision' was designed to reveal beneath the accrued 'rust' of superficial

[16] Lawrence E. Klein, *Shaftesbury and the Culture of Politeness: Moral Discourse and Cultural Politics in Early Eighteenth-Century England* (Cambridge: Cambridge University Press, 1994).

[17] Lord Shaftesbury, *Characteristics of Men, Manners, Opinions, Times*, ed. Lawrence E. Klein (Cambridge: Cambridge University Press, 1999), 77.

[18] Ibid. 87 and 75.　　　[19] Ibid. 89.

[20] Ibid. 231.　　[21] Ibid. 233.

[22] For two recent accounts of *The Tatler* and *The Spectator* in relation to gossip, see Rebecca Bullard, *The Politics of Disclosure, 1674–1725: Secret History Narratives* (London: Pickering and Chatto, 2009), esp. 111–32, and Nicola Parsons, *Reading Gossip in the Early Eighteenth-Century England* (Houndmills: Palgrave Macmillan, 2009), esp. 92–118.

manners or custom (a much used metaphor in the modernizing discourse of conversation) a 'universal plastic nature'.[23] Its values are affiliated to the great classical texts, especially Plato's, transcending questions of time and place. In this respect Shaftesbury's use of the Socratic dialogue, derived from Plato's example, contrasts with what we might call the more novel-ized representations of conversation found in Addison and Steele essays.[24] Their regular invocations of Horace and Cicero may present the world they describe as continuous with classical values, but their readers are made continually aware of the busy eighteenth-century world in and about which they write, including a regular survey—far from being always positive—of its distinctive turns of phrase and colloquial neologisms.[25] Shaftesbury's dialogues are not colloquial in this way; they are not marked by the details of their contemporary location, as the adoption of classical names for the discussants of his philosophical dialogues suggest. Where the 'amicable collision' of Shaftesbury's polite world is defined in assert-ively masculine terms, seemingly unafraid of a clash of contraries in the service of revealing general nature, Addison and Steele's ideas on politeness are much more emollient. So, for Shaftesbury, ridicule can operate as an acid test of truth, including the truths of religion, but in *The Tatler* and *The Spectator* several papers warn against the danger of ridicule going too far, in case its acidity leads to violence and contention. Their desire for agreeableness aims to leave an altogether sweeter taste in the reader's mouth than Shaftesbury's stoicism.

The differences between Shaftesbury and *The Spectator* have been well marked by David Solkin in relation to the social portraiture of the early eighteenth century. The rise of the conversation piece as a genre in the 1720s and 1730s, after a series of earlier false starts, indicates the pervasive appeal of the cultural shift identified with *The Spectator* project. Looking at earlier attempts at social portraiture, Solkin compares John Closter-man's picture of Shaftesbury and his brother Maurice (see Fig. 1) with the series of portraits Sir Godfrey Kneller painted for the Kit-Cat Club, whose members included Addison, as well as the painter himself. Solkin notes that Closterman 'made a point of showing them as oblivious to the viewer's presence; a presentation consistent with Shaftesbury's resistance to the notion of the individual as role-player, his refusal as an autonomous

---

[23] Shaftesbury, *Characteristics*, 31 and 93.

[24] I take the term 'novelized' from M. M. Bakhtin. See *The Dialogic Imagination: Four Essays*, ed. Michael Holquist, trans. Caryl Emerson and Michael Holquist (Austin: University of Texas Press, 1981), 5–6.

[25] Adam Potkay notes that Cicero provides many of the mottoes to essays in *The Spectator*. See *The Fate of Eloquence in the Age of Hume* (Ithaca/London: Cornell University Press, 1994), 11.

Fig. 1. John Closterman, 'Maurice Ashley-Cooper; Anthony Ashley-Cooper, 3rd Earl of Shaftesbury' (1702). Courtesy of the National Portrait Gallery, London.

citizen to engage in the characteristic relations of the marketplace'.[26] Shaftesbury directed the whole enterprise as part of an effort to raise the estimation of portraiture towards the classical status of history painting. Closterman's full-length portrait shows the brothers in pseudo-classical dress, conversing in a copse before a small temple. Their situation, as Solkin remarks, 'reworks the familiar Horatian topos of virtuous retirement, staging an implicit contrast between the wholesomeness of a tranquil country life and the active and self-interested pursuits associated with the city or the court'.[27] Naturalizing the role of the brothers as landowners, the wooded landscape in which they appear aims to confirm these Whig aristocrats as natural rulers. Kneller's paintings are much more aware of the involvement of their subjects in circuits of exchange, which include the viewers of the picture. This 'audience-oriented subjectivity', to use Habermas's term, looks to bind its viewers into its construction of a conversable community.[28]

James Thornhill's group portrait 'Andrew Quicke in Conversation with the 1st Earl of Godolphin, Joseph Addison, Sir Richard Steele, and the Artist' (*c.*1711–12) provides a striking contrast with the portrait of Shaftesbury and his brother (see Fig. 2). The classicized background seeks to present the new commercial sociability not as a rupture but a natural development of the values of the classical past affirmed by Shaftesbury. Addison and his friends here participate in the world of goods that fuelled the conversations described in *The Spectator*. They share a bottle of wine (the two glasses between five, as Solkin suggests, pointing to a moderate restraint separating this clubbable world from the tavern), but also practise conversation as a form of polite exchange between equals that puts to one side hierarchy and inequality. The Earl of Godolphin, the nobleman at the centre of the group, patron to most of those involved, like Augustus among his courtiers in *Spectator* 280, does not exercise his superiority of rank. The note that Addison receives from a servant entering the left-hand edge of the picture shows the circle's involvement in the larger world, but the relationship between the world of business and the conversability on display here is better managed in the picture than in *Spectator* 280. Here the awareness of a world of making deals does not break up their equipoise as conversationalists, and like the glances that serve to knit together the participants with the viewer, only emphasizes the

---

[26] David H. Solkin, *Painting for Money: The Visual Arts and the Public Sphere in Eighteenth-Century England* (New Haven/London: Yale University Press, 1993), 36.

[27] Ibid. 12.

[28] See Jürgen Habermas, *The Structural Transformation of the Public Sphere: An Inquiry into a Category of Bourgeois Society*, trans. Thomas Burger with the assistance of Frederick Lawrence (Cambridge, MA: MIT Press, 1989), 49.

Fig. 2. James Thornhill, 'Andrew Quicke in Conversation with the 1st Earl of Godolphin, Joseph Addison, Sir Richard Steele, and the Artist' (*c.*1711–12). Private collection. Photograph courtesy of the Paul Mellon Centre for Studies in British Art, London.

idea of a community beyond this particular circle. The exact context for the painting of Thornhill's picture is unknown, but Kneller's pictures were explicitly designed to be part of this conversable world, as they were to hang together in the room in Joseph Tonson's house in Barn Elms, where the Kit-Cat Club held its meetings. Solkin describes it as 'a new kind of portrait gallery', designed not to support dynastic authority, but rather to illustrate an emergent concept of sociability predicated on a community of politeness operating in a commercial society.[29]

The confidence of the Thornhill painting and those portraits Kneller painted for the Kit-Cat Club may spring from the fact that they were intended to be placed in a relatively constrained conversable circle, where the subjects of the paintings mingled with the select numbers of the viewers. In this regard, the audience towards which its version of subjectivity was directed was a very restricted one. The coffee house world onto

---

[29] Solkin, *Painting for Money*, 37.

which *The Spectator* sometimes vertiginously opens is not part of the more limited nexus of glances represented and presumed by these paintings. There may be a look beyond the frame in Thornhill's picture, but it is likely to have been received by those already in the picture, probably literally, and certainly metaphorically. *The Spectator* describes a much less limited and knowable terrain, and often represents the experience as discomforting. The Addisonian culture of politeness sought, among other things, a flattening out of this broader world of contention and competition. The principle of abstraction that the project's egalitarianism depends upon operates as a limit on the novelization of their discourse. Writing in *Spectator* 49, for instance, Steele offers a lively picture of one coffee house, identifying two kinds of clients, students from the inns of court, who rise early only to laze around in the coffee house, before being replaced by 'Men who have Business or good Sense in their Faces, and come to the Coffee-house either to transact Affairs or enjoy Conversation'. The latter include Beaver, a haberdasher, surrounded by his court of admirers, who do not let their own opinions be known until they know his. Men of this class seem unable to abstract themselves from their socio-economic situation in commercial society. Steele prefers to be with people for whom 'the pretended Distinction in Company is only what is raised from Sense and Understanding' (*T* 225, III: 173), the modern equivalent of the men of enlarged views in the court of Augustus. Ironically, in *Spectator* 280, 'pretended distinction' is displaced onto the merits of social performance and conversation, which functions here to divert the reader from questions of wealth and class. *Spectator* 49 had made the same point, placing its faith in those 'as have not Spirits too Active to be happy and well pleased in a private Condition, nor Complexions too warm to make them neglect the Duties and Relations of Life' (*S* 49, I: 210). The performance of the happy medium imagined here depends upon the avoidance of desire and dissent in the name of the easy reproduction of social relations.

The Tatler and *The Spectator* are often quite explicit about the forms of conversation that qualify as polite. Indeed the increasingly conversable tone and format of the essays themselves better serve to negotiate the contradiction of teaching a mode meant to be all about tact, learning through the experience of good company, than the often clumsy didacti-cism of the conduct books. Nevertheless, at times, the periodicals *are* explicitly didactic about their interventions into conversational conduct. Steele describes one 'common Fault', for instance, as 'growing too inti-mate, and falling into displeasing Familiarities'. An easy commerce is distinct from the collapsing of hierarchies or the induction of the vulgar into the conversable world. The 'robust Pleasantries practised by the rural

Gentry of this Nation' are regularly criticized by both Addison and Steele, part of their Whig antagonism to the Tory squirearchy, but even more readily both police the behaviour of those who inhabit the new commercial culture of the town: 'even among those who should have more polite Idea's of Things, you see a Set of People who invert the Design of Conversation, and make frequent Mention of ungrateful Subjects' (*T* 225, III: 172). Addison and Steele position themselves above the conversability of the coffee houses in this regard. From this elevated vantage point, they can see that the 'present Grandeur of the *British* Nation' is not matched by any 'rise in our Publick Diversions, and Manner of enjoying Life'. Such regressive behaviour threatens the modernizing narrative that *The Spectator* wants to suggest is already marvelously shaping the future. Coffee houses are frequently presented as a babble of many voices, '*a barren Superfluity of Words*' (*S* 476, IV: 187), rather than an arena of polite conversation.[30] In *The Tatler*, Steele had complained that the quality of conversation did not keep up with the nation's commercial grandeur: 'you'l [*sic*] find, Rakes and Debauchees are your Men of Pleasure; Thoughtless Atheists, and Illiterate Drunkards call themselves Free-Thinkers; and Gamesters, Banterers, Biters, Swearers, and Twenty new-born Insects more, are, in their several Species, the modern Men of Wit' (*T* 12, I: 104). Although Addison and Steele may sometimes seem to be in favour of a free trade in wit, identifying conversation with an open 'flow' of pleasurable communication, they identify certain kinds of talk as below the ideal of polite conversation they promote.

From the perspectives of the discourse of politeness, figurative language was often associated with the primitiveness of vulgar speech, on the one hand, or the irresponsibility of aristocratic ornament on the other.[31] Addison and Steele certainly seek to regulate the indulgence of wordplay in conversation. Punning, for instance, is to be treated with suspicion; its tendency towards opening up a sexual horizon in polite conversation threatens to interrupt the flow, throwing up physical obstacles—the language of the body—in the kind of talk that ought to aim at more decorous and 'abstracted' forms of interaction. In *Spectator* 504, Steele complains that 'Punning is therefore greatly affected by Men of small Intellects':

---

[30] Addison took the phrase from Samuel Garth's poem *The Dispensary* (1706).
[31] See Simon Alderson's, 'The Augustan Attack on the Pun,' *Eighteenth-Century Life*, 20 (3) (1996), 1–19, and Potkay, *The Fate of Eloquence*, 70–1. Hester Lynch Piozzi's *British Synonymy; or, An Attempt at Regulating the Choice of Words in Familiar Conversation*, 2 vols (London, 1794), dismissed punning as 'mock rainbow wit' (II: 184).

These Men need not be concerned with you for the whole Sentence, but if they can say a quaint thing, or bring in a Word which sounds like any one Word you have spoken to them, they can turn the Discourse, or distract you so that you cannot go on, and by Consequence if they cannot be a witty as you are, they can hinder your being any wittier than they are.

Unintentionally confirming the distracting nature of puns, Steele himself can't help but pause in his essay to give a few examples, but then goes on to discuss the more egregious error of

another Kind of People of small Faculties, who supply want of Wit with want of Breeding; and because Women are both by Nature and Education more offended at any thing which is immodest than we Men are, these are ever harping upon things they ought not to allude to, and deal Mightily in double Meanings.

These 'double Meaners', Steele complains, are 'dispersed up and down through all Parts of Town or City' (*S* 504, IV: 288). In *Spectator* 155, Addison had already discussed the 'indecent License taken in Discourse, wherein the Conversation on one Part is involuntary, and the Effect of some necessary Circumstance', for instance, suddenly finding oneself thrown into intimacy with strangers in a coach or other form of public assembly. The situation is one that reiterates Addison's preference for conversable situations with gentlemen much like himself, and preferably, as in the Thornhill picture, with those to whom he is already personally known. Conversation, which might be thought of as a means to produce familiarity, is ironically for Addison better supported among those who are already familiars. Typically, however, he uses the question of relations between the sexes to unpack his discomfort, and proceeds to a series of letters of complaint from 'that Part of the Fair Sex, whose Lot in Life it is to be of any Trade or publick Way of Life' (*S* 155, II: 107).

The first letter is from the proprietor of a coffee house who complains at the fact her customers 'strive who shall say the most immodest things in my Hearing'. Addison goes on to report:

They tell me that a young Fop cannot buy a Pair of Gloves, but he is at the same Time straining for some ingenious Ribaldry to say to the young Woman who helps them on. It is no small Addition to the Calamity, that the Rogues buy as hard as the plainest and modestest Customers they have; besides which they loll upon their Counters half an Hour longer than they need, to drive away other Customers.

Double entendres here quite literally block the flow of trade. Addison claims to have had numerous other letters from Change Alley complaining of 'light Conversation of commonplace-Jests, to the Injury of her whose

Credit is certainly hurt by it'.[32] Conversation is meant to improve the flow of 'commerce', but predatory male sexuality is a diversion from this smooth system of exchanges. The young fops would be better off restraining their conversation to a form of politeness that facilitates the flow of goods: 'they ought with Cash to supply their want of Eloquence.' To be fair to Addison, of course, he does not use these situations as a reason to exclude women from the conversable world, but their role is a relatively passive one, and depends upon men regulating their desires into a polite circuit of trade: 'A Woman is naturally more helpless than the other Sex; and a Man of Honour and Sense should have this in his View in all Manner of Commerce with her' (107–9).

The Tatler had been quite explicit about its address to women from early on. Indeed its title—unlike *The Spectator*, a point to which I'll return below—suggested a proximity to the world of tittle-tattle, like chat and gossip a form of conversation most often negatively associated with women. *The Tatler* contained several papers from Mrs Distaff arguing for the admission of women to the world of learning.[33] Steele's writing valorized the domestic world as one of the overlapping spheres of sociability that constituted the privatized world of commercial culture:

> To manage well a great Family, is as worthy an Instance of Capacity, as to execute a great Employment; and for the Generality, as Women perform the considerable Part of their Duties, as well as Men do theirs; so in their common Behaviour, those of ordinary Genius are not more trivial than the common Rate of Men; and in my Opinion, the playing of a Fan is every whit as good an Entertainment as the beating a Snuff-box. (*T* 172, II: 444–5)

The Spectator frequently returned to the same theme, acknowledging different tendencies as natural to the sexes, but presenting both as capable of amelioration by the practice of politeness: 'Men should beware of being captivated by a kind of savage Philosophy, Women by a thoughtless Gallantry' (*S* 128, II: 8). Recast in more strictly conversational terms, the two sides of Addison's warning could be understood as addressed to

---

[32] Swift's parody of an entrepreneur of conversation, Simon Wagstaff, complains that 'Double-entendres...often put Ladies upon affected Constraints...they break, or very much entangle the Thread of Discourse.' See *A Complete Collection of Genteel and Ingenious Conversation* (hereafter *Polite Conversation*), in *A Proposal for Correcting the ENGLISH TONGUE, Polite Conversation etc.*, *Prose Writings of Jonathan Swift*, Vol. IV, ed. Herbert Davis with Louis Landa (Oxford: Basil Blackwell, 1957), 109. Swift was much less concerned than Addison about the smooth flow of mercantile discourse. See the discussion of Swift's satire on Whig conversation below.

[33] See Stephen Copley, 'Commerce, Conversation and Politeness in the Early Eighteenth-Century Periodical', *British Journal for Eighteenth-Century Studies*, 18 (1995), 63–77 (73).

Shaftesbury's dialogues, on the one hand, and fashionable forms of feminized conversation on the other. *The Spectator* confirms its address to
female readers in terms of an aim 'to make Woman-kind…entirely amiable', but now the danger seems not so much empty-headedness as over-
much political engagement. Mr. Spectator wishes to turn them away from
'that Party Rage which of late Years is very much crept into their [women's]
Conversation'. These vices Addison defines as 'Male' and implies that the
involvement of women in polite conversation is valued precisely because
they might be expected to bring with them 'the Softnes (*sic*), the Modesty,
and those other endearing Qualities which are natural to the Fair Sex'. Out
of their natural sphere, caught up in political wrangling, however, women
are even less likely than men to be able to temper their behaviour: 'a
Woman is too sincere to mitigate the Fury of her Principles with Temper
and Discretion, and to act with that Caution and Reservedness which are
requisite in our Sex' (*S* 57, I: 242–3). Women may serve to regulate the
temper of conversation, they may even participate in print culture, contributing essays and correspondence to *The Tatler* and *The Spectator*, as
some did, but women are also represented as all too liable to be over-
whelmed by political and other passions. Steele can insist that one can see
'in no Place of Conversation the Perfection of Speech so much as in an
accomplish'd Woman' (*T* 62, I: 430), but the example he presents is Lady
Courtly discussing dress. If Steele is raising the status of such private concerns, making them a potential object of virtuous discourse, when they
properly conform to the codes of politeness, then he is also demarcating
the areas in which he expects women to practise their conversational skills.[34]

In *The Spectator*, a significant shift in title from *The Tatler*, the essayist
is still intent on creating a species of relatively open discourse with his
readers, but equally remaining outside the complex world of clubs and
coffee houses that he frequents and describes. The very idea of the
spectator is of someone outside and inside—within but above—this
modern theatre of manners. Mr. Spectator observes rather than fully
participates in what is going on around him. When the paper was restarted
in 1714, Addison soon made his commitment to this role explicit. In
Spectator 556, he experiments with a series of more participatory positions,
but after a series of troubling encounters soon thinks better of it. He ends
by recommitting himself to his role as 'an indifferent SPECTATOR…it
shall be the chief Tendency of my Papers to inspire my Countrymen with
a mutual Good-will and Benevolence' (*S* 556, IV: 501). Even this ambivalent position had its detractors, who felt it still sacrificed too much of the

---

[34] See ibid. 73–4.

traditions of courtly and classical civility to the commercial world. Jonathan Swift, for instance, although formerly a friend of Addison, and an advocate of the importance of politeness in the classical tradition, always maintained a different perspective on its origins and most appropriate forms, including a deep scepticism about its compatibility with commercial society. Contrary to Addison's more Whig-republican genealogy of conversation, Swift believed that English politeness had some things to learn from French courtliness, among them the importance of female participation in conversation: 'If there were no other Use in the Conversation of Ladies, it is sufficient that it would lay a Restraint upon those odious Topicks of Immodesty and Indecencies, into which the Rudeness of our Northern Genius is also apt to fall.'[35] The proper English model for such a conversable world Swift took to be the Stuart court: 'I take the highest Period of Politeness in *England*...to have been the peaceable Part of King *Charles* the First's Reign.'[36]

Swift's essay 'Hints towards an Essay on Conversation'—probably written in by 1710, but only published posthumously in 1736—affirmed that the 'two chief Ends of Conversation' were 'to entertain and improve'. Like Cicero in his *Offices*, he expresses surprise that 'so useful and innocent a Pleasure, so fitted for every Period and Condition of Life, and so much in all Men's Power, should be so much neglected and abused'. Whatever Swift's taste for controversy in other forms of discourse, he agreed with Addison that 'the Itch of Dispute and Contradiction' was at odds with proper conversability. Where he vehemently disagreed with him was on the idea that commercial society could sustain the polish of courts or the wisdom of traditional learning. Swift seems to aim a swipe at *The Spectator* when he complains of the wits at Will's coffee house filling the heads of young students 'with Trash, under the Name of Politeness, Criticism, and Belles Lettres'. Too much familiarity for Swift was 'a dangerous Experiment in our Northern Climate, where all the little Decorum and Politeness we have are purely forced by Art, and are so ready to lapse into Barbarity'.[37] The eighteenth century's plethora of handbooks on conver-

---

[35] Jonathan Swift, 'Hints towards an Essay on Conversation', in *Prose Writings of Jonathan Swift*, Vol. IV, ed. Davis, 95. I've found at least two examples of Swift's essay being reprinted in later periodicals: see 'Hints towards an Essay on Conversation', *St. James's Magazine*, 1 (September 1762), 22–31, and 'An Essay on Conversation', *Universal Magazine of Knowledge and Pleasure*, 48 (March 1771), 119–22.

[36] Swift, 'Hints', 94.

[37] Swift, 'Hints', 92, 88, 94, 90, and 92. For Cicero's comments on this matter in *De Officiis*, see *On Duties*, ed. and trans. M. T. Griffin and E. M. Atkins (Cambridge: Cambridge University Press, 1991), 51: 'Guidance about oratory is available, provided by the rhetoricians, but none about conversation, although I do not see why that could not also exist.'

sation were partly an anxious response to this perceived danger, despite the
contradiction of attempting to define a form whose chief attraction was
purported to be its easy colloquial flow, a point that Swift made into a
biting joke in his satirical *Treatise on Polite Conversation* (1738). Far from
being an advocate of the conversational freedoms of the new commercial
society, Swift feared that its coffee shops and clubs—and their neophyte
clientele—could not command the wisdom of the humanist inheritance.

The supposed author of *Polite Conversation*, Simon Wagstaff, is a
zealous Whig, committed to the Addisonian project, but much more
crudely explicit about the alliance between Whiggism, commerce, and
polite conversation. Much of the material for the parody was probably
gathered by 1714, certainly not much longer after the demise of
The Spectator.[38] The collocation 'polite conversation' seems not to have
occurred in a book title prior to Swift's parody.[39] As late as 1738 'polite'
was still a relatively novel term, in book titles at least, usually laying claim
to 'the refinement and learning appropriate to high social status', but
suspect because of its association with the Whig desire to create a virtuous
dress to cover the moral nakedness of the new commercial society.
'Conversation', however, was still mainly associated with a concept of a
community living together under God, and still used more prevalently in
this sense, in book titles at least, rather than the encroaching modern
notion of what Rumbold calls 'social talk'.[40] Where the collocation does
appear inside printed sources, instances are rarely positive, with the
exception 'of authors [including Addison and Steele] of Whig and modernizing views'. From this perspective, Swift's title page operates as a
jarring statement of the brash new order's colonizing of an older sense
of social and religious life fully intertwined, revealing 'the contrast between superficial refinement and the vacuous brutality of a Whiggish
commercializing culture'.[41]

Wagstaff himself is certainly a brash proponent of social talk as a crude
and mechanical means of securing advancement. He affects knowledge of

---

[38] See Davis's 'Introduction' to *Prose Writings of Jonathan Swift*, IV: xxviii, xxx.

[39] The matter is complicated by the different claims of the Dublin and London editions
of 1738. The former is the one overseen by Swift himself with the title *A Treatise on Polite
Conversation*, but after the introduction it also has a half-title: *A Compleat Collection of
Genteel and Ingenious Conversation, according to the most Polite Mode and Method, now Use at
Court, and in the best Companies of England: In several Dialogues*. The London edition
effectively reverses the order. It gives as the title *A Complete Collection of Genteel and
Ingenious Conversation, according to the Most Polite Mode and Method now Use at Court,
and in the Best Companies of England.* There follows *Polite Conversation in Three Dialogues* as
a half-title. Rumbold, 'Locating Swift's Parody', 256–7, notes that English readers
quickly adopted *Polite Conversation* as the work's short title.

[40] Ibid. 257.   [41] Ibid. 255–6.

'Persons of Quality', and even promises to polish 'all Parts of [their] Conversation', whether at 'Meals, Tea, or Visits'. The little-mindedness of his ambitions is captured for Swift in the banality of visiting and taking tea; the shallowness of his grasp of his elite culture fixed by his perception that he needs to explain to his readers that Horace is 'a *Roman* Poet'. Indeed he is 'proud to own, that except some Smattering in the *French*, I am what the Pedants, and Scholars call, a Man wholly illiterate'. The horizon of his sense of tradition is set by 'at least an hundred Years, without any Change in Phraseology'. Any link to Cicero or the humanist tradition is beyond him. Fashion is much more Wagstaff's concern, and with it the marketplace: he omits his collection of useful oaths not out of concern for standards, but because 'it would not only double the Charge, but likewise make the Volume less commodious for Pocket Carriage'. The parody also makes clear Swift's concern about the aping of social superiors and the decline of hierarchy if conversation is really regarded as a democratization of the social arts. Wagstaff with typical tactlessness notes the objection that 'the Publication of my Book, may, in a long Course of Time, prostitute this noble Art to mean and vulgar People.' He insists that a footman cannot swear like a lord, but then lets the cat out of the bag: 'unless he be a Lad of superior Parts, of good Memory, a diligent Observer, one who hath a skilful Ear, some Knowledge in Musick, and an exact Taste'. Wagstaff's idea of the public provides a proleptic travesty of Habermas's public sphere: 'I can produce the Stamp of Authority from Courts, Chocolate-houses, Theatres, Assemblies, Drawing-rooms, Levees, Card-meetings, Balls, and Masquerades; from Persons of both Sexes, and of the highest Titles next to Royal.' Here is a vision of a new world of small change challenging the older public authority of traditional learning with a vengeance![42]

The Spectator figures conversation as a way of adding polish + social ease: Shaftesbury + Swift disagree

HUME AND 'THE FUND OF CONVERSATION'

In some senses, Simon Wagstaff won the day. At least, his vision of the circulation of conversation in a commercial society is recognizably the world, for instance, of Boswell's *London Journal* (1762–3) or Fanny Burney's *Evelina* (1778), both discussed in my next chapter. Certainly the idea of society as a conversation sustained by the circulation of goods and defined by the familiar interactions of its people became increasingly accepted, if not always celebrated. David Hume, for instance, may have

[42] Swift, *Polite Conversation*, 110, 112, and 114.

had more time for the role of courts as arbiters of taste than Addison or Shaftesbury (or Wagstaff), but he had no doubt that commercial society added to the 'fund of conversation'.[43] In her classic account of the Scottish Enlightenment, Gladys Bryson defined the chief insight of Hume and his fellow Scots as their perception of man as a social being. They explored sympathy as a foundational human attribute that could assuage the fear that social coherence might be sacrificed to commercial culture. Following up on Bryson's insight, scholars such as John Dwyer and Richard B. Sher have shown that the conversable literary culture of the Scottish Enlightenment, embodied in clubs, societies, newspapers, and periodicals, often overtly acknowledged their Addisonian model. George Drummond's student essay on conversation was written as this world was taking shape. It also provided the context to sustain the priority Hume and his friends gave to sympathetic understanding over abstract reason and the consolidation of the reorientation of literature away from old-fashioned learning and towards the conversable.[44]

The hegemony of this conversable world was far from being uncontested, however, even in Edinburgh. Its most immediate challenge there was the problem of reconciling traditions of Presbyterian godliness to politeness. Sher has shown how the 'Moderate' party in the Church of Scotland, led by Hume's friends the clergymen William Robertson, Hugh Blair, Adam Ferguson, and John Home, formed itself out of the protracted struggle with those members of the Kirk who believed doctrine and a religious life more important than the social virtues.[45] Sociability in Moderate circles was defined against the perceived rancorousness of Presbyterian culture. Hume insisted too much religion made polite culture unsustainable. Friendship with him was itself a matter of public controversy for the Moderates in the 1750s. The 'Popular' party of the Church of Scotland regarded clergymen associating on terms of easy familiarity with an atheist

---

[43] David Hume, 'Of Luxury' [published later as 'Of Refinement in the Arts'], in *Essays and Treatises on Several Subjects*, 2nd edn (Edinburgh, 1758), 159.

[44] See Gladys Bryson, *Man and Society: The Scottish Inquiry of the Eighteenth Century* (Princeton: Princeton University Press, 1945), John Dwyer, *Virtuous Discourse: Sensibility and Community in Late Eighteenth-Century Scotland* (Edinburgh: Donald, 1987), 3, and Richard B. Sher, *Church and University in the Scottish Enlightenment: The Moderate Literati of Edinburgh* (Princeton: Princeton University Press, 1985). Dwyer describes the influence of Addison and *The Spectator* in Scotland as 'immense' (17). The view is reiterated by most scholars of the Scottish Enlightenment: see, for instance, Nicholas Phillipson, 'Politics, Politeness and the Anglicisation of Early Eighteenth-Century Scottish Culture', in Roger A. Mason (ed.), *Scotland and England 1286–1815* (Edinburgh: John Donald, 1987), 226–46. Phillipson points out that 'in Edinburgh the *Tatler* and *Spectator* were reprinted as soon as they had appeared in London, and were discussed and imitated by city wits in magazines like *The Tatler of the North*' (235).

[45] Sher, *Church and University*, esp. 45–92.

philosopher as a degraded willingness to sacrifice religious truth to the polite virtue of being agreeable. The aging clergyman George Anderson, for instance, excoriated the Moderates for mixing with Hume and Lord Kames, asserting the obligation of Christians to exclude infidels 'from their communion and fellowship, not only in sacred things, but likewise from all unnecessary conversation upon other subjects'.[46] Notwithstanding Anderson's critique, Blair, Home, and Robertson joined Hume and Adam Smith as founding members of the Select Society set up on 22 May 1754. Although they shied away from matters relating to revealed religion in their debates at the Select Society, such topics were not necessarily excluded from the 'free conversation' at the convivial suppers that followed the meetings.[47] An equally fraught controversy followed in 1756 when the Moderate clergyman John Home's play *Douglas* was performed in Edinburgh with the support of his friends among the clergy.[48] For many members of the Kirk, this was going too far in worldliness and several Moderates were suspended. Hume's open letter in support of Home did not help matters.[49] Support from such a source was a provocation, only compounded by its praise for the 'liberty of thought' of the ancients, a rhetorical move that always incensed men like Anderson by implying pagan authority was comparable to the Bible's. Acknowledging that he and Home differed in their religious beliefs, Hume went on to offer his own work as a monument to their 'mutual amity', the fruit of a world where the social virtues and free enquiry were more important than religious denomination:

I have been seized with a strong desire of renewing these laudable practices of antiquity, by addressing the following dissertations to you, my good friend: For such I will ever call and esteem you, notwithstanding the opposition which prevails between us, with regard to many of our speculative tenets. These differences of opinion I have only found to enliven our conversation.[50]

---

[46] George Anderson, *An Estimate of the Profit and Loss of Religion, Personally and Publicly stated: Illustrated with references to Essays on Morality and Natural Religion* (Edinburgh, 1753), 77.

[47] The 'free conversation' at the suppers given by the wine merchant Robert Alexander is described in Alexander Carlyle's *Autobiography*, quoted in Ernest Mossner, *The Life of David Hume*, 2nd edn (Oxford: Oxford University Press, 1980), 282.

[48] See the account in Sher, *Church and University*, 74–88.

[49] See David Hume, *Four Dissertations* (London, 1757), i–vii, reprinted in the *Scots Magazine*, 19 (June 1757), 293–4, and various other journals. Hume was warned off publication by his friends, dithered, but then finally published the letter. See Mossner, *Life of Hume*, 361–2. Even Mossner's account of Hume finds the letter 'inexpedient' and recognizes it 'could only result in further inflaming the bigots'.

[50] Hume, *Four Dissertations*, iii.

Given the volume he was dedicating to Home contained his opinions on natural religion, one of the targets of Anderson's attack, the letter implies the primacy of sociability over religious faith. Edinburgh in the 1750s was a crucible in which the older godly idea of 'conversation' reacted powerfully against a modern notion of secular interactions between individuals.

Our own modern perspectives should not distract us from the interested nature of what the Moderates were doing in constructing their conversable world. John Witherspoon, for instance, mocked their coordinated defence of their interests: *'All moderate men are joined together in the strictest bond of union, and do never fail to support and defend one another to the utmost*, be the cause they are engaged in what it will'.[51] From an extremely constrained social base, which wielded a hugely disproportionate amount of power in Scottish society, Hume's friends defended patronage and the influence of the landowning classes in the governance of the Church of Scotland against one of their society's 'few democratic strains'.[52] Without encouraging any anachronistic understanding of the Popular Party as democrats, the position of the Moderates on the patronage question at least illustrates the exclusivity of politeness in its campaign against enthusiasm and fanaticism.[53] Nor should we assume that the opponents of politeness were simply dull, unsociable Puritans. A reading of Witherspoon's witty and sophisticated attacks on the Moderates in his *Ecclesiastical Characteristics* (1753), which went into eight editions in the 1750s and 1760s, the title itself a jibe at Shaftesbury's politeness, ought to be enough to challenge this idea. Presbyterianism had a social world of its own, even if it might not be recognized in terms of the select sociability of their Moderate opponents; it was one centred on the congregation and

---

[51] John Witherspoon, *Ecclesiastical Characteristics: Or, The Arcana of he Church Policy. Being an Humble Attempt to Open up the Mystery of Moderation*, 5th edn (Edinburgh, 1763), 63.

[52] Ebenezer Erskine, for instance, believed church vacancies ought to have been filled by the decision of an electorate of male heads of households. See Sher, *Church and University*, 49. On the social composition of the Moderates, see Roger L. Emerson, 'The Social Composition of Enlightened Scotland: The Select Society of Edinburgh, 1754–1764', *Studies on Voltaire and the Eighteenth Century*, 64, (1973), 291–329 (308). Most of the founder members had been at school together or were related. Many were either members of the Moderate party in the Church or the legal profession. Emerson makes the point that politics in Scotland was controlled by a very few aristocratic patrons, most of whom were close to the Select Club, if not members, while Edinburgh itself was small enough to allow this group the kind of hegemony impossible in London at the time.

[53] John R. McIntosh, *Church and Theology in Enlightenment Scotland: The Popular Party, 1740–1800* (East Linton: Tuckwell, 1998), 94–5, notes that after Erskine's secession in 1740 few in the Kirk believed that 'the congregation, or heads of families, [had] the sole right of calling a minister'. McIntosh describes the position of the Popular Party as 'constitutional' in their belief that direct voting ought to be qualified by the authority of the elders and other officials of the Church.

inclined to controversy and contention as part of godly concern with theological truth. Witherspoon believed that the Moderates had contempt for those who made '*a high profession of religion, and a great pretence to strictness in their walk and conversation*'.[54] He brilliantly parodies a series of other Moderate doctrines, for instance: '*A minister must endeavour to acquire as great a degree of politeness in his carriage and behaviour, and to catch as much of the air and manner of a fine gentleman, as possibly he can.*'[55] Above all, he suggested, the Moderates 'avoid all the high flights of evangelical enthusiasm, and the mysteries of grace, which the common people are so fond of'.[56] Witherspoon's worry was that a 'corruption in doctrine, looseness in practice, and slavish submission in politics, had overspread the church of Scotland'. Twenty-first-century literary readers and scholars, in many ways the descendants of Hume and Blair, may too easily underestimate the opportunities for participation in a peculiar kind of conversable world provided by the Popular Party in the Kirk.[57] Certainly the Popular Party had its own distinctive sense of what constituted good conversation.

The Hume best known to his eighteenth-century contemporaries was the man of letters who had followed Addison in using the essay as the form most appropriate to bringing philosophy out of the cloister and into the sociable world. He had switched from the more technical philosophical style of *A Treatise of Human Nature* (1739–40) after it 'fell *dead-born from the Press*; without reaching such distinction as even to excite a Murmur among the Zealots', and reinvented himself as a polite man of letters in his *Essays Moral and Political* (1741–2).[58] These essays together with the 'enquiries' that came with them in later editions aimed at a polite,

---

[54] Witherspoon, *Ecclesiastical Characteristics*, 61.
[55] Ibid. 35. [56] Ibid. 27.
[57] John Witherspoon, *A Serious Apology for the Ecclesiastical Characteristics* (Edinburgh, 1763), 45. For an account of the Popular Party as an enlightened intellectual movement, see McIntosh, *Church and Theology*, 32–91. Alex Benchimol relates the antagonism between the Moderates and the Popular Party to Geoff Eley's critique of Habermas's account of the emergence of the public sphere: 'At the very moment of its institutional consolidation, the Scottish Enlightenment public sphere was faced with a popular intellectual movement that, as Eley put it in a more general historical context, was both "combative *and* highly literate".' See Alex Benchimol, 'Cultural Historiography and the Scottish Enlightenment Public Sphere', in Alex Benchimol and Willy Maley (eds), *Spheres of Influence: Intellectual and Cultural Publics from Shakespeare to Habermas* (Oxford: Peter Lang, 2007), 105–50 (128).
[58] On the fate of the *Treatise*, see Hume's 'My Own Life' (1776) in *The Letters of David Hume*, 2 vols, ed. J. Y. T. Greig (Oxford: Oxford University Press, 1932), I: 2. An account of Hume's 'careful management and cultivation of his career as an author' appears in Richard B. Sher, *The Enlightenment and the Book: Scottish Authors and Their Publishers in Eighteenth-Century Britain, Ireland, and America* (Chicago/London: University of Chicago Press, 2006), 45–52. Tom Beauchamp in his edition of *Enquiry concerning the Principle of Morals* notes that the word 'polite' occurs only once in the *Treatise*, but is ubiquitous in

conversable style addressed to the needs of a modern society. The first collection opened with 'Of Essay-Writing' and set out Hume's most direct account of 'the conversable world' he now addressed. The essay begins by contrasting the 'elegant Part of mankind' with those 'immers'd in the animal Life'.[59] This 'elegant' world Hume took to be constituted out of a partnership between the 'learned and conversable'. Echoing both Addison and Shaftesbury, the separation of the learned and the conversable he deemed to be 'the great Defect of the last Age'. His essay explains his aim of rescuing the conversable world from an idea of social talk as merely 'a continued series of gossiping Stories and idle Remarks'. However, he makes it quite clear that belles-lettres cannot be left to scholars; for they are too often 'without any Taste of Life or Manners, and without that Liberty and Facility of Thought and Expression, which can only be acquir'd by Conversation'. Conversation then is defined as a form of vernacular discourse, closely associated with the literary, that can save ordinary life from vacuity, but also properly socialize the scholarly world. The experience that is essential to true scholarship and philosophy can only be found 'in common Life and Conversation'. Learning is being reoriented away from scholasticism and towards the ordinary relations of the everyday world and vernacular language. Even Lockean reasoning and observation take second place to an idea of 'experience' based on living in society. Sceptical about both metaphysics and divinity, philosophy for Hume had to become a human and social science, but ought to tend towards the conversational in its ease and freedom of address. As he explained in his *Enquiry concerning the Principles of Morals* (1751), the very foundations of moral behaviour were to be built out of the conversable world: 'the more we converse with mankind, and the greater social intercourse we maintain, the more we shall be familiarized to these general preferences and distinctions, without which our conversation and discourse could scarcely be rendered intelligible to each other.' Daily conversation with others shakes us out of the point of view peculiar to ourselves and extends our range of sympathies: 'The intercourse of sentiments, therefore, in society and conversation, makes us form some general unalterable standard, by which we may approve or disapprove of characters and manners.' We may maintain a preference for ourselves and what is close to us, and so find it easiest to sympathize with our friends, as Addison and Steele had suggested when writing about conversation, but

---

Hume's writing thereafter. See David Hume, *An Enquiry Concerning the Principle of Morals*, ed. Tom Beauchamp (Oxford: Oxford University Press, 1998), 166.

[59] See David Hume, 'Of Essay-Writing', in *Essays, Moral and Political*, 2 vols (Edinburgh, 1741–2), II: 1–8.

Hume's theory of sympathy aimed to show how moral standards derived from the experience of conversation served perfectly well 'in company, in the pulpit, on the theatre, and in the schools'.[60]

What constituted 'conversable' behaviour and writing for Hume? Rather than looking for the kind of masculine or heroic virtue inherent to Shaftesbury's regime of politeness, Hume in general sought a gendered softening of both philosophy and social life. 'Of Essay Writing' goes so far as to declare women, or, at least, 'Women of Sense and Education (for to such alone I address myself)', to be 'the Sovereigns of the Empire of Conversation', even suggesting that he 'shou'd resign into their fair Hands the sovereign Authority over the Republic of Letters'. Although Hume acknowledged his 'particular pleasure in the company of modest women', as he put it in 'My Own Life', the conditional 'should' in 'On Essay Writing' is significant. For Hume reiterates that his primary commitment is to his 'Countrymen, the Learned, a stubborn independent Race of Mortals, extremely jealous of their Liberty', reasserting the select homosociality of Edinburgh's literati. What he will offer women is 'a League, offensive and defensive, against our common Enemies of Reason and Beauty, People of dull Heads and cold Hearts' (the last epithet most obviously intended for the Popular Party).[61] The idea of such leagues was to be an important discursive opportunity for women in the decades ahead, most notably for women like Elizabeth Montagu discussed in my next chapter. Conversation often continued to be understood as a feminized zone of practice, but even Hume did not cede it to women without conditions. Women's participation was predicated on tight constraints and taken to be primarily concerned with softening male manners and operative only in certain kinds of spaces. The presence of virtuous women provided a perfect school for manners, according to Hume, 'where the delicacy of that sex put every one on his guard, lest he gives offence by any breach of decency', but that did not mean necessarily the best school for conversation in his eyes.[62] If Hume delighted in his experiences of the French salons, then he also registered nostalgia for the rough and tumble of Edinburgh groups like the Poker Club. Writing from Paris towards the end of 1763, he told Adam Ferguson: 'I really wish for the plain roughness of the Poker, and particularly the sharpness of Dr Jardine, to correct and qualify so much lusciousness.'[63] Gatherings like the Poker and the Select

[60] Hume, *Enquiry concerning the Principle of Morals*, 44.
[61] Hume, 'Of Essay Writing', 5.
[62] David Hume, 'Of the Rise and Progress of the Arts and Sciences', in *Essays and Treatises on Several Subjects*, 2nd edn (Edinburgh, 1758), 70–85 (83).
[63] Quoted in Mossner, *Life of Hume*, 285.

Club practised forms of candour widely regarded as inappropriate for female company. Female 'complacency', the ability of women 'to engage in sympathetic exchange with one's fellow man', was generally regarded as mollifying the potential asperities of the new society, as one poet in the *Scots Magazine* put it:

> Woman!—to her the task assign'd,
> To harmonize man's rugged mind![64]

Increasingly, after Hume, writers such as Hugh Blair in his extremely popular *Sermons* (1777–1801) and Henry Mackenzie in his periodical essays and novels stressed the importance of the domestic virtues to the welfare of the nation.[65] Moderate preachers such as James Fordyce developed the idea that the domestic space ought to be the bedrock of the larger and more complex series of social spaces. 'To form the manners of men', he wrote, 'various causes contribute; but nothing, I apprehend, so much as the turn of the women with whom they converse. Those who are most conversant with women of virtue and understanding will be always found the most amiable characters.'[66]

Hume's ideas on the spread of conversation in a society built out of these private virtues was aimed not only against the Puritan elements within the Kirk, but also at those zealous proponents of the civic humanism whose hostility to the effeminizing refinements of commercial society he dismissed in his essay 'Of the Rise and Progress of the Arts and Sciences'. Hume acknowledged that 'eloquence certainly arises more naturally in popular governments', but saw 'civilized monarchy' as the best context for its sustenance. Like Swift, he saw the emulative context of royal courts—'an inclination to please his superiors, and to form himself upon those models'—as the genuine origin of 'mutual deference or civility', distancing himself from the 'high political rant' of republican discourse. Hume's idea of a civilized monarchy was defiantly modernizing. His essay provocatively asserts the coarse nature of the ancients in comparison: 'the arts of conversation were not brought so near perfection among them as the arts of writing and composition.'[67] Their philosophy

---

[64] 'An Apostrophe in Favour of Love', *Scots Magazine*, 40 (March 1778), 158. The definition of complacency is taken from Dwyer, *Virtuous Discourse*, 118.

[65] In 1807 the *Critical Review* declared Blair's *Sermons* the most popular works in the language after *The Spectator*. See Sher, *Enlightenment and the Book*, 33.

[66] James Fordyce, *Sermons to Young Women*, 2 vols (1766), I: 22. See also Dwyer, *Virtuous Discourse*, Chaps 4 and 5.

[67] Hume, 'Of the Rise and Progress of the Arts and Sciences', 74 and 78–9. See Potkay, *The Fate of Eloquence*, 77–8, on Hume's view of the historical role of chivalry in softening the classical virtues.

and learning is represented as unsociable metaphysics, oriented away from and not circulating within an open society, a point he makes when comparing Aristotle and Cicero at the opening of the *An Enquiry Concerning Human Understanding*. Aristotle is placed among the 'abstract reasoners', while Cicero is a proponent of the Addisonian 'easy philosophy' that 'enters more into common life; moulds the heart and affections; and, by touching those principles which actuate men, reforms their conduct, and brings them nearer to that model of perfection which it describes'.[68] In the general polemic against the virtues of classical republicanism in 'Of the Rise of the Arts and Sciences', however, even Cicero doesn't escape Hume's wit: 'I must confess, I have frequently been shocked with the poor figure under which he represents his friend ATTICUS, in those dialogues where he himself is introduced as a speaker.' Classical culture lacked 'polite deference and respect', qualities that Shaftesbury, of course, disapprobated where he inferred the effeminacy of modern commercial culture. To Hume, even Augustus's court—contrary to Steele's praise for its egalitarianism—is culpable for having not quite worn off the rough manners of the republic. Shaftesbury is dismissed as one those misguided 'zealous partisans of the ancients' who see modern refinements as 'foppish and ridiculous'. Indeed the failure to recognize the importance of women to proper conversation is what marks ancient manners (and Shaftesbury's school of republican virtue) as a form of barbarity for Hume.[69]

What Shaftesbury regarded as suspect effeminacy, Hume often saw as a necessary refinement of culture. Hume's version of the conversable world, as one might expect, has much more room for sympathy and even sex than any of the other writers I've discussed so far. He seems even less nervous of gallantry than Addison, regarding it as a socialized form of the sympathy and sexuality that he represents as a natural part of social processes: 'NATURE has implanted in all living creatures an affection betwixt the sexes, which even in the fiercest and most rapacious animals, is not merely confined to the satisfaction of the bodily appetite, but begets a friendship and mutual sympathy, which runs thro' the whole tenor of their lives.'[70] Although Hume mentions Addison favourably, the emphasis on sympathy strikes a different note from *The Spectator*'s idea of politeness, not least because Humean intellectual sociability retains more room

---

[68] David Hume, *An Enquiry Concerning Human Understanding*, ed. Tom L. Beauchamp, Oxford Philosophical Texts (Oxford: Oxford University Press, 1999), 6.
[69] Hume, 'Of the Rise and Progress of the Arts and Sciences', 79–80 and 82.
[70] Ibid. 82.

for collision and what he called 'disputation', if 'never of animosity'.[71] Notwithstanding his commitment to polite exchange as the basis of the republic of letters, the sometimes provocative and often paradoxical style of his own essays indicates something of the way Humean conversability retained a space for 'vehement reasoning'.[72] James Boswell, an ardent admirer of Addison's standards, certainly thought his compatriots, including Hume, failed to live up to English standards of politeness:

They would abolish all respect due to rank and external circumstances, and they would live like a kind of literary barbarians [*sic*]. For my own share, I own I would rather want their instructive conversation than be hurt by their rudeness. However, they don't always show this. Therefore I like their company best when it is qualified by the presence of a stranger.[73]

The last sentence suggests the freedoms taken by Hume and their friends when the company was 'select'. Looking back on this period from 1800, William Smellie viewed the freedom Boswell criticized as part of the distinctive brilliance of Edinburgh literary culture:

In London, in Paris, and other large cities of Europe, though they contain many literary men, the access to them is difficult; and, even after that is obtained, the conversation is, for some time, shy and constrained. In Edinburgh, the access to men of parts is not only easy, but their conversation and the communication of their knowledge are at once imparted to intelligent strangers with the utmost liberality. The philosophers of Scotland have no nostrums. They tell what they know, and deliver their sentiments without disguise or reserve. Their generous nature was conspicuous in the character of Mr Hume. He insulted no man; but, when the conversation turned upon particular subjects, whether moral or religious, he expressed his genuine sentiments with freedom, with force, and with a dignity which did honour to human nature.[74]

---

[71] Hume, *Four Dissertations*, ii.

[72] Potkay, *The Fate of Eloquence*, 101–2, but note his description of Hume's style more generally as 'sparkling blandness'. Potkay also points out that Smith described English politeness to his students in terms of its 'calm, composed, unpassionate serenity noways ruffled by passion', a fact that may imply that, like Boswell, he took the Scottish literary sociability familiar to his audience to be more vehement. See Smith's *Lectures on Rhetoric and Belles Lettres*, ed. J. C. Bryce (Indianapolis: Liberty Fund, 1985), 198. Smith distinguishes differences of behaviour in conversation between the English, French, and Spanish, ascribing them to their different national notions of 'politeness'.

[73] James Boswell, *London Journal* (12 July 1763), 300. I am grateful to John Havard for drawing this comment to my attention.

[74] William Smellie, *Literary and Characteristical Lives of Gregory, Kames, Hume, and Smith* (Edinburgh, 1800), 162, but Smellie himself had reason to inveigh against the select nature of this world when he was blocked from the Edinburgh chair of natural history. See the account in Steven Shapin, 'Property, Patronage, and the Politics of Science: The Founding of the Royal Society of Edinburgh', *British Journal of the History of Science*, 7 (1974), 1–41.

Certainly, for all Boswell's asseverations, politeness and refinement continued to be crucial concepts for thinkers of the Scottish Enlightenment, not least because much of their work worried away at the question of the moral implications of developing a society based on economic improvement, but these questions were oriented around the dynamic of sympathy and the science of its operations. Compared to such investigations into the principles at work behind human action, Addison's essays could seem—in Hume's words—'agreeable Triffling'.[75]

Politeness and conversation were increasingly open to being seen as operations of affect. Sympathy between participants appears more and more to be a pre-condition of conversation taking place at all. In this regard, the word 'sympathy' sometimes retained the aura of its earlier occult sense, potentially taking its mysterious operations beyond the friendship and socio-economic compatibility advertised in Addison and Steele's writing on polite conversation.[76] The Scottish tradition was far from seeing conversation as a form of straightforwardly 'open' sympathetic discourse. Hume was capable of being quite arch about the need to 'counterfeit' so as to remain in control of this theatre of affect and not cause offence to others. The ancients he complained often lacked the 'civility [that] obliges us either to express or counterfeit towards the persons with whom we converse.'[77] Even for many of those committed to the project of politeness, in whatever form, the idea of 'counterfeit' could seem to go too far towards sacrificing truth to social forms. These included those English Dissenters who were to play such an important part in the English provincial enlightenment and for whom one of the key figures was Isaac Watts.

ISAAC WATTS AND GODLY CONVERSATION

Hume may seem relatively relaxed about the diversity of exchanges that he took to make the complex machinery of modern society. Recognizing the

[75] David Hume to William Strahan, 7 February 1772, in *Letters*, ed. Greig, II: 257.

[76] See the discussion in Mary Fairclough, 'The Sympathy of Popular Opinion: Representations of the Crowd in Britain, 1770–1849', unpublished PhD thesis, University of York, 2008, especially 39–67 and 72–91.

[77] Hume, 'Of the Rise and Progress of the Arts and Sciences', 79. On the need to 'counterfeit' in Hume, see Jenny Davidson, *Hypocrisy and the Politics of Politeness: Manners and Morals from Locke to Austen* (Cambridge: Cambridge University Press, 2004), 95. James Fordyce's *The Character and Conduct of the Female Sex* (London, 1776) claimed that the greatest ages of civilization had always acknowledged the importance of femininity, but admitted 'the allurement of female softness was perhaps not always sufficiently understood, owing probably to that passion for public interests, and extensive fame' (6).

diversity of interests separating modern manners from the unitary virtue associated with the classical republic, <u>Hume imagined a conversable world</u> <u>of diffuse and complex exchanges.</u> In a figure some of his eighteenth-century readers may have found rather impolite, Hume described the relations between the scholarly and the conversable in terms of 'a Balance of Trade'. 'The Materials of this Commerce', he continues, 'must chiefly be furnish'd by Conversation and common Life: The manufacturing of them alone belongs to Learning.'[78] It is worth pausing over this metaphor for a while. 'Conversation and common Life' as forms of primary production may accord well with the empiricist desire to ground thought in experience, but they sit less well with the Addisonian identification of conversation with polish. Rather than conversation working on what learning will provide, here it seems productive of the materials of thought. Without suggesting Hume did not also believe conversation had a role within secondary and even tertiary processes, here it gives it a key role in the *production* of knowledge.

Improvement was not just a matter of civility. The members of the Edinburgh Select Society, for instance, also met again in the context of societies for the improvement of trade and agriculture in Scotland.[79] <u>Many</u> <u>of the clubs and societies that bloomed across Britain in the eighteenth</u> <u>century had as their focus not just the burnishing of politeness or the</u> <u>promotion of cordiality, but the discovery of truth.</u>[80] <u>From this perspec-</u> <u>tive, conversation was not just the means of consolidating polite sociability,</u> <u>but itself a crucial motor of 'improvement',</u> even a pedagogic medium. Nonconformist writers like Watts often appealed to the idea that truth needed to struggle with error in an open contest. Certainly conversation played its part in the pedagogy of moderate English Dissent via the influential writing and teaching of men like Philip Doddridge and Watts. As a teacher at his Northampton dissenting academy, Doddridge, influenced by his own tutor John Jennings, has been credited with the development of the 'modern pedagogical ideals of discursive interchange and free discovery'.[81] Students were encouraged to interrupt lectures to ask questions, but also to experience divergent opinions on a range of issues:

[78] Hume, 'Of Essay Writing', 4.

[79] See Emerson, 'Social Composition of Enlightened Scotland', 27.

[80] Perhaps the most obvious example is the Lunar Society. Many of the participants were Dissenters or their associates and directly or indirectly would have been aware of the ideas on conversation and improvement discussed by Watts in *Improvement of the Mind* expounded below.

[81] Daniel E. White, *Early Romanticism and Religious Dissent* (Cambridge: Cambridge University Press, 2006), 25. See also Philip Doddridge's 'An Account of Mr. Jennings's Method' (1728), in *Dissenting Education and the Legacy of John Jennings, c.1720–c.1729,* ed. Tessa Whitehouse, available at http://www.english.qmul.ac.uk/drwilliams/pubs/jennings%

you will not by any means imagine that I intend to recommend the particular notions of all the writers I here mention, which may, indeed, sufficiently appear from their absolute contrariety to each other in a multitude of instances; but I think that, in order to defend the truth, it is very proper that a young minister should know the chief strength of error.[82]

The question of conversation itself as a pedagogical mode is explicitly explored in Part I of Isaac Watts' *Improvement of the Mind, or A Supplement to the Art of Logick* (1741), one of the most widely circulated books of the eighteenth century.[83]

Samuel Johnson, not usually a friend to Dissent, singled out the book for particular praise in his 'Life of Watts':

Few books have been perused by me with greater pleasure than his *Improvement of the Mind*, of which the radical principles may indeed be found in Locke's *Conduct of the Understanding*, but they are so expanded and ramified by Watts, as to confer upon him the merit of a work in the highest degree useful and pleasing. Whoever has the care of instructing others, may be charged with deficience in his duty if this book is not recommended.[84]

Johnson's predilection for a little roughness in conversation, as we shall see, often discomforted and disappointed his more Addisonian admirer James Boswell. Possibly his admiration for Watts had to do with the nonconformist's commitment to creative collision in the cause of truth:

In free and friendly *Conversation our intellectual Powers are more animated and our Spirits act with a superior Vigour in the quest and pursuit of unknown Truths.* There is a Sharpness and Sagacity of Thought that attends Conversation beyond what we find whilst we are shut up reading and musing in our Retirements. Our souls may be *serene* in Solitude, but not sparkling, though perhaps we are employed in reading the Works of the brightest Writers. Often has it happened in *free Discourse* that new Thoughts are strangely struck out, and the Seeds of Truth sparkle and blaze through the Company, which in calm and silent Reading would have never been excited. By *Conversation* you will both give and receive this Benefit; as *Flints* when put into Motion and striking against each

---

20legacy.html. The importance to Jennings of 'mutual Converse' is apparent throughout this extremely interesting document (19).

[82] Quoted in Isabel Rivers, *Reason, Grace and Sentiment: A Study of the Language of Religion and Ethics in England, 1660–1780*, 2 vols (Cambridge: Cambridge University Press, 1991–2000), I: 182. Rivers notes the allusion to Milton's *Areopagitica*.

[83] William St. Clair, *The Reading Nation in the Romantic Period* (Cambridge: Cambridge University Press, 2004), 131. In print throughout the eighteenth century, an edition was brought out in Edinburgh as late as 1868.

[84] Samuel Johnson, 'Life of Watts', in *Lives of the Most Eminent English Poets; with Critical Observations on their Works*, ed. Roger Lonsdale, 4 vols (Oxford: Oxford University Press, 2006), IV: 109.

other produce living Fire on both Sides, which would never have risen from the same hard Materials in a State of Rest.[85]

Watts wrote these remarks in a comparison of the relative merits of various means of instruction. Disapproving of John Locke on innate ideas, he was more generally in agreement with him, not least in stressing the educational importance of observation and experience to the acquisition of knowledge: 'Tis this that furnishes even from our Infancy with a rich variety of Ideas and Propositions.' Next he assesses reading and the great advantage it gives in terms of access to 'the learned World, in the most remote Nations, and in former Ages, almost from the Beginning of Mankind'. Lectures attended in silence are also mentioned, but there is a clear preference for a more dialogic mode of instruction. Conversation is included as '*by mutual Discourse and Enquiry we learn the Sentiments of others, as well as communicate our Sentiments to others in the same Manner*'. Significantly, for Watts, unlike writers on politeness such as Addison and Swift, 'under this Head of *Conversation* we may also rank *Disputes* of various Kinds'.[86]

Watts goes on explicitly to compare these different forms of knowledge production. Observation has the advantage of being at first hand, and so 'these Ideas are more lively.' Conversation in comparison is only a 'Copy' of experience. Reading opens up a larger range of opinion than conversation.[87] Reading also allows us to review what has been read, whereas, for all its vivacity, 'what we obtain by *Conversation* and in *Lectures*, is oftentimes lost again as soon as the Company breaks up.' Lectures can provide a vivid experience, within which the lecturer can focus on particularly knotty problems, possibly, as Doddridge did, even allowing the students to ask questions. Interaction, predictably enough, provides one of the chief advantages of conversation: 'When we *converse* familiarly with a learned Friend, *we have his own Help at hand to explain to us every Word and Sentiment that seems obscure* in his Discourse.' '*Friendly Conference*', as Watts puts it, may resolve difficulties found in books, but it is the superiority of conversation to cloistered virtue that really makes him wax lyrical:

CONVERSATION calls out into Light what has been lodged in all the Recesses and secret Chambers of the Soul: By occasional Hints and Incidents it brings old useful Notions into Remembrance; it unfolds and displays the hidden Treasures of Knowledge which *Reading, Observation* and *Study* had before furnished the Mind. By mutual Discourse the Soul is awakened and allured to bring forth its

---

[85] Isaac Watts, *Improvement of the Mind, or A Supplement to the Art of Logick* (1741), 42–3.
[86] Ibid. 30–3.   [87] Ibid. 35.

Hoards of Knowledge, and it learns how to render them most useful to Mankind. A Man of vast Reading without Conversation is like a *Miser* who lives only to himself.[88]

If there are echoes of Milton's *Areopagitica* in such passages, an equally striking presence is the language of circulation and trade, imbued with the kind of moral imperative that was such a distinctive aspect of eighteenth-century thinking about conversation. As with both Addison and Hume, conversation is associated with the breaking open of monkish solitude and retirement. The social situatedness of conversation is a key value for all these writers, but what distinguishes Watts's version from Addison's writing on the subject is the weight given to these metaphors of collision and contention. His account is less concerned to restrict the most effective kinds of conversation to the pre-selected circle of friends. Watts warns against 'conversing only with Persons of the same Sentiments'. When in the company of sailors, farmers, mechanics, or milkmaids, a situation almost unimaginable for Addison and Hume, 'we ought to turn the subject to what they know: 'By this means you may gain some Improvement in Knowledge from every one you meet.' Here the emphasis on practical knowledge trumps the model of conversation predicated on polite avoidance of talking shop.[89]

Watts does believe these interactions can bring with them the sort of polish associated with Whig advocates of politeness:

A Hermit who has been shut up in his Cell in a College, has contracted a sort of Mould and Rust upon his Soul, and all his Airs of Behaviour have a certain awkwardness in them; but these awkward Airs are worn away by degrees in Company: The Rust and the Mould are filed and brusht off by polite Conversation. The *Scholar* now becomes a *Citizen* or a *Gentleman*, a *Neighbour* and a *Friend*.[90]

Johnson's 'Life of Watts' credited him with being 'one of the first authors that taught the Dissenters to court attention by the graces of language', swiftly following up by restating the widespread association of Dissent with enthusiasm rather than the social arts:

Whatever they had among them before, whether of learning or acuteness, was commonly obscured and blunted by coarseness and inelegance of style.

---

[88] Ibid. 37–42.
[89] Ibid. 125.
[90] Ibid. 44. Shaftesbury believed: 'All politeness is owing to liberty. We polish one another and rub off our corners and rough sides by a sort of amicable collision. To restrain this is inevitably to bring rust upon men's understandings' (*Characteristics*, 31).

He showed them, that zeal and purity might be expressed and enforced by polished diction.[91]

Johnson's emphasis on Watts's civility should alert us to the fact that he was no puritanical controversialist. His pedagogical interests were orienting Dissent towards a more worldly engagement with polite circulation. If Hume's writing often presented both English Dissenters and the Popular Party of the Kirk as fanatics impatient of refinement and polish, overly eager to install a godly republic of truth in place of the conversable world, Watts was part of a long process working from the other side to open a negotiation between English nonconformity and politeness.

The process was not an easy one, as Isabel Rivers's thoughtful investigation of 'affectionate religion' has shown. Rivers reveals the anxiety many felt that making room for the affections in religious life might be mistaken for a defence of enthusiasm. Other anxieties anticipated some of the tensions fought out in the Church of Scotland in the 1750s and 1760s. 'Moderation' was a term favoured by both Doddridge and Watts, and their anxieties about enthusiasm were often expressed in terms of the need for rational and polite intercourse between Dissenters and other Christians, but they were also leery of substituting civility for godliness.[92] Like Anderson and other opponents of Hume, they were wary of anything that substituted the refinement of the passions for what they regarded as the higher reason of Christianity. Watts was particularly sharp on Shaftesbury's politeness as a cover for infidelity, a target he shared with John Witherspoon. The comments come in the context of his detailed discussion 'Of Reading and Books'. Watts recommends forms of social reading—much like the seminar—whereby people come together for 'conversation, and [...] communicate mutually their Sentiments on the Subject, and debate about it in a friendly Manner.' This sociable context does not simply encourage polite deference to the author's point of view. His students were 'to consider whether their Opinions are right or no, and to improve your own solid Knowledge'.[93] Later he recommends reading Addison and Steele and other polite writing from the periodicals, but when it comes to Shaftesbury's *Characteristics* he insists on the importance of not allowing the smoothness of the text to substitute for the question of its truth. Advising his readers against 'a lively Pertness, a Parade of Literature, and much of what some Folks now a Days call *Politeness*', for Watts the end of reading remains 'the Conformation of our Hearts and

[91] Johnson, 'Life of Watts', 107.
[92] See the detailed discussion of 'affectionate religion' in Rivers, *Reason, Grace and Sentiment*, I: 164–204. On 'moderation', see I: 168 and 178.
[93] Watts, *Improvement of the Mind*, 62–3.

Lives to the Duties of true Religion and Morality'. '*Free Conversation*', Watts believes, is designed for 'mutual Improvement in the Search of Truth'.[94]

The potential tensions here between politeness and a higher reason of theological truth can be glimpsed in William Rose's reviews of Hume's essays. Rose was a Scotsman who had assisted Doddridge at Northampton, before starting a school of his own at Chiswick. In the pages of the *Monthly Review*, he was one of the earliest and most consistently positive of Hume's reviewers. Rose was sympathetic to Hume's freedom of enquiry and praised the elegance and sprightliness of his style, but there were limits to the latitude he was willing to grant. The 'Essay on Suicide' went too far in its challenge to religious thinking for Rose:

> Were a drunken libertine to throw out such nauseous stuff in the presence of his bacchanalian companions, there might be some excuse for him; but were any man to advance such doctrines in the company of sober citizens, men of plain sense and decent manners, no person, we apprehend, would think him entitled to a serious reply, but would hear him with silent contempt.[95]

Interestingly, the transgression is figured in terms of a fall into the rough talk of the tavern. Even to entertain such ideas is to ignore the real values of rational conversation for Rose. The practice of rational conversation promoted by Dissenters was for most of them still governed by ideas of an ultimate religious truth. Figures like Watts and Rose may seem to be participating in the development of modern secular liberalism, but it is worth reminding ourselves that the discussion of conversation in *Improvement of the Mind* ends with a vision of the Last Days. If 'the errors of conversation are Infinite', then we may look beyond 'the Errors and the Incumbrances of Flesh and Blood', when 'our Conversation shall be with Angels, and more illuminated Spirits in the upper Regions of the Universe'.[96] The polite virtues mattered for a man like Watts, but not so much as the hope that conversation might bring believers closer to God.

A great deal of eighteenth-century sociability still took place with an idea of this ultimate context for conversation in mind. Its contours may be found, for instance, in the 'sociality' of David Hartley's influential *Ob-*

---

[94] Ibid. 82, 73, and 138.

[95] William Rose, *Monthly Review*, 70 (1784), 427–8. See also James Fieser, 'The Eighteenth-Century British Reviews of Hume's Writing', *Journal of the History of Ideas*, 57 (1996), 645–57.

[96] Watts, *Improvement of the Mind*, 148. Watts is careful to make sure his readers do not fall into the enthusiasm of thinking such visionary company can be enjoyed in the here and now: 'Happy should we be could we but converse with *Moses*, *Esaiah* and *St. Paul*, and consult the Prophets and Apostles, when we meet with a difficult Text! But that glorious Conversation is reserved for the Ages of future Blessedness' (41).

servations on Man (1749), which also tends towards a final union with God.[97] Even so, for Doddridge, Watts, and, ultimately, John Wither-spoon, the godly needed to come to terms with a new world of commerce whose differences had to be to be mediated through complex social interactions.[98] Polite conversation offered itself as a chart for navigating these turbulent waters, but, perhaps especially for the religious, the proliferation of conversable worlds seemed to offer only so many reefs on which the good soul might be wrecked and cast away. If human sociability became a key idea of the eighteenth century, so too did conversation as the chief paradigm for understanding this aspect of human beings become ever more contested, and not only by those primarily committed to godly conversation.

SMITH, ROUSSEAU, AND THE CRITIQUE OF POLITE CONVERSATION

For Hume the diversified fund of conversation available in a modern, polite society produced a superior moral being. Although committed to select company and agreeableness, his version of conversation, at least in some situations, allowed for a degree of disputatious rough and tumble. Not everyone, even in Hume's circle, was so willing to allow the passions, even of a moderate kind, such relatively free play in the formation of the social virtues. In his *Theory of Moral Sentiments* (1759), Hume's close friend Adam Smith, another participant in the clubbable world of Edin-burgh, also saw the operations of sympathy mediated by conversation and other forms of sociability as working to abate the gloomier passions:

Society and conversation, therefore, are the most powerful remedies for restoring the mind to its tranquility, if, at any time, it has unfortunately lost it; as well as the best preservatives of that equal and happy temper, which is so necessary to self-satisfaction and enjoyment. Men of retirement and speculation, who are apt to sit brooding at home over either grief or resentment, though they may often have

---

[97] David Hartley, *Observations on man, his frame, his duty, and his expectations*, 2 vols (1749), I: 472, defines 'sociality' as 'the Pleasure which we take in the mere Company and Conversation of others, particularly of our Friends and Acquaintance, and which is attended with mutual Affability, Complaisance, and Candour'.
[98] John Witherspoon emigrated to the United States in 1768, where he became President of the Presbyterian New College of New Jersey, now Princeton University. He was the only clergyman to sign the American Declaration of Independence. Among other things, he lectured on rhetoric and belles-lettres at Princeton. See Thomas P. Miller, *The Formation of College English: Rhetoric and Belles Lettres in the British Cultural Provinces* (Pittsburgh: University of Pittsburgh Press, 1997), 2.

more humanity, more generosity, and a nicer sense of honour, yet seldom possess the equality of temper which is so common among men of the world.[99]

Smith develops this Humean paradigm towards a more nuanced modelling of the way sympathy produced the moral virtues. Hume's sense of the positive effects of the relatively open trade of sentiments in social talk became a process whereby the innate human proclivity for sympathy was part of a dynamic process of socialization. Our sympathetic experience with others brings with it an anxiety for how our actions might appear in their eyes. A process of reflection on our place within this theatre of sympathy, both feeling subject and object of the judgments of others, transforms Addisonian agreeableness into an 'impartial spectator' who moderates our behaviour from within. In what we might conceive of as a theorization of some of Addison's ideas on the matter, especially the spectatorial metaphor, conversation represented one function by which this social tuning of virtue took place, but the qualifications evident in Smith's acknowledgment of the potential superiority of the man of retirement and speculation are significant.

Even in the first edition of *Theory of Moral Sentiments* conversation makes a much less frequent appearance in his account of the way sympathy creates the social virtues than it does in most of Hume's writing. Later editions grow increasingly dubious about too close a relationship between ideas of virtue and public opinion, distancing themselves from the conversational interactions going on around Smith. Sympathy and sociability too broadly construed might only lead us back into the world of sensual consumption from which a desire for the approvals of one's fellows was meant to save us. Chitchat and gossip might set themselves up as regulators of moral behaviour. From this perspective, public opinion derived from conversations in coffee houses and taverns seemed an uncertain foundation for society (a point the Attorney General memorably made at Thomas Paine's trial in 1792).[100] 'The great pleasure of conversation and society, besides', wrote Smith, 'arises from a certain correspondence of

---

[99] Adam Smith, *The Theory of Moral Sentiments*, ed. D. D. Raphael and A. L. Macfie (Indianapolis: The Liberty Fund, 1984), 23.

[100] The Attorney General scoffed at the idea that 'the sense of this nation is to be had in some pot-houses and coffee-houses in this town of his own choosing.' Paine had written to the court from Paris a few weeks earlier to say that 'I have gone into coffee-houses, and places where I was unknown, on purpose to learn the currency of opinion, and I never yet saw any company of twelve men that condemned the book.' See *The Whole Proceedings of the Trial...against Thomas Paine* (1793), in *Trials for Treason and Sedition 1792–1794*, ed. John Barrell and Jon Mee, 8 vols (2006–7), I: 85.

sentiments and opinions, from a certain harmony of minds, which like so many musical instruments coincide and keep time with one another.'[101] Smith's moral philosophy has a much more stoical emphasis than Hume's in this regard. Even Smith's vaunted spectatorial metaphor, and the correlative emphasis on the visual imagination, might be seen as a turn away, relatively speaking, from conversation as part of the material practices of the society around him.[102] Increasingly Smith emphasized the importance of 'the manhood of self-command', although his model is more often the prudent man of worldly affairs than either Shaftesbury's or Rousseau's classical civic virtue.[103] By the final edition of *The Theory of Moral Sentiments*, the impartial spectator within the breast of such a man has become a secular version of conscience.[104] Worldlier than the enthusiasm of the Kirk, on the one hand, but, on the other, possibly responding to the challenge of Rousseau's spartan views on virtue, its place is above social talk. Here was a fuller exploration of the 'indifference' of the spectatorial metaphor than any found in Addison's writing. While clubs of like-minded friends might have seemed a secure basis for a morality derived from reciprocal human interaction, the further the horizons of sociability extended, then the more troubling the perspective against which the Edinburgh intelligentsia erected their ideas of the conversable world became.[105]

John Dwyer has noted a growing preference in Scottish Enlightenment ideas of sociability for the little group: the club of like-minded friends whose intimacy offers a guarantee of select conversation rather than mere gossip, coffee-shop house talk, or the rough and tumble of theological and political controversy. Henry Mackenzie explicitly developed an Addisonian politeness in his periodicals *The Mirror* and *The Lounger*, both of which grew directly out of literary clubs in Edinburgh with those names.[106] Admiring commentators in both England and Scotland saw the figure of the Lounger as continuous with Mr. Spectator as a man who 'conversed with men of the world, and drew from life'. Their praise echoed the by-now standard account of periodical essayists as 'the daily visitants of the

---

[101] Smith, *Theory of Moral Sentiments*, 337.
[102] On the spectatorial metaphor, see the account given in David Marshall, 'Adam Smith and the Theatricality of Moral Sentiments', *Critical Inquiry*, 10 (1984), 592–613.
[103] Smith, *Theory of Moral Sentiments*, 152.
[104] See Raphael and McFie's introduction to their edition of *Theory of Moral Sentiments* on the evolution away from notions of popular opinion (15–16). Parallels between the developments in Smith and Rousseau are discussed in Fonna Forman-Barzilai's 'Sympathy in Space(s): Adam Smith on Proximity', *Political Theory* 33 (2) (2005) 189–217.
[105] Dwyer, *Virtuous Discourse*, 178.
[106] Ibid. 10.

parlour, not the seldom consulted oracles of the library'. This modesty of address gave the periodicals 'a powerful influence on the public taste and the public manners'. Explicitly acknowledging the well-worn anti-scholastic trope, commentators credited Mackenzie with following Addison in avoiding 'the cold declamations of the cloistered monk on the vanity of human life' in favour of 'the voice of man, warm from the heart, and pointing to action'. Indeed the view from England was that this spirit was better in Edinburgh than in a London increasingly being torn by the 'rage for politics'.[107] In this regard, the language of the heart espoused by Mackenzie often veered away from the verbal exchanges celebrated in someone like Smellie's account of Scottish literary culture, especially where the latter appeared too mired in the 'Debates of Politics and the clamour of Party'.[108] Dwyer suggests Smith's stoicism can make the emphasis on the gentle affections found in Mackenzie and the moderates seem rather trivial. Both suggested an anxiety at work about the authority of the language of feeling circulating in the community.[109] Both Lord Chesterfield and Jean Jacques Rousseau were depreciated in *The Mirror*. The former's idea of politeness was too much like courtly hypocrisy; the latter's emphasis on virtue was guilty of the kind of primitivism Hume despised, but Rousseau was less culpable from Mackenzie's point of view because he appealed to a sense of virtue beyond the tittle-tattle of the world at large.[110] Rousseau is not often regarded as a conversationalist, but his influence more generally is worth dwelling upon here, as it has important consequences for ideas of conversation later in the century, not least in its anxieties about verbal exchange and social mediation.

Unlike the Scottish desire to reinvent virtue in a commercial society through properly regulated networks of circulation, Rousseau starkly warned his readers not to flatter themselves that they would ever 'see Sparta revive in the bosom of commerce and sordid gain'.[111] His *Letter to d'Alembert* (1759) has the flavour of his Calvinistic origins in its attacks on the theatre. Its date encourages a comparison with the defences of the stage against their Calvinist opponents made by the Moderates in Scotland. Adam Ferguson's contribution to the *Douglas* controversy, *The Morality of*

---

[107] 'The Lounger. A Periodical Paper, published at Edinburgh in the years 1785 and 1786', the *Scots Magazine*, 49 (July 1787), 342–4. The article reproduces admiring accounts originally published in the *English Review* and *European Magazine*.
[108] Quoted in Sher, *Church and University*, 305. •·
[109] See Dwyer, *Virtuous Discourse*, 178.
[110] Ibid. 83.
[111] Jean Jacques Rousseau, *A letter from M. Rousseau, of Geneva, to M. d'Alembert, of Paris, concerning the effects of theatrical entertainments on the manners of mankind* (London, 1759), 85.

stage-plays seriously considered (1757), argued that the theatre was much preferable to the 'rude cabals, which the more decent conversation and manners of civilized times, have in a great measure abolished'.[112] Ferguson was generally not ill disposed to the Spartan virtues, but he was much more tolerant towards the theatre than Rousseau, who represented it as corrupting his native Geneva. A key issue for Rousseau is the participation of women (and by association the kind of feminized politeness advocated by Hume). He praises the tone of Geneva's 'circles', where, without the constraints of a feminized politeness, conversation can be more contentious, and more productive of truth: 'they do not spare one another in disputes: each man finding himself attacked by the whole collected force of his adversary, is obliged to make use of all his power to defend himself; and thus it is that the mind acquires precision and vigour.'[113] Politeness in Rousseau's eyes tends towards a formalistic hypocrisy contrasted with the more open and genuine interactions of the people. Even more than his conversational 'circles', Rousseau prefers public entertainments, comparable to Spartan festivals, where people are participants themselves rather than spectators at a theatrical show: 'They are lively, gay, and fond; their heart is then in their eyes, as it is always on their lips; they endeavour to communicate their joy, their pleasures; they invite, they press, they force, they dispute with their guests. The several societies form but one, and every thing is common to all.'[114] This tendency in Rousseau's writing means that he is continually looking for verbal discourse to be corroborated or even replaced by more direct forms of sentiment. John Home, who Ferguson had been writing to defend, took Rousseau's pamphlet to be an attack on the veneration of sociability at the heart of the Scottish Enlightenment. 'He who has libeled society itself', he told Lord Bute, had now turned his misanthropy against 'the most refined entertainment of social life'.[115]

By the 1770s and 1780s, estimating Rousseau's critique of conversation had perhaps become a more complex matter, speaking as it did to the increasing anxiety that the language of the everyday world was too corrupted to be a true medium of the affections. From this perspective, conversation was liable to be identified with the empty forms of social talk rather than what was construed as the deeper communion based on sympathy exemplified by Henry Mackenzie's character Harley in *The Man of Feeling* (1771). Like many of Rousseau's characters, Harley puts his faith more in signs of sympathy than verbal communication. The

---

[112] Adam Ferguson, *The Morality of stage-plays seriously considered* (Edinburgh, 1757), 22.
[113] Rousseau, *Letter to d'Alembert*, 141.   [114] Ibid. 175.
[115] Home to Bute, 12 December 1758. Quoted in Sher, *Church and University*, 87.

literary language of sentiment, as James Chandler puts it, increasingly comes to consist in 'a mostly wordless exchange in a face-to-face setting'.[116] Laurence Sterne's writing both explores and parodies this tendency. Like most of the writers I've looked at in this chapter, Sterne placed great emphasis on the softening and civilizing effects of female conversation. Parson Yorick's pays tribute to their participation in urban commerce in *A Sentimental Journey*:

The women—by a continual higgling with customers of all ranks and sizes from morning to night, like so many rough pebbles shook long together in a bag, by amicable collisions, they have worn down their asperities and sharp angles, and not only become round and smooth, but will receive, some of them, a polish like a brilliant.[117]

For all Yorick's satisfaction at this analysis, the reader is continually presented with situations where conversation opens up to the double entendre and the sort of commerce that disturbed Addison. If the solution is to trust to unspoken expressions of sincerity identified in the female body, this proves hardly less unstable. When presented with a handkerchief warm from the lovely Maria's breast, the Parson's sympathy, as so often in Sterne, borders on an improper concern for the palpitations of her body.[118] 'Writing, when properly managed, (as you may be sure I think mine is) is but a different name for conversation,' Tristram Shandy tells us, but Sterne's writing revels in the problem of polite regulation of meaning, winking at his reader's knowledge of the multifarious forms of social talk and their instability.[119] His peculiarly quixotic sense of the conversability of literature spilled into his social life as a celebrity author in the 1770s, possibly represented in the painting by J. H. Mortimer that provides the cover for this book.[120] In these spaces, sympathy could veer towards a libertine desire for embodied conversation. Elizabeth Montagu found Sterne an extraordinarily beguiling example of the importance of sympa-

---

[116] James Chandler, 'The Languages of Sentiment', *Textual Practice* 22 (2008), 21–39 (23).
[117] Laurence Sterne, *A Sentimental Journey through France and Italy. By Mr. Yorick*, 2 vols (London, 1768), II: 171–2. See Potkay, *The Fate of Eloquence*, 150.
[118] Sterne, *A Sentimental Journey*, II: 177. Focusing on precisely this passage, Chandler sees a shift 'from representation to metonymy in its mode of signifying affective states' ('Languages of Sentiment', 24).
[119] Laurence Sterne, *The Life and Opinions of Tristram Shandy, Gentleman*, 9 vols (London, 1760–7) II: 179.
[120] The central figure baring his breast to reveal a heart-shaped locket has been identified as Sterne. See John Sunderland, *John Hamilton Mortimer: His Life and Works* (London: Walpole Society, 1988), 133–5, who dates the painting to the mid-to-late 1760s. See also, Arthur Cash, *Laurence Sterne, the Later Years* (1986), 365–72. Among others who have been identified in the painting are Thomas Arne and Francis Grose.

thetic conversation to literary culture, but ultimately, she decided, it was not one that could be respectably enjoyed.[121] If women were to be the sovereigns of the conversable world of literature, they found themselves on a throne subject to a restrictive and tightening statute of limitations.

weak ending

[121] For Montagu's relationship with Sterne, see Felicity A. Nussbaum, *The Limits of the Human: Fictions of Anomaly, Race, and Gender in the Long Eighteenth Century* (Cambridge: Cambridge University Press, 2003), 101–2 and 107–8.

2

Proliferating Worlds, 1762–1790

This chapter examines the proliferation of conversational spaces in the later part of the eighteenth century. If household visits continued as the 'elementary form of polite socializing', conversation also multiplied across the new spaces of the urban renaissance.[1] Many of these spaces were created with the express intention of encouraging talk, either in informal social gatherings or in the many clubs and societies that were such a striking phenomenon of eighteenth-century urban life.[2] Associations were formed for 'literary conversation' in the broadest sense, that is, to discuss the knowledge, events, and other forms of news increasingly available in print. One such group Benjamin Franklin called his 'Club of Honest Whigs'. They met in the 1760s and 1770s as 'friends of liberty and science', first at St. Paul's Coffee House and after 1772 at the London Coffee House, for supper on fortnightly Thursday evenings.[3] Apart from Franklin, its members included many of the leading dissenting clergymen and schoolmasters of the metropolis: among them James Burgh, Richard Price, Joseph Priestley, and William Rose, the sympathetic reviewer of Hume at the *Monthly*. James Boswell, not a regular visitor, described the rambunctious atmosphere of a meeting on 21 September 1769: 'We have wine and punch upon the table. Some of us smoke a pipe, conversation goes on pretty formally, sometimes sensibly, and sometimes furiously…Much was said this night against the Parliament.'[4] Quasi-professional gatherings of authors, artists, and actors, like the Honest Whigs or Samuel Johnson's Literary Club, founded in 1764, were a crucial part of the scene of culture in the 1760s and the decades that followed.[5]

---

[1] Peter Clark, *British Clubs and Societies, 1580–1800: The Origins of an Associational World* (Oxford: Oxford University Press, 2000), 190.

[2] Ibid. 229.

[3] Verner W. Crane, 'The Club of Honest Whigs: Friends of Science and Liberty', *William and Mary Quarterly*, 3rd ser., 23 (1966), 210–33.

[4] James Boswell, *Boswell in Search of a Wife 1766–1769*, ed. Frank Brady and Frederick A. Pottle (Melbourne/London: William Heinemann, 1956), 319.

[5] On the role of such groups in Edinburgh, see D. D. McElroy, 'The Literary Clubs and Societies of Eighteenth Century Scotland, and Their Influence on the Literary Productions of the Period from 1700 to 1800', Unpublished doctoral thesis, University of Edinburgh, 1952.

Books like Joseph Priestley's *History of and Present State of Electricity* (1769) and, more famously, Boswell's *Life of Johnson* (1791) were the products of their discussions. Not infrequently, they made conversation a form of intellectual fight, sometimes, like Johnson, celebrating the triumphs of 'talking for victory'.

Book clubs also proliferated along similar lines, if with less celebrated participants, all over the country. Frequently setting up their own libraries, they usually subscribed to the periodicals that did so much to facilitate the idea of culture as a conversation.[6] Literary and Philosophical Societies, like those in Manchester (1781), Derby (1783), and Newcastle-upon-Tyne (1793), formed to circulate principles of 'improvement' understood to be 'put into motion by collision' through 'meeting and conversing together'.[7] The spread of such conversations was intrinsic to the eighteenth century's sense of its own modernity, but to some commentators they threatened an inundation of talk about the wrong kinds of subjects from the wrong sort of people. So, the Newcastle-upon-Tyne Lit. and Phil. at its inception in 1793 banned 'wrangling about politics or controversial divinity'.[8] Many contemporaries, like the comedian John Bernard, saw the ideological conflicts of the 1790s as bringing the sad demise of 'the era of Clubs'. The idea of the 1790s as the death of a convivial culture conversation has often been repeated, but at the time some thought it was an overdue response to a longer term process of corruption that had been fouling the channels of communication.[9] The specific question of whether the 'small change' of women's talk was sustaining, enhancing, polluting, or diluting the national conversation was a constant feature of these arguments (sometimes explicitly discussed at debating societies).[10] Most voluntary

---

[6] See William St. Clair, *The Reading Nation in the Romantic Period* (Cambridge: Cambridge University Press, 2004), 235–67. According to the *Monthly Magazine*, 51 (June 1821), mispag., the first book club was formed at Leicester in 1740 and its members included John Aikin, Senior. The same article estimated the number of such institutions in 1821 as 6500 with 'above 1000 new ones being formed in the last three years' (398).

[7] *Memoirs of the Literary and Philosophical Society of Manchester*, 1 (1785), vi.

[8] As reported in the Edinburgh paper *The Bee*, 16 (10 July 1793), 26. Thomas Spence had been thrown out of the earlier Newcastle Philosophical Society after giving a lecture on his radical theory of property rights in 1775. See Malcolm Chase, *The People's Farm: English Radical Agrarianism 1775–1840* (Oxford: Oxford University Press, 1988), 21. *A Memoir of Thomas Bewick written by Himself*, ed. Iain Bain (Oxford: Oxford University Press, 1979), gives a sense of the disorder that could attend political debates in its description of the fight that broke out between Bewick and Spence over a vote in another society. The Manchester Lit. and Phil. had banned 'Religion' and 'British politics' from its discussions. See *Memoirs*, I (1785), xviii.

[9] See John Bernard, *Retrospections of the Stage*, 2 vols (London, 1830), II: 170.

[10] On 22 March 1780, for instance, The Palladium, or Liberal Academy of Eloquence debated the question: 'What reason can be assigned for precluding the Fair from the privilege of Civil Society, or from a liberal participation in their discussions?' See Donna

associations that met for talk were dominated by men and continued to meet in taverns and other older and rougher forms of social space, but many of the new forms of urban sociability deliberately made room for women, most obviously the assembly rooms and public promenades built at centres of leisure like Bath and Tunbridge Wells. For a time, especially in the decades after 1760, the Bluestocking circles associated with Elizabeth Montagu and her friends seemed to be fulfilling Hume's notion of female sovereignty over the conversable world, but the participation and authority of women always remained conditional and sometimes subject to fierce hostility, especially from those nostalgic for the masculine values of a civic humanism. These anxieties had a complex place in more general fears about the breaking down of social identities in the new urban spaces. While coffee shops, assembly rooms, and public promenades were sources of civic pride, proof of progress and of the triumph of civil society, they were also places where social boundaries were felt to be melting away, gender differences undermined, and national identity eroded. From this perspective, the retired domestic circle could appear the safest place for conversation, but even those who staked their reputations on their domestic virtues, as Anna Laetitia Barbauld often did, were not necessarily averse to intervening in the 'general conversation' around public affairs.

Particularly at times of national crisis, such as the loss of the American colonies and the political turmoil of 1780, the proliferation of conversation could seem as much a source of unhealthy dissemination as the lifeblood of a healthy body politic. Addison and Steele's project had always been oriented against 'the Rabble of Mankind that crowd our Streets, Coffee-houses, Feasts, and publick Tables'. Steele could not 'call their Discourse Conversation, but rather something that is practiced in Imitation of it' (*T* 153, II: 361).[11] The ambivalence about conversation I ascribed to Adam Smith in my last chapter has been understood as part of broader 'strategic withdrawal' among Scots moralists, which aimed to orient readers away from 'the public arena of contract and calculation' towards 'the private domain of heartfelt sociability and a more genuine converse'.[12] The jeremiads of improving Scots were directed especially

T. Andrew, *London Debating Societies, 1776–1799* (London: London Record Society, 1994), 81.

[11] All references to *The Tatler* are to Donald F. Bond's edition, 3 vols (Oxford: Clarendon Press, 1987), as *T*, followed by original issue number and then volume and page number.

[12] John Dwyer, ' "A Peculiar Blessing": Social Converse in Scotland from Hutcheson to Burns', in John Dwyer and Richard Sher, *Sociability and Society in Eighteenth-Century Edinburgh* (Edinburgh: Mercat Press, 1993), 1–22 (18).

towards London, whose teeming public entertainments seemed a world away from any Humean version of 'select' company. On the other hand, for Samuel Johnson, notoriously hostile to Scotland, only 'London talk' could claim to offer the genuine pleasures of conversation, but even he defined his idea of 'solid' and 'manly' conversation against the oceans of talk lapping at the walls of his Literary Club at the Turk's Head:

To study manners however only in coffee houses: is more than equally imperfect; the minds of men who acquire no solid learning, and only exist on the daily forage they pick up by running about, and snatching what drops from their neighbours as ignorant as themselves, will never ferment into any knowledge valuable or durable.[13]

Rather than celebrating open collision, Johnson's 'talking for victory' often aimed to suppress certain kinds of exchange, especially from religious nonconformists when they broached questions of freedom of conscience or theological controversy. When it came to female conversation, he could be welcoming, but only within certain regulatory limits. At the home of Hester Lynch Piozzi and her first husband, Henry Thrale, for instance, he pursued his own version of strategic withdrawal, sometimes even submitting to female regulation of his conversation, at least in a 'private' context. After his death, Johnson's conversation became a matter of national pride and a source of public controversy fought between biographers, but it was also mocked by satirists who thought the heroic claims made for his life and writings was undermined by the tittle-tattle of his conversation.

MEN'S TALK

The aspiration to form a conversation of culture out of dispersed exchanges between private citizens fuelled the proliferation of clubs and societies that grew up (and, often quickly, died) in the eighteenth century. Extending from informal coffee shop gatherings or familiar visits to private homes to more formalized societies with official membership rolls, rules, and often rituals, these clubs and societies were remarkably varied in their forms, but they did retain certain consistent features: 'The great mass of societies remained concentrated in towns, limited mainly to men, holding their meetings in public drinking houses, and with a variety of ritual activities.'[14] Older forms of male sociability were not always so intent

---

[13] Hester Lynch Piozzi, *Anecdotes of the Late Samuel Johnson*, 4th edn (1786), 267.
[14] Clark, *British Clubs and Societies*, 95.

on improvement or sober rationality, although Boswell's account of the Club of Honest Whigs suggests reform did not have to go hand in hand with sobriety. Sometimes clubs met to create a space for male behaviour that indulged itself in more libertine and bibulous forms of talk. One of the most spectacularly successful of these clubs was the Society of Dilettanti, set up in 1735 by aristocrats returning from the Grand Tour. The society originally met in a series of taverns, but by the end of the century had acquired its own dedicated space in Almack's Club. The trajectory of the Dilettanti in certain respects confirms a narrative from aristocratic excess to a more specialized and professional role followed by other clubs towards the end of the century, but it was not a straightforward journey. The club played a part in the foundation of the Royal Academy and won repute for sponsoring a series of scholarly projects, including the magnificent folios of *The Antiquities of Athens and other Monuments of Ancient Greece* (first volume 1762) and then *Ionian Antiquities* (1769), but it was quite a while before it cast off its associations with libertine sociability. Conversation in such strictly male gatherings was valued for its wit and obscenity. 'Friendly and social intercourse', wrote Robert Wood somewhat blandly in the preface to *Ionian Antiquities*, 'was undoubtedly the first object in view.'[15] More frankly, the Society conformed to a libertine-aristocratic notion of sociability grounded in 'heavy drinking, ceremonies and ritual, old-style masculinity, client-patron relationships, and selectivity'.[16] As Horace Walpole waspishly noticed, 'the nominal qualification is having been in Italy, and the real one, being drunk.'[17]

The Society may have celebrated a classical republican genealogy, but it lacked the focus on practical politics that had distinguished the Kit-Cats a few decades earlier.[18] The Dilettanti did follow Addison and his friends by commissioning a series of ensemble portraits painted by a single artist (in their case George Knapton) to hang in their meeting room. Rather than the relatively direct, even approachable portraits painted by Kneller for the

---

[15] Robert Wood, 'Preface' to *Ionian Antiquities*, quoted in Bruce Redford, *Dilettanti: The Antic and the Antique in Eighteenth-century England* (Los Angeles: J. Paul Getty Museum and Getty Research Institute, 2008), 2.

[16] Clark, *British Clubs and Societies*, 471. See also, Jason M. Kelly, *The Society of Dilettanti: Archaeology and Identity in the British Enlightenment* (New Haven, CT/London: Yale University Press, 2009), 7–59, and Shearer West's 'Libertinism and the Ideology of Male Friendship in the Portraits of the Society of Dilettanti', *Eighteenth-century Life*, 16 (1992), 76–104. West gives much more credence to the republican slant of the original club than Redford.

[17] Letter to Sir Horace Mann on 14 April 1743, in *The Yale Edition of Horace Walpole's Correspondence*, ed. W. S. Lewis, 48 vols (New Haven: Yale University Press, 1937–83), XVIII: 211.

[18] Redford, *Dilettanti*, 3–4.

Kit-Cats, the Society commissioned a series of much more playfully self-conscious pictures, privileging witty performance over sincerity. They included a painting of the notorious libertine Francis Dashwood dressed as a monk, self-consciously flaunting conventional religion and morality. The paintings emphasize the display of elite status and a sense of freedom from the rules applied to ordinary citizens. Knapton was succeeded as painter to the Society by 'Athenian' Stuart and then, in 1769, by Sir Joshua Reynolds, who contributed two memorably opulent group portraits to the Society's collection. Reynolds himself described the pictures in a letter to Lord Grantham: 'They are employed according to the intent of the Society in drinking and Virtù. The new Room and these Pictures have given something of a reviving spirit to the Society.'[19] Bringing together 'drinking and Virtù' captures the combination of a civic humanist concern for public values, at least in relation to classical art, and what Redford calls a 'private realm of ritual, recollection, and gratification'.[20] In many ways, the Society's aristocratic insouciance registers a degree of resistance to the correlation of private and public morality, but Wood's preface may be a straw in the wind of changing times in its insistence that the Dilettanti 'have not…abandoned the cause of *virtù* in which they are engaged, or forfeited their pretension to that character which is implied in the name they have assumed'.[21] Committed as he was to a serious concern for questions of public taste and knowledge of classical antiquity, no wonder Wood drew a veil over the less morally improving aspects of their meetings.

Such gatherings could seem a form of masculine self-indulgence falling well short of a modernizing and moralizing discourse of politeness. Some time around 1762, Elizabeth Montagu decided to make a public protest when it came to her attention that the Society had designs on using an area in Green Park to build an 'edifice' for the display of their antique casts.[22] Showing a typical concern for public morality, Montagu argued that such a grant would usurp a space intended for the entertainment of the people at large for a use that would potentially 'alienate the public hearts'. The

---

[19] 1 October 1777, *The Letters of Sir Joshua Reynolds*, ed. John Ingamells and John Edgcumbe (New Haven: Yale University Press, 2000), 70. West suggests that in Reynolds's two group portraits the libertine aspects of the Knapton paintings are 'not obliterated, but presented in a more acceptable—and more public—form' ('Libertinism and Ideology', 91).

[20] Redford, *Dilettanti*, 4.

[21] Quoted ibid. 2.

[22] The letter from the Huntington Library's collection (MO3000) has been reproduced in *Bluestocking Feminism: Writings of the Bluestocking Circle, 1738–1785*, vol. 1: *Elizabeth Montagu*, ed. Elizabeth Eger (London: Pickering and Chatto, 1999), 167–8. The letter seems never to have been published. The Dilettanti shelved their proposal for the new building. See Lionel Henry Cust, *The History of the Society of Dilettanti*, ed. Sidney Colvin (London: Society of Dilettanti, 1914), 60.

Dilettanti, she argued, would be perceived by the populace as foreign interlopers; their building 'a place where foreign fashions, foreign follies, foreign fopperies, foreign arts, & foreign artists are to be encouraged'. She implicitly associates the Dilettanti's classicism with an aristocratic republicanism when she connects it with the Beefsteak Club: 'Can such a compliment be made to the Dilettanti & refused to the English beef stake club?' For Montagu, the aristocratic republicanism associated with such clubs was simply a form of factionalism, patriot posturing at the expense of the public good. Including the Beefsteak Club brings within the purview of her letter the patriot politics of John Wilkes, which would turn a public space intended for the promotion of polite sociability into 'a scene of riot & debauchery'. The creation of public parks was part of the urban renaissance's programme of encouraging virtuous sociability.[23] Montagu's letter imagines Green Park being polluted by a 'school of luxury, the Academy of Vice, & the Palaestra of Faction'. Her idea of the feminized conversable world is implicitly being ranged against the homosociality of 'independent gentlemen'. The vaunted 'independence' of civic humanism is no more than self-indulgence, the breeding ground of political faction inimical to the national interest, an affront to the Christianized idea of improvement at the heart of Montagu's own project.[24]

I'll be returning to Montagu's own staging of the conversable world later in this chapter, but it's worth inquiring further into the varieties of masculine sociability she was at least partially defining herself against. The Beefsteak Club mentioned in her letter had been set up in the theatre at Covent Garden in 1735. Its motto was 'Beef and Liberty'.[25] A gridiron inscribed with the motto was hung over their meetings. Not unlike the Dilettanti, the meetings themselves were focused mainly on the consumption

---

[23] See Peter Borsay's 'The Rise of the Promenade: The Social and Cultural Use of Space in the English Provincial Town *c.* 1660–1800', *British Journal of Eighteenth-Century Studies*, 9 (2) (1986), 125–40.

[24] For attacks on the Dilettanti that share something of Montagu's perspective, see West, 'Libertinism and Ideology', 94–5. On Montagu's emphasis on public integrity and a patriotism beyond what she perceived as party factionalism, see Harriet Guest, 'Bluestocking Feminism', *Huntington Library Quarterly*, 65 (2002), 59–80; Emma Major, 'The Politics of Sociability: Public Dimensions of the Bluestocking Millennium', ibid. 175–92; ead. *Madam Britannia: Women, Church, and Nation, 1712–1812* (Cambridge: Cambridge University Press, forthcoming); and Elizabeth Eger ' "The Noblest Commerce of Mankind": Conversation and Community in the Bluestocking Circle', in Barbara Taylor and Sarah Knott (eds), *Women, Gender and Enlightenment: A Comparative History* (Basingstoke: Palgrave Macmillan, 2005), 288–305. Major's work, especially, emphasizes the self-presentation of Montagu as participating in genuinely patriotic debate by virtue of her perception of the Church of England's role as a national institution.

[25] See the description in *Boswell's London Journal 1762–1763*, ed. Frederick A. Pottle (London: William Heinemann, 1950), 51–3.

of alcohol and conversation salted with displays of obscene wit. Although Boswell described the company there as 'mixed', presumably in political affiliation, it contained at least a strong tendency towards the patriot politics implied in Montagu's letter. John Wilkes and the patriot satirist Charles Churchill, for instance, were among the company Boswell met when he attended: 'We had nothing to eat but beefsteaks, and had wine and punch in plenty and freedom. We had a number of songs.'[26] The same roistering atmosphere and patina of opposition politics were still prevalent in 1787, when John Bernard was proposed as a member. Graduating from the more provincial sociability of a Bath 'catch' club, Bernard remembered thrilling at the 'galaxy of table wits in whose lustre the Royal Brothers delighted to sun themselves, and whose union formed an epoch in the convivial history of London.'[27]

Bernard's galaxy of stars comprised, among others, Richard Brinsley Sheridan, who sometimes brought Charles James Fox, Miles Peter Andrews, Edward Topham, Robert Merry, and Capt. Charles Morris, secretary and songwriter to the company.[28] Unlike the Bath Catch Club and despite Morris's role, this was more a 'talking' rather than a 'singing' society. In its boozy circles, punning was a highly valued skill, at which Merry in particular excelled.[29] These men scribbled newspaper squibs, dashed off prologues and epilogues for the theatre, flaunting their facility for rapid composition, while all the time indulging in alcohol-fuelled banter.[30] Bernard recalled that 'the members were all men of the world, and (London being a large cauldron, in which society is kept continually in a ferment, and something new is hourly rising to the surface,) they had well-stored heads to unburthen on coming together.'[31] Those from outside the elite, such as Bernard, were welcomed if they could add to this stock of scurrilous merriment. Neither politeness nor even hygiene were necessary: John Williams, alias Anthony Pasquin, satirical poet and

[26] Lord Sandwich, 'a jolly, hearty, lively man', according to Boswell, was in the chair. He was associated with Churchill and Wilkes in the notorious orgies at Medmenham Abbey, but later expelled from the Beefsteaks when he impeached Wilkes in the Lords.

[27] Bernard, *Retrospections*, II: 114. Bernard had gone to Covent Garden to join the company as principal comedian. The musical aspect to the Bath Club was necessary, 'so little stirring in the town, to furnish food for conversation' (*Retrospections*, II: 117). Other clubs mentioned by Bernard during this period include the Earl of Barrymore's Blue Bottle Club, for which Anthony Pasquin acted as secretary, and a club of actor comedians known as 'The Strangers at Home'.

[28] Bernard estimated the membership at 40, a third of the membership seem to have been noblemen, *Retrospections*, II: 114.

[29] Ibid. II: 116.

[30] John Taylor's *Records of My Life*, 2 vols (London, 1832), gives a flavour of this world, including Merry's participation, see, esp., II: 266–7.

[31] Bernard, *Retrospections*, II: 116.

	Good humour	Wit	Humour
Sheridan	0	3	0
Selwyn	2	2	0
Andrews	2	2	0
Merry	3	1	2
Topham	2	1	0
Woodfall	3	1	0
Bate Dudley	3	1	0
Taylor	3	1	3
Hewardine	3	1	3
Saville Carey	3	1	3
G. A. Stevens	2	1	2
Major Arabin	3	1	3
Bearcroft	2	1	0
Bannister	3	2	3

sidekick of the arch libertine the Earl of Barrymore, was 'filthy', but tolerated for his powers of conversation. In his published recollections, Bernard purports to reproduce his notes, much like Boswell in his *Life of Johnson*, to give a flavour of the conversation. He even prints a 'scale' of sociability to register the different kinds of conversational talents on display (see table above).[32]

Sheridan he described as a 'satirist', mainly talking 'under the excitement of the general attention', especially when Fox was there to impress. If Sheridan displayed a 'comparative coldness and indifference to the general sources of merriment', then 'never was a man's a greater echo to his character than Merry's'. Bernard's close friend Merry may have excelled at punning, but his conversation, like his poetry, displayed a more 'benevolent mould of mind'. Indeed he was mocked by the club for appearing in the pages of *The World* as Della Crusca, the poet of fashionable sensibility, providing the playwright Richard Cumberland with an opportunity for another pun: 'they [Merry's poems] put him in mind of a bouquet of artificial flowers; they had all the bloom, without the *scents*.'[33] Those present at the Beefsteak Club may have contributed articles and squibs to the newspapers that sponsored Merry's poetry, but these were very different from the softened heterosexual eroticism of Della Cruscan poetry, and more in line with the general ambience of the club itself. Its

[32] Ibid. II: 140. Hester Piozzi wrote up a similar table in her *Thraliana*. Johnson scored full marks for 'general knowledge' and zero for 'person and voice'. The table was drawn up differently for her women friends and included a column for 'powers of conversation'. See *Thraliana: the Diary of Mrs. Hester Lynch Thrale (Later Mrs Piozzi) 1776–1809*, ed. Katharine C. Balderston, 2 vols (Oxford: Oxford University Press, 1942), I: 329–31.

[33] Bernard, *Retrospections*, II: 143, 146–9.

masculine boisterousness was at odds with public displays of fragile sensibility. Like many critics of Merry's poetry, the company probably took the sighing and panting of Della Cruscanism as a risible sign of the degeneration of British culture into effeminacy.[34]

Bernard was one of many who believed that 'the Era of Clubs' was destroyed by the ideological polarization brought by the French Revolution. Previously, he claimed, 'the safety of the country was not at that period threatened. It was the spirit of harmony and fellowship which brought men together of all kinds and classes to cement, once a week, the pleasurable "chains of the heart".'[35] He represents the associational world of the 1780s as a meritocracy open to talents and the democracy of feeling. Whether this was the more general atmosphere of the club at the time is another matter. His own sentimental language, written from exile in America decades later, implies a strong preference for the 'amiability' he always shared with his friend Merry. The more generally masculine, aristocratic, and libertine world drawn in his descriptions of the Beefsteak Club suggests the teasing of Merry may have been a defensive gesture by the company there, lending support to the idea that such clubs functioned as bastions of masculinity against a perceived movement of women into the public sphere.[36] Bernard himself was something of a victim of this increasingly out-dated world, forced to emigrate partly through the debts he faced as the club's secretary, run up by some of his more insouciant aristocratic club mates.[37]

TALKING FOR VICTORY

Clubs like the Beefsteak practised a more wittily combative and profane idea of conversation than the politeness proposed in *The Spectator*. Punning was a form of verbal duelling for Merry and his friends, part of a competitive ethos that did not always spare the feelings of those involved. An equally masculine ethos of competition defined the Literary Club set up by Samuel Johnson and his friends at the Turk's Head in 1764. There the emphasis was on 'manly' or 'solid' conversation rather than flashing puns. Johnson in particular was quick to quash the indecency associated with punning. Ability in conversation for Johnson always had a moral aspect: 'it is when you come close to a man in conversation, that you

---

[34] The classic attacks on the effeminacy of Merry and the other Della Cruscans were William Gifford's satirical poems *The Baviad* (1793) and *The Maeviad* (1795).

[35] Bernard, *Retrospections*, II: 171.

[36] Clark, *British Clubs and Societies*, 203.

[37] See John Bernard, *Retrospections of America 1797–1811*, ed. Mrs. Bayle Bernard (New York: Benjamin Blom, 1887), 23.

discover what his real abilities are.'[38] Solid conversation had to draw on a breadth of reading and other weighty weapons that properly armed the participants for combat:

There must, in the first place, be knowledge, there must be materials;—in the second place, there must be a command of words;— in the third place, there must be imagination, to place things in such views as they are not commonly seen in:—and in the fourth place, there must be presence of mind, and a resolution that is not to be overcome by failures; this last is an essential requisite; for want of it many people do not excel in conversation. (*BLJ* IV: 166)

In the process, Johnson sometimes made a differentiation between 'talk' and 'conversation', a common enough distinction in the eighteenth century, if one far from easy to stabilize into a positive definition. Boswell noted:

Though his usual phrase for conversation was *talk*, yet he made a distinction; for when he once told me that he dined the day before at a friend's house, with 'a very pretty company;' and I asked him if there was good conversation, he answered, 'No, Sir; we had *talk* enough, but no *conversation*; there was nothing *discussed*.' (*BLJ* IV: 186)

'Pretty' here implies that the company included women, before whom Johnson obviously felt some constraint, although he was far from always practising it, even in their presence. Johnson's conversation was often a very robust version of Fielding's turning things round together. John Dunning thought that 'in his company we did not so much interchange conversation, as listen to him' (*BLJ* III: 240), but Johnson respected those who could give as good as they got. Pre-eminent among these was Edmund Burke. Although Johnson sometimes thought Burke's conversation too jocular and 'low' (*BLJ* V: 32; see also IV: 276), he once admitted to Boswell: 'That fellow calls forth all my powers. Were I to see Burke now it would kill me.' 'So much was he accustomed to consider conversation as a contest', commented Boswell, 'and such was his notion of Burke as an opponent.' For Boswell himself Johnson's roughness in conversation could be a problem, a matter I'll return to at the end of this chapter.[39]

---

[38] *Boswell's Life of Johnson*, ed. G. B. Hill, rev. L. F. Powell, 6 vols (Oxford: Clarendon Press, 1934–50), IV: 179. Further references to this edition appear as *BLJ* in parentheses, with volume and page numbers.

[39] When Johnson was near to his death, his friend Bennett Langton told him he had sometimes 'contradicted people in conversation' (*BLJ* IV: 280). Boswell told him: 'I suppose he meant, the *manner* of doing it; roughly—and harshly.' Johnson replied: And who is the worst for that?'

> BOSWELL: 'It hurts people of weak nerves.'
> JOHNSON: 'I know no such weak-nerved people.'

Johnson may have practised something akin to the frictive model of conversation found in Watts's *Improvement of the Mind*, but without the celebration of freedom of enquiry. On the contrary, his roughness was very often directed at Dissenters when they dared to express heterodox opinions in his company. His praise of Watts for bringing Dissenters into the range of what he considered polite culture gives some clue as to what he expected of them in conversation with him. He frequently tolerated them in private company, *if* they conformed to his perception of proper behaviour.[40] When his friend the minister Dr. Henry Mayo insisted on the right to liberty of conscience, Johnson retorted: 'People confound liberty of thinking with liberty of talking' (*BLJ* II: 249). Boswell engineered a return to the topic in 1783. Having justified the right of the magistracy to drive away a Quaker, Johnson asserted: 'Now the vulgar are the children of the State. If any one attempts to teach them doctrines contrary to what the State approves, the magistrate may and ought to restrain him.' Boswell records William Seward asking in return: 'Would you restrain private conversation, Sir?' to which Johnson replied:

'Why, Sir, it is difficult to say where private conversation begins, and where it ends. If we three should discuss even the great question concerning the existence of a Supreme Being by ourselves, we should not be restrained; for that would be to put an end to all improvement. But if we should discuss it in the presence of ten boarding-school girls, and as many boys, I think the magistrate would do well to put us in the stocks, to finish the debate there.' (*BLJ* IV: 216)

For all his reputation for Toryism, Johnson was no enemy to 'improvement', but he did not think progress demanded freedom of political and religious enquiry. He claimed for himself the right to exercise a monitory power through his conversation as in his writing.

Edward Gibbon, who joined the Literary Club in 1774, after the death of Oliver Goldsmith, was more comfortable with continental modes of

---

Told of the exchange by Boswell, Burke commented: 'It is well, if when a man comes to die, he has nothing heavier upon his conscience than having been a little rough in conversation.'

[40] See G. M. Ditchfield, 'Dr. Johnson and the Dissenters', *Journal of the John Rylands Library*, 68 (1986), 373–409. Ditchfield believes historians have exaggerated Johnson's antipathy towards Dissenters. He sees Johnson as comfortable with 'educated, urban Dissenters, clergy or laity, who had some literary conversation, who did not urge the promotion of Dissenting causes in politics and whose Calvinism had lost some of its extreme rigour without being replaced or superseded by Arianism or its variations' (378). This underestimates the degree of tacit compliance implied even in his own description of Johnson's views. Ditchfield makes a great deal of Mayo's presence in Johnson's circle, but the clergyman was known as 'THE LITERARY ANVIL' because of Johnson's 'reiterated blows' (*BLJ* II: 252). Hardly, then, a relationship based upon reciprocity.

politeness than the combativeness displayed in Johnson's talk.[41] Although
he wrote to Garrick from Paris in August 1777, to assure the Club that he
had not 'lost my relish for *manly* conversation and the society of the
brown table' (Gibbon's emphasis), the underscoring suggests an awkward
self-consciousness about his failings in this regard.[42] The ethos of the Club
was neither one of polite moderation nor the glitter associated with the
French salon. Johnson's loved to thrash out opinion, although he was
quite capable of a playful spirit of contradiction. Significantly, the Club
was more professional in its membership than the Dilettanti, originally
comprised of men making names for themselves as authors and painters:
Johnson, Edmund Burke (not yet an MP), Oliver Goldsmith, and
Sir Joshua Reynolds. Although bishops and peers were later to swell
their numbers, Johnson was famously hostile to aristocratic patronage
and prided himself on his independence. To an extent, the Literary
Club was a demonstration of the pre-eminence its membership had
achieved in the world of letters. If their exclusivity was proof of Oliver
Goldsmith's claim that the 'the truly great seldom unite in societies',
placing themselves above and beyond the 'anarchy of literature', then
the rapid circulation of their bon mots in print could only promote a
general aspiration to imitate 'men of the first wit and conversation'.[43]
Their conversation invited endless imitation from the numerous literary
societies up and down the nation.

Quite possibly Johnson's sense of his independence as an author was
confirmed by his famously plain-speaking conversation, an exaggerated
version of what was taken to be a national virtue.[44] For many of his
contemporaries, on the other hand, his failures to moderate his conversation were a disgraceful blight on the reputation of British letters. Elizabeth
Montagu was furious at his disruption of her assemblies.[45] Lord Chesterfield branded him a 'respectable Hottentot' for his transgressions against
'all the regards of social life':

[41] See W. B. Carnochan, 'Gibbon's Silences', in James Engell (ed.), *The Age of Johnson*,
Harvard English Studies 12 (Harvard, MA/London: Harvard University Press, 1984), 367–85.
[42] Quoted ibid. 376, who makes the point about Gibbon's self-consciousness.
[43] See Oliver Goldsmith, *The Citizen of the World*, 2 vols (1769), I: 80 and *Johnsoniana;
or A Collection of Bon Mots* (1776), iii. Johnson regarded *Johnsoniana* as 'a mighty impudent
thing' (*BLJ* II: 432). It quickly went into a second edition, to his chagrin outselling
A Journey to the Western Islands (*BLJ* III: 325).
[44] See Peter Burke, *The Art of Conversation* (Cambridge: Polity Press, 1993), 108–12.
[45] See, for instance, her letter to Vesey quoted in *Mrs Montagu 'Queen of the Blues': Her
Letters and Friendships from 1762 to 1800*, ed. Reginald Blunt (London: Constable, 1923)
II: 162. Elizabeth Vesey's reputation for bringing harmony out a discord had some effect on
Johnson's conversation apparently. Montagu told Elizabeth Carter: 'Even Samuel Johnson
was seldom brutally rude in her society.' Quoted ibid. II: 5.

He disputes with heat, and indiscriminately, mindless of the rank, character, and situation of those with whom he disputes; absolutely ignorant of the several gradations of familiarity and respect, he is exactly the same to his superiors, his equals, and his inferiors.[46]

Even Sir Joshua Reynolds wondered that a man who could be so gentle in tête-à-tête could be so violent in other conversational situations:

In mixed company he fought on every occasion as if his whole reputation depended upon the victory of the minute, and he fought with all the weapons. If he was foiled in argument he had recourse to abuse and rudeness.[47]

Contrary to Chesterfield's criticism and Reynolds description, Johnson himself often claimed to believe that company needed to be select if it was really to aim at intellectual combat. Told that some Oxford colleges had excluded students from conversation with the fellows, he commented: 'They are in the right, Sir, for there can be no real conversation, no fair exertion of mind amongst them, if the young men are by' (*BLJ*, II: 443). When the membership of the Literary Club started to swell, first to twelve in 1768, then thirty in 1777, Johnson became dissatisfied, setting up the Essex Head Club in 1783, with a membership limited at 24 (and a rule book he drew up himself).[48] At other times, he preferred a more domestic setting for his talk, where conversation could be more relaxed, most obviously at the Streatham villa of Hester Piozzi, then Mrs Thrale, where he felt, as William Cook put it, most '*at home*' (Cook's italics).[49] Even at Streatham, however, his conduct was far from easy to bear, although he did submit to chastisement at Piozzi's hands on some occasions.[50] Boswell may have brought forward Johnson's power as a

[46] Lord Chesterfield, *Letters*, ed. David Roberts (Oxford: Oxford University Press, 1992), 220. Boswell took the portrait to be of Johnson, but acknowledged it may have been meant for George, Lord Lyttelton, among others (*BLJ* I: 266–7). Boswell insisted Lyttelton never acted with the 'violence' described here.

[47] See Charles Leslie and Tom Taylor, *The Life and Times of Sir Joshua Reynolds*, 2 vols (London, 1865) II: 462.

[48] For an account of the setting up of the club, see William Cook, *The Life of Samuel Johnson*, 2nd edn (London, 1785), 65–9. Hester Piozzi's *Anecdotes of Johnson* claims that when it grew in numbers Johnson became 'less fond of the meeting, and loudly proclaimed his carelessness *who* might be admitted, when it was become a mere dinner club' (122).

[49] See Cook, *Life*, 84. Cook was close to Goldsmith, to whom he had letters of introduction when he came over from Ireland. John Taylor claimed he was the first person Johnson nominated as a member of the Essex Head Club. See the brief sketch of Cook in Taylor, *Records of My Life*, II: 365–7.

[50] See Piozzi, *Anecdotes*, 293. Frances Burney gives an account of the attack made on William Pepys, an ally of Lyttelton and Montagu's. The next day Hester Piozzi 'read him a very serious Lecture upon giving way to such violence' (*Early Journals and Letters of Fanny Burney*, IV, Part II, ed. Betty Rizzo (Montreal/Kingston: McGill-Queen's University Press, 2003), 371.

sign of British mastery, but it was far from providing a model that could comfortably be emulated in the sublunary worlds of literary associations forming around the country.[51]

what is the point of all this?

DEBATING THE NEWS

For those who regarded Johnson's talk as a sign of cultural mastery, it provided the most illustrious example of the more general British taste for 'mutual improvement by liberal conversation and rational enquiry'.[52] Even at its zenith, the era of clubs and associations celebrated by John Bernard and dominated by the figure of Johnson and his friends was fraught with anxieties about the limits of sociability and the threat of 'social invasion'. Classical ideas of civic conversation were being both emulated and put under pressure by the proliferation of conversation proposing to give the opinions of private men on public affairs. Such talk, fuelled by newspapers and periodicals, kept pace with the expansion in the market for books. Notwithstanding Johnson's strictures against the 'forage' of the day, newspapers became 'essential lubricants for public and social discourse' (including stories of Johnson and his circle).[53] Often stocked by conversation clubs and reading groups who advertised meetings in their pages, newspapers and periodicals provided a wealth of topics, from gossip to political news, to reviews of books, with plentiful extracts, which members might otherwise never read. Most learned societies remained generalist, committed to improvement, attempting to keep abreast of the increasing volume and diversity of information available. The press presented itself as an ongoing conversation, frequently printing the correspondence of its readers (fictional or otherwise), reporting on their gatherings, and priding itself as the bastion of British freedom of speech.

Plenty of the participants in the burgeoning world of voluntary associations were eager to see eighteenth-century London as fulfilling or even outdoing the civic ideals of Athens or Rome. From mid-century, informal discussion groups in coffee shops and taverns proposed themselves as clearing houses of opinion by transforming themselves into debating clubs. By the late 1770s many were leaving the taverns and pubs they

---

[51] For a general account of Johnson and emulation, see Isobel Grundy, *Samuel Johnson and the Scale of Greatness* (Leicester: Leicester University Press, 1986).

[52] The description of the aims and ambitions of the Rankenian Society of Edinburgh given in the *Scots Magazine*, 33 (July 1771), 340. The Rankenian was a precursor of Hume's Select Club, which met in the tavern after which it was named. Hume was a member.

[53] Clark, *British Clubs and Societies*, 172.

had begun in and setting up as commercial ventures in special rooms, charging a fee. They were even reputed to be patronized by parliamentarians, some of whom, including Burke and William Pitt the Younger, were supposed to have honed their debating skills there. The result by 1780 was 'a cacophony of open debating societies discussing a medley of topics'.[54] The worry remained whether this cacophony could be orchestrated into a harmonious sense of public opinion. In 1781, the president of the Westminster Forum presented its debates as providing a site for the integration of what he calls 'public conversation'.[55] More forthrightly than its president, 'Junius Junior' defended the Forum as the best means of keeping up the spirit of liberty against 'effeminacy of manners, and a mean servility of mind'. The benefits of instructive conversation, he argued, could be supported just as well in these situations as in more refined and select company:

Is there a more pleasing, a more interesting channel through which instruction can flow, than a lively animated conversation? And when gentlemen meet together for the purpose of communicating their sentiments to each other on any particular subject proposed for their discussion, although the company be very numerous, 'tis nevertheless in a more enlarged sense of the word, conversation.[56]

Unusually confident about such meetings, 'Junius' sees the participants at the Westminster as 'gentlemen', where satirists more often represented debating clubs as populated by pretentious mechanics. At a time when too many public institutions appeared to be corrupted, his article is willing to imagine the debating societies, 'animated by an ardent love of their country', taking on the role abdicated by Parliament. Samuel Johnson would have regarded such opinions as dangerous Whig pretension. When Johnson and Boswell encountered Sir Adam Fergusson at the Pantheon in March 1772, the knight expressed a concern that the luxury of places like the Pantheon 'corrupts a people, and destroys the spirit of liberty'. Johnson mocked his veneration for the ancient republics, insisting they were barbarically ignorant of modern politeness, even compared to the Pantheon, and denounced Fergusson as a 'vile Whig' (*BLJ* II: 169–70).

Not untypically, Johnson insisted on his delight in modern improvement with a provocative force at odds with most eighteenth-century ideas of polite conversation. Most others hoped that if Britons took care to manage their conversation properly, then their social talk could fulfil at

---

[54] Clark, *British Clubs and Societies*, 119.
[55] [David Turner], *A Short History of the Westminster Forum: containing some Remarks upon the Laws; wherein the Nature of such Societies is Examined*, 2 vols (1781), II: 131 and 216.
[56] *The Morning Chronicle* (11 January 1780).

least a version of a classical idea of civic conversation. Johnson's early biographer, William Cook, a member of the Essex Head Club, brought out *Conversation: A Didactic Poem* (1796) to affirm precisely this case. In it, conversation is hymned as a form of 'moral happiness—and social use' and imagined as a proving ground for public virtue after the manner of the Romans:

> at their baths—their meals—the public hall,
> 'Twas Conversation took the lead in all.
> Here rights were canvass'd—manners understood,
> And laws develop'd for the public good.

British conversation becomes a belated version of the talk of independent men free from tyranny:

> 'tis that perpetual school,
> Which moulds the manners, free from tyrant rule,
> Gives flow of speech, and readiness to scan
> The various habitudes of active man.[57]

Cook's poem brings Burke and Johnson forward as examples of mighty prowess, although their contentious manner is marked as exceptional. 'Minds gigantic', like theirs, can enjoy 'contention strong', but the next page gives the more usual line against 'contention's sound'.[58] Cook's poem may be a hymn to conversation, but its laboured didacticism has scarcely learned to turn conversation's charms into an appropriate poetic form, especially when contrasted with the supple ease of Cowper's conversation poems. *Conversation* was popular enough to be reissued twice more over the next twenty years, in 1807 and again in 1822, but the preface to the last (dated 1815) bemoans the triumph of commerce and politics, topics that have driven the elegant arts of conversation too close to political debate. By 1815, Cook seems to have abandoned his civic aspirations. Echoing the descriptions of travellers like Goede, the conversable assembly is now merely '*a crowd* where *a man of sense dares not be himself*, and where, striving to be like others calling themselves *Company*, he must put on the *fool's coat* for the evening, or make his exit.'[59]

---

[57] William Cook, *Conversation: A Didactic Poem, in Three Parts* (London, 1796), 42 and 40.

[58] Ibid. 9–10.

[59] Cook, *The Pleasures of Conversation*, rev edn (1822), xx: 'the spirit of commerce… now began to appear as one of the prominent features of the English character, and being followed by the general interests which men of all ranks and talents found in politics, they cultivated business and debate more than refined and enlivened society.'

By this stage, Cook's poem had been infused with a powerfully nostalgic sense of the 1770s and 1780s as a golden age of talk. He added a new
extended passage on individual members of the Literary Club (Johnson,
Burke, Reynolds, and his friend Goldsmith among them) who dwarf the
chatter of the present.[60] Back in the 1770s and 1780s, participants were
far from certain that they were living through a period of conversational
greatness. Even the president of the Westminster Forum felt bound to
admit that its debates sometimes failed to transcend their 'ale-house'
origins, notwithstanding that they managed to attract the moderating
presence of 'a few ladies'. The roughness of the debates, he believed,
discouraged the attendance of those who genuinely commanded a 'classical
erudition'.[61] Others, like William Young, tried to negotiate the differences
between the classical past and the new commercial society by insisting that
Athens itself had been a trading nation and as such offered 'a model of
modernity'.[62] Its glory was to be measured in its openness to a great variety
of talk generated by the people's involvement in the fate of their city:

The frequent assemblage of the people on the public concerns must have made
every one conversant in political subjects; and the minds too of men must thence
have become strong, and fitted for abstruse discourse, penetrating in disquisitions
of serious moment, lively in common chat, and communicative at all times; for no
restriction silenced the boldest champion of discontent, or merriest advocate of
scandal.[63]

Young's version of Athens countenances a very open and democratic idea
of civic discourse, dismissive of the objections of 'fine gentlemen' to 'their
grossness of conversation'.[64] If political conversation in Athens fed into a
more general vivacity of communication, then Young feared that the
diversity of commercial Britain could not recreate a true sense of the
unity of the polis:

Then, individuals formed a community; *now*, more properly a community may be
said to be of individuals; *then*, the interest of the whole was deemed that of each; *now*,

[60] Cook, *Pleasures of Conversation*, 82–91.

[61] Turner, *Short History*, I: 20 and 29.

[62] Peter Liddel, 'William Young and the *Spirit of Athens*', in *Reinventing History: The
Enlightenment Origins of Ancient History*, ed. James Moore et al. (London: School of
Advanced Study, University of London, 2003), 57–85 (65).

[63] William Young, *The Spirit of Athens, Being a Political and Philosophical Investigation of
the History of that Republic* (London, 1777), 162.

[64] Ibid. 164. Later editions were more circumspect in certain regards. Liddel, 'William
Young', 76, notes that by 1786 the word 'free state' had replaced 'democracy' in a key
passage where Young discusses the political arrangements 'best calculated for general
happiness'. Liddel believes events in America influenced the shift.

the inverse is adopted, and each would operate on the whole. The genius of patriotism, which animated every breast no longer exists—we wonder at its effects.[65]

For many commentators there was little difference between the civic pretensions of the debating clubs and the fashionable ambitions of places like the Pantheon, at least when it came to the potential for social confusion. A letter addressed to Lord North 'On Places of Public Diversion' in the *General Evening Post* for 21–3 January made no distinction between debating clubs and the theatres and pleasure gardens when it came to the degeneracy of the times. The correspondent complained that statutes existed to stem this tide of errant sociability, but still it was 'winked at by the inferior magistracy'.[66] Despite the pretensions to regularity and order manifested in the move away from the pubs and taverns, debating clubs remained a constant source of concern, suggesting a presumption to debate the affairs of the nation outside Parliament.

The winter of 1779–80 produced a spike in the numbers of such societies amid the anxieties generated by the American War, the petitioning of the Yorkshire Association, and the activities of the Protestant Association that culminated in the Gordon Riots of the summer.[67] The Society for Free Debate at Coachmakers' Hall provoked a satirical poem written by one Harum Skarum, who reports 'our introductory sixpences, like *death* and *stage-coaches*, had levelled all distinctions, and jostled wits, lawyers, politicians, and mechanics, into the confusion of the last day.' The debate that follows—between stock figures such as Sam Simple and Dick Frantic—presents the main topics as anti-popery (suggesting the occasion of the poem may have been the Gordon Riots of 1780) and 'our corrupt and traiterous Administration'.[68] Boswell got wind of another debate at the same venue by the Religious Society for Theological Inquiry in 1781, describing the meeting as 'a kind of religious Robinhood Society, which met every Sunday evening, at Coachmakers'-hall, for free debate.' He asked Johnson if he should go to hear debated 'the text which relates, with other miracles, which happened at our SAVIOUR'S death, "And the graves were opened, and many bodies of the saints which slept arose".'

---

[65] Young, *The Spirit of Athens*, 9.

[66] The letter includes 'PATRIOTIC CLUBS' and 'Disputation Clubs, including the ROBIN HOOD' as part of the crisis of urban sociability. See the discussion in Gillian Russell, *Women, Sociability, and Theatre in Georgian London* (Cambridge: Cambridge University Press, 2007), 4 and 6.

[67] Using the advertisements for the commercial debating societies in the daily press, Donna T. Andrew, 'Popular Culture and Public Debate: London 1780', *Historical Journal*, 39 (2) (1996), 405–23, shows that that there were 295 debates advertised in 1780 compared to 418 over the whole of the proceeding seven years.

[68] 'Harum Skarum', *Account of a Debate in Coachmaker's Hall* (London, 1780), 2, 18.

Johnson was decidedly against it: 'One would not go to such a place to hear it,—one would not be seen in such a place—to give countenance to such a meeting' (*BLJ* IV: 92–3).[69] Johnson thought popular debating societies had no business discussing what he perceived as the established truths of the national religion, especially when the audience was socially mixed or if women were present. He was not sure such conversations even had a place in private. What Boswell's published account of their exchange over Coach-makers' Hall omits is the presence of Mrs Hall and her curiosity over the question of the resurrection of the body.[70] Johnson's 'anger' recorded in Boswell's journal suggests his uneasiness at her being there, especially when the topic aroused her interest. Johnson did not want such things to be discussed in front of women. When Bennett Langton asked him for his opinion of those who preached against the Trinity, Boswell records Johnson took offence: 'I wonder, Sir, how a gentleman of your piety can introduce this subject in a mixed company' (*BLJ* II: 254). For Johnson the division between private and public conversation was fraught when it came to such topics in such company. By the 1790s, Harum Skarum's nightmare of the political consequences of such conversations seemed on the verge of being realized. The Royal Proclamation of May 1792 now urged the magistracy to act against such societies. John Thelwall, who was to become one of the radical movement's main orators, had learned many of his skills at Coachmakers' Hall, which he had attended from his teenage years. As manager of the Society for Free Debate by the early 1790s, he fought and lost the battle to keep it alive.[71]

TALKING ABOUT THE BLUES

My next chapter will return to the fate of public conversation at Coach-makers' Hall, but I now want to return to anxieties about female partici-pation in the associational world. The explosion of debating societies in 1780 included several that explicitly invited women to take part in their debates. By the end of 1780 there were four where only women could speak.[72] Female conversation in these and other contexts was often

[69] The debate took place on 15 April 1781, under the auspices of the Religious Society for Theological Enquiry. The charge for the 'admittance to Gentlemen and Ladies' was sixpence. See Andrew, *London Debating Societies*, 139.

[70] James Boswell, *Laird of Auchinleck 1776–1782*, ed. Joseph W. Reed and Frederick A. Pottle (New York/London: McGraw-Hill Book Company, 1977), 325–7.

[71] See the discussion of Thelwall in my next chapter, pp. 151–6.

[72] See Andrew, 'Popular Culture', 410, and Mary Thale, 'Women in London Debating Societies in 1780', *Gender and History*, 7 (1995), 5–24. Topics discussed included whether women should have the right to representation in parliament; see Thale, 18–19. By 1781 La Belle Assemblee and the other women's debating societies had disappeared, possibly

represented as trivial gossip, or when it presumed to organize, especially outside the home, tending towards chaos and anarchy, 'without a leader', as William Hutton put it, 'every one speaking at the same time'.[73] In this context, attempts by those like Elizabeth Montagu to develop the possibilities inherent in the feminized conversable world offered by Hume were always liable to satirical attack, either for mistaking trivial talk for conversation or for dangerously usurping male prerogatives.

Female debating clubs were careful to advertise themselves as 'rational', but the participation of women was usually seen as corrupting the very qualities that made female conversation an improving cultural force. Quite apart from the discomfort at the idea of women participating in religious and political disputes, disliked by Addison and Steele, sharply attacked by Samuel Johnson, plenty of commentators were even uncertain as to the propriety of urban recreations that laid no claim to debating public issues: 'The tenderest part of the creation', the *General Evening Post* claimed, 'owe, many of them, the origin of their darkest infamy to the licentious lessons conveyed to the giddy mind from these abandoned schools of pleasure.'[74] The anxiety lay in the paradox that the private virtues of women were being increasingly seen, however indirectly, as intrinsic to the health of the public. Places of pleasure like the Pantheon were worrying not only to those like Sir Adam Fergusson, who feared they distracted the people from public affairs, but also to those who feared they distracted women from the home.[75] The *Annual Register* praised the Pantheon when it first opened in the 1771–2 season as 'a striking instance of the elegance and profusion of modern times', but showed signs of discomfort at the 'olio of all sorts; peers, peeresses, honourables and right honourables, jew brokers, demireps, lottery insurers, and quack doctors'. An 'olio' was precisely a mixed rather than select company. In order to distinguish itself from its plebeian rival at Spa Fields, the endorsement of a peeress was required for a subscription at the Oxford Street establishment, but at least one correspondent to the press doubted the durability of this barrier. Such was the decadence of the times that the nobility themselves might be desperate to turn a penny 'by letting out tickets to *Anybodies*, to

---

because the prospects for parliamentary reform waned, possibly because of the alarm caused by the Gordon Riots, or possibly because of the kind of reactions outlined in this section.

[73] See William Hutton's *Courts of Requests: Their Nature, Utility, and Powers Described* (Birmingham, 1787), 263. Hutton's attitude is all the more striking as he was generally an enthusiast for the proliferating world of provincial conversation.

[74] *General Evening Post* (21–3 January 1773).

[75] The Pantheon assembly rooms opened in Oxford Street for masquerades, concerts, promenading, and conversation. See the excellent discussion in Russell, *Women, Sociability, and Theatre*, 88–118. There was also a Spa Fields Pantheon catering mainly for apprentices, journeymen, and maidservants that opened in 1770.

Nobodies, and to *Everybodies*'.[76] Johnson regarded the private pleasures of 'people here [at the Pantheon] who are watching hundreds, and who think hundreds are watching them' (*BLJ* II: 169) as less of a concern than popular debating societies, but the dividing line between private pleasures and public virtue at such venues seemed more insecure to others. In Burney's *Evelina*, something of a conspectus of the conversable worlds of the early 1770s, the bluff English sea captain Captain Mirvan cuts through the language of politeness and refined pleasure to give a blunt estimation of the Pantheon as a sexual marketplace: 'You may talk what you will of your eye here, and your eye there…but we all know they both squint one way' (107).[77] The spectre of criminal conversation, adulterous flirtation rather than polite or improving talk, continually haunted fashionable resorts in the late eighteenth century. Under this pressure, the Pantheon soon became more strictly redefined as a venue for music: 'The galleries, where patrons had prom-enaded, gossiped, and stared at each other, were filled with benches, and a gallery was erected over the entrance, in which was placed a royal box.'[78]

Select societies gathered for more literary conversation may not have needed to be kept under the eye of a royal box (this was supposedly a republic of letters after all), but the question of the organization of their talk had always been a sensitive one. Early in the 1750s the novelist Samuel Richardson had taken on a monitory role in 'the female senate' he gathered around himself at North End (his suburban address in Fulham) when writing his final novel, *Sir Charles Grandison*.[79] He told Hester Mulso that 'the whole piece abounds, and was intended to abound, with situations that should give occasion for debate, or different ways of thinking.'[80] Many of the letters that make up the text of *Sir Charles Grandison* are reports of conversa-tions (and feed into others), sometimes taking up topics Richardson dis-cussed with his 'senate', including the topic of 'Man's usurpation, and woman's natural independency' (III: 242).[81] The novel is quite explicit about the national glory to be won from female participation: 'O my

---

[76] *Annual Register*, 15 (1772), 69, and *Gazetteer* (12 December 1771).

[77] References to Burney's novel are to *Evelina*, ed. with an intro. Edward A. Bloom (Oxford: Oxford University Press, 1982) with page numbers given in the body of the text as here.

[78] Russell, *Women, Sociability, and Theatre*, 117.

[79] See Anna Laetitia Barbauld's 'The Life of Mr. Richardson', in *The Correspondence of Samuel Richardson*, ed. Barbauld, 6 vols (London, 1804), where she refers to the '[g]reat debates' that 'took place in the author's female senate' (I: cxxiii).

[80] 'To Hester Mulso', 21 August 1754, in *Selected Letters of Samuel Richardson*, ed. John Carroll (Oxford: Clarendon Press, 1964), 311.

[81] All references to *The History of Sir Charles Grandison* are to the World's Classics edition, ed. Jocelyn Harris, 3 parts (Oxford: Oxford University Press, 1972) and given in the text with part number and page.

Charlotte…how I love my Country! ENGLAND is the *only* spot in the world, in which this argument *can* be properly debated!' (III: 242). Sir Charles takes women seriously in conversation (in contrast to the sarcasms of Mr Walden). He recognizes that conversation allows women to both better themselves in terms of knowledge and 'improve a man of sense, sweeten his manners, and render him a much more sociable, a much more amiable creature, and, of consequence, greatly more happy in himself than otherwise he would be from books and solitude' (III: 250). Nevertheless Sir Charles always retains his place as the moderator. He praises the *debate* on female independence, but makes it quite clear he does not endorse his sister's *practice* of it. Charlotte is granted considerable latitude to speak her mind, but ultimately she has to accept submission to a husband the novel makes clear is no match for her either in intellectual resources or conversational spark.[82] Ultimately it is the domestic space of family relations that is the proper sphere of female conversation, but it also defines the virtues of Richardson's hero. Although he makes it clear that Sir Charles's operates in a larger world, not very convincingly described in the Italian sections of the novel, his chief glory is 'to behave commendably in the *private* life' (III: 99). The family circle helps 'to make up worthily, and to secure, the great community of which they are so many miniatures' (I: 25).

The circulation of the 'small change' of domestic conversation matters immensely to Richardson's novels, but male monitors must continually check the value of the coinage. Exchange takes place within a circum-scribed quasi-domestic space of the sort shown in Susanna Highmore's drawing of Richardson reading his manuscript to a circle of admirers at North End (see Fig. 3).[83] Richardson was praised as a 'constant patron' (6) of women in John Duncombe's *Feminiad* (1754), one of several books and poems that began to praise advances in female learning in Great Britain from around this time.[84] Duncombe, who finally married Susanna Highmore in 1761 after a long courtship, represents the 'deeply read' (11) woman as the perfect wife, but emphasizes the importance of carrying

---

[82] See Betty A. Schellenberg, *The Conversational Circle: Rereading the English Novel, 1740–1775* (Lexington: University of Kentucky Press, 1996), 65. Schellenberg reads *Sir Charles Grandison* as an attempt to fulfil the programme of feminized sociability laid out in *The Spectator* and Hume's 'On Essay Writing'. See also E. J. Clery's account along similar lines in *The Feminization Debate in Eighteenth-Century England: Literature, Commerce and Luxury* (Palgrave Macmillan: Basingstoke, 2004), 132–70.

[83] The picture was bound in with the second volume of Barbauld's edition with the title 'Mr. Richardson reading the Manuscript of Sir Charles Grandison in 1751 to his Friends in the Grotto of His House at North End, from a drawing made at the time by Miss Highmore'. I am grateful to Harriet Guest for first drawing the picture to my attention.

[84] Harriet Guest, *Small Change: Women, Learning, Patriotism, 1750–1810* (Chicago: University of Chicago Press, 2000), 49–69.

Fig. 3. Joseph Constantine Stadler after Susannah Highmore, 'Mr. Richardson reading the Manuscript of Sir Charles Grandison in 1751 to his Friends in the Grotto of His House at North End, from a drawing made at the time by Miss Highmore'. Private Collection.

learning with 'studious ease' (11).[85] The keyword is 'ease'. Duncombe correlates reading with 'social care' (11) and the refinements of a 'polish'd land' (9), not to mention its 'domestic excellence' (11). The concatenation of these terms confirms how far the definitions of the literary in this period were being reoriented away from ideas of pedantic learning towards a conversability at odds with the life of the secluded scholar. *The Feminiad* places the revaluation of women writers and their involvement in a form of literary culture defined by domestic conversation at the centre of this process.[86]

Several of the women who corresponded and conversed with Richardson were to be important to the Bluestocking phenomenon of the middle to late decades of the eighteenth century.[87] Felicity Nussbaum notes that

---

[85] John Duncombe, *The Feminiad: A Poem* (1754). The poem was reissued in a second edition in 1757. References are given to this edition in the text.

[86] See Guest, *Small Change*, 61.

[87] Perhaps the chief of these was Catherine Talbot. Clery, *Feminization Debate*, 155, claims she 'became so closely involved with the writing and revising of *Sir Charles Grandison* that she might have claimed co-authorship'. Others include Hester Mulso (see above,

these circles appropriated for themselves 'a peculiar kind of moral agency and power while shaping a critical realm in which reasoned opinion can be shaped in the public and private spheres to provide a principled under-girding of the country through women's virtue'.[88] These women used conversation as part of a conscious attempt to shape the variety of opinion into a national culture, factionalism was downplayed, and politics frowned upon as a subject for discussion.[89] Certainly Elizabeth Montagu's brilliant gatherings in Hill Street and then in the grandeur of Portman Square are perhaps the closest the eighteenth century came to realizing Hume's vision of an empire of conversation reigned over by women. Not that even the inner circle of Bluestocking women maintained exactly the same version of con-versation. Montagu's rather tightly organized groups of talkers, often literally arranged in a semi-circle of chairs, differed from Vesey's looser gatherings, for instance, where talk was allowed to disperse around the room.[90] These differences should alert us to the danger of using the term 'Bluestocking' as if it denoted a homogenous group organized purely around gender affilia-tions.[91] Gender was an absolutely crucial issue in the formation and under-standing of the associational world, but conversation did not always simply form itself around a polarized binary opposition between the sexes.

This caveat does not mean women did not self-consciously form convers-able worlds around gendered identities. Whatever the variety in its organiza-tion, Bluestocking conversation was celebrated as a distinctive formation by Hannah More in her poem 'Bas Bleu, Or Conversation'. Written in 1783 and dedicated to Elizabeth Vesey, the poem circulated in manuscript around literary London for some months before it was published in 1786.[92] In her 'Advertisement' to later editions of the poem, More defined the Bluestock-

---

p. 102), who had a long debate with Richardson over the duty of filial obedience, and Elizabeth Carter.

[88] Felicity A. Nussbaum, *The Limits of the Human: Fictions of Anomaly, Race, and Gender in the Long Eighteenth Century* (Cambridge: Cambridge University Press, 2003), 90.

[89] See note 24 above for the emphasis on patriotic unity in Bluestocking assemblies.

[90] See Elizabeth Eger and Lucy Peltz, *Brilliant Women: 18th-Century Bluestockings* (London: National Portrait Gallery, 2008), 22. and Eger, *Bluestockings: Women of Reason from Enlightenment to Romanticism* (Basingstoke: Palgrave Macmillan, 2010), 107–14. Frances Burney recalled that Vesey's 'fears were so great of the horror, as it was styled, of a circle, from the ceremony and awe which it produced, that she pushed all the small sofas, as well as chairs, pell-mell about the apartments, so as not to leave even a zig-zag path of communication free from impediment' (see Madame D'Arblay [Burney], *Memoirs of Doctor Burney*, 2 vols (London, 1832), II: 264).

[91] See the discussion of this issue in Major's *MADAM BRITANNIA*, forthcoming.

[92] On the pre-publication circulation of the poem, see Anne Stott, *Hannah More: The First Victorian* (Oxford: Oxford University Press, 2003), 62–5. The poem was first published in *Florio: A Tale for Fine Gentlemen and Fine Ladies and The Bas Bleu; or, Conversation: Two Poems* (London, 1786).

ings as 'composed of persons distinguished in general, for their rank, talents, or respectable character, who met frequently at Mrs. *Vesey*'s and at a few other houses, for the sole purpose of conversation, and were different in no respect from other parties, but that the company did not play at cards'.[93] Conversation here was being opposed to frivolous fashionable pursuits that the group, no less than Mary Wollstonecraft later, regarded as a distraction from the proper exercise of women's rational faculties. In her earlier essay 'Thoughts on Conversation' (1777), More insisted:

It has been advised, and by very respectable authorities too, that in conversation women should carefully conceal any knowledge or learning they may happen to possess. I own, with submission, that I do not see either the necessity or propriety of this advice. For if a young lady has that discretion and modesty, without which all knowledge is little worth, she will never make an ostentatious parade of it, because she will rather be intent on acquiring more, than on displaying what she has.[94]

More reaffirms the role of feminized conversation in the process of bringing learning out into the world. In the poem itself, changing the terms of Hume's metaphor of trade between the worlds of learning and 'conversation and common life', she apostrophizes conversation as 'polisher of rugged man'. Conversation is valuable precisely because it takes the potentially barbaric stuff of learning and turns it into something socially useful:

> Our intellectual ore must shine,
> Not slumber, idly, in the mine.
> Let Education's moral mint
> The noblest images imprint;
> Let Taste her curious touchstone hold,
> To try is standard be the gold;
> But 'tis thy commerce, Conversation,
> Must give it use by circulation;
> That noblest commerce of mankind,
> Whose precious merchandize is MIND! (ll. 242–51)

Conversation's role is not simply one of refining by circulation. Perhaps because of her increasingly evangelical perspective, More also sees conversation as a form of knowledge production, a process that could 'strike new light by strong collision' (l. 267), but her dominant emphasis is on overcoming differences:

---

[93] The later advertisement can be found in *Sacred Dramas and Other Poems* (London, 1827), 154. I have not found it in any edition of the poem before 1800. More's increasingly evangelical position on conversation may have brought with it more need for definition. See my discussion in Chapter 5.

[94] Hannah More, 'Thoughts on Conversation', in *Essays on Various Subjects, Principally Designed for Young Ladies* (London: 1777), 37–8.

> Conversation, soothing power
> Sweet goddess of the social hour. (ll. 212–13)

Indeed only a prior context of conformity, a community of like-minded 'congenial' souls, provides a safe context for collision:

> But sparks electric only strike
> On souls electrical alike;
> The flash of intellect expires,
> Unless it meet congenial fires:
> The language to th'Elect alone
> Is, like the Mason's mystery, known;
> In vain th'unerring sign is made
> To him who is not of the Trade.
> What lively pleasure to divine,
> The thought implied, the hinted line,
> To feel Allusion's artful force,
> And trace the Image to it's source! (ll. 286–99)[95]

Harmony is guaranteed by the fact that the participants are an 'Elect,' prechosen by a qualifying examination of taste. The religious implication of 'elect' becomes more powerful in More's later work where godly conversation develops an increasingly tense relationship with the kind of politeness central to Bluestocking conversation.[96]

If not as evangelical as More became, Montagu's own exploitation of conversation was always tied to a programme of moral regeneration. In this regard, her ambitions for literary conversation also overlapped somewhat with Johnson's, but there was always tension between them. Elizabeth Carter introduced Johnson to Montagu in 1759. He visited her assemblies more than once, after 1775 often as a guest at the house on Hill Street, but connections were often strained, particularly after publication of *Lives of the Poets* in 1781, which contained an attack on Montagu's friend and collaborator Lord Lyttelton. Nussbaum is surely right to see a struggle between them for authority intensified by their different gendered conceptions of conversability.[97] Montagu found his behaviour at the assemblies often rough and shocking and felt he introduced sexual equivocation into the discussion. Johnson acknowledged the importance of her assemblies and was wounded at the idea he might be dropped.[98] Competition between

---

[95] See 'Bas Bleu', in More, *Florio*, 82–3, 84, 80, and 85–6.

[96] See the discussions of More's *Coelebs in Search of a Wife*, 2 vols (1808) Chapters 4 and 5.

[97] See Nussbaum's lucid survey of relations between Montagu and Johnson in *Limits of the Human*, 73–82.

[98] In March 1781, Johnson bemoaned the fact he had been dropped by Montagu, telling Boswell at Streatham, 'there are people whom one should like very well to drop, but would not wish to be dropped by' (*BLJ* IV: 73).

the pair began early. Montagu certainly wrote her *Essay on Shakespeare* (1769) with Johnson's preface to the plays very much in mind. They were competing for the role of guardian of the nation's literary reputation, especially against the French, specifically Voltaire's criticisms of Shakespeare, a competition conducted not just via the printed text but also in the conversable worlds they created in literary London.[99] For Montagu, Johnson's conversation lacked the 'ease' that she associated with polite letters, but also offended against morality in its masculine roughness. The idea of masculine letters softened by feminine politeness is clearly at play in her collaboration with George, Lord Lyttelton in his *Dialogues of the Dead* (1760), to which she anonymously contributed the final three dialogues.[100] The volume explicitly confirms the moral programme of politeness found in Addison, nowhere perhaps more clearly than in the dialogue—written by Lyttelton—between Addison and Swift, where the polite values of *The Spectator* are preferred to the rough lash of satire.[101] Montagu's contributions are careful to elaborate this position by refusing any affirmation of mere fashionable ease over learning. The first of her dialogues—between Hercules and Cadmus—affirms the importance of 'the united strength of civil community' against the Herculean preference for military virtues, but also acknowledges the threat of luxury and effeminacy. So, in her next, she parodies the vacuity of a bookseller who argues: 'No book is fit for a Gentleman's reading which is not void of Facts and of Doctrines, that he may not grow a Pedant in his morals or conversation.' From the bookseller's perspective, 'modern conversation flows gentle and easy, unencumbered with matter and unburthened of instruction.'[102] Where Lyttelton's dialogues failed for some contemporaries was in their awkward commitment to politeness over feeling and character. At least one critic bemoaned their '*monotony of manner*' and found them 'considerably deficient in those characteristical, or what we may call dramatical, distinctions which ought to constitute the essence of dialogue.'[103] The taste for conversational

---

[99] See Nussbaum, *Limits of the Human*, 74–82, which contains some arresting remarks about Montagu's views of the effeminacy of Johnson's 'finical' prose style. The latter revolves primarily around the issue of his Latinate ornamentation. In terms of his conversation, I'd suggest she more often reads him in the kind of racialized terms implied by Chesterfield's 'Hottentot' (see p. 93 above), that is, as someone whose barbarity tends towards aberrant aggression rather than what she regarded as English manners and 'ease'.

[100] Montagu contributed 'Dialogue XXVI: Cadmus and Hercules', 'Dialogue XXVII: Mercury And a Modern Fine Lady', and 'Dialogue XXVIII: Plutarch, Charon, and a Modern Bookseller'. See *Dialogues of the Dead* (London, 1760), 291–320.

[101] See *Dialogues of the Dead*, 28, where Hermes tells Addison 'how much does [Swift] yield to you in all the polite and elegant Graces; in the fine touches of delicate sentiment.'

[102] Ibid. 292, 310, 311.

[103] *Candid and Critical Remarks on the Dialogues of the Dead* (London, 1760), 76 and 6. The judgment supports Prince's claims about the turn against 'abstract metaphysical

flow expounded by the bookseller in Montagu's dialogue looked towards the novel's increasing commitment to the back-and-forth of conversation beyond the Addisonian polite learning expounded in *Dialogues of the Dead*.

The conversations Montagu organized at her assemblies were orchestrated against the association of feminized culture with unlearned froth. Her idea of 'ease' opposed the roughness of Johnson, but also disparaged social talk uninterested in moral improvement. That did not stop her being accused of reducing conversation to ostentation and show. Assemblies of intellectual women were always vulnerable to being represented as transgressively public in this regard, too much brilliant surface, and not enough of either learning or genuine sentiment, depending on the critic's point of view.[104] Hester Piozzi's attitude to Montagu, like several other women, was often ambivalent in this regard. She acknowledged Montagu's power in the literary world, and attended her assemblies, but she also competed with them, if indirectly, by offering a more self-consciously sentimental space for conversation to flow around. 'Mrs. Montagu's Bouquet is all out of the Hot-house', she once wrote, 'mine out of the Woods & Fields & many a Weed there is in it.'[105] The position as an authority on conversation Piozzi claimed in the preface to *British Synonymy* was predicated not only on the association of familiar talk with femininity, but also drew on her role as a mediator of Samuel Johnson's reputation. Her *Anecdotes of Johnson* (1786) placed him firmly in the domestic circle of her home in Streatham Park. While Johnson was still alive, Montagu had written to Piozzi noting that he 'is very polite, but I want him to be tender.'[106] Montagu was effectively acknowledging that Piozzi had managed to create a domesticated relationship with him. In May 1780, Piozzi wrote to Johnson: 'I have no care about enjoying undivided empire, nor any thought of disputing it with Mrs. [Montagu]. She considers her title as indisputable most probably, though I am sure I never heard her urge it. Queen Elizabeth, you remember, would not suffer her's [*sic*] to be enquired into—and I have read somewhere the great

disquisitions'. See Michael Prince, *Philosophical Dialogue in the British Enlightenment: Theology, Aesthetics and the Novel* (Cambridge: Cambridge University Press, 1996), 244–5, a development that may have also influenced the approach to Johnson's biography taken by Boswell and Piozzi.

[104] See Guest, *Small Change*, 101.

[105] Quoted in James L. Clifford, *Hester Lynch Piozzi (Mrs. Thrale)*, 2nd edn (Oxford: Clarendon Press, 1952), 153, from a note on a card at GB 133 Eng MS 629 in the Thrale-Piozzi Manuscripts Collection, John Rylands University Library, Manchester.

[106] Letter from Montagu to Piozzi, January 14 (no year), 'Thrale-Piozzi Manuscripts', GB 133 ENG MS 551.

Mogul is never crowned.'[107] The disavowal of competition, here, only serves to signal her difference from Montagu's 'empire'. Where Piozzi constructs Montagu's conversation in terms of dominion, Oriental despotism even, she implies her own literary gatherings were less exotic and more '*at home*' (to use Cook's phrase).

When Helen Maria Williams described 'the elegant retirement at Streatham Park' in 1792, the word 'retirement' marked a difference from the sparkling assemblies associated with Montagu.[108] Piozzi aspired to 'Virtue in the contracted Sense'.[109] In the edition of Johnson's letters Piozzi brought out in 1788, she celebrated his correspondence as 'familiar chat spread upon paper': 'The good taste by which our countrymen are distinguished, will lead them to prefer the native thoughts and unstudied phrases scattered over these pages, to the more labored elegance of his other works—as bees have been observed to reject roses, and fix upon the wild fragrance of a neighbouring heath.' The parallel with her comments on Montagu's hothouse flowers is telling. Again she represents her own taste as an uncultivated meadow, affiliating English conversation to an idea of domestic virtues in two senses (as it had been for Addison and others).[110] Piozzi's importance for the literary world of the 1780s is frequently overlooked, but she played an important part in creating a more sentimental idea of conversability, distinct from the glitter of Montagu's diamonds, but equally from Johnson's 'talking for victory'.[111] For Boswell, in competition with Piozzi for ownership of Johnson's memory, her picture of the great man's conversation was an unwelcome qualification to his image of the masculine colossus. Or, perhaps more to the point, she aimed to mediate Johnson in terms of her own 'contracted' feminine virtues, as it were, against the heroic version Boswell was known to be building in his *Life*, even if his own methods threatened to subvert what he

---

[107] Piozzi to Johnson, May 1780, *Letters to and from the Late Samuel Johnson, LL.D*, 2 vols (London, 1788), II: 92.

[108] Helen Maria Williams to Piozzi, 9 September 1792, 'Thrale-Piozzi Manuscripts', GB 133 ENG MS 570.

[109] The context was Piozzi's table of the social qualities of her women friends (see n. 32 above). She took these virtues to be more serious achievements than mere fashionable accomplishments: 'they must possess Virtue in that contracted Sense or one w^d not keep em Company, so that is not thought about, & I would not be contracted about Beauty neither; it is general Appearance rather than Beauty that is meant by Person Mien & Manner the useful Knowledge we can all comprehend' (*Thraliana*, I: 330).

[110] *Letters to and from the Late Samuel Johnson*, I: iv–vi.

[111] Among other things, she was to have an important role in the development of Robert Merry's poetic persona as Della Crusca in the 1780s. Their correspondence is in 'Thrale-Piozzi Manuscripts' at GB 133 ENG MS 558.

was about by an insistence on minute transcription that shrank Johnson to the less exalted world Piozzi claimed as her own.[112]

Piozzi's villa at Streatham had quite deliberately restaged the Literary Club in a familial and domesticated setting. The portraits of its members painted for her by Sir Joshua Reynolds reconfigured the closed gender relations associated with the club pictures of the Kit-Cats and Dilettanti. At the very time Reynolds was painting his two memorable group portraits of the Dilettanti, he was also working on a commission from the Thrales to paint a set of ensemble portraits for their newly expanded villa. Impressive in many ways Streatham Park may have been, but it was also situated away from those aristocratic areas of London where Montagu presided and the Dilettanti caroused. Nevertheless Redford draws a parallel between Reynolds's two commissions in so far as both were designed to decorate 'a capacious private space that would form the center, both social and symbolic, of an inner circle.'[113] Lined with over two thousand volumes, many purchased under the direction of Johnson, the library-cum-dining room at Streatham was completed with twelve half-length portraits, which Fanny Burney described as 'the chain of Streatham worthies'.[114] Each portrait was accompanied by 'Characters in Verse' written by Hester Piozzi. Each was interactive in itself and grouped into a circuit of private exchanges. Reynolds has his ear cupped to listen. Although dressed in formal academic robes, Charles Burney looks as if he is ready to engage in conversation with the viewer. Placed in its original context with the others, even the picture of Johnson suggests the gathering storm of a response to an inopportune remark.[115] What Redford doesn't make anything of is the presence of Hester Piozzi and her daughter, Queeny, in the chain, which makes this a very different kind of ensemble from those found either at the Kit-Cat Club or at the Dilettanti Society.

Hester Piozzi venerated Samuel Johnson, but in a way that brought him into a domestic setting, registered by the mother and daughter pair presiding over the Library, but domestication here is not in any simple sense a retreat into a privatized world. Piozzi became a public character through

---

[112] Boswell succeeded in fomenting trouble between Piozzi and Montagu by revealing that she and Johnson had agreed they could not get through *Essay on Shakespeare*. See Mary Hyde, *The Impossible Friendship: Boswell and Mrs. Thrale* (London: Chatto and Windus, 1973), 100–4.

[113] See Redford, *Dilettanti*, 107.

[114] D'Arblay, *Memoirs of Doctor Burney*, II: 81.

[115] Several of the portraits were hung together in the 'Reynolds and Celebrity' exhibition held at Tate Britain in 2005. See Martin Postle, *Joshua Reynolds: The Creation of Celebrity* (London: Tate Publishing, 2005). Postle describes the intention 'to convey the idiosyncratic manner of Johnson's conversation' (174).

her manipulation of domestic conversation and the language of affect.[116] By domesticating Johnson, Piozzi was also reorienting the idea of feminized literary conversation away from the kind of glamorous gathering associated with Montagu. The brilliant visibility of the conversation staged by Montagu provided, as Harriet Guest puts it, 'on the one hand a shining spectacle for the civilized progress of the nation, and on the other a figure of vanity whose learning is tainted by the doubtful glitter of fashionable display'.[117] This ambivalence towards Montagu informed the responses of other women besides Piozzi involved in Bluestocking circles, who were also evolving a taste for a more intimate and domestic idea of the conversational circle. Fanny Burney, for instance, seems to have felt much more at home in the quasi-domestic gatherings at Streatham than with Montagu.[118] In 1832, she looked back with pleasure at the 'colloquial elegance' of the assemblies of the time:

And such meetings, when the parties were well assorted, and in good-humour, formed, at that time, a coalition of talents, and a brilliancy of exertion, that produced the most informing dissertations, or the happiest sallies of wit and pleasantry, that could emanate from social intercourse.[119]

If 'Mrs Thrale' could not muster the 'splendour' of Mrs. Montagu's gatherings, or 'so curious a selection of distinguished individuals as those of Mrs Vesey', then still they were 'held of equal height with either in general estimation'.[120] Nor did the distance of time and change in Burney's social circumstances resolve the ambivalence of her feeling that they were also perhaps too much the construction of art in Montagu's conversations: 'her reputation for wit seemed always in her thoughts, marring their natural flow, and untutored expression.'[121] Johnson, who was introduced to *Evelina* by Hester Piozzi, encouraged Burney to compete with Montagu: 'No, no,—fly at the *Eagle*!—*down* with Mrs. Montagu herself!— I hope she will come *full* of Evelina!'[122] His puerile excitement at the thought of these women in combat affirms his idea of public discourse as a

---

[116] Guest, *Small Change*, 195, notes the emergence in patriotic discourse of the 1770s and 1780s of 'the association between femininity and the private virtues appropriate to the domestic and maternal role that underpins the alliance, and affords femininity an acceptable public face'.

[117] Guest, *Small Change*, 131.

[118] Margaret Anne Doody, *Frances Burney: The Life in the Works* (Cambridge: Cambridge University Press, 1988), 66–70, notes that after the success of *Evelina* her father took her to Streatham where she was 'drawn out, encouraged to talk as well as to listen' (68).

[119] D'Arblay, *Memoirs of Burney*, II: 276.

[120] Ibid. II: 275.

[121] Ibid. II: 271.

[122] *The Early Journals and Letters of Fanny Burney*, ed. Lars E. Troide and Stewart J. Cooke, 3 vols (Oxford: Clarendon Press, 1988–94), III: 153.

form of contention, but the Thrale household, where these conversations about Montagu took place, also represented a more comfortable social space for Johnson than the 'superb House' being built on Portman Square.[123]

When she was moving in these circles, Burney was capable of being stinging about Montagu and her friends. She wrote a play called *The Witlings*, parodying their pretensions. Although the play was never performed in public, for fear of offending Montagu, it was read aloud by her father in a domestic setting at the home of a family friend, Samuel Crisp, before a small, largely female audience in August 1779.[124] In the play Lady Smatter's club represents a conversable world that is far from forming the bridge to the world of learning imagined in Montagu's contributions to *Dialogues of the Dead*. As the hero, Beaufort, tells Censor:

My good aunt has established a kind of Club at her House, professedly for the discussion of literary Subjects; and the Set who compose it are about as well qualified for the Purpose, as so many dirty Cabbin Boys would be to find out the Longitude. To a very little reading, they join less Understanding, and no Judgement, yet they decide upon Books and Authors with the most confirmed confidence in their abilities for the Task. And this Club they have had the modesty to nominate the Esprit Party.[125]

When Lady Smatter appears herself, it quickly emerges that she reads only in order to talk. Nor is her conversation a pleasure in itself, only part of her display of power:

Well to be sure, we are all Born with sentiments of our own, as I read in a Book I can't just now recollect the name of, so I ought not to wonder that yours and mine do not coincide; for, I declare, if my pursuits were not made public, I should not have any at all, for where can be the pleasure of reading Books, and studying authors, if one is not to have the credit of talking of them?[126]

Burney, who wrote the play under the soubriquet of 'a sister of the order', is not attacking feminized sociability as such, but parodying the aristocratic display of polite learning and the problems that caused for notions

---

[123] Ibid. 152. The house was designed by 'Athenian' Stuart. Begun in 1777, Montagu took up residence there at the end of 1781.

[124] In fact it was her father and Crisp's fear of giving Montagu offence that crushed any idea of it being sent to Sheridan with a view to performance, despite his and Arthur Murphy's continuing encouragement. Charles Burney insisted 'not only the Whole Piece, but the *plot* had best be kept secret, from every body'. See *Early Journals*, III: xi–xiii and 346 n.

[125] *The Witlings* (I.195 n), in *The Complete Plays of Frances Burney*, ed. Peter Sabor (London: Pickering and Chatto, 1995), 12–13.

[126] Ibid. 21.

of candour and sincerity, increasingly important in judging the value of conversable worlds.

Predictably enough, male critics of Montagu often eagerly joined in the critique. Take this exchange from April 1791 between Samuel Rogers, William Seward, and Robert Merry. During a discussion of Elizabeth Montagu, Seward described her as a 'composition of art' who mocked guests at her assemblies behind their backs. Smartly picking up on the allusion to Tom Paine's attack on Edmund Burke in *Rights of Man*, Rogers retorted: 'the genuine soul of nature has forsaken her.'[127] The entire conversation is informed by the fact that 'Mrs. Montagu… entertains all the aristocrats,' as Barbauld put it in a letter to her brother from the same year.[128] Misogyny structures the exchange, but it's also informed by competing ideas of class, religion, and politics, not to mention sociability. Nor were the participants opposed to the feminization of the conversable world per se. The exchange took place not in the closed world of a male club, but a salon presided over by Helen Maria Williams.[129] The conversation shows Merry far from his Beefsteak circumstance, among the sort of literary company to whom Piozzi had been praising his poetry, that is, those more inclined to associate conversation with sentiment and society than libertine bawdry.[130] Critiques of Montagu were often made in situations like this one, antagonistic to her glittering aristocratic world, one as sceptical of its ambiance as they were of the libertinism of the nobleman's club. The boundaries between these worlds were frequently porous, especially for men like Merry and William Seward, who slipped easily between the interstices, retailing conversations from many of them to an eager reading public.[131] The Anglican complexion of Montagu's idea of moral regeneration did not exclude leading Dissenters such as Richard Price or Anna Laetitia Barbauld, but their participation often depended on them conforming themselves to the larger

[127] P. W. Clayden, *The Early Life of Samuel Rogers* (London, 1887), 173. The person she is supposed to have mocked is Richard Price, whose religious and political views this company would have been particularly quick to defend against Montagu's perceived sense of aristocratic superiority.

[128] 'To John Aikin', Hampstead, 1791, in *The Works of Anna Lætitia Barbauld, with a Memoir by Lucy Aikin*, 2 vols, ed. Lucy Aikin (London: 1825), II: 159.

[129] Williams had been made a literary celebrity in the 1780s by her poem 'Sensibility'. A friend of Piozzi's in the 1780s, see above, p. 110, they remained close even in the 1790s, when they differed on politics. See the 'Thrale-Piozzi manuscripts', MS 570.

[130] See Piozzi's recommendations to a rather unimpressed Anna Seward in the 'Thrale Piozzi Manuscripts', MS 565.

[131] Seward appears in Boswell's *Life of Johnson* reasonably often. See Seward's *Anecdotes of some Distinguished Persons*, 4 vols (London, 1795–6).

cultural hegemony, at least in their manners.[132] Montagu and her circle conceived of conversation more in terms of the organization of difference in the name of a harmony manifested in the Church and State than the encouragement of the collision between a diversity of views.

RETIRED CONVERSATION

One way or another, Fanny Burney and Hester Piozzi were close to the heart of literary London in the 1770s and 1780s. Nor were they by any means hostile to Church and State. Burney may have found appearances at Montagu's assemblies testing, but her journals show she was present at some memorable conversational gatherings and clearly enjoyed recording them.[133] Piozzi developed an identity as a creature of sentiment, but she could be very robust in conversation and certainly enjoyed her celebrity. Many other women self-consciously developed a situation further from London talk than either Burney or Piozzi, but not defined in terms of solitude. Provincial or domestic conversation could function as a source of authority, even if very different from either the glittering polish of Montagu's circle or the professionalized combat of Johnson and the Literary Club.[134] The literary activities of women writing from these positions, even if they ended up published in metropolitan periodicals, often presented themselves as part of a much more mundane but necessary worldliness, such as caring for a family, visiting friends and relatives, and corresponding with networks of similarly situated women. Katherine Plymley, who never published any of her writing, and the much better known Anna Laetitia Barbauld, for instance, wrote from within family networks of a provincial cast, if ones that were far from ignorant of the metropolitan world.[135]

---

[132] Samuel Rogers recalled another conversation at Helen Maria Williams's salon in which William Seward complained that Montagu was 'an aristocrat and a friend to the slave trade. But I suspect her of art. She has often diverted me with instances of Dr. Price's simplicity.' See Clayden, *Early Life of Samuel Rogers*, 173.

[133] For Burney's often stated fear of public ridicule, see Burney, *Early Journals and Letters*, III: 163.

[134] I am not suggesting Montagu somehow floated above worldly cares. She managed a household and a large estate, including a coalmine after her husband's death in 1775. Her correspondence frequently adverts to her pleasure in business, but these identities are very different from the self-consciously modest versions of domesticity I explore in this section.

[135] Another case in point is Anna Seward (no relation to William), identified with Johnson's birthplace in Lichfield, but self-consciously opposed both to his idea of literary professionalism and to the fashionable London world identified with Montagu. Seward played an important if to some extent covert role in contesting the heroic view of Johnson's conversation created by Boswell. She was involved in the circles of local literati, which overlapped with those of Derby and Birmingham associated with the Lunar Society. In

A key text in developing definitions of domestic virtue against both fashionable display and housewifely labour was John Gregory's *A Father's Legacy to his Daughters* (1774). Gregory's book had a typically Scottish emphasis on the civilizing powers of female manners. He addresses women not as 'domestic drudges' or 'slaves of our [men's] pleasures', but as 'companions and equals'. Anything 'in reading or conversation' which 'warms the imagination, which engages and softens the heart and raises the taste above the level of common life' threatens the modest virtues Gregory enjoins on his daughters. Written in the shadow of the early loss of their mother, Gregory communicates to his daughters a deep sense of the uncertainty of conversation out in the world: 'You will hear, at least for once in your lives, the genuine sentiments of a man who has no interest in flattering or deceiving you.'[136] In Burney's *Evelina*, Lord Orville proves to be one man at least whose words can be trusted, although the novel reveals conversation more generally to be far from reliable. Some of Burney's readers, the poet Anna Seward included, believed Evelina was taken too far from home and too much into the fashionable world to make her discovery.[137] Interestingly, Burney had met one of Gregory's daughters, Dorothea, several times at Streatham.[138] Dorothea Gregory was a ward of Elizabeth Montagu at the time, but the relationship with her guardian was soon to sour when Dorothea fell in love with the Scottish clergyman and author Archibald Alison. Montagu thought Alison's worldly prospects limited and anyway intended Dorothea for her nephew Matthew Robinson, who had adopted the surname Montagu in 1776. When these plans were thwarted and Dorothea married Alison in 1784, she was cast off.[139]

A version of these events was given to the Shropshire watercolourist Katherine Plymley when she spent two days with Dorothea Alison in 1794 (*KPN* 23).[140] Plymley was particularly impressed by Dorothea's contentment with her newly retired situation:

1804 she published a controversial biography of its brightest luminary, Erasmus Darwin. See John Brewer, *The Pleasures of the Imagination: English Culture in the Eighteenth Century* (London: Harper Collins, 1997), 573–612; Guest, *Small Change*, 252–67; and Seward's correspondence with Piozzi, 'Thrale-Piozzi Manuscripts', MS 565.

[136] See Gregory, *A Father's Legacy to his Daughters* (Edinburgh, 1774), 6 and 117. On Burney's knowledge of Gregory's book and the meeting with his daughter, see Joyce Hemlow, 'Burney and the Courtesy Books', *PMLA*, 65 (1950), 732–61 (738).

[137] In January 1790, Seward wrote to Piozzi to complain that in *Evelina* 'low & insipid Characters are too frequently obtruded upon our attention…I no more like attending to their conversation upon paper than I shou'd like their society in real life.' See 'Thrale-Piozzi Manuscripts', MS 565.

[138] See Burney, *Early Journals and Letters*, III: 151, 153, 156, 158–61.

[139] There was later a partial reconciliation.

[140] See the notebooks of Katherine Plymley at the Shropshire Archives, Shrewsbury, MS 1066/1–197. The first diary starts in October 1791. All in-text references are to the relevant notebook number preceded by *KPN*.

there is something very interesting, in seeing a woman who after being educated by her Father (Dr Gregory) in every elegant accomplishment, & who after his death, which happened when she was 18, was adopted & treated by Mrs Montague as her daughter, was not only introduced by her to court & the circles of fashion, but to all who are most celebrated in the literary & talking world, & who after living ten years in this society sits down […] in a situation uncommonly retired, & discharges with the utmost cheerfulness all the duties of a wife, mother & mistress of a family, without once discovering that she has figured in higher circles by anything but her knowledge, which not at all obtrusive, & by real good-breeding quite free from affectation. (*KPN* 23)

For neither Plymley nor her new friend did retirement signify solitude, silence, or any lack of interest in public affairs.[141] At their first meeting over dinner in April 1792, Archibald Alison spoke warmly about events in France and advocated reform in Britain (*KPN* 10). Plymley's diary records her pleasure when her brother tried 'to lead the conversation in company that it may contribute to spread the cause of truth' (*KPN* 10).[142] Although she deferred to her brother and his male friends, she was not simply a passive observer. On a visit to neighbours, Katherine and her sister Ann sprang to the defence of her family's politics when aspersions were cast on their loyalty (*KPN* 15).[143] These women's sense of their provincial virtues was defined precisely by their distance from the London *ton*, but also formed the basis of their opinions on public matters.[144]

Many of Plymley's early diary entries are taken up with the abolition of the slave trade, with which her family was centrally involved. She began it out of an eagerness to record the thoughts of luminaries like Wilberforce and Thomas Clarkson, who came to consult her brother on strategy and principles, but the early years of the journal also discuss the French Revolution and reform at home. Passionately committed to freedom of enquiry, an entry for spring 1793 records her anxiety that groups like the Association for Preserving Liberty and Property against Republicans and

[141] Plymley was also eager to learn all she could about female literary figures like Montagu, More, and Piozzi. Dorothea Alison told her that Piozzi had masculine manners from being so often in the company of men (*KPN* 24). When Piozzi married Mr. Thrale, Alison told Plymley, she found 'no woman of fashion at the other end of town wou'd visit in the city'.

[142] Her brother Joseph was an Anglican clergyman who became archdeacon of Shropshire in 1792, inherited the Corbett family estates in 1804, and took the surname of Corbett in 1806.

[143] She reports 'false accusations' against her family from 'violent aristocrats' and reflects with 'pride' that 'I & Ann, who was present, held fast our integrity, & were steady to our friends, unmoved by anything we heard except with contempt & indignation' (*KPN* 15).

[144] Archibald Alison, for his part, regretted that they were 'distant from the literary world living and dead'. He had joined a reading group in Shrewsbury, although 'this only supplies him with the publications of the day' (*KPN* 24).

Levellers seemed to wish 'even for questioning opinions deliver'd in conversation' (*KPN* 15). She also reported with concern Wilberforce's revelation that after the Two Acts aimed against treason and sedition passed at the end of 1795 he would no longer entertain Clarkson in his home because 'his conversation was so very unguarded in politics' (*KPN* 41). Conversation matters for Plymely because as with many other women it was a major source of information. She refers to Paine's *Address to the Addressers* (1792) approvingly, for instance, but admits she only knows the book through hearing it discussed (*KPN* 13). Although she travelled to London and Bath, most of her experience of conversation was in domestic and familial environments, often mediated through her brother and his visitors. She does supply accounts of her copious reading, but often her quotations are from reviews, rather than the books themselves, suggestive of the restrictions that made women relatively reliant on conversation as a source of information. Among the books she read in review was Barbauld's *Remarks on Mr. Gilbert Wakefield's Enquiry into the Expediency and Propriety of Public or Social Worship* (1792).[145] Plymley transcribed the review's approbation of the sentiment that public worship brings 'men together on the footing of equality' (*KPN* 177). She also recorded Barbauld's view that 'The temple is the only place where human beings, of every rank & sex & age, meet together for one common purpose.' Among the other transcriptions is one that could be read as a direct comment on Montagu and her gatherings: unlike meetings 'for the purposes of splendor & amusement [where] the bulk of the inhabitants are of necessity excluded', Barbauld wrote, 'Every time social worship is celebrated, it includes a virtual declaration of the rights of man.' Rather like Dorothea Alison, Barbauld was someone who had been involved with the Montagu circle, but developed a more critical attitude towards its perceived ostentation.

During the 1770s Montagu and her friends made an effort to recruit Barbauld (or as she was then, Aikin) to their conversable world. Already a well-received poet at this early stage in her career, Barbauld's desire to distance herself from the perceived uncouthness of her Presbyterian past may have drawn her to the politeness associated with the supposedly national culture of Anglicanism. No doubt part of the attraction of Montagu for Barbauld was also the prospect of female solidarity in a project of moral reformation, but this particular gendered identity came with conditional terms, including costs that Barbauld was ultimately

---

[145] She transcribes from the *Monthly Review*, new series 8 (1792), 429–31. The reviewer was Barbauld's friend William Enfield, a member of Warrington's conversable world. For the attribution, see Benjamin C. Nangle, *The Monthly Review Second Series 1790–1815: Indexes of Contributors and Articles* (Oxford: Clarendon Press, 1955), 78.

unwilling to pay. The biography written by Barbauld's niece, Lucy Aikin, provides a neat way into this issue:

At the splendid mansion of her early and constant admirer Mrs Montague [*sic*], Mrs Barbauld beheld in perfection the imposing union of literature and fashion;—under the humbler roof of her friend and publisher, the late worthy Joseph Johnson of St. Paul's Church-yard, she tasted, perhaps with higher relish, 'the feast of reason and the flow of soul'.[146]

'Splendid mansion', 'imposing', and 'fashion' are all words intended to send alarm bells ringing for those Dissenters who might be expected to prefer 'humbler' forms of sociability. Montagu had originally approached Barbauld after reading her *Poems* (1773). The essays Barbauld then published with John Aikin, Jr., her brother, as *Miscellaneous Pieces in Prose* (1773), appear to have made Montagu feel 'still more intimately acquainted with the turn of your mind'.[147] Montagu may have been even more delighted to read another Barbauld essay, published soon afterwards. Her 'Thoughts on Devotional Taste' (1775) offers 'devotion' as a term that could provide a bridgehead between the sectarian theological commitments of Dissent and the hegemonic culture associated with the Church of England (the kind of bridgehead of politeness Samuel Johnson praised Isaac Watts for building). Animating Barbauld's essay is a fear that her fellow Dissenters were in danger of perpetuating the 'critical and disputatious spirit' of their seventeenth-century forebears in their separation from the Anglican culture of politeness.[148]

Barbauld never retreated from thinking of the social and religious affections as inherently compatible, but she did not always see eye-to-eye with Montagu and her circle as to what constituted sociable feelings. In the 1770s, Barbauld's main concern when reflecting on her Dissenting background was still the destabilizing pressures generated by too much candour in religious enquiry.[149] From at least Watts and Doddridge's time onwards, Dissent's attempt to distance itself from the uncouthness of its Presbyterian past had concerned itself with the difference between the affections and those passions that smacked of enthusiasm. Another participant in the collaborative culture at Warrington, William Enfield, recognized Barbauld's essay as part of an ongoing project 'to remove the

[146] *Works of Anna Lætitia Barbauld*, ed. Aikin, I: xxxii.
[147] Montagu to Barbauld, 22 February 1774, in Anna Letitia Le Breton, *Memoir of Mrs. Barbauld, including Letters and Notices of her Family and Friends* (London: George Bell, 1874), 39.
[148] Anna Lætitia Barbauld, 'Thoughts on Devotional Taste. on Sects, and on Establishments', in *Devotional Pieces, copied from the Psalms and the Book of Job* (London, 1775), 1–50 (29).
[149] Ibid. 35.

disgrace which enthusiasm in its several forms has brought upon devotion'.[150] Enthusiasm in this context could imply a dogmatic insistence on
theological controversy. For most commentators in the late eighteenth
century, including many disapproving Dissenters, the chief generator of
the factious 'opinion' in Dissenting circles was believed to be Joseph
Priestley. He certainly identified himself as the target of Barbauld's
critique.[151] Barbauld objects primarily to the candour of Priestley's idea
of religious enquiry as against the kind of feminized yet also regulated
sensibility approved in the Montagu circle. Barbauld had written to her
brother in 1774 that '*You* are hardly social creatures till your minds are
humanized and subdued by that passion which alone can tame you to
"all the soft civilities of life".'[152] These 'soft civilities' are precisely what the
Montagu circle sought to bring to the discussion of political and religious
affairs. If they were opposed to the aggression of Samuel Johnson's
orthodoxy, they were perhaps even more opposed to disputatious Dissenters, but they also offered someone like Barbauld a way out of some of
the constraints of Dissent.[153] The vigorous exchanges of places like the
Club of Honest Whigs and even the Lunar Society, frequented by Priestley, were not usually open to female participation.

Elizabeth Montagu's first overture to Barbauld in February 1774
claimed 'the genuine effect of polite letters is to inspire candour, a social
spirit, and gentle manners.'[154] Montagu had also told Barbauld that 'to live
under the benign empire of the muses, on the conditions of a naturalized
subject, who, not having any inherent right to a share of office,
credit, or authority, seeks nothing but the protection of the society is all I
aim at'.[155] For Priestley, this kind of 'taste' was inherently disposed against
candour of the kind he exercised at the Club of Honest Whigs. Priestley
believed that what Barbauld was seeing as the disputatious enthusiasm of
sects was the astringent means of keeping the road to religious and civic
truth open, but she did not need Priestley to point out the benefits of a
culture of candour and open enquiry. Condemned in some reviews for

---

[150] [William Enfield], *Monthly Review*, 53 (1775), 419.
[151] See Deirdre Coleman, 'Firebrands, Letters, and Flowers: Mrs. Barbauld and the
Priestleys', in Gillian Russell and Clara Tuite (eds), *Romantic Sociability: Social Networks
and Literary Culture in Britain, 1770–1849* (Cambridge: Cambridge University Press,
2002), 82–103; Anne Janowitz, 'Amiable and Radical Sociability: Anna Barbauld's
"Free Familiar Conversation"', ibid. 62–81; and Jon Mee, *Romanticism, Enthusiasm, and
Regulation: Poetics and the Policing of Culture in the Romantic Period* (Oxford: Oxford
University Press, 2003), 177–90.
[152] *Works of Anna Lætitia Barbauld*, ed. Aikin, II: 4.
[153] See Eger, *Bluestockings*, 169–70.
[154] Le Breton, *Memoir*, 38.
[155] Ibid. 38–9.

being too masculine, her early poetry had shown itself quite capable of moving from celebrations of feminine virtues to 'unambiguous classical republicanism'.[156] Her education in the vigorous culture of Dissent at the Warrington Academy, where she had enjoyed conversation with Priestley and his wife, Mary, had inculcated the importance of 'instructive conversation' centred in the family circle.[157] Her father, John Aikin, Sr., followed his tutor Doddridge in developing this idea as part of his pedagogic practice. Outside of the lectures at Warrington, 'he had frequent small parties to drink tea with him, unbend, and enter with them into the most free and familiar conversation.' Following the suggestions made by Watts in *Improvement of the Mind*, he would listen to and try and resolve the difficulties students had found with their lectures.[158] Priestley may have given the idea a less domestic inflection, but he too recommended that lecturers encourage their pupils 'to enter occasionally into the conversation by proposing queries or remarks which may occur to them'.[159] Barbauld inherited with her brother John a model of intellectual work as a collaborative family enterprise, first bearing fruit in their *Miscellaneous Pieces*. This sense of family extended to the other tutors and their families at the Warrington Academy, including, at different times, Joseph and Mary Priestley, Gilbert Wakefield, and William Enfield, and continued after Barbauld left in 1774. Barbauld's writing constructs these relationships as 'a civilizing force of sympathy that would emerge from private households to reform the corrupt masculine world of public power'.[160] If the thematization of sympathy in this writing offered to meliorate the 'gloom' of Puritan dogma associated with Dissent, then it did not imply a retreat from nonconformity's commitment to conversation as a species of enquiry after truth.

Nowhere is this clearer perhaps than in Aikin and Barbauld's other major collaboration, the six-volume collection for children, *Evenings at Home* (1792–6).[161] The collection defines itself in terms of the family 'budget' developed by the Fairborne family in the collection's frame

---

[156] Guest, *Small Change*, 228. The most obvious example is her poem *Corsica*, written in 1769.

[157] The phrase 'instructive conversation' appears in the story 'The Ship', *Evenings at Home*, 6 vols (London, 1792–6), I: 135.

[158] V.F., 'Historical Account of the Warrington Academy [cont.]', *Monthly Repository of Theology and General Literature*, 8 (1813), 161–72 (161). I am grateful to Felicity James for this reference.

[159] Joseph Priestley, *An Essay on a Course of Liberal Education for Civil and Active Life* (London, 1765), 29.

[160] Daniel E. White, *Early Romanticism and Religious Dissent* (Cambridge: Cambridge University Press, 2006), 51–2.

[161] See the discussions in White, *Early Romanticism*, 70–86, and Michelle Levy, 'The Radical Education of *Evenings at Home*', *Eighteenth-Century Fiction*, 19 (2006), 123–50.

narrative. The 'budget' is a box of literary endeavours to which all members of the family contribute and later draws upon for their entertainment (a model not unlike the *Johnsoniana* built up by the Thrale family). Not only when they explicitly collaborated in *Miscellaneous Pieces* and *Evenings at Home*, but also in their other work, both Aikin and Barbauld circulated their writing around family and friends in much this way. Aikin 'would have everything he wrote read aloud by one member of the family to the others, and he encouraged comments even from the youngest'.[162] Barbauld too had circulated her poetry around the community at Warrington, also reaching out via Joseph Johnson to the larger community of provincial and metropolitan Dissent. Her early poem on the departure of the Priestleys from Warrington had celebrated the 'brightening influence' of the 'social circle joined' to 'raise [...] my pensive mind'.[163] For both Aikin and Barbauld, such exchanges were seen as entering into a 'mart of commerce' in which people exercised their right to 'examine, compare, choose, reject'.[164] The commercial metaphor, of course, speaks to the idea of conversation as integral to the progress of national improvement to which the provincial networks of Dissent were very much committed. Moreover, as Levy points out, the version of domestic space found in their *Evenings at Home* 'is neither feminized nor privatized, but rather is populated by men, women, and children, from within and outside the family'.[165] The dialogues were explicitly questioning of political and religious orthodoxy. Pieces such as 'The Cost of War' were quickly denounced by loyalists such as Sarah Trimmer for questioning received idea of military heroism.[166]

In pamphlets such as her *Address to the Opposers of the Repeal of the Corporation and Test Acts* (1789), Barbauld was unapologetic about the association between Dissent and conversation as a form of sober enquiry after truth:

If, by the continued peaceableness of our demeanour, and the superior sobriety of our conversation, a sobriety for which we have not yet quite ceased to be

---

[162] Betsy Rodgers, *Georgian Chronicle: Mrs Barbauld & Her Family* (London: Methuen, 1958), 122. At Warrington writing by Barbauld and others was dropped into the work bag of Mary Priestley for circulation.

[163] See 'On Mrs. P[riestley]'s Leaving Warrington', in *The Poems of Anna Letitia Barbauld*, ed. William McCarthy and Elizabeth Kraft (Athens/London: University of Georgia Press, 1994), 1–3 (ll. 41–2).

[164] See 'The Hill of Science', in *Miscellaneous Pieces in Prose* (1773), 62–3, and the discussion of this passage in White, *Early Romanticism*, 78–9.

[165] Levy, 'Radical Education', 127.

[166] Quoted ibid. 123.

distinguished; if, by our attention to literature, and that ardent love of liberty which you are pretty ready to allow us, we deserve esteem, we shall enjoy it.[167]

'Sobriety of conversation' is a phrase gesturing back to the truth-oriented conversation of Presbyterianism. What is distinctive about her political writing is the continual linking back of political critique to the virtue of domestic arrangements. When she addresses the emergent popular radical movement in her *Civic Sermons for the People* (1792), she locates its authority in the private virtues of its members: 'Love then this Country; unite its idea with your domestic comforts...remember that each of you, however inconsiderable, is benefited by your Country; so your Country, however extensive, is benefited by every one of the least of you.'[168]

Domestic conversation for Barbauld ought to underpin the civic virtues of public debate and thereby create an important space for female participation. Her disagreement with Gilbert Wakefield suggests she thought of the chapel in the same kind of way. Quite explicitly for Barbauld, social worship offers a conversable world that cuts across class and gender boundaries and challenges Wakefield's masculine assumptions that would separate religious (and political) duty from the social affections. Freedom for women to participate in public on this kind of debate didn't conform to most Bluestocking ideas of conversability (nor Samuel Johnson's for that matter). In 1780, the year female debating societies boomed in the metropolis, Elizabeth Carter wrote an outraged letter about religious matters being discussed by women in such venues:

There is a new school of oratory set up, where, on a Sunday evening, for the price of sixpence, people may go and hear the discussion of knotty points of divinity. There were five hundred people there on Sunday. The subject was Predestination. The opponent to this doctrine said it was a damnable opinion, on which a gentlewoman (for I am not sure that ladies go to divinity lectures) who was probably on the other side of the question, hissed the speaker. She was rebuked for this by the moderator, and told it was only for serpents to hiss. All the other oratorical institutions will only make people impertinent; but such a method of treating subjects of divinity will certainly help to make them mad.[169]

---

[167] *An Address to the Opposers of the Repeal of the Corporation and Test Acts*, 4th edn (London, 1790), 22.

[168] *Civic Sermons to the People*, no. 2 (London, 1792), 22. See also the discussion in Guest, *Small Change*, 236.

[169] 8 May 1780, *Letters from Elizabeth Carter to Mrs Montagu between the Years 1755 and 1800*, 3 vols (London, 1817), III: 129. Although the topic of predestination was debated several times in the 1770s and 1780s at such societies, the advertisements collected by Andrew show none around this time, unless Carter is referring to debates on biblical texts Luke 19.26 and 1 Corinthians 13.3 at the University for Rational Amusement and the Religious Association, respectively, on April 30, which was a Sunday. See Andrew, *London Debating Societies*, 96, for details.

Barbauld may well have also worried that such spaces were too raucous for the sociable affections to work their charms, but she was not opposed in principle to women debating theology. For her part, Montagu was often condescending in her comments on Barbauld's background. In November 1774 she had written to Carter: 'I had last night a charming letter from Mrs. Barboult. [*sic*] I find she is in a very uncouth neighbourhood, but she speaks of her situation with that resignation I shd expect. I have a more exquisite sense of her superior merit than she has, & I am chagrined at what does not mortify her.'[170] The situation was her decision to marry the Revd Rochemont Barbauld and set up a school for boys at Palgrave, Norfolk, which they ran from 1774 to 1785. Predictably enough, her decision also brought derision from Samuel Johnson: 'If I had bestowed such an education on a daughter, and had discovered that she thought of marrying such a fellow, I would have sent her to the *Congress*' (*BLJ* II: 408–9). Barbauld would more probably have regarded her situation as an affirmation of the domestic virtues that underwrote her political interventions.[171] Barbauld became increasingly sceptical about the kind of fashionable elegance associated with Montagu. She wrote to her brother in January 1784 to say: 'Mrs Montagu, not content with being the Queen of literature and elegant society, sets up for the Queen of fashion and splendour. She is building a very fine house,...and I am afraid will be as much the woman of the world as the philosopher.'[172] The word 'Queen' here, I'd suggest, is being used very deliberately to associate Montagu with the court. The idea of the woman of the world implied fashionable display and illusory surface compared to values of enquiry and engagement underpinned by the domestic virtues espoused in most of Barbauld's writing.

POZZY AND BOZZY: AN AFTER-LIFE OF CONVERSATION

Domestic ideology placed increasing certain kinds of pressure on conversable worlds such as Montagu's, predicated on splendour and display, but it also created issues for Johnson's reputation as the nation's greatest con-

---

[170] 12 November 1774, 'Montagu correspondence', MO3350.

[171] My approach is in general agreement with that taken by Guest, *Small Change*, 228–9, who notes that Barbauld's notion of domestic duty did not imply a choice between 'sensibility and politics'. Guest is arguing against the version of this choice laid out in G. J. Barker-Benfield, *The Culture of Sensibility: Sex and Society in Eighteenth-Century Britain* (Chicago: University of Chicago Press, 1992), 222 and 266.

[172] 'Letter to John Aikin', January 1784, in Le Breton, *Memoir*, 55.

versationalist. Nussbaum's argument about Johnson's competition with Montagu suggests that events in the American colonies in the 1770s had made his conversation increasingly important as a monument of national pride: the proof of British power was related to the presence among its literati of such a powerful talker as Johnson. Ironically, power has no part in the definition Johnson offered for 'conversation' in his *Dictionary* (1755–6). There it appears in more Addisonian guise as 'familiar discourse; chat; easy talk; opposed to a formal conference'. 'Conversableness' he defined as 'the quality of being a pleasing companion; fluency of talk'.[173] When James Boswell came to London in 1762, he expected to find this kind of conversation. Boswell consistently attempted to comport himself in an Addisonian manner, even going to places described in *The Spectator* and imagining his own position in terms of its prior scripting of politeness:

At three o'clock I went to Westminster Abbey and the verger politely showed me into one of the prebend's stalls, where I sat in great state with a purple silk cushion before me. I heard service with much devotion in this magnificent and venerable temple. I recalled the ideas of it which I had from *The Spectator*.[174]

He drove through the city with his head full of ideas suggested by Addison and Steele 'such as I could not explain to most people'. The paradox of participatory exclusiveness implied by the last expression speaks volumes for what he learned from *The Spectator*, but his journal also reveals the difficulties involved in self-fashioning this position both outside and inside the crowd: 'We endeavoured to work our minds into the frame of the Spectator's, but we could not. We were both too dissipated.'[175] For Boswell the world of consumption threatened to drown, often literally in alcohol, the polite sociability Addison and Hume thought it ought to encourage.

Frequently, Boswell reacted to his own dissipation by despising himself. Projecting the self-loathing outwards, he was particularly dismissive of the possibility of a properly spectatorial sociability emanating from his birthplace, Scotland, disdaining the 'familiarity' practised by his countrymen even when gathered together in the metropolis: 'I find that I ought not to keep too much company with Scotch people, because I am kept from acquiring propriety of English speaking, and because they prevent my mind from being filled with London images, so that I might as well be in

[173] See Johnson's *A Dictionary of the English language: in which the Words are deduced from their Originals, and illustrated in their different Significations*, 2 vols (London, 1755–6) under 'conversation' and 'conversableness'.

[174] *London Journal 1762–1763*, 29 May 1763, 270.

[175] Ibid. 8 January 1763, 130, and 13 April 1763, 240.

Scotland.'[176] Boswell was committed himself to studying the 'polite reserved behaviour' of the English: 'Mr. Addison's character in sentiment, mixed with a little of the gaiety of Sir Richard Steele and the manners of Mr Digges, were the ideas which I aimed to realize.'[177] For all he recognized the 'instructive conversation' to be found with men like Hume, he thought their enquiring minds too destructive of politeness in his English sense.[178] As a bulwark against his own failings in politeness and morals, for which he constantly chided himself, Boswell turned to the bulk of Samuel Johnson, resting his hero's reputation primarily on his conversation.

All Johnson's biographers commented on Johnson's pleasure in conversation. Even the ponderous Sir John Hawkins reported that 'the great delight of his life was conversation and mental intercourse,' Hester Piozzi told her readers that 'conversation was all he required to make him happy,' but neither she nor Hawkins gave their readers the copious transcriptions that made up the bulk of Boswell's book.[179] Boswell boasted of 'the peculiar value' of his work as 'the quantity that it contains of Johnson's conversation' (*BLJ* I: 31), but he acknowledged 'objections which may be made to the minuteness on some occasions of my details of Johnson's conversation' (*BLJ* I: 33). For her part, although she and her family had collected Johnson's sayings from early on, Piozzi was capable of being acid about Boswell's method. When Johnson was with Boswell on their tour of the Hebrides, she wrote to say 'I am glad Mr. Boswell is with you— nothing that you say for this week at least will be lost to Posterity.'[180] Among other things, of course, the letter also implies Johnson colluded with the transcription and circulation of his conversation, recognizing that his own reputation might depend on the details of his private talk. He had after all in taken this view in *The Rambler*: 'The business of the biographer is often to pass slightly over those performances and incidents, which produce vulgar greatness, to lead the thoughts into domestick privacies, and display the minute details of daily life.'[181]

---

[176]   *London Journal 1762–1763*, 3 February 1763, 177.
[177]   *London Journal 1762–1763*, 1 December 1762, 61–2.
[178]   Ibid. 12 July 1763, 300. See the discussion of Boswell's comments on Hume in Chap 1, p. 66–7.
[179]   Sir John Hawkins, *The Life of Samuel Johnson, LL.D.* (London, 1787), 219, and Piozzi, *Anecdotes*, 4th edn, 275.
[180]   See *Letters* II: 209 (Piozzi-Thrale MS.540/72).
[181]   See *The Rambler*, ed. W. J. Bate and Albrecht B. Strauss, *The Yale Edition of the Works of Samuel Johnson*, 16 vols (New Haven: Yale University Press, 1969), III: 321. Boswell quotes the passage in defence of his own method (*BLJ* I: 32). See also Helen Deutsch, *Loving Dr. Johnson* (Chicago: University of Chicago Press, 2005), 2–4.

To an extent, it was an approach Johnson had practised himself in *Lives of the Poets*, but Boswell's obsessive concern with the transcription of private conversation risked implying that his hero's life *'consisted in little else than talking'* (*BLJ* I: 343).[182] The situation was worsened by the unstable status of biography as a genre more generally because of 'its possible infection of the masculine purity of the public sphere of history'.[183] Against the feminizing implications of its conversational approach, Boswell's *Life* was careful to note those occasions when Johnson manifested a sterling manliness in his conversation, but his hero could not always stop himself talking for victory in ways that spilled over into barbarity. One notorious instance was Johnson's clash with the Quaker Mary Knowles over the decision taken by a young woman named Jane Harry to leave the Church of England. Encountering Johnson at a gathering at Dilly the booksellers, Knowles wanted to use the case to discuss substantial issues of belief and freedom of conscience. Typically, Johnson did everything he could to thwart any serious discussion of these issues. In Boswell's published version of the exchange (*BLJ* III: 298–300), Knowles told Johnson that Harry was 'sorry at finding that he was offended at her leaving the Church of England, and embracing a simpler faith'. Johnson dismissed Harry as 'an odious wench' insisting she could know nothing of the issues. When Knowles patiently pointed out Harry had studied the New Testament carefully, Johnson 'rose again into passion, and attacked the young proselyte in the severest terms of reproach'.[184] At this point, Boswell shifts into a general account of the company's delight with Johnson's performance that evening: 'Notwithstanding the occasional explosions of violence…I compared him at this time to a warm West-Indian climate, where you have a bright sun, quick vegetation, luxuriant foliage, luscious fruits; but where the same heat

[182] Boswell quotes from and is attempting to ameliorate the implications of Piozzi's *Anecdotes*, 23.

[183] Guest, *Small Change*, 55.

[184] Anna Seward, who was present, had an important role in circulating accounts of the incident unfavourable to Johnson. See *Letters of Anna Seward: written between 1784 and 1807*, 6 vols (Edinburgh, 1811). In 1785, she wrote to Knowles herself about Boswell's request for 'records of the life of his despot', including 'the tremendous conversation at Dilly's between you and him, on the subject of Miss Harry's commencing quaker' (i.47–8). A note points out that 'Mr Boswell has strangely mutilated, abridged, and changed the minutes sent him of this conversation.' She told Piozzi that she regretted helping Boswell with his request for materials (see Hyde, *Impossible Friendship*, 122). The version published in Seward's letters was reproduced in the *Monthly Repository of Theology and General Literature* 6 (1811), 519–25, which invited its readers to compare it with the Knowles version. For a further analysis of Boswell's account of the incident, see Felicity Nussbaum, 'Boswell's Treatment of Johnson's Temper: "A Warm West-Indian Climate"', *Studies in English Literature, 1500–1900*, 14 (1974), 421–33.

sometimes produces thunder, lightning, and earthquakes, in a terrible degree.' Boswell construes Johnson's conversation as varied, fertile, and sublime, even if sometimes the site of unpredictable violence, but he was also aware that there were other versions in circulation less willing to translate what had happened into an incidence of Johnsonian sublimity. In the circumstances, Boswell felt obliged to add a note to the second edition admitting that he had omitted an account of the evening sent to him by Knowles herself.

This account had already been published in the *Gentleman's Magazine* for June 1791 as a direct challenge to his omission: 'It chiefly relates to the principles of the sect called *Quakers*,' noted Boswell sarcastically, 'and no doubt the Lady appears to have greatly the advantage of Dr. Johnson in argument as well as expression.' He leaves it to any readers to judge for themselves who 'have the curiosity to peruse it' (*BLJ* III: 299).[185] For those of us who do have the curiosity, the version in the *Gentleman's Magazine*, republished as a separate pamphlet in 1799, is unequivocal in its account of the conversational virtues of Knowles against Johnson's:

Very striking is the mild fortitude of modest Truth; and it is finely contrasted with the boisterous violence of bigoted Sophistry, so long accustomed to victory over feigned or slight resistance, and, in a certain circle, to timid and implicit submission.

In this account, Johnson accused the Quaker directly of seducing Harry 'from the Christian religion' and insists 'I cannot forgive the little slut, for presuming to take upon her self as she has done.' Knowles for her part insists the Church cannot take over responsibility for anyone's moral agency: 'A Nation, or State, having a conscience, is a doctrine entirely new to me.' Where she expects candid discussion, Johnson answers only with abuse, growing furious '*at the space of time the Gentlemen insisted on allowing his antagonist wherein to make her defence*'. When Knowles offers the conciliatory hope that he will meet Harry again in heaven, he brusquely retorts: 'Meet *her!* I never desire to meet fools any where.' Of course, there is no way of knowing whether this account is any truer than Boswell's. No less than his, the Knowles account is shaped by its own set of assumptions about what constituted proper conversation. Conversation for Knowles could be both polite and a medium of enquiry, as it could for

---

[185] See *Gentleman's Magazine*, 61 (June 1791), 500–2, reprinted as *Dialogue between Dr. Johnson and Mrs Knowles* (London, 1799). There is a brief record of the conversation in Boswell's journal. See *Boswell in Extremes 1776–1778*, ed. Charles McC. Weis and Frederick A. Pottle (London: Heinemann, 1971), 288–9. There the comparison of Johnson to a tropical storm actually follows a violent disagreement with Anna Seward over the American colonies. I'm grateful to David Fallon for pointing this out to me.

Barbauld, where moral agents of whatever sex turned religious principles around together. For Johnson, there is a necessary limit to such enquiries, even within relatively select conversational circles, especially if women were to be involved. Talking for victory as a conversational mode meant using all the resources at one's disposal to put a stop to this kind of enquiry. In Nussbaum's analysis, 'Johnson encouraged heated debate as rather more manly than gentlemanly.'[186] Conversation became, as Boswell put it, 'a trial of intellectual vigour and skill' (*BLJ* IV: 111), but Johnson often exercised those skills to stop debate. No doubt Nussbaum is correct to follow Michèle Cohen in seeing Boswell bringing Johnson forward as a colossus of English manliness, but the project contained uncomfortable contradictions for a man, like Boswell, who had sometimes at least aspired to an Addisonian idea of polite conversation.[187]

Something of the problem for Boswell is expressed in his journal's account of the very first time he met Johnson. Describing 'his dogmatical roughness of manners' as 'disagreeable', Boswell resolves nevertheless to 'mark what I remember of his conversation', a commitment that evolved into the *Life of Johnson*.[188] Boswell labours mightily in the biography to show his subject's 'roughness was only external and did not proceed from his heart' (II: 362). Although Boswell claimed Johnson himself had sanctioned this minute method, it caused a great outcry in the press when first revealed in his *Tour of the Hebrides* (1785). Johnson's conversation there is not just a record of witty performance or solemn utterance, the older idea of what constituted the *ana* or table talk of great men, but also a great deal of entirely mundane talk. The anonymous *Remarks on the journal of a tour to the Hebrides* (1785) complained it was Johnson's writing not his convivial conversation that would recommend him to posterity. Boswell has 'forced upon the Public, a six shilling book replete with small talk and ill-natured remarks'.[189] Satirists and caricaturists, such as Peter Pindar in his *Poetical Epistle to Boswell* (1786), made great sport with the image of Boswell as a 'charming haberdasher of small ware!'[190] What these criticisms missed, but Boswell, unconsciously at least, understood, was

---

[186] Nussbaum, *Limits of the Human*, 90.

[187] See Michèle Cohen, 'Manliness, Effeminacy and the French: Gender and the Construction of National Character in Eighteenth-century England', and Philip Carter, 'James Boswell's Manliness', in Tim Hitchcock and Michèle Cohen (eds), *English Masculinities 1660–1800* (London/New York: Longman, 1999), 44–61 and 111–30, respectively. See also Nussbaum's *The Autobiographical Subject: Gender and Ideology in Eighteenth-Century England* (Baltimore/London: Johns Hopkins University Press, 1989), 103–26.

[188] *London Journal*, 16 May 1763, 260.

[189] Verax, *Remarks on the Journal of a Tour to the Hebrides* (London, 1785), 19.

[190] Peter Pindar, *A poetical and congratulatory epistle to James Boswell, Esq*, (London, 1786), 9.

the growing interest of readers in the everyday aspects of the lives of the great, which sustained so many of the newspapers that eagerly reported the gossip and the developing competition between Bozzy and Pozzy after Johnson's death.[191] The public rushed to buy both the *Tour* and, when it eventually came out, the *Life of Johnson*, as they also rushed to buy Piozzi's *Anecdotes of Johnson* (1786) and the *Letters to and from the Late Samuel Johnson* (1788).

As a woman presuming to manage the reputation of Johnson, Hester Piozzi was even more open to mockery than Boswell, especially as her work centred on the domestic details of life at Streatham, easily parodied as the female confusion of gossip with solid conversation. the *Monthly Review*, for instance, reported the frustration of its expectation of 'learned observations, with moral reflections, and profound disquisitions—such as beam like luminaries of resplendent beauty, in so many parts of his works; and, if we have not been misinformed, commonly united to render his conversation, at once splendid and instructive.'[192] Furious at being side-lined in Piozzi's accounts of her relationship with Johnson, Boswell joined in the sport of baiting her, but also admitted privately that her versions revealed his hero to be less than the giant he wanted people to believe.[193] Boswell did what he could to edit out 'Johnson's dependency on the feminine world of household economy', but his own emphasis on repro-ducing so much of Johnson's conversation threatened to drown his hero in a welter of everyday talk.[194] The point was driven home in a series of satirical attacks on Boswell's *Life* even before it came out, the best of them probably the anonymous 'Lessons in Biography or How to write the Biography of a Friend', published in several newspapers in July 1791:

We talked of wind I said I knew many persons much distressed with that complaint—POZZ. 'Yes, Sir, when confined, when pent up.' I said I did not know that, but I questioned if the Romans ever knew it.—POZZ 'Yes, Sir, the

---

[191] See Pindar's satire *Bozzy and Piozzi, or, the British Biographers, A Town Eclogue* (London, 1786), in which the pair traded in inane details about Johnson's life for the laurels to be awarded by a bored Sir John Hawkins.

[192] *Monthly Review*, 74 (1786), 374. Piozzi copied the review into her *Thraliana*, II: 704.

[193] See James Boswell, *Boswell: The English Experiment, 1785–1789*, ed. Irma S. Lustig and Frederick A. Pottle (Heinemann, 1986), 194–5, on his response to Piozzi's edition of letters. For Boswell's feeding of the press with stories hostile to Piozzi in this period before his *Life* came out, see Hyde, *Impossible Friendship*, 110–13 and 130–6. Always paranoid about women intellectuals, he told Edmund Malone 'it is *clear* that she *means* to bite me as much as she can, that she may curry favour with Mrs. Montague.' Quoted in Hyde, *Impossible Friendship*, 106.

[194] Deutsch, *Loving Dr. Johnson*, 185.

Romans knew it'—BOZZ 'Livy does not mention it'.—POZZ 'No, Sir, Livy wrote History. Livy was not writing the Life of a Friend'[195]

The satire carries on for two newspaper columns before noting that it has included only such extracts 'as will tend to impress our readers with an high idea of this vast undertaking'. Johnson's reputation—supposed to be of such import to the national character—is being reduced to mere flatulence by the over-concentration on the detail of his conversation. Boswell begged his readers 'to endeavour to keep in mind his deliberate and strong utterance' (*BLJ*, II: 326), but his attempt to produce a monumental Johnson against the domesticity of Piozzi's account undermined itself by the minuteness of its account of his idol's conversation.

The fight over the corpus of Johnson's conversation offers a framework for thinking about major shifts in the field of literary production in the Romantic period. For all its caveats, anxieties, and regulatory ambition, *The Spectator* committed itself to conversation out in the world of coffee shop and tavern as a constitutive part of literary relations. By the early nineteenth century, even Johnson's idea of London talk is being treated with increasing scepticism. For some commentators, even by the 1780s, it was flourishing better in Edinburgh than a London torn by political dissension. Even 'the literary colossus' Samuel Johnson, according to the *European Magazine* in 1787, had been too mired in politics to sustain an Addisonian equipoise in his essays.[196] At his death, one correspondent to the *Gentleman's Magazine* mourned the fact that Johnson had been born too late for his erudition to be appreciated: 'I fear, a compleat victory obtained by News-papers, Magazines…Translations, Abridgements, Beauties, Reviews, and Fugitive Pieces, with the light Summer Infantry to compleat the rout over the heavy-armed Legion of the Learned.'[197] Twenty years later, Hannah More's evangelical novel *Coelebs in Search of a Wife* (1808) has its hero go to London fired by Johnson's famous praise of conversation in the capital. He finds instead merely superficial chatter fuelled by the newspapers. In a world now so thick with social mediation, the fungible role Hume applied to conversation appeared unsustainable. There was just too much stuff to be processed and too many people eager to involve themselves. One response was to displace the understanding of literary culture in terms of conversation onto a Wordsworthian

[195] See, among others, *The Morning Herald* (5 July 1791) and the discussion in Lucyle Werkmeister, *Jemmie Boswell and the London Daily Press, 1785–1795* (New York: New York Public Library, 1963), 32–7.

[196] 'The Lounger', in the *Scots Magazine*, 344, reproducing a discussion from the *European Magazine*.

[197] See the *Gentleman's Magazine*, 54 (December 1784), 883.

communion with 'something far more deeply interfused'. Such constructions were not necessarily conservative, at least not in intention. For Mary Hays and for Wordsworth himself, they offered the prospect of reaching beyond social distinctions to a pure language of the heart, an issue returned to frequently in the second part of this book. The cost was the abandonment of sweaty bodies in rooms or out in the street. Rather than barter with difference, better to transcend it, from this of point of view. A similar reflex fed into Coleridge's thinking and underpinned his tendency to identify literary culture with an organic whole rather than the messiness and potential for misapprehension embodied in metaphors of verbal exchange. For Coleridge, literariness had to be cleared of thekind of chat and gossip identified with women and directed towards a grandeur that forms like the familiar essay could never reach. Addison he identified with a taste for loose and unconnected writing that had feminized literary culture. Better, for Coleridge, to go back to the scholasticism of seventeenth-century divines, texts hard for anyone to think of as conversable. When it came to biography, Coleridge complained at the way 'huge volumes of biographical minutae' fail to 'illustrate those qualities which distinguished the Subject of them from ordinary men'. The same essay compares such biographers to 'the most garrulous female Chronicler' who scribbles 'on the Marble Monument, sacred to the memory of the departed Great'.[198] It is hard not to believe that he is deliberately representing Boswell as a womanly writer in wolf's clothing.

By the end of the eighteenth century, many forms of Georgian sociability—pleasure gardens, promenades, assemblies, masquerades, and even the theatre—were being abandoned by the elite. The political turmoil of the 1790s reinforced the process. The emergence of a separation of spheres between the sexes, comprising with it an antipathy to the kind of display associated with Montagu, may be part of same historical phenomenal, but the example of Barbauld, for instance, shows that any such development was far from straightforward. Conversation at home, as it were, could remain the basis of public interventions that took their authority from the domestic virtues. Even so, for both women and men, if in different ways, there was a broader historical process emptying out or segregating many of the mixed public places through which the vivifying conversation of culture had been perceived to be circulating. Many clubs

---

[198] See Samuel Taylor Coleridge, 'A Prefatory Observation on Modern Biography', *The Friend*, 21 (25 January 1810), 2 vols, *The Collected Works of Samuel Taylor Coleridge*, Vol IV, ed. Barbara Rooke (Princeton: Princeton University Press, 1969), II: 285–7. He distinguishes *The Friend* from *The Spectator* by 'the greater Length of the separate Essays, by their closer Connection with each other, and by the Predominance of one Object, and the common Bearing of all to one End' (II: 19).

moved to private sometimes purpose-built spaces and abandoned any sense of an open urban terrain across which conversation could flow relatively freely. Retrenchment involved a complex reassessment of the eighteenth-century idea of conversation that formed a defining part of the cultural context of the Romantic period. Literature continued to define itself in terms of conversation, but often redefined against circulation in mixed social spaces. Literary ideas of conversation were increasingly either domesticated or displaced into ideas of higher forms of communion, but those shifts must also be weighed against the continuation of the wider context of ongoing talk about literature, politics, and other issues that continued in an array of places, including bookshops, clubs, and in the home.

PART II

PARTS 3.4

3

Critical Conversation in the 1790s: Godwin, Hays, and Wollstonecraft

This chapter addresses the fate of conversation in the fraught atmosphere of the 1790s, as it was played out in the circles associated with William Godwin, Mary Hays, and Mary Wollstonecraft. Their ideas on conversation were borne out of participation in a particular kind of conversable world located in the expanding metropolis of London.[1] They mixed primarily among literary and professional people of the middling sort; many disposed to Dissent, often reform-minded in politics, eager to debate the news of the day as well as various larger issues. This group focus helps get away from 'the fiction of the autonomous writer and the fiction of the passive reader' (one might add the myth of the solitary interpreter), but I also want to show that their ideas were the product of three interlaced but distinct trajectories that maintained a complex tension with each other.[2] Much has been written about the Godwin and Wollstonecraft relationship from a genetic-familial point of view.[3] My focus is instead on a nexus of assumptions about conversation, politeness, and sociability that each of these writers developed in distinctive ways in their writing and in their relationships with others.

[1] For details of the expansion of the metropolis into the areas where Godwin, Hays, and Wollstonecraft lived, see Linda Clarke, *Building Capitalism: Historical Change and the Labour Process in the Production of the Built Environment* (London/New York: Routledge, 1992).

[2] Gregory Clark, *Dialogue, Dialectic, and Conversation: A Social Perspective on the Function of Writing* (Carbondale and Edwardsville: Southern Illinois University Press, 1990), 32.

[3] See, for instance, Williams St Clair's *The Godwin's and the Shelley's* (London/Boston: Faber, 1989), and Julie Carlson's *England's First Family of Writers: Mary Wollstonecraft, William Godwin, Mary Shelley* (Baltimore: Johns Hopkins University Press, 2007). Both of these studies make major contributions to our understandings of the development of the writing of Godwin and Wollstonecraft, but my approach stresses the more contingent web of social relations, in the 1790s at least, in which their lives and writings were caught up.

Not that a shift away from a familial perspective implies this social text is to be regarded as somehow distinct from the private and domestic spheres. Much of the interaction between Godwin, Hays, and Wollstonecraft took the form of tea taking and visiting around a specific area of North London, near what is now the British Library, even if the conversations over tea were sometimes about issues as weighty as philosophical necessity and the nature of revolutions.[4] As my previous chapter showed, the domestic situation was increasingly represented as the safest place for conversation in the later eighteenth century. Pressure in this direction intensified once the print war over the French Revolution made family relations a battlefield for cultural politics, but this point should not obscure the emphasis on conversational improvement even in the more theoretical discourse of Godwin's *Political Justice* (1793). Between its first edition and the essays gathered in *The Enquirer* (1797), Godwin shifted between two different paradigms of conversation. In the writing of both Godwin and Wollstonecraft, an earlier idea of 'rational' conversation is to some extent revised and overtaken by a more affective model of the conversable world, one with debts to Addison and Hume, but both still continued to hold open the possibility of conversation functioning as a republican political modality.

FORCIBLE, INSTRUCTIVE, AND ENTERTAINING

Godwin's diary entry for 22 November 1791 reads: 'Holcroft calls: talk of the Widow. Webb calls: talk of necessity virtue & perception. Call on Jacob, fr. Sup at Hollis's, talk of David, Canaanites, and the use of conversation.'[5] The entry suggests both the sociable texture of Godwin's intellectual life at the time and the self-consciousness about conversation in it. Godwin's succinct note does not explain what he and Hollis said about conversation. Quite possibly, they reflected on the constraints placed on

---

[4] Godwin's diary shows that on the evening of 24 April 1792, he spent the evening with the artist George Dyson talking about 'truth, necessity & revolutions'. See Godwin's Diary, MS. Abinger e.4, Bodleian Library. A complete scan of the diary and a searchable database is now available as part of the Oxford Digital Library. The editorial team of Victoria Myers, David O'Shaughnessy, and Mark Philp have rendered me invaluable assistance. Unsurprisingly, the topics mentioned here recur often in the diary over the next few years. Judging by their subsequent correspondence, philosophical necessity and the nature of revolutions were among the subjects with which Mary Hays 'almost harassed him' when they first met at Paragon Place. See her letter of 6 May 1795 in *The Correspondence of Mary Hays (1779–1843), British Novelist*, ed. Marilyn L. Brooks (Lewiston/Queenston/Lampeter: Edwin Mellen Press, 2004), 390–2. The original letter is in the Pforzheimer Collection of the New York Public Library at MH 4.

[5] Abinger e.4.

conversation by social convention. The reflection was common in such circles at the time. In *Vindication of the Rights of Men* (1790), Wollstone-craft had complained that European civilization had refined 'the manners at the expence [*sic*] of morals, by making sentiments and opinions current in conversation that have no root in the heart, or weight in the cooler resolves of the mind'.[6] She took this kind of conversation to be typical of the false gallantry found in a commercial society in thrall to a fashionable elite. In *Vindication of the Rights of Woman* (1792), the perception that politeness obstructed rational relations between the sexes (and between people in general) moves to the heart of her critique of 'the cold unmeaning intercourse of gallantry'.[7] Plenty of radical novels from the early 1790s presented polite conversation as failing in candour. Charlotte Smith's *Desmond* (1792), for instance, satirizes both the 'delectable conversation' of the sensualist Lord Newminster and the prejudiced political calculations of a circle of local tradesmen, 'so expressive of the candour and disinterested conduct of British electors'. Smith's hero, Lionel Desmond, on the other hand, displays an 'open, ingenuous countenance'. His face corroborates the candour of the hero's conversation, as in many sentimental novels of the time, a point I will return to later in this chapter. In her preface, Smith framed her novel as 'drawn from political conversations to which I have been a witness in England, and France, during the last twelve months'. If the word 'witness' suggests an alert presence rather than participation, the position recommended for women by so many conduct books, then Smith defended her own right to use fiction as a 'vehicle of political discussion'. Her refutation of claims that 'women…have no business with politics' drew the approbation of a review by Wollstonecraft.[8]

Smith and Wollstonecraft were not critical of conversation as such, but only of its practice in the fashionable world or corrupted political circles.

---

[6] Mary Wollstonecraft, *A Vindication of the Rights of Men, in a Letter to the Right Honourable Edmund Burke*, 2nd edn (London, 1790), 11. The final part of the sentence doesn't appear in the first edition.

[7] See Mary Wollstonecraft, *A Vindication of the Rights of Woman with Strictures on Moral and Political Subjects* (London, 1792), 216. Wollstonecraft described John Gregory's claim that his daughters would seldom hear the genuine sentiments of men as a 'mournful truth'. Nevertheless, she chastised him for not encouraging women to aspire to rational conversa-tion rather than accept as a fact of life the empty gallantry of men's conversation. On Gregory, see above pp. 116–17. See also Gregory Claeys, 'The Divine Creature and the Female Citizen: Manners, Religion, and the Two Rights Strategies in Mary Wollstonecraft's *Vindications*', in Glenn Burgess and Matthew Festenstein (eds), *English Radicalism, 1550–1850* (Cambridge: Cambridge University Press, 2007), 115–34, and Jenny Davidson, *Hypocrisy and the Politics of Politeness: Manners and Morals from Locke to Austen* (Cambridge: Cambridge University Press, 2004), 76–80, 86–91, and 100–1.

[8] Charlotte Smith, *Desmond: A Novel*, 3 vols (1792), I: 31, III: 172, II: 6, and I: ii–viii. For Wollstonecraft's review of Smith's novel, see *Analytical Review*, 13 (1792), 428–35.

'It is in such conversation, if conversation it may be called, that I am to pass the tedious days of the next month,' complains Fanny Waverly in *Desmond*, reflecting on what she hears around her in the fashionable circles of Bath.[9] Early on in the 1790s at least, the possibilities of 'conversation' were separable for Godwin and Wollstonecraft from their scepticism about politeness. Both were the products in differing ways of the culture of Rational Dissent, Godwin by upbringing, and Wollstonecraft through her social contact in the 1780s with James Burgh, Richard Price, and Joseph Johnson, among others. The emphasis in Rational Dissent on conversation as a form of strenuous intellectual exchange privileged candour and sincerity over polish and politeness. Godwin wrote to a neighbour, Fredrick Norman, in 1793: 'Conversation I rank among the highest gratifications of human life & the most prolific sources (*sic*) of improvem^t.'[10] Conversation as a pleasure was usually allied to its capacity for improvement in such circles. Mary Hays believed 'the great bane to the pleasures of conversation is affectation, or the wish to appear to possess what nature has denied.'[11] She too had received an intellectual schooling in English Dissent. The Baptist meetinghouse in Southwark that she attended with her family provided a crucial nurturing environment for her intellectual development.[12] Among her connections was the minister Robert Robinson, whose attention to the education of his daughters Priestley praised in the oration he gave at his friend's funeral.[13] When his younger daughter married and moved to London, Robinson worried that she might submit to pulpit commandments not to criticize others.[14] To Hays, he wrote: 'take nothing for granted...I love the inquisitive, the *reasoner*, who never takes my sayso, and who wants to know the why, and the wherefore.'[15] Hays went on to mix with other prominent dissenters

[9]   Smith, *Desmond*, III: 110.
[10]   MS. Abinger c. 17. See *The Letters of William Godwin*, vol. 1: *1778–1797*, ed. Pamela Clemit (Oxford: Oxford University Press, 2011), 78.
[11]   See her *Letters and Essays, Moral and Miscellaneous* (London, 1793), 192.
[12]   See Gina Luria Walker, *Mary Hays (1759–1843): The Growth of a Woman's Mind* (Aldershot: Ashgate, 2006), 34. For a very different kind of Baptist sociability, see Tim Whelan's ' "For the Hand of a Woman, has Levell'd the Blow": Maria de Fleury's Pamphlet War with William Huntington, 1787–1791', *Women's Studies*, 36 (2007), 431–54.
[13]   See Joseph Priestley, *Reflections on Death, A sermon, on occasion of the death of the Rev. Robert Robinson, of Cambridge, delivered at the new meeting in Birmingham, June 13, 1790* (London/Birmingham, 1790), 23. For Hays's early debts to Robinson, see Gina Luria Walker, 'Mary Hays (1759–1843): An Enlightened Quest', in Sarah Knott and Barbara Taylor (eds), *Women, Gender and Enlightenment* (Palgrave Macmillan: Basingstoke, 2005), 493–518 (496–8).
[14]   Robinson to Hays, 4 March 1789, *Correspondence*, 259–61 (Pforzheimer, misc. ms: 2160).
[15]   Ibid. 261.

such as Joseph Priestley, Theophilus Lindsey, and John Disney from the late 1780s.

If some dissenting circles were willing to transgress conventional gendered roles in social life, women were still excluded from formal education at their academies.[16] Given women's '*conditional* access to knowledge', conversation was an important conduit of the Enlightenment for women, as we have already seen in the case of Kathryn Plymley.[17] Sometimes more acceptable than solitary reading, usually easier to come by than formal instruction, it is no surprise that both Hays and Wollstonecraft give it serious attention in their writing. Like nearly all eighteenth-century writers on education, Wollstonecraft finds a key role for conversation in republican pedagogy: 'The elements of religion, history, the history of man, and politics, might also be taught by conversation, in the socratic form.'[18] Phrases such as 'rational conversation' and 'social converse' recur throughout her writing as desirable goals for women.[19] 'We then wish to converse', she writes of her intellectual ambitions for women, 'not to fondle; to give scope to our imaginations as well as to the sensations of our hearts.'[20] Many observers recorded Wollstonecraft's combative flair for talk. Generally, she practised an idea of conversation that exceeded in candour and forthrightness even what someone like Barbauld hoped and expected of Dissenters. For Barbauld, the next generation of Wollstonecraft and Hays were, among other things, practising a different kind of discourse—verbal and written—from the social and domestic circle she had participated in at Warrington. The extent of their emphasis on candour pressurized Barbauld's understanding of the 'soft maxims' of domestic conversation.[21]

---

[16] See Kathryn Gleadle's ' "Opinions deliver'd in conversation": Conversation, Politics, and Gender in the Late Eighteenth Century', in Josie Harris (ed.), *Civil Society in British History: Ideas, Identities, Institutions* (Oxford: Oxford University Press, 2003), 61–78 (75). Marilyn L. Brooks thinks it possible that Hays attended some lectures at the New College, Hackney. See Hays, *Correspondence*, 237, and George Dyer to Mary Hays, 28 February 1794, 286 (Pforzheimer, misc ms 2170).

[17] See Michèle Le Doueff, *The Sex of Knowing*, trans. Kathryn Hamer and Lorraine Code (New York/London: Routledge, 2003), 24.

[18] Wollstonecraft, *Vindication of the Rights of Woman*, 388.

[19] See, for instance, ibid. 407 and 326.

[20] Ibid. 151.

[21] When Maria Edgeworth wrote to Barbauld to suggest they join together to edit a literary paper for women, Barbauld responded: 'there is no bond of union among literary women, any more than among literary men; different sentiments and different connections separate them much more than the joint interest of their sex would unite them. Mrs Hannah More would not write along with you or me, and we should probably hesitate at joining Miss Hays, or if she were living, Mrs. Godwin [Wollstonecraft].' Barbauld to Edgeworth, 30 August 1804 in Le Breton, *Memoir*, 86–7. In *Vindication of the Rights of Woman*, 113, Wollstonecraft expressed disappointment that 'even women of superior

After Joseph Johnson introduced them in 1792, Hays described Wollstonecraft's 'conversation, like her writings, [as] brilliant, forcible, instructive, and entertaining'.[22] Godwin famously recalled dining at Johnson's
hoping to hear Thomas Paine only to spend the entire evening arguing
with Mary. Even Hazlitt, never too quick to praise women intellectuals
(apart from Wollstonecraft, as it happens), recalled the easy way she dealt
with Godwin in debate and also passed on to his readers Coleridge's 'great
idea of [her] powers of conversation' in 'My First Acquaintance with
Poets'.[23] But Wollstonecraft herself was also clear-eyed about the latitude
extended to women in private conversation. After Mary Hays sent her the
draft preface to *Letters and Essays* (1793), Wollstonecraft warned against the
overly effusive gratitude shown to her male patrons: 'Your male friends will
still treat you like a woman—and many a man, for instance Dr. Johnson,
Lord Littleton, and even Dr. Priestley, have insensibly been led to utter warm
elogiums in private that they would be sorry openly to avow with cooling
explanatory ifs.'[24] The 'even' acknowledges that both Hays and Wollstonecraft had been the beneficiaries of Priestley's conversation, but equally
implies an awareness of the sometimes tenuous place of conversation between private and public, especially for women, even among liberal Dissenters.

At this stage in their careers at least, Hays allowed more room for the
play of affect in conversation than Wollstonecraft, but sincerity rather
than refinement is still the keynote. Her essay 'Remarks on Conversation

sense' could represent women as merely smiling flowers. Her note refers to Barbauld's poem
'To a Lady, with some Painted Flowers' commenting that 'virtue must be acquired by *rough*
toils, and useful struggles with worldly *cares*'. Here Wollstonecraft invokes Barbauld's poem
'To Mrs. P[riestley], with some Drawings of Birds and Insects' (ll. 98–102), indicating her
more general respect for the plainer virtues of Rational Dissent. Barbauld responded with
'The Rights of Woman', reiterating the importance of the 'soft maxims' that she implies
Wollstonecraft's rough treatment of her had ignored. See *The Poems of Anna Letitia
Barbauld*, ed. William McCarthy and Elizabeth Kraft (Athens/London: University of
Georgia Press, 1994), 77, 6–9, and 121–2. For an illuminating discussion of the dispute
that explores Barbauld's emphasis on domestic manners as the basis of a public morality, see
Harriet Guest, *Small Change: Women, Learning, Patriotism, 1750–1810* (Chicago: University of Chicago Press, 2000), 222–3 and 226.

[22] Perhaps from Hays's journal, now lost, the description was given after she breakfasted
with Wollstonecraft alone at her Store Street apartment: see *The Love Letters of Mary Hays
(1779–1780)*, ed. A. F. Wedd (London: Methuen, 1925), 5.

[23] See *The Complete Works of William Hazlitt*, ed. P. P. Howe, 21 vols (London: Dent,
1930-4), XVII: 111–12. All further references to Hazlitt's writing are to this edition and
given in the main text.

[24] Wollstonecraft to Hays, 25 November 1792, in *The Collected Letters of Mary
Wollstonecraft*, ed. Janet Todd (London: Penguin, 2005), 210. Wollstonecraft appears to
have met Samuel Johnson not long before his death. Lyttelton acknowledged that some of
the pieces in *Dialogues with the Dead* came from another hand, but not that the contributor
was Elizabeth Montagu or even that his collaborator was a woman. See the discussion of
their collaboration above, pp. 108–9.

and Friendship' insisted that 'general converse' should be 'unaffected, open, ingenuous'. These virtues are anchored in the 'devotional affections', although, like Barbauld, whose terminology Hays echoes here, she makes it clear that 'the precepts and duties of religion are all included in benevolence.'[25] The first thing Hays ever published was a contribution to the controversy with Gilbert Wakefield on public worship. Her *Cursory Remarks* (1792) reiterates Barbauld's sense of the importance of the sociability associated with religious communion as a source of enlightenment for women: 'I have myself', she wrote, 'experienced so much satisfaction, intellectual entertainment, and improvement, from an attendance on the public ordinances of religion.' Hays implies the benefits of the conversations she had enjoyed with various groups of Dissenters from the 1770s. Private worship of the sort recommended by Wakefield, 'a religion purely mental and contemplative', as Hays puts it, would exclude women from participation in one of the relatively few spheres in which they could take a part in intellectual debate.[26] Tentative about her own participation in public controversy, especially after Wakefield ridiculed the first edition of her reply, she nevertheless insisted on the importance of 'the spirit of freedom and enquiry universally disseminated'.[27]

Providing an explicitly political role for conversation, Godwin made it a key engine of progress in *Political Justice* (1793): 'if there be such a thing as truth, it must infallibly be struck out by the collision of mind with mind.' To bring about revolutions required 'free and unrestricted discussion': 'we must write, we must argue, we must converse.'[28] For Coleridge, trying to wean John Thelwall from Godwin's atheist influence, the emphasis on conversational candour in Godwin's private conduct was simply self-indulgence: 'Godwin, whose very heart is cankered by the love of singularity & who feels no disinclination to wound by abrupt harshness, pleads for absolute Sincerity,' he wrote to Thelwall, 'because such a system gives him a frequent opportunity of indulging his misanthropy.'[29] My next chapter

---

[25] Hays, *Essays*, 199–200. Earlier, she applauds George Dyer's praise of Barbauld (and Wollstonecraft), 11.

[26] Mary Hays, *Cursory remarks on An enquiry into the expediency and propriety of public or social worship: inscribed to Gilbert Wakefield*, 2nd edn (1792), 15 and 13.

[27] Ibid. 19, and see her postscript (22–8) for her reaction to Wakefield's response.

[28] William Godwin, *An Enquiry Concerning Political Justice*, ed. Mark Philp, vol. III of *Political and Philosophical Writings of William Godwin*, 7 vols, gen. ed. Mark Philp (London: William Pickering, 1993), 15 and 115. All other references to Godwin's prose, except his *Memoirs* of Wollstonecraft, will be to this edition and will be cited as *PPW* with volume and page numbers in the main text.

[29] 'Coleridge to Thelwall', 13 May 1796, *The Collected Letters of Samuel Taylor Coleridge*, ed. E. L. Griggs, 6 vols (Oxford: Oxford University Press, 1956–71), I: 214. All other references to Coleridge's letters are given in the text to this edition as *CL* with volume and page number.

will return to Coleridge's own conversational practice, especially in his poetry, but I do not want to reproduce the knee-jerk casting of Godwin as an automaton with no social skills found in much Romantic literary criticism. Godwin regarded 'the art of conversation', as he told Amelia Alderson with awkward gallantry, as 'the art of arts'.[30] After the success of *Political Justice*, a cringeworthy flirtatiousness often took over his relations with women, but generally when it came to candour Godwin more or less practised what he preached, not least with Mary Hays.[31] Encouraged by her experiences with Robinson and other dissenting clergymen, Hays had written to Godwin in October 1794 asking to borrow a copy of *Political Justice*. She had read the *Analytical*'s review and heard the book praised by William Frend. In the autumn of 1795 she moved close to Somers Town partly for 'the pleasure of *more frequent* conversations with you'.[32] There followed a heady round of conversation and quickly fired-off follow-up letters. In October 1795, she breathlessly wrote to Godwin: 'Your conversation excites the curiosity & the activity of my mind.'[33] For all the adulation, she was quite confident enough to feel she could disagree with him: 'Not that I am prepared to accord with you on every subject, for though I felt the force of many things you [said] in the discussion, which took place the last time I [had the] pleasure of seeing you, they did not bring conviction.'[34] Although some of the conditional nature of this relatively open space in terms of gendered hierarchies may be glimpsed in Hays's description of Godwin as her 'tutelary genius', for most of the 1790s Godwin, Hays, and Wollstonecraft were each of them, sometimes together, the beneficiaries of a rich culture of literary and intellectual sociability in London.[35]

GODWIN AND THE COLLISION OF MINDS

Abandoning a career as a dissenting minister, Godwin had moved to London in 1782 to be close to the heart of the national book trade.

---

[30] 'Godwin to Alderson', 'Correspondence of Amelia Alderson Opie (1794–1854)', Box 1, Op. 3, Huntington Library, San Marino, California; *Letters of Godwin*, 165. I am grateful to Harriet Guest and David O'Shaughnessy for drawing this letter to my attention.

[31] For a sympathetic account of Godwin's encouragement of women writers, especially in conversation, see Pamela Clemit, 'Godwin, Women, and "The Collision of Mind with Mind"', *Wordsworth Circle*, 35 (2004), 72–6.

[32] Hays to Godwin, 1 October 1795, *Correspondence*, 401 (Pforzheimer MH7).

[33] Hays to Godwin, 13 October 1795, ibid. (Pforzheimer MH8).

[34] Hays to Godwin, 28 July 1795, ibid. 395 (Pforzheimer MH6).

[35] Hays to Godwin, 10 May 1795, ibid. 393 (Pforzheimer MH5).

Participation in the sociable world of publishers and writers in the metropolis, centred in places like the Chapter Coffee House in St Paul's Churchyard, was important for anyone planning a career as a professional writer.[36] The bookshops of the Robinson brothers and Joseph Johnson were places of business, but also lounging rooms.[37] Johnson, like other publishers, also held more select dinners for his authors and others, in his case in the home above his shop (where the company, often disputatious, had at different times included Barbauld, Godwin, and Wollstonecraft). Godwin's diary and letters give a crowded picture of the sociable world of a writer often presented as an isolated rationalist, and it is worth remembering Hazlitt's account in *The Spirit of the Age* ends by acknowledging that the philosopher had 'kept the best company of his time' (xi.28).[38] Deliberately drawing attention to his own sociable world, Godwin's *Enquirer* essays announced his delight in 'the vivacity, and, if he may be permitted to say it, a richness, in the hints struck out in conversation, that are with difficulty attained in any other method'. The outcome of these conversable origins means that the essays come to the reader 'not as dicta, but as the materials of thinking'. Godwin signals a switch from the rational deliberation of *Political Justice* to an essayistic mode 'principally the result of conversations' (*PPW*, V: 78).

Taking him at his word, Rajan reads *The Enquirer* as a foundational 'Romantic' moment in the turn to hermeneutics. Unfortunately, Rajan doesn't address the conversational trope directly in her account of Godwin's hermeneutic turn. Her main focus is on his essay 'On Choice in Reading' and its discussion of ideas of 'morality' and 'tendency' in the making of meaning.[39] She understands Godwin's idea of 'tendency' as

---

[36] St. Clair, *The Godwins and the Shelleys*, 18–19.

[37] Johnson and the Robinsons were canny businessmen and their sociable networks certainly aided them in what Aikin and Barbauld thought of as the 'mart' of knowledge. See Peter Clark's discussion of the role of eighteenth-century sociable clubs in helping trade: *British Clubs and Societies, 1580–1800: The Origins of an Associational World* (Oxford: Oxford University Press, 2000), 152–5.

[38] Johnson is first mentioned in the diary as the host of the dinner for Paine in 1791. Godwin only attends the dinners regularly after 1797, which is not to say he didn't frequent the bookshop or even the dinners before then. See Beth Lau, 'William Godwin and the Joseph Johnson Circle: The Evidence of the Diaries', *Wordsworth Circle*, 33 (3) (2002), 104–8. On the richness and diversity of Godwin's conversational life from the 1780s to the late 1790s, see Clemit, 'Godwin, Women, and "The Collision of Mind"'; Mark Philp, *Godwin's Political Justice* (London: Duckworth, 1986), 35–7, 80–1, and 86; and Daniel E. White, *Early Romanticism and Religious Dissent* (Cambridge: Cambridge University Press, 2006), 97–106. Godwin's diary suggests he saw the Barbaulds quite often after 1789, although it is not always clear whether it is Anna Laetitia or her husband Rochemont—or both—who is mentioned.

[39] See Tilottama Rajan, *The Supplement of Reading: Figures of Understanding in Romantic Theory and Practice* (Ithaca/London: Cornell University Press, 1990), 168–9.

freeing the reader from an auxiliary relation to the text and its 'announced moral'. From this point of view, 'history' becomes 'the site of difference rather than of a vindication of authorial identity'. Rajan writes brilliantly about authorial anxieties surrounding texts opened up to a multiplicity of readers, including the 'divinatory hermeneutics' that allowed Godwin to impose 'a teleological direction on the history of reception'. She has very little to say about practices of reading and their relation to the social life of conversation shared by Godwin, Hays, and Wollstonecraft. 'Inscription of reading' within their texts is the primary focus of her analysis. Analysis of the sites of difference where reading took place and judgments were discussed need not imply any crude reflective relationship between social ground and textual production. Study of the social text as a form of mediation in itself has often been neglected in Romantic-period criticism, at least until very recently, but it represents a crucial perspective for understanding the writing of Godwin, Hays, and Wollstonecraft.[40]

Before going on to discuss *The Enquirer*, I want to expand further upon the version of conversation Godwin elaborates in *Political Justice*, where it appears much closer to what Habermas calls 'rational-critical debate' than it does in the later work. Victoria Myers has already offered an excellent account of the development of Godwin's ideas about conversation in *Political Justice*. She sees the key context as the tension between oratory and conversation in the Whig-republican political tradition. Oratory was identified with institutions such as the courts and Parliament, but its 'eloquence' was often perceived 'as dangerous to free institutions because of its ability to rouse the passions and put them under the control of a talented speaker'.[41] Myers argues that Godwin imagined new institutions of conversation and the press would come to replace the civic function of oratory and its dangerous appeal to the passions. Godwin 'absorbed classical oratory into the dialogic mode to make it appropriate to an anarchic system, a system in which decision-making under the authoritative headship of government would be replaced by local community and *ad hoc* discussion'. The result, as Myers sees it, represents a *via media* whereby Godwin is 'both more radical than the Whigs and less authoritarian than the revolutionaries in France'.[42] Later in this chapter I'll return to the question of where this formulation leaves British radical associa-

---

[40] See Gillian Russell and Clara Tuite, 'Introducing Romantic Sociability', in *eaedem* (eds), *Romantic Sociability: Social Networks and Literary Culture in Britain, 1770–1849* (Cambridge: Cambridge University Press, 2002), 4.
[41] Victoria Myers, 'William Godwin and the *Ars Rhetorica*', *Studies in Romanticism*, 41 (2002), 415–44 (415).
[42] Ibid. 419.

tions, who certainly thought themselves capable of maintaining a conversable world of their own.

The aspects of *Political Justice* discussed by Myers constitute a radicalization of ideas of civic conversation already associated with classical culture.[43] Its 'voluntary pledges of mind', as William Cook put it in the poem he published just three years after *Political Justice*, allowed 'rights' to be 'canvass'd' and 'laws develop'd for the public good'. Civic conversation was always conceived of as a relatively open medium of exchange beyond the coercive pressures associated with oratory. Conversation was understood to flourish in and play its part in maintaining societies 'free from tyrant rule'.[44] Acknowledging the classical republican aspects of Godwin's thinking explored by Myers, I would like to follow up the influence of ideas on conversation derived from the traditions of Rational Dissent in which Godwin was trained. Rowland Weston believes this aspect of Godwin's thinking produces an idea of '"conversation" conceived of as a disembodied "intercourse of mind with mind"'.[45] I think this rather underestimates the complexity of the commitment to conversation to be found both in Rational Dissent and in *Political Justice* itself. I'm confident that Godwin's metaphor of 'the collision of mind with mind' has its origins in those passages from Watts discussed in my first chapter. Watts was a friend of Godwin's grandfather's and his book would have been a set text in the Hoxton academy he attended, but Weston's broader analysis rather assumes Rational Dissent was an unsociable world of theological dispute.[46] Rational Dissent as a cultural formation tended to give at least as much emphasis to social discourse as private reflection or disembodied intellectuality. Watts negotiated between a commitment to truth and the polite taste Johnson credited him with giving to Dissent. Priestley may have been more sceptical about ideas of taste, but he enjoyed the vigorous sociability of places like the Club of Honest Whigs. Their combative ideas of conversation were scarcely disembodied, and often placed emphasis on the importance of the affections: 'A Hermit who has been shut up in his Cell in a College, has contracted a sort of Mould and Rust upon his Soul...The Rust and the Mould are filed and brusht off by polite Conversation. The *Scholar*

---

[43] See my introduction, p. 17 above.

[44] See the discussion of Cook's *Conversation* (1796) above, pp. 97–8.

[45] See Rowland Weston, 'Politics, Passion and the "Puritan Temper": Godwin's Critique of Enlightened Modernity', *Studies in Romanticism*, 41 (2002), 445–71 (448, quoting *PPW*, II: 505). Weston concentrates on the philosophical sources of Godwin's thinking rather than either his imagining of cultural geography or his social practices.

[46] On Watts's friendship with Godwin's grandfather, see St Clair, *The Godwins and the Shelleys*, 2.

now becomes a *Citizen* or a *Gentleman*, a *Neighbour* and a *Friend*.'[47] Books for Godwin, as they are for Watts, are primarily a preparative to 'candid and unreserved conversation' where those involved will 'compare their ideas...suggest their doubts...remove their difficulties' (*PPW*, III: 121). Where this formation of thought about conversation melds into the classical tradition is that conversation is an explicitly civic and improving process for both, one that transforms the solitary 'scholar' into the sociable 'citizen'.

Through ancestry, education, and in his social life, Godwin was a beneficiary of a culture of vigorous conversational exchange. In the wake of the publication of *Political Justice* (1793), he became an energetic participant in metropolitan talk. He criss-crossed London from John Horne Tooke's dinner table in Wimbledon to less salubrious gatherings in Joseph Gerrald's cell in Newgate. Godwin was a sociable animal, but within limits. Godwin always feared that large assemblies threatened to cloud the process of rational deliberation. Even when they were preaching his own doctrines, Godwin was concerned that popular speakers might be 'propagating blind zeal, where we meant to propagate reason' (*PPW*, III: 118). Writing after the French Revolution and the emergence in Britain of a popular radicalism, he saw an expansion of public debate on political matters that Watts never faced. The classical republican tradition discussed by Myers tended to oppose its civic idea of conversation to more populous forms of political debate, notwithstanding Junius Junior's spirited defence of the debating societies in 1780. Oratory was suspect precisely because of assumptions about the malleable passions of the crowd: 'If once the unambitious and candid circles of enquiring men be swallowed up in the insatiate gulf of noisy assemblies', as Godwin put it, 'the opportunity of improvement is instantly annihilated' (*PPW*, III: 122). Godwin did mix with radicals from the London Corresponding Society and Society of Constitutional Information, including, especially, John Thelwall, whom he first met at one of John Horne Tooke's dinners in Wimbledon.[48] Godwin even visited them in prison in Newgate in 1793, but he joined neither the London Corresponding Society (LCS) nor the

---

[47] Isaac Watts, *The Improvement of the Mind: or, a Supplement to the Art of Logick* (London, 1741), 44.

[48] Godwin's diary first records a meeting with Thelwall on 24 March 1793 at Horne Tooke's, along with other members of the SCI. See Abinger e. 4. Tooke had played an important role in Thelwall's political development from 1790. Thelwall regarded him 'in the light of his intellectual and political father'. See Cecil Thelwall, *The Life of John Thelwall by his Widow* (London, 1837), 76.

Society for Constitutional Information (SCI), nor does he seem to have attended their sometimes riotous anniversary dinners.[49]

[handwritten annotation: that Godwin was a Stalker but a rational one. Didn't like big groups? or not]

'DISCORDANT OPINIONS'

Although there was always a strain of metropolitan radicalism associated with tavern 'free-and-easies', other gatherings—often with the same personnel—aspired to a politer and even domestic practice.[50] Popular radical associations were also conversable worlds, at least in their own eyes, if not Godwin's or the anti-Jacobins who tried to shut them down. Richard Newton's two prints of social life among the state prisoners in Newgate, 'Promenade in the State Side of Newgate' and 'Soulagement en Prison, or Comforts in Prison' (both 1793), represent visitors (but not Godwin), at convivial conversational gatherings in the prison (see Figs. 4 and 5). The purpose may have been to show the enlightened civility of radical associations being sustained even under duress. 'The open countenances, the eager, genial expressions' of those participating, Iain McCalman suggests, imply 'ethical candour and benevolence'. At the far left of 'Soulagement en Prison', the presence of William Holland's wife and daughter suggests even the preservation of 'domestic virtue in an inhospitable setting'.[51] Members of the LCS set up their own 'conversazione' at their homes or

---

[49] At those relatively rare meetings attended by reformers from across the social spectrum, there were often complaints about the riotous behaviour of the LCS. See, for instance, the Privy Council interviews after the arrests for treason in 1794. John Wharton, MP for Beverly, was embarrassed by his participation at the SCI anniversary dinner on 2 May 1794, where he claimed 'many members of the London Corresponding Society were admitted as visitors, and certainly behaved very improperly' (TS11/963 ff 256–7, National Archive, Kew, London). The LCS member John Baxter was more robust about what his interrogators called 'persons of very inferior stations' (f 653). 'Whatever they were', Baxter replied (f 654), 'they were Persons who thought they had a good Right to express their Opinions on Public Matters.' Characteristically, Horne Tooke behaved as boisterously as anyone at the dinner. See Albert Goodwin, *The Friends of Liberty: The English Democratic Movement in the Age of the French Revolution* (Cambridge, MA: Harvard University Press, 1979), 330–1. Tooke's dinners at Wimbledon and other gatherings often showed something of the old libertine radicalism associated with Wilkes or the Beefsteak Club. Thelwall thought that Tooke's political principles were not 'sufficient to atone for all deficiencies of heart and morals' (*Life of Thelwall*, 352).

[50] On the tavern free-and-easy in radical culture, See Iain McCalman, *Radical Underworld: Prophets, Revolutionaries, and Pornographers in London, 1795–1840* (Cambridge: Cambridge University Press, 1988); David Worrall, *Radical Culture: Discourse, Resistance, and Surveillance, 1790–1820* (Detroit: Wayne State University Press, 1992); and James A. Epstein, *Radical Expression: Political Language, Ritual, and Symbol in England, 1790–1850* (New York/Oxford: Oxford University Press, 1994).

[51] See Iain McCalman, 'Newgate in Revolution: Radical Enthusiasm and Romantic Counterculture', *Eighteenth Century Life*, 22 (1998), 95–110 (96–8).

Fig. 4. Richard Newton, 'Promenade on the State Side of Newgate' (1793). Courtesy of the Huntington Library, San Marino, California.

shops, the word itself indicating the aspiration to participate in the civility of the eighteenth-century republic of letters and perhaps implying their own domestic virtues.[52] When she called on the shop of the radical publisher Daniel Isaac Eaton in 1794, Amelia Alderson was warmly welcomed by his wife and they 'so fraternized' that the shop was shut and the chairs drawn round for talk about the recent arrests in Edinburgh.[53] Godwin visited several radical gatherings for 'tea', as his diary

---

[52] When the informant James Powell, a member of the LCS, wrote to his government handlers, probably early in 1795, to complain of neglect, he gave an insight into this culture: 'Just after his acquittal, Thelwall established what was called a conversatione every Monday evening at his house to which the principal men of the party were invited. I also for the purpose above mention'd, knowing from the place I had then & your generosity I could afford it (indeed the expence was trifling bread & cheese & porter only being allowed) mine was more numerously attended even than Thelwalls.' Powell's undated letter is at the National Archives in Kew, London, at PC 1 23/38A.

[53] See Cecilia Brightwell, *Memorials of the Life of Amelia Opie*, 2 vols (Norwich, 1854), I: 43. Also present were Alderson's host in London, John Boddington, and a stranger who turned out to be Charles Sinclair, delegate of the SCI at the British Convention of November 1793. He had been arrested, but his trial was abandoned. The group discussed Sinclair's release. Alderson and Boddington were 'so charmed with his manners and conversation, that we almost fancied we had known him before'.

Fig. 5. Richard Newton, 'Soulagement en Prison' (1793). Courtesy of the Lewis Walpole Library, Yale University.

puts it, even meeting men like the ultra-radical Richard 'Citizen' Lee with Thelwall there, but his social life was usually more 'select'. Godwin shied away from encountering these men in more raucous situations.[54] *Political Justice* had warned that even 'the conviviality of a feast may lead to the depredations of a riot' (*PPW*, III: 118).

Godwin's attack on his sometime friend John Thelwall's political lecturing in *Considerations on Lord Grenville's and Mr. Pitt's Bills* (1795) certainly owes something to the selectivity of Addison's belief that 'Conversation is never so much streightened and confined as in numerous Assemblies' (*S* 68, I: 289).[55] Godwin's metaphors of friction in *Political Justice* suggest an open engagement with difference, but the kaleidoscopic

[54] Four times during January to February 1795 Godwin's diary shows that he took 'tea' at what seems to be Powell's conversazione in a group that included Thelwall and Citizen Lee. See Bodleian MS. Abinger e.4. On the 'Select Club', see below, 152.

[55] For a fuller account of the dispute between Godwin and Thelwall, see Jon Mee, '"The Press and Danger of the Crowd": Godwin, Thelwall, and the Counter-Public Sphere', in Robert Manaquis and Victoria Myers (eds), *Godwinian Moments: From the Enlightenment to Romanticism* (Toronto: Toronto University Press, 2011), 83–102. All references to *The Spectator* are to Donald F. Bond's edition, 5 vols (Oxford: Clarendon Press, 1987) as *S* followed by original issue number and then volume and page number.

possibilities revolved within a fairly tight circumference. His disagreement with Thelwall over the modalities of reform focused on whether the radical movement was capable of sustaining the open enquiry identified with conversation in *Political Justice*. In terms of his own associational practice beyond dinners and household visits, Godwin cultivated a regulated and circumscribed form of conversation. Between 1793 and 1796, for instance, Godwin was an active member of the Philomathian Society, which met in London every week or so to discuss philosophical and political issues. John Thelwall had composed an anniversary ode for the society in 1791 and in Godwin's time the society also welcomed men such as the Irish plumber John Binns (a leading LCS member from 1794).[56] Written and published before Thelwall joined the LCS, the anniversary poem he wrote for the society celebrates 'Wine, and Wit, and Jest, and Song', but also positions its meetings beyond 'the sordid herd, profane of vulgar joys'.[57] The Philomaths could countenance a social mix and celebrated convivial discussion, but it was a much more controlled environment than the popular debating clubs Thelwall frequented in the 1780s and 1790s. Twenty-one was the maximum number allowed at the Philomathian discussions, an hourglass regulated the time taken by each speaker.[58] The environment was close to that proposed at the 'Select Club' Godwin had discussed setting up with Maj. Alexander Jardine to debate *Political Justice*. Its 'Prospectus' speaks of a meeting of 'philosophic *minds,* in search of *truth*'. The list of names Godwin provided is made up of doctors, lawyers, 'intelligent artists', and leading Whigs such as Fox and Sheridan. There are '*No Rules,*—only to remember that truth, knowledge, mind being the chief object, no subject is to be excluded from conversation.' The paradox of unlimited enquiry within strictly regulated limits that runs through the eighteenth-century ideas on conversation here reappears in a distinctive form.[59]

---

[56] On the Philomathians, see St Clair, *The Godwins and the Shelleys*, 92–3, and John Thelwall, *Ode to science. Recited at the anniversary meeting of the Philomathian Society, June 20, 1791* (London 1791). Thewall's ode is dedicated to Henry Amory, a staunch dissenter who was educated at the Hoxton Academy, possibly with Godwin. I owe this information to David O'Shaughnessy. See his forthcoming essay '*Caleb Williams* and the Philomaths: Recalibrating Political Justice for the Nineteenth Century', *Nineteenth-Century Literature*.

[57] Thelwall, *Ode to science*, 8 and 5.

[58] John Binns, *Recollections of the Life of John Binns: Twenty-Nine Years in Europe and Fifty-Three in the United States* (Philadelphia, 1854), 45. Binns points out that the only speakers who had to be curtailed by the glass were Godwin and Thomas Holcroft. O'Shaughnessy suggests that John Fenwick, another LCS member and husband of Eliza Fenwick, may also have been a member. See '*Caleb Williams* and the Philomaths'.

[59] William Godwin, 'Prospectus for a Select Club', MS. Abinger c. 32. 'Truth' and 'knowledge' are added to 'mind' in the manuscript. See St Clair, *The Godwins and the Shelleys*, 91–2.

Thelwall was a member of the Philomathians from at least 1791, but he became a star of the more raucous space of the Society of Free Debate at Coachmakers' Hall, which he had attended from as early as 1783.[60] Encouraged by the Royal Proclamation of May 1792, magistrates began to take the action against this kind of gathering long advocated in newspapers.[61] Sir John Sewell called for the suppression of 'these clamorous theatres', even though he had been once 'an habitual frequenter'. What once he was willing to tolerate as a medium of healthy improvement, he now attacked as a dangerous vehicle of dissension. His *Critique on the French Revolution* (1793) is the transcript of his speech given at the Society in answer to 'a most flaming eulogium on the excellence of the new [French] constitution'.[62] The eulogist may well have been Thelwall, who was at the time battling to keep the Society in operation. In April 1792, the landlord of Coachmakers' Hall came to Thelwall with 'repeated indications of terror and alarm', and informed him that 'on account of the threats which had been directed against him by certain persons in authority, he could not venture to renew his agreement with us, unless we would covenant not to bring forward any questions of a political nature.' The Society moved to a tavern in Cornhill before being driven out of existence early the next season.[63]

The point of my continuing account of this one debating club is that Thelwall had practical experience of the way opinions could form themselves in the supposedly unpromising circumstances of popular debate. Like Junius Junior, Thelwall saw no necessary disconnection between such venues and the idea of conversation as a form of improvement. Indeed Thelwall's rebuttal of Godwin's criticisms was bitter against his restrictive view of what qualified as political conversation:

I was not *frantic enough*, though the 'Lover of Order' is, to suppose that this *consent of wills*, this 'magnificent harmony, expanding itself through the whole community', was to be produced by writing quarto volumes, and conversing with a few speculative philosophers by the fire side.[64]

---

[60] See the 'Prefatory Memoir' to Thelwall's *Poems written Chiefly in Retirement*, 2nd edn (Hereford, 1802), xxiii. Thelwall claimed his 'public career commenced at the debating society at Coachmakers' Hall'. He first appeared there when he was nineteen, taking Pitt's side on the India Bill against the Fox–North Coalition. His politics changed after his involvement with Horne Tooke at the 1790 Westminster election.

[61] Mary Thale, 'London Debating Societies in the 1790s', *Historical Journal*, 32 (1989), 57–86 (62).

[62] Sir John Sewell, *Critique on the late French Revolution, in a speech delivered at the Society for Free Debate* (London 1793), 7, 2, and 8.

[63] John Thelwall, *Political Lectures (No. 1) on the Moral Tendency of a System of Spies and Informers* (London, 1794), iii.

[64] John Thelwall, *The Tribune*, 3 vols (1795–6), II: xvii. Thelwall's reissue of *The Tribune* included his attack on Godwin in a preface from which this quotation comes.

Even before their dispute, Thelwall subscribed to a model of civic conversation that could interlace private conversation, debating societies, and other forms of popular association. He had given a speech at Coachmakers' Hall on precisely this topic. His position gives an account of the benefits of conversation much like the one found in Watts and Godwin: 'I never knew an instance of men of any principle frequently discussing any topic, without mutually correcting some opposite errors, and drawing each other towards some common standard of opinion; different perhaps, in some degree from that which either had in the first instance conceived, and apparently more consistent with the truth.' Like them, he also acknowledged the importance of private judgment in consolidating the discoveries made in discussion; it was, he believed, 'in the silence and solitude of the closet, that long rooted prejudices are *finally renounced*, and *erroneous* opinions changed.' Using the idea of discussion as a form of primary production developed by Hume, Thelwall went on to insist that 'the materials of truth are collected in conversation and debate; and the sentiment at which we most revolt, in the warmth of discussion, is frequently the source of meditations, which terminate in settled conviction.' The conviction was framed by an anticipation of a Godwinian gradualism: 'The harvest, it is true, is not instantaneous, and we must expect that the seed should lie raked over for a while, and apparently perish, before the green blade of promise can begin to make its appearance, or the crop be matured.' Even so, from Thelwall's perspective only democratizing conversation could bring about enlightenment:

But how is this to be discovered, unless the parties freely compare their sentiments?—If discussion be shackled, how are discordant opinions to be adjusted, but by tumult and violence? If societies of free inquiry are suppressed, what power, what sagacity, in such an age as this, shall preserve a nation from the convulsions that follow the secret leagues and compact of armed conspiracy.[65]

Although it was almost certainly made no later than 1792, there is much in the speech that sounds like the Godwin of *Political Justice*. Thelwall's account of the collision of mind balanced against the final authority of the deliberations of the closet are typical of Godwin's writing, as is the slow harvest of truth, but what is really striking about the speech is the place where it was made. Its most likely occasion would have been the debate of 24 May 1792, just after the Royal Proclamation against seditious writings. The debate that day addressed the question of whether 'Associations for Political Purposes [are] likely to promote the happiness of the people, by informing their minds, or to make them discontented without

[65] Thelwall, *Life of Thelwall*, 51–2.

redressing their grievances?'[66] In answer to this question, Thelwall was promoting a debate far beyond the confines of the kind of conversation encouraged by Godwin and doing it in a place that the philosopher was to define as inappropriate to deliberative reasoning. The associations of the site were still strong enough in 1811 for Coleridge to reject Coachmakers' Hall as a venue for his lecture series on Shakespeare.[67]

Thelwall was not without his own political ambiguities on such matters, as the comments about the 'vulgar herd' in his Philomathian ode suggest, but he continued to insist 'mixed assemblies' were as capable of promoting the deliberative achievements of rational conversation as 'the domestic tranquility of the fireside'.[68] In 1795 he disrupted a meeting of the Philomathians to confront Godwin about the attack on his lecturing.[69] Defending himself in print against Godwin's attack, Thelwall insisted:

It is by conversation that the mind is quickened and the obstinacy of dogmatic confidence softened: it is in 'mixed and crowded audiences' [terms used by Godwin in his attack] ...—'in theatres and halls of assembly' [again Godwin's terms] that the real lover of his species must principally expect to inspire that generous sympathy—that social ardour, without which a nation is but a populous wilderness, and the philosopher only a walking index of obsolete laws and dead-lettered institutes.[70]

Thelwall made no sharp distinction between his participation in free debate and his domestic situation. Beaufort Buildings provided him not only with a lecture theatre, but also a bookshop, a meeting place for the LCS, and a home for his family.[71] Nor were the political meetings only on official LCS business. Beaufort Buildings was also where Thelwall set up his own 'conversazione' early in 1795, opening a space that included political with other forms of sociability. Godwin himself attended a lecture and then supped with Thelwall and other radicals afterwards in the lecturer's apartment.[72] Government repression after 1792, and, especially,

[66] Donna T. Andrew, *London Debating Societies, 1776–1799* (London: London Record Society, 1994), 321.

[67] See Gillian Russell, 'Spouters or Washerwomen: The Sociability of Romantic Lecturing', in Russell and Tuite (eds), *Romantic Sociability*, 123–44 (139).

[68] Thelwall, *Tribune*, II: xiv–v, again throwing Godwin's own phrases back at him.

[69] Godwin's diary for 22 December 1795 records 'Philomths, statesmen; explanation w. Thelwal'.

[70] Thelwall, *Tribune*, II: xiv–v.

[71] See Russell, 'Spouters or Washerwomen', 126, and Judith Thompson, 'From Forum to Repository: A Case Study in Romantic Cultural Geography', *European Romantic Review*, 15 (2004), 177–91.

[72] See Godwin's diary entry for 12 June 1795: 'Thelwal's Lecture: sup at Thelwal's, w. Richters, Warren, Ritson{,} Walker & Mannings; adv. Wadstrom'. I am grateful to James Grande for this information.

after the Two Acts of 1795, which so alarmed Katherine Plymley, was also often represented by radicals like Thelwall in terms of an invasion of privacy. The scandal of informants straining 'to catch and to betray the idle conversation of your unguarded moments', whether in coffee shops or in more domestic circumstances, became a staple of radical protest against Pitt's Terror.[73]

A POLITE ENQUIRER

Godwin's dispute with Thelwall and the intensification of government intervention against radical associations must have played their part in the production of *The Enquirer* essays. Defined as the products of conversation, promising to generate even more talk among their readers, they also repudiate the more abrasive model of conversation Godwin imagined in *Political Justice*. Furthermore, conversation appears as a distinctive political modality there, even if defined within prescribed limits; now in *The Enquirer* conversation is largely defined against political discourse. The process may be anticipated in *Caleb Williams* (1794), where Godwin reconfigures the possibility of conversation as a variety of public discussion in order to 'draw its reader into a private individualized conversation with the text'.[74] As well as Godwin's immediate situation in the 1790s, these changes must be placed in relation to the larger story of the withdrawal of conversation from mixed social space. Much as *Political Justice* seems resistant to such changes, the lectures on rhetoric and belles-lettres Godwin heard from Andrew Kippis at the Hoxton Dissenting academy in 1773 had emphasized the importance of politeness to 'the genteel &

[73] See Thelwall's *Moral Tendency of a System of Spies and Informers*, 7. See also Corinna Wagner, 'Domestic Invasions: John Thelwall and the Exploitation of Privacy', in Steve Poole (ed.), *John Thelwall: Radical Romantic and Acquitted Felon* (London: Pickering and Chatto, 2009), 95–106. Thomas Muir was prosecuted on the basis of snatches of his conversation overheard by a domestic servant: see *An Account of the Trial of Thomas Muir* (Edinburgh, 1793), 113–16. For other cases where the defence claimed coffee shop conversations were 'private', see John Barrell, *The Spirit of Despotism: Invasions of Privacy in the 1790s* (Oxford: Oxford University Press, 2006), 75–102, and James Epstein, '"Equality and No King": Sociability and Sedition—The Case of John Frost', in Russell and Tuite (eds), *Romantic Sociability*, 43–61.

[74] See Kristen Leaver, 'Pursuing Conversations: *Caleb Williams* and the Romantic Construction of the Reader', *Studies in Romanticism*, 33 (1994), 589–610 (606). Leaver constructs a polarity between the public sphere and privatized conversation that rather ignores the possibility of 'public conversation'. For an analysis more in tune with my own approach, which sees *Caleb Williams* as creating 'only to foreclose the promise of an ameliorative public opinion' (245), see Nicolle Jordan, 'The Promise and Frustration of Plebeian Public Opinion in *Caleb Williams*', *Eighteenth-Century Fiction*, 19 (2007), 243–66.

affable part of the Dissenters' (and recommended 'Hume's Essay on the delicacy of Taste & passion').[75] Godwin knew and mixed socially with Dissenters who were committed to a version of public discourse based on the domestic virtues promoted by, for instance, the Aikin family, as his diary shows. Turning towards the possibilities of this more domestic idea of conversation, *The Enquirer* essays quite self-consciously turn away from the method of *Political Justice*, 'a work upon the principles of political science, published by the same author four years ago'. The transformation is figured as a move from high political discourse into the 'humbler walks of private life':

He ardently desires that those who shall be active in promoting the cause of reform, may be found amiable in their personal manners, and even attached to the cultivation of miscellaneous enquiries. He believes that this will afford the best security, for our preserving kindness and universal philanthropy, in the midst of the operations of our justice. (PPW, V: 77 and 79)

From this perspective, a revised version of conversation becomes a way of keeping alive at least the possibility of political change—a utopian micro-cosm against Pitt's anti-Jacobin repression—but also modulates Godwin's commitment to reform into a more personal and affective discourse.

The two-part essay 'Of Politeness' in *The Enquirer* is a key text in this development. Godwin notes there that men of 'sublime virtues'—impli-citly the republican tradition in either its classical or Rousseauvian inflec-tion—have been apt to disparage the discourse of politeness as a form of exclusion. Confirming that such uses of politeness deserve 'decisive disap-probation' (*PPW*, V: 221), he nevertheless goes on to offer an alternative account, in the process providing a (false) etymology connected to 'polis', that is, consonant with the idea of conversation as a version of civic virtue. These virtues are examples of the 'lesser morality', a phrase with a distinctly Addisonian flavour, which 'the heart can record, but which the tongue is rarely competent to relate' (*PPW*, V: 222).[76] In this regard, Godwin acknowledges the importance of conversation as small change in the circulation of virtue, but the cadences go beyond Addison and antici-pate the Wordsworthian moment of 'Tintern Abbey'. No wonder that Rajan and others have so often understood *The Enquirer* as Godwin

---

[75] Andrew Kippis, 'Introductory Lectures to the Belles Lettres', Lecture III, Harris Man-chester College, Oxford, Ms, Belsham 4, f. 36. I am grateful to Stephen Burley for supplying me with a transcript of the Kippis lecture.
[76] The essay echoes *Spectator* no. 93, where Addison addresses himself explicitly to 'those only who are not always engaged in Scenes of Action' (*S* 93, I: 395). See the discussion of Addison's essay pp. 40–2. Godwin had been reading Addison for the essay on English style in *The Enquirer*.

making a Romantic turn towards something far more deeply interfused. Yet Godwin does not entirely abandon the republican principles of *Political Justice*. The redefinition of conversation in terms of politeness is an uneasy and uneven process. Godwin signals his awareness that for writers like Hume and Swift the ideas of courtliness and politeness had gone together.[77] Defensive of his own republican heritage, even as he prepares a strategic retreat, Godwin insists that it 'does not seem reasonable to suppose that the abolition of servility should be the diminution of kindness' (*PPW*, V: 225). Moving on from the discomforting prospect of political default, the second part of the essay addresses 'the reciprocal claims of politeness and sincerity' (*PPW*, V: 81).[78] In the process, he touches on some of the issues surrounding Barbauld's notion of devotional taste and the implicit question of where politeness left candour, contention, and moral truth. While warning against sincerity for its own sake, he nevertheless insists on the important civic function of candour among 'the cardinal interests of a human being, the great stamina of his happiness'. Godwin continues to assert that 'politeness is of a humbler nature', but now it appears a more necessary virtue. And the essay ends with a somewhat melancholy closing shot of this humble virtue personified: 'It follows in the same direction, like a gleaner in a cornfield, and picks up and husbands those smaller and scattered ears of happiness, which the pride of Stoicism, like the pride of wealth, condescended not to observe' (*PPW*, V: 231). The uneasy weighing of the different virtues here casts a melancholy eye backwards on the republican civic virtues. *The Enquirer* backs away from the culture of candid enquiry expounded in *Political Justice* towards a more polite and affective idea of conversation.

The Spectator had frequently figured the virtues of conversation in feminized terms, but also continually worried about the dangerous proximity of a lighter world of gossip and chit-chat. There may be a similarly ambivalently gendered aspect to the melancholy retreat at the end of Godwin's essay, a kind of sad acceptance of the feminized virtues of the gleaner (a task often, of course, left to women workers and children in the fields). In his *Memoirs* of Wollstonecraft, first published in 1798, Godwin self-consciously represented himself as the beneficiary of a dialectical relationship between his rationalism and the sensibility of his recently

---

[77] Swift is discussed in the essays on English style in *The Enquirer*. Godwin's diary has many references to reading Hume during this period, including the *Essays*. He was also reading Shaftesbury, who definitely did not see the relationship between conversation and politeness as a species of courtliness. For the relevant essays in *The Enquirer*, see *PPW*, V: 268–77.

[78] Godwin's list of contents gives this phrase as the subtitle of the second section of the essay.

deceased wife.[79] The resultant portrait of Wollstonecraft downplayed her own commitment to a rational-critical ideal of conversation—those 'brilliant, forcible, instructive' aspects of Wollstonecraft's talk that delighted Mary Hays—in the interests of playing up her sensibility to his own advantage. Godwin subsumes the feminine into an image of himself as a more complete being. In the process, he may redefine rather than abandon the Whig-republican version of conversation as a civic institution, but the acceptance of the feminized conversable world is equivocal, and effaces what he knew of the combative conversation of women in the circles he and Wollstonecraft frequented. Rajan has suggested that 'the dialogical nature of conversation makes us aware that understanding cannot simply posit something by negating something else, but is made up of differences.'[80] She is equally acute on the ways that Romantic writers exploited the participatory attractions of the conversational turn to shore up their authority. In *The Enquirer*, Godwin reconfigures himself as an everyman attuned to the humbler walks of life, matured by exposure to the particularities of difference. Conversation now, as with Addison and Hume's view of the importance of the 'select' club, is understood in this rewriting to work best when it narcissistically encounters difference as the familiar. Instead of a field of historical difference, reception of the writer's work turns out to be an affirmation of the self.

'SENTIENT LANGUAGE'

This change in Godwin's understanding of conversability can be related to developments in the thinking of Hays and Wollstonecraft, found, especially, in two of their texts he was reading (and discussing) only weeks before he began writing *The Enquirer* essays.[81] Wollstonecraft increasingly adjusted her attitude to refinement and manners, although in a much more complex manner than Godwin's representation of her as a creature of sensibility allows. Her *Letters written during a short residence in Sweden, Norway, and Denmark* (1796) is a book that could be described as conversational for more than one reason. Her preface affiliates the book with travel writing that orients itself towards an affective relationship with the reader rather than the delivery of facts and figures:

---

[79] See White, *Early Romanticism*, 113–18, and *Memoirs of the Author of A Vindication of the Rights of Woman*, ed. Pamela Clemit and Gina Luria Walker (Peterborough, Ont.: Broadview, 2001).

[80] Rajan, *The Supplement of Reading*, 124.

[81] Godwin read Wollstonecraft's *Letters written during a short residence in Sweden, Norway, and Denmark* (1796) in January and Hays's *Memoirs of Emma Courtney* (1796) in March before he began writing the essays for *The Enquirer* in July 1796. See 'Godwin's Diary', MS. Abinger e. 7.

I therefore determined to let my remarks and reflections flow unrestrained, as I perceived that I could not give a just description of what I saw, but by relating the effect different objects had produced on my mind and feelings, while the impression was still fresh.[82]

Earlier signs of Wollstonecraft thinking about the question of reader relations in these terms are present in her review of Hester Piozzi's *Observations and Reflections made in the Course of a Journey through France, Italy, and Germany* (1789). Piozzi was chided by a number of critics for using 'language not suited to the printed page'.[83] 'Colloquial expressions' and those 'childish feminine terms, which occur in common novels and thoughtless chat' marred Piozzi's book for Wollstonecraft too.[84] Nevertheless, Wollstonecraft's review does acknowledge a potential in Piozzi's conversational style:

These travels are very desultory, and have all the lax freedom of letters without that kind of insinuating interest, which slightly binds a nosegay of unconnected remarks, and throws a thin, but graceful veil over egotism; the substitution of one for I, is a mere cobweb.[85]

The 'Advertisement' to *A short residence in Sweden, Norway, and Denmark* suggests Wollstonecraft saw herself as exploiting the potential in her own travel book:

A person has a right, I have sometimes thought, when amused by a witty or interesting egotist, to talk of himself when he can win on our attention by acquiring our affection. Whether I deserve to rank amongst this privileged number, my readers alone can judge—and I give them leave to shut the book, if they do not wish to become better acquainted with me.

If Wollstonecraft's conversational style undergoes an affective turn here, it is not exactly 'polite' in its assertion of independence. Amelia Alderson, like a number of reviewers, believed Wollstonecraft's book had given her a glimpse of 'the woman' behind 'the philosopheress':

---

[82] Mary Wollstonecraft, *Letters written during a short residence in Sweden, Norway, and Denmark* (London, 1796), 'Advertisement' [np]. On 'affective realism' in late eighteenth-century travel writing, see Nigel Leask, *Curiosity and the Aesthetics of Travel Writing 1770–1840* (Oxford: Oxford University Press, 2002), 42.

[83] See James L. Clifford, *Hester Lynch Piozzi (Mrs. Thrale)*, 2nd edn (Oxford: Clarendon Press, 1952), 343.

[84] *Analytical Review*, 4 (June 1789), 142–6, and 4 (July 1789), 301–6. Quotations from 301. See also the criticism of Piozzi in Wollstonecraft, *Vindication of the Rights of Woman*, 227–8.

[85] *Analytical Review*, 4 (June 1789). 142.

I saw nothing but the interesting creature of feeling, & imagination, & I resolved if possible, to become acquainted with one who had alternately awakened my sensibility & gratified my judgement.[86]

Alderson was subtle enough to recognize that the affective turn had not abandoned other kinds of question. Given Alderson herself had grown up a participation in the vigorous civic culture of Norwich, her ability to value Wollstonecraft's appeal to 'sensibility' *and* 'judgement' [my italics] is unsurprising.[87] If Wollstonecraft's travel book represents a reorientation of her ideas on the importance of manners, anticipating and possibly influencing Godwin's shift in *The Enquirer*, there is a continuing dialogue within her text between spartan republican values and her expressed need for the literary and cultural refinements of modernity: 'Still nothing so soon wearies out the feelings as unmarked simplicity. I am, therefore, half convinced that I could not live comfortably exiled from the countries where mankind are so much further advanced in knowledge...My thoughts fly from this wilderness to the polished circles of the world.'[88] The question of which conditions best conspire to provide good conversation is a constant theme in the book. Early on she notes how the restricted 'sphere of observation' in country towns prevents good political talk.[89] At the end of *A short residence in Sweden, Norway, and Denmark*, 'the conversation ever flowing in the muddy channels of business' fuels Wollstonecraft's disgust with the commercial port of Hamburg.[90]

Another kind of debate with Rousseau also sustains Wollstonecraft's book. The imaginative reveries, strategically placed throughout, impressed

---

[86] 'Alderson to Wollstonecraft', 28 August 1796, MS. Abinger c. 41.

[87] A visitor to Katherine Plymley's home in 1795 noted that 'the ladies in general, on the eastern side the kingdom are well versed in politics, & conversed with freedom on the subject' (*KPN* 35). See the notebooks of Katherine Plymley at the Shropshire Archives, Shrewsbury, MS 1066/1-197. All in-text references are to the relevant notebook number preceded by *KPN*. Among them was Catherine Buck, the future wife of the abolitionist Thomas Clarkson, who was recalled as 'in conversation quite brilliant sometimes'. See Gleadle's '"Opinions deliver'd in conversation"', 74–5. Alderson mixed and talked politics with people like Godwin and Robert Merry, not to mention Thomas Hardy, secretary of the LCS. See, for instance, her letter to Godwin of 5 February 1796, MS. Abinger c. 3, ff. 16–17, where she mentions having passed him a message via Hardy. On Norwich and political associations and societies in this period, see C. B. Jewson, *The Jacobin City: A Portrait of Norwich in Its Reaction to the French Revolution 1788–1802* (Glasgow: Blackie, 1975), and Penelope J. Corfield and Chris Evans (eds), *Youth and Revolution in the 1790s: Letters of William Pattison, Thomas Amyot and Henry Crabb Robinson* (Stroud: Allan Sutton, 1996). See Corfield and Evans, 189, for Alderson's contributions to *The Cabinet* (1794–5), a product of the city's reformist and literary circles.

[88] Wollstonecraft, *A short residence in Sweden, Norway, and Denmark*, 116–17.

[89] Ibid. 20, see also 32–3. [90] Ibid. 259.

many early readers, including, predictably enough, Coleridge and Southey, but they are increasingly repudiated in favour of a return to social and political questions ('*men's questions*' as she calls them early on, recoding the sometimes surprised responses of her interlocutors to her directness of address). What this doesn't mean is any easy acceptance of a relationship between refinement and commerce found in Addison and Hume as the bitter comments on Hamburg at the end of the book make clear.[91] Unlike her *Historical and Moral View of the French Revolution* (1794), largely written during the Terror, the travel book has a more confident statement of the imminence of universal revolution:

> An ardent affection for the human race makes enthusiastic characters eager to produce alteration in laws and governments prematurely. To render them useful and permanent, they must be the growth of each particular soil, and the gradual fruit of the ripening understanding of the nation, matured by time, not forced by an unnatural fermentation. And, to convince me that such a change is gaining ground, with accelerating pace, the view I have had of society, during my northern journey, would have been sufficient, had I not previously considered the grand causes which combine to carry mankind forward, and diminish the sum of human misery.[92]

The idea of 'each particular soil' determining the outcome of the revolutionary decade might sound like Godwinian gradualism, but her faith that change is 'gaining ground' sounds a more urgent note. *A short residence in Sweden, Norway, and Denmark* in this regard at least, retains rather more political force in the reorientation towards manners than it was allowed to keep in *The Enquirer*.

Godwin was an ardent admirer of Wollstonecraft's book and it profoundly influenced his estimation of his future wife. It may also have played its part in the revision of his thinking about the affections, but perhaps not as directly as the conversation—both verbally and by letter – he kept up with Mary Hays from late 1794.[93] Hays herself praised Wollstonecraft's book as 'a work that addresses itself to the heart, and

---

[91] On 'men's questions', see Wollstonecraft, *A short residence in Sweden, Norway, and Denmark*, 13. For Coleridge and Southey on Wollstonecraft's book, see 'To Thomas Southey, April 28, 1797', *The Life and Correspondence of the Late Robert Southey*, ed. C. C. Southey, 6 vols (London, 1849), II: 311, and John Livingston Lowes, *The Road to Xanadu: A Study in the Ways of the Imagination*, 2nd rev. edn (London, 1951), 161.

[92] Wollstonecraft, *A short residence in Sweden, Norway, and Denmark*, 'Appendix' [np].

[93] Wollstonecraft was a participant in this conversable circle from January 1796, as Godwin's diary shows. For Godwin's opinion of Wollstonecraft's book, see *Memoirs*, 129: 'The occasional harshness and ruggedness of character, that diversify her Vindication of the Rights of Woman, here totally disappear. If ever there was a book calculated to make a man in love with its author, this appears to me to be the book.'

seizes on its affections'.[94] Compared to either Godwin or Wollstonecraft, Hays always had a much stronger emphasis on the role of the affections in human relations. Her correspondence with Godwin frequently discussed the subject (his answers, often quoted back to him in her letters, usually came in face-to-face conversation). As early as her second letter to Godwin, from 7 December 1794, she was writing that 'notwithstanding I had multiplied sorrows in the indulgence of private affections, I started at the idea of their annihilation, & could not but regard them as the centre of humanity from whence embracing a wider, & still wider, circle, emanated that sublimer sympathy which acknowledges no other limits than those of animated nature.'[95] Whereas Godwin insisted on a 'disinterested benevolence', she described herself as 'a materialist': 'Man appears to me to be but of one substance, capable of receiving from external impressions sensible ideas, successively formed into various combinations & trains, carried on, by means of sympathy & association with mechanical exactness, in an infinite series of causes & effects.'[96] One consequence of this emphasis was that she often perceived conversation in terms of an open-hearted intercourse able to transcend verbal expression. Whereas for Hume, for instance, it was from social talk that one could learn sympathy, for Hays sympathy sometimes became a pre-requisite of conversation taking place at all.

The narcissistic strain found in writing on conversation from very early on in the century, the preference for select groups reflecting back one's own social identity or aspirations, is increasingly taken to a new level in the literary treatments of conversation from around the 1770s. Often the turn is represented as a reaction against the emptiness of fashionable chat. In *Memoirs of Emma Courtney*, Hays distinguishes 'genuine effusions of the heart and mind' from 'the vain ostentation of sentiment, lip deep, which, causing no emotion, communicates none'.[97] One result of this kind of distinction, as in Sterne and Mackenzie, could be an emphasis on the body, but this response tended to bring with it a further anxiety about sex tainting the purer affections (a reason Hays upbraided Godwin's veneration of Sterne).[98] At one point at least, Emma Courtney expresses a preference for 'conversing at a distance' by letter, because of the awing

---

[94] Mary Hays, 'Memoirs of Mary Wollstonecraft', *Annual Necrology, 1797–8* (London, 1800), 411–60 (439).

[95] Hays to Godwin, 7 December 1797, *Correspondence*, 385 (Pforzheimer MH2).

[96] Hays to Godwin, 1 October 1795, *Correspondence*, 400 (Pforzheimer MH7).

[97] Mary Hays, *Memoirs of Emma Courtney*, 2 vols (London, 1796), II: 14.

[98] See Hays to Godwin, 1 October 1795, *Correspondence*, 399 (Pforzheimer MH7). 'The *mere ribaldry* of *Tristram Shandy*', she tells Godwin, 'is, in my opinion, on every account more censurable, for it has not even the merit of simplicity.'

presence of the 'penetrating glance' of Mr. Francis.[99] These issues gain extensive treatment in Hay's complex novel, much of it based on the correspondence and conversations with Godwin and with William Frend over 1794–6. *Emma Courtney* charts the development of an ardent young woman who is educated first through solitary reading ('conversing only with books').[100] Emma then graduates to the sociable conversation at her father's table, an uneven mix of fashionable gallantry and worldly intellectualism. It is there she first meets Mr. Francis, who provides her with the rational conversation for which she hungers. The conversations with Mr Francis—literal and epistolary—fulfill the notion of the medium's ability to give vigour and spark to intellectual life. Later isolated with her unsympathetic relations at Morton Park, she relies on Francis's letters to provide the social converse without which her mind 'wanted *impression*, and sunk into languor' (an echo of Wollstonecraft's *A short residence in Sweden, Norway, and Denmark*, read by Hays as she wrote her novel).[101] Emma also finds relief in the conversation of a neighbour, Mrs Harley (the surname, of course, of Mackenzie's hero in *The Man of Feeling*), but her incessant return to the virtues of her son Augustus so impresses Emma that her enthusiastic nature converts him into a version of Rousseau's St Preux. Gazing at Harley's picture in the library, she imagines a communion with it that allows her to 'read in the features all the qualities imputed to the original by a tender and partial parent'.[102] The kind of vigorous conversation Hays had practised intensely with Godwin and others is substituted for Emma by a kind of experience centred on sensibility. 'Cut off from the society of mankind', as Emma puts it herself, she gives in to a tendency to 'reverie' associated with Rousseau (a pattern, of course, also explored in Wollstonecraft's book).[103] When Emma actually encounters Harley, they do enjoy a happy form of domestic sociability: 'our intervals from study were employed in music, in drawing, in conversation, in reading the *belles lettres*—in—"The feast of reason, and the flow of souls".'[104] Emma understands Pope's ubiquitous line as a form of mind matching, a transparent communion, not the conviviality of a bookseller's suppers Barbauld's niece had used it to describe. What she discovers is that others do not always respond as she wishes. Emma finds not the pure communion her enthusiasm demands but resistance and rejection. Even Augustus's mother adopts a new reserve when faced with the arduous freedom of Emma's conversation.

---

[99] Hays, *Emma Courtney*, I: 73 and 85.
[100] Ibid. I: 86.   [101] Ibid. I: 89.   [102] Ibid. I: 113.
[103] Ibid. I: 113.   [104] Ibid. I: 139.

Part of Emma's response to rejection and the drying up of the flow of conversation is to dream of a language that transcends the mediations of the language and to an extent even those of the body. She writes to Augustus Harley wishing 'we were in the vehicular state, and that you understood the sentient language; you might then comprehend the whole of what I mean to express, but find too delicate for *words*.'[105] The phrase 'sentient language' was taken from Abraham Tucker's *The Light of Nature Pursued* (1768–77), a huge rambling work, popular in Rational Dissenting circles, where it represents the possibility of 'raising certain figures or motions on our outsides which communicate the like to our neighbour and thereby excite in him the same ideas that gave rise to them in ourselves, making him as it were feel our thoughts'.[106] The problem explored in the novel is that the yearning for a sympathy that transcends the quagmire of verbal mediation continually leads Emma astray, offering precisely the kind of critique that Barbauld and Thelwall were to offer to Coleridge's poetry around this time. What Hays adds to this analysis is a gender politics that presents Emma's enthusiasm as the reaction of a powerful mind to the paucity of opportunity to participate in candid conversation (whether personally with Augustus Harley or more generally).[107] Faced with the 'insipid *routine* of heartless, mindless intercourse', 'an ardent spirit, denied a scope for its exertions!' inevitably projects communion onto its surroundings.[108] When Mr. Francis recommends 'independence', abstracting herself from her feelings, Emma replies, 'why call her to *independence*—which not nature, but the barbarous and

---

[105] Ibid. I: 177–8.
[106] See Abraham Tucker's *The Light of Nature Pursued*, 7 vols (1768–77), IV: 135. For a discussion of its use in *Emma Courtney*, see James Chandler, 'The Languages of Sentiment', *Textual Practice*, 22 (1988), 21–39. Hazlitt abridged the book for Joseph Johnson in 1807. Coleridge had proposed the idea and Godwin acted as Hazlitt's mediator with the publisher. See Duncan Wu, *William Hazlitt: The First Modern Man* (Oxford: Oxford University Press, 2008), 87 and 105.
[107] The critique was anticipated to some degree by Eliza Fenwick's *Secresy*, 3 vols (London, 1795), another novel produced from within these circles. Fenwick's novel opens with Caroline Ashburn pleading with the guardian of her young friend Sibella: 'Gladly would I devise a means by which to induce you to lay aside this prejudice against us, and in the language of reason, as from one being to another, discuss with me the merits or defects of your plan' (I: 3). Where the guardian wishes to educate his ward in seclusion, Caroline is an advocate of the merits of rational conversation for women. Later (I: 128), Caroline tells Lady Barlowe that Sibella only 'wishes for communication, for intercourse, for society; but she is too sincere to purchase any pleasure, by artifice and concealment'. The novel's love plot ends tragically because of the failure of the hero and heroine to find an adequate means of communication.
[108] Hays, *Emma Courtney*, I: 168 and 169. For the relevant letter to Godwin, 28 July 1795, see *Correspondence*, 394 (Pforzheimer MH 6).

accursed laws of society, have denied her.'[109] Faced with a similar situation on her trip to Scandinavia, disentangling herself from her relationship with Gilbert Imlay, Wollstonecraft had insisted on her right still to ask 'men's questions' about politics and society within an affective idea of conversation, a complexity of response that the gendered binaries at work at the end of Godwin's essay 'Of Politeness' struggle to allow (even as he struggled to allow it room in his account of Wollstonecraft as a creature of feeling in the memoir).

The drive to telepathy as described in Hays is not a simple conservative disavowal of the collisions of the public sphere, but an exploration of a pathology of the radical desire for reciprocity without mediation or contact, found also, for instance, in Rousseau (and perhaps even Habermas). Godwin, Hays, and Wollstonecraft lived out their developing ideas of the conversable world after Mary's return to London and her marriage to the philosopher, but they did so in an atmosphere of paranoia about Pitt's government's desire to restrict freedom of speech even in quasi-domestic situations. To increase the claustrophobia, they faced numerous satirical representations of their conversations in the anti-Jacobin novels that flooded from the press after 1795. For Godwin himself, even as he adapted to the new situation of the literary world in the 1790s, there remained a sense of the passing away of the civic conversation of the eighteenth-century republic of letters. What remained for Godwin was a melancholy sense of loss, including his own version of Emma's pangs before the portrait of Augustus when he wrote to Robert Merry on 27 July 1797. Reading *The British Album* (1790), a volume that gathered together the Della Cruscan poetry that had made Merry's name, Godwin turned to the portrait that provided the frontispiece to the volume:

I formerly despised it. But now the distance between us is so immense, I can look at it with pleasure, can trace in fancy the mind of the author while I contemplate. & can almost talk to it. I recollect at the same time the social qualities of the ~~author~~ original, dearer to my mind than his poetical emanations.[110]

As we have already seen, Merry was noted for his abilities as a conversationalist. He had become close to Godwin after escaping France in 1793. From 1794, he flourished as a talker in those Norwich circles well known for their open conversation, but he was unable to make a living in the theatre because of his radical associations. In September 1796, he

[109] Hays, *Emma Courtney*, II: 107. Compare the letter to Godwin, 6 February 1796, *Correspondence*, 426 (Pforzheimer MH 12).
[110] MS. Abinger c. 21. I am grateful to Pamela Clemit for supplying me with a transcription of this letter. See *Letters of Godwin*, 232.

emigrated to the United States with his wife, the actress Anne Brunton (where they were to be joined by John Bernard). Amelia Alderson, charmed like many others by Merry's conversational powers, was unable to imagine how he would get on there. She wrote to Godwin:

I wish much to know how he looked & talk'd when he bade you adieu—whether he was most full of hope, or dejection—My heart felt heavy when I heard he was really gone, & gone too where I fear the charms of his conversation, and his talents will not be relished as they desire to be.[111]

Alderson and Godwin shared an assumption that the United States was either too primitive or too commercial to sustain a conversable world. They were making calculations in London akin to Wollstonecraft's in Scandinavia as they began to experience the disappearance and erasure of its vigorous culture of critical conversation. Godwin's mournful communion with Merry's portrait speaks for a sense of the loss of conversation felt by many in the 1790s and afterwards. In it we might see a trace of a particular kind of displacement as compensation, Emma Courtney's dream of 'a sentient language' whereby a conversational world thick with socialized and gendered mediation, not to mention the unwelcome attentions of government spies, could be transcended. It was a dream of intellectual flow without collision that was to become a recurrent trope in the poetry of British Romanticism.

---

[111] 'Alderson to Godwin', 14 October 1796, MS. Abinger c. 3. Contrary to the expectations of Alderson and Godwin, Merry actually celebrated the 'social converse' he found in Philadelphia in America. See Jon Mee, 'Morals, Manners, and Liberty: British Radicals and Perceptions of America in the 1790s', in Ella Dzelainis and Ruth Livesey (eds), *The American Experiment and the Idea of Democracy in British Culture, 1776–1914* (Aldershot: Ashgate, 2011, forthcoming).

4

'Language Really Used by Men': Cowper, Coleridge, and Wordsworth

The promise of a sentient language able to bypass the muddy mediations of verbal exchange became crucial to the poetry of the Romantic period, particularly to the innovations brought by Samuel Taylor Coleridge and William Wordsworth in the 1790s, but the conversational paradigm was transformed rather than abandoned. The process involved various representations of what Rajan calls the 'scene of reading' in terms of conversational exchange. The position of the reader was prefigured and to some extent conscripted by representations of an addressee within the text.[1] For Wordsworth, especially, poetry was explicitly being defined by a series of experiments in 'the language of conversation' of 'the middle and lower classes of society', but 'modern' poetry was being conceived in terms of conversational style long before *The Lyrical Ballads* (1798). My primary case is William Cowper, who, in 1798 anyway, Coleridge believed to be 'the greatest of modern poets'.[2] Like much of the poetry of the late eighteenth and early nineteenth century, Cowper aspired to a loose and agreeable style that approximated to conversational ease.[3] Often defining itself against the urbanity of Pope's poetry, later eighteenth-century poetry of this ilk aimed for a less epigrammatic and more relaxed

---

[1] Tilottama Rajan, *The Supplement of Reading: Figures of Understanding in Romantic Theory and Practice* (Ithaca/London: Cornell University Press, 1990), 4.

[2] See the 'Advertisement' to *The Lyrical Ballads* (1798) in *The Prose Works of William Wordsworth*, ed. W. J. B. Owen and Jane Worthington Smyser, 3 vols (Oxford: Oxford University Press, 1974), I: 116. References to Wordsworth's prose are to this edition and given in the text. Assuming Hazlitt's account in 'On My First Acquaintance with Poets' is accurate, Coleridge moved from giving this judgment of Cowper to talking about 'the experiment about to be tried by him and Wordsworth' in *Lyrical Ballads*, possibly implying his sense of their relatedness. See *The Complete Works of William Hazlitt*, ed. P. P. Howe, 21 vols (London: Dent, 1930–4), XVII: 120; all further references to Hazlitt's writing are to this edition. Cowper's influence on Coleridge has been widely recognized, at least since Humphrey House's *Coleridge* (London: Rupert Hart-Davis, 1962), 71–3.

[3] See William St Clair, *The Reading Nation in the Romantic Period* (Cambridge: Cambridge University Press, 2004), 214.

style.[4] Cowper criticized Pope's 'mechanic art' ('Table Talk', l. 654) from precisely this perspective.[5] His preference was for 'charming Ease' (I: 9), as he told William Unwin in a letter indignant at Samuel Johnson's attack on Matthew Prior's loose style. Cowper insisted that 'the familiar stile, is of all stiles the most difficult to succeed in' (ibid. 10).[6]

Cowper's poetry circulated as a commodity in a rapidly expanding world of book production and consumption. His books were consumer goods for the middle classes, as Leonore Davidoff and Catherine Hall's research into the reading habits of provincial families has shown, but they also contained a critique of the morals and manners of the aristocracy and those who aped them in London.[7] These families would have found confirmed in Cowper's pages the moral superiority of the domestic virtues. Unsurprisingly, then, Katherine Plymley transcribed Cowper's poetry and letters into her journal (*KPN* 168), noting down particularly his letter to William Unwin of 26 November 1781[8]:

There is a pleasure annex'd to the communication of one's ideas, whether by word of mouth or by letter, which nothing earthly can supply the place of, and it is the delight we find in this mutual intercourse, that not only proves us to be creatures intended for social life, but more than any thing else perhaps, fits us for it. (I: 543–4)

Cowper's version of conversation was amenable to the domesticity Plymley celebrates in her journals, defined against the *ton*, but far from uninterested in public affairs and definitely committed to 'mutual intercourse'.[9] The domestic circle imagined as a family relationship, much less explicitly oriented

[4] Pope may have been aiming at conversational ease in his own eyes, but Cowper's response is an index of a broader cultural shift that increasingly regarded it as unnatural (a judgement also reproduced by Coleridge in the discussion with Hazlitt, XVII: 121) . For a useful account of Pope's 'conversable' style, see J. Paul Hunter's 'Couplets and Conversation', in John Sitter (ed.), *The Cambridge Companion to Eighteenth-century Poetry* (Cambridge: Cambridge University Press, 2001), 11–35.

[5] All quotations of Cowper's poetry are from *The Poems of William Cowper*, ed. John D. Baird and Charles Ryskamp, 3 vols (Oxford: Oxford University Press, 1980–95) with the line and—for *The Task*—book numbers given after the quotation. The text of *Poems* (1782) is found in vol II and *The Task* in vol III.

[6] In a letter written on 5 January 1782 (II: 3), Cowper described Pope as 'a mechanical maker of verses'. References to Cowper's letters and prose are to *The Letters and Prose Writings of William Cowper*, ed. James King and Charles Ryskamp, 5 vols (Oxford: Oxford University Press, 1979–86) with volume and page number given in the text.

[7] Leonore Davidoff and Catherine Hall, *Family Fortunes: Men and Women of the English Middle Class, 1780–1850*, rev. edn (Chicago: University of Chicago Press, 2002), 112–13, 155–66, and 172.

[8] Plymley read Hayley's *Life of Cowper* carefully. She quotes from it in several times in her diary. See her notebooks at the Shropshire Archives, Shrewsbury, MS 1066/1–197. All in-text references are to the relevant notebook number preceded by *KPN*.

[9] In a letter to Mrs. John Newton *c*.6 August 1781, Cowper described his poem 'Conversation' as designed 'to convince the world that they make but an indifferent use of their tongues, considering the Intention of Providence when he endued them with the faculty of Speech; to point out the Abuses, which is the jocular part of the Business, and to prescribe the Remedy, which is the grave and sober' (I: 506).

towards intellectual conversation than the moral mission of Bluestocking sociability, became a place in retirement where the talk of the town could be processed into more acceptable forms of speech.[10]

In *The Task* (1785) Cowper remains committed to literature as circulating truth within the body politic, but his sense of the corruptions of 'gain-devoted cities' (i.682) is in stark contrast with Addison's tears of joy at the Royal Exchange.[11] 'London, opulent, enlarged, and still | Increasing London' (i.721–2) has become a place of dispersal that has lost any capacity for moral integration, at least within its boundaries:

> Thither flow,
> As to a common and most noisome sewer,
> The dregs and faeculence of ev'ry land (i.682–4)

Outside those boundaries, Cowper's conversable poetry offered those families who gathered to hear his poetry read aloud, as Jane Austen's did, a sense of an ongoing community of conversation beyond the empty talk of the town.[12] In their daily lives many of these listeners may have been caught up in a world of trade, but gathered together to read from Cowper they could congratulate themselves on not being the showy talkers of London. Their domestic lives could be imagined—as his poetry imagined his own—as a space where a moral perspective oriented to higher things could be articulated. From this vantage point, the inundation of daily news might be worked into a sense of larger community.

'The Address to domestic happiness' in Book iii of *The Task* goes so far as to praise its sweet sociability as:

> thou only bliss
> Of Paradise that has survived the fall! (iii.41–2)

Out of this 'divine Chit chat' might be created a distinctively poetical version of a public sphere.[13] 'Retirement' becomes a space wherein 'sweet converse' (iii.391) could transform London talk into a deeper communion.

---

[10] Cowper tried to ingratiate his cousin Lady Hesketh with Montagu's circle by writing 'On Mrs Montagu's feather hangings', which appeared in the *Gentleman's Magazine*, 58 (June 1788), 542. Apparently, it didn't work. On 21 August he wrote in more typically Cowperian vein: 'To me my Dear it seemeth that we shall never by any management make a deep impression on Mrs. Montagu. Persons who have been so long accustom'd to praise, become proof against it' (II: 202). See below, p. 176 for Hannah More's claim that she was the only one of the Montagu circle who had a taste for Cowper's poetry.

[11] The comparison is also drawn by Julie Ellison, 'News, Blues, and Cowper's Busy World', *Modern Language Quarterly*, 62 (2001), 219–37, who suggests: 'For Cowper, the newspaper, not the marketplace, offers a global array signifying different races and nationalities available for sublimation' (236).

[12] See Chap 5, pp. 226–8.

[13] Coleridge to John Thelwall, 17 December 1796, *The Collected Letters of Samuel Taylor Coleridge*, ed. E. L. Griggs, 6 vols (Oxford: Oxford University Press, 1956–71), I:

Both Coleridge and Wordsworth took up this challenge in their differing ways, but perhaps with more ambitious and possibly even more extended notions of community. To this extent at least, their poetry was in dialogue with the radicalism of the 1790s. No less than Godwin, with whom they both kept up an ambivalent relationship, their ideas of conversation were also shaped by a more general retreat from socially mixed spaces. Certainly Coleridge felt government intrusion as a powerful presence after the Two Acts.[14] For these and other reasons, Coleridge, especially, developed and intensified Cowper's strong sense of a Christian communion as the proper object of conversational poetics. Less concerned than Coleridge with this kind of transcendence, Wordsworth famously represents the diversity of London in Book VII of *The Prelude* (1805), but his response gives a disenchanted sense of the empty disarticulated talk to be found there, reminiscent in some regards of *The Task*.[15] More important to his poetry than to either Cowper or Coleridge's is the encounter with strangers. The problem of how to negotiate the risky space of social mediation is an important one in much of Wordsworth's poetry from the mid-1790s. Possibly he was aware of the rendering of such scenarios in John Thelwall's *The Peripatetic* (1793), although the trope was widespread in the period's magazine poetry. In Thelwall's generically mixed prose adventure, difference is continually acknowledged; it cannot be wished away, as it often was in the magazine poetry of the later eighteenth century, but conversation continues to be explored, if only in a form of imperfect barter. At times, Thelwall's prose and poetry turns towards a sentimental communion of transcendence, but at others 'sweet converse' is conceived as a form of exchange with the potential to reach out into a democratized idea of the public.[16] In contrast, Wordsworth's 'convers[ation] with general nature' (I: 140), as he put it in the 1800 preface, is often in dialogue with a

279 (all future references to Coleridge's letters given in the text are to this edition as *CL* with volume and page number). The context was the ongoing disagreement between Coleridge and Thelwall over religious poetry.

[14] See John Barrell on Coleridge's alarm about the Treasonable Practices Bill in particular in *Imagining the King's Death: Figurative Treason, Fantasies of Regicide 1793–1796* (Oxford: Oxford University Press, 2000), 587–8.

[15] Wordsworth read *The Task* as early as 1785 and returned to it in the 1790s; see Duncan Wu, *Wordsworth's Reading 1770–1799* (Cambridge: Cambridge University Press, 1993), 38–9.

[16] The phrase 'sweet converse' appears twice in Thelwall's 'Lines Written at Bridgewater, in Somersetshire, on the 27th of July 1797, during a long excursion, in quest of a peaceful retreat', written soon after he left Coleridge in Somerset. The passage is explicitly addressed to 'my Samuel', although the trope is ubiquitous in eighteenth-century poetry. See Thelwall's *Poems written Chiefly in Retirement*, 2nd edn (Hereford, 1802), 129–30. Judith Thompson sees Thelwall's conversation poems as promoting the complementarity of the domestic and patriotic virtues against 'the solitary, self-solacing power of the

mystery of feeling figured as music rather than social talk, but the collision of conversation, the risk in social encounter, remained at the heart of his poetry of the 1790s.

COWPER'S 'DIVINE CHIT CHAT'

Cowper participated in the polite world of letters in the 1750s, contributing essays on conversation to magazines like *The Connoisseur* and writing poems to Richardson in praise of *Sir Charles Grandison*, but the defining moment of his life was the breakdown he suffered in 1763.[17] He abandoned a promising legal career and entered an asylum in St. Albans. The following year he experienced a religious conversion that culminated in the Olney hymns, written (1764–72) in collaboration with the evangelical clergyman John Newton. From 1765, Cowper was living with the family of Morley Unwin, an Anglican priest, but after his death in 1767, he moved with Unwin's widow, Mary, and her two children to the small village of Olney in Buckinghamshire, where he met Newton. Religious poetry excluded all other forms until a relapse in Cowper's mental health in 1773. In recovery, he started to write again, discovering a new conversational ease and familiarity in the poetry published by Joseph Johnson as *Poems by William Cowper, of the Inner Temple, Esq* (1782).

When Cowper returned to writing poetry, his self-consciously conversational model was increasingly defined by his situation outside 'the *busy* and the *gay* world'.[18] Provoked by Samuel Johnson's attacks on Matthew Prior in *Lives of the Poets*, Cowper gave William Unwin an account of the difficulty of the task he was setting himself:

To make sense speak the language of prose without being prosaic, to marshal the words of it in such order as they might naturally take in falling from the lips of an extemporary speaker, yet without meanness; harmoniously, elegantly, and

imagination engaged with and activated by nature in "This Lime Tree" '. See Thompson, 'An Autumnal Blast, a Killing Frost: Coleridge's Poetic Conversation with John Thelwall', *Studies in Romanticism*, 36 (1997), 427–56 (444).

[17] See 'An Ode on Reading Mr. Richardson's History of Sir Charles Grandison', *Poems*, I: 53–4 and 471 n. The poem was a response to *Critical Remarks on Sir Charles Grandison* (1754), a sceptical attack on the novel's religiosity.

[18] The phrase is taken from John Newton's suppressed 'Preface' to Poems (1782). See *Poems*, I: 568. Joseph Johnson was concerned that the preface might 'recommend the volume to the Religious, [but] it would disgust the profane.' Cowper had been anxious that poems like 'Table Talk' and 'Conversation' might be deemed too frivolous. Some copies of the 1782 edition do exist with the preface bound in.

without seeming to displace a syllable for the sake of the rhime, is one of the most arduous tasks a poet can undertake. (II: 10)

In many ways, the passage looks towards Wordsworth's desire to experiment with the language of conversation in *Lyrical Ballads*, not least in the emphasis placed on metre as a means of creating harmony from prosaic language, but Cowper presents himself as a participant in a feminized cottage industry in a 'snug parlour' in his letters from this period: 'one lady knitting, the other netting, and the Gentleman winding worsted' (29 March 1784, II: 229). Unlike the heroic version of masculinity that Boswell tried to enshrine in his *Life of Johnson*, Cowper stood for a gentler idea of male identity, combining 'manliness and sweetness', whose literary labours were not oriented towards conflict, but the production of domestic virtues in a country whose public life is constantly seen as degenerate.[19] 'He was the first English poet', as Julie Ellison puts it, 'to gentrify the press by means of a provincial aesthetic of retired masculinity.'[20]

Cowper's interest in conversation had emerged early in his writing career. Before his breakdown, his essay on conversation in *The Connoisseur* magazine for 16 September 1756 (V: 23–7) was attempting a staple subject of periodical essayists. Under the Juvenilian epitaph 'Always observing the rules and laws of language' (V: 23), Cowper endorses Fielding's identification of conversation as 'one of our principle distinctions from brutes' (ibid. 26). Among its predictable contents is the clichéd contrast between 'the graces of conversation' displayed by the French as opposed to the 'sullen and uncommunicative disposition' of the English. Where his countrymen come up trumps for Cowper is in their liberty to be different: 'the *English* consist of very different humours, their manner of discourse admits of great variety: but the whole *French* nation converse alike' (ibid, 23). At this time in his life, Cowper was a member of the Nonsense Club, associating with men like Bonnell Thornton and George Colman, who conducted *The Connoisseur*.[21] The essay's easy manner and pleasure in agreeable informality articulate the aspirations of the London clubs of the mid-century. Whatever the problems with particular deviations from the golden mean of Addisonian politeness, the essay is confident that the generality of talk can be reformed into a more polished form of conversation (not least by following the example of Cowper and his friends). The contrast drawn between English heterogeneity and French sameness suggests a much more relaxed attitude to variety than many felt later in the

[19] Davidoff and Hall, *Family Fortunes*, 112–13.
[20] Ellison, 'Cowper's Busy World', 220.
[21] See Arthur Sherbo, 'Cowper's Connoisseur Essays', *Modern Language Notes*, 70 (1955), 340–2.

century. By the 1780s, not only had Cowper's own world darkened, but also the task being set for conversation appeared both more urgent and more doubtful of success out in society broadly construed.

To some extent, Cowper versified his essay of the 1750s into the poem 'Conversation', first published in his 1782 collection, but the conversable world is rather less secure in the later redaction. The poem's opening lines—even as they celebrate the virtues and pleasures of conversation— foreground the fraught distinction between 'talking' and 'converse':

> Though nature weigh our talents, and dispense
> To ev'ry man his modicum of sense,
> And Conversation in its better part,
> May be esteemed a gift and not an art,
> Yet much depends, as in the tiller's toil,
> On culture, and the sowing of the soil.
> Words learn'd by rote, a parrot may rehearse,
> But talking is not always to converse,
> Not more distant from harmony divine
> The constant creaking of a country sign (ll. 1–10)

Conversation is here defined against artfulness, which might be tainted with hypocrisy, much more so here than in the 1756 essay's relatively relaxed celebration of the diversity of English conversation. 'Talking' is not always to 'converse' for Cowper (as Samuel Johnson also sometimes acknowledged). 'Culture' is an interesting option for Cowper to choose as the ground of his distinction, especially when kept so closely in touch with its agricultural origins in 'the sowing of the soil'.[22] The metaphor implies that conversation depends on a kind of 'second nature', internalized within the individual through habits of reflection and tact, as Wordsworth was to suggest in his preface to *Lyrical Ballads*.[23]

The organic 'culture' metaphor might be taken as a simple expression of Cowper's preference for rural retirement over city life were it not for the fact that he also satirizes 'the constant creaking of a country sign'. Whether it is in the country or the city, the tavern is a place of suspicion for Cowper's domestic morality. For all the potentially democratic aspects of Cowper's opening invocation of conversation as 'a gift', not everyone has it nor is it easily supplied by 'rote' learning. Partly, perhaps, the target of this last phrase is the scholasticism against which Addison and Hume ranged their conversable worlds. The reference to 'the harmony divine' might be a gesture

---

[22] See the important discussion of the word and its development in Raymond Williams, *Keywords: A Vocabulary of Culture and Society*, rev. edn (London: Fontana, 1983), 87–93.

[23] See James Chandler, *Wordsworth's Second Nature: A Study of the Poetry and the Politics* (Chicago: University of Chicago Press, 1984).

towards Shaftesbury's idea of conversational dialogue as a manifestation of a deeper communion in Nature. The difference, of course, is that for Cowper's evangelical temper, unlike Shaftesbury's deism, 'plastic Nature' was imbued with a very Christian sense of the divine presence.[24] Coleridge developed this aspect of Cowper's 'divine Chit chat' from *The Task*, but the loose couplets of Cowper's earlier poems struggle to communicate the air of harmony he wanted to convey.[25] Like the conduct books and the myriad periodical essays on conversation, which rarely pretend to teach what ought to be done in any positive sense, the poem 'Conversation' proceeds instead to outline a series of familiar solecisms that prevent people participating fully in cultured conversation. Only at its conclusion does it arrive at a more surprising and insistently evangelical vision of conversation.

In the 1782 collection, the moral satires that precede 'Conversation' dwell on the hypocrisy of forms of sociability out in the world. 'Table Talk' frames the volume's wider interest in conversation in terms of British and Protestant freedom of speech:

> The soul, emancipated, unoppress'd,
> Free to prove all things and hold fast the best,
> Learns much, and to a thousand list'ning minds,
> Communicates with joy the good she finds (ll. 273–5)

The word 'liberty' echoes around the poem, but the values of civic disinterestedness appear to be in terminal decline. 'The Progress of Error' defines a world where:

> Accomplishments have taken virtue's place,
> And wisdom falls before exterior grace (ll. 417–18).

Lord Chesterfield is attacked as a 'polish'd and high finish'd foe to truth' (l. 341). His 'poison all high life pervades' (l. 347). 'Polish'd manners' become 'a mask we wear' (l. 166) in 'Conversation'. In an evangelical gesture towards conversation as a search for moral truth, the freedom of contradiction becomes necessary, as it did for Watts, who used the same trope, 'to brush the surface and to make it flow' (l. 102). Cloistered virtue is not an option. Conversation's role as 'sacred interpreter of human thought' is affirmed, even if 'few respect or use thee as they ought' (ll. 23–4). The problem was how to combine evangelical urgency with 'modesty and ease' (l. 104). How to stop proper Protestant 'freedom of dissent' (l. 97) becoming

---

[24] See the attack on Shaftesbury's 'rant and rhapsody in virtue's praise' in *The Task* (V: 677–94).

[25] Coleridge told Thelwall that a love of Shaftesbury's platonism had to be supplemented by a love of Jesus (*CL*, I: 214).

fractious dispute? Interestingly Hannah More was immersed in Cowper's poetry before she began writing her *Coelebs in Search of a Wife* (1808), a novel that wrestles with precisely these issues. In 1808, she told Sir W. W. Pepys 'more than twenty years ago...I was the only one of the old school, who strongly relished Cowper, but then he had not published the Task.' Elizabeth Montagu, she notes, was 'never brought over to the faith'. More immediately moves from her comments on Cowper's poetry to a more general judgment on conversation in contemporary society: 'And so you agree with me that conversation is absolutely extinct.'[26]

Cowper's 'Conversation' anticipates this godly perspective on the state of worldly conversation, but its conclusion struggles to find a way of mediating its evangelical urgency in the easy style. Instead, it turns to an extended account of the conversation of Christ with the Apostles on the road to Emmaus. Isaac Watts had alluded to the future felicity of transparent conversation with the prophets in his *Improvement of the Mind*, but deferred such aspirations as otherwise too enthusiastic. Perhaps he would have found fault with 'Conversation' in this regard, as Cowper insists that future felicity may at least glimpse within certain sorts of communicative exchange in this world:

> True bliss, if man may reach it, is composed
> Of hearts in union mutually disclosed (ll. 679–80)

Cowper is evangelically hostile to those who disparage such aspirations as 'fanatic and absurd' (l. 578). He was determined to make conversation 'always active on the side of truth' (l. 602). The problem remained of how to balance these perspectives with his sense of the importance of tasteful ease to poetry. Hannah More, for instance, felt the fluidity of his poetry sometimes licensed those who had more interest in conversational ease than in its moral content:

The determined imitator of an easy writer becomes insipid, of a sublime one, absurd. Cowper's ease appeared his most imitable charm: but ease aggravated his insipidity. His occasional negligences, his disciples adopted uniformly. In Cowper, there might sometimes be carelessness in the verse, but the verse itself was sustained by the vigour of the sentiment. The imitator forgot that his strength lay in the thought; that his buoyant spirit always supported itself; that the figure though amplified was never distorted; the image though bold was never incongruous, and the illustration though new, was never false. (II: 200–1)

---

[26] See William Roberts, *Memoirs of the Life and Correspondence of Mrs. Hannah More*, 2nd edn, 4 vols (1835), III: 251, and Anne Stott, *Hannah More: The First Victorian* (Oxford: Oxford University Press, 2003), 273–4. For his part, Cowper told Newton in February 1788 that More was 'a favorite writer with me', III: 103.

Certainly 'Conversation' gives little indication of how to engage with the world without simply reproducing a 'tasteless journal of the day before' (l. 276). Instead the poem simply shifts gears to the evangelical ending that would surely have at least earned More's approval for its insistence on the place of piety within polite conversation.

In its melodic blank verse, Cowper's major poem *The Task* (1785) employs a much more flexible medium for conveying a sense of the divine harmony. In the process, it also develops at length a picture of the domestic circle as the mediating space between celestial felicity and the flow of worldly information. Kevis Goodman sees the poem as self-consciously revising the georgic tradition by setting itself the task of producing a coherent national imaginary from the desiccated forms of worldly conversation.[27] The large audience of provincial readers who delighted in it would have experienced the 'simultaneous consumption' Benedict Anderson has identified with the newspaper, the sense of national community emerging out of a dispersed community of readers.[28] What ought to be added to the secularist assumptions of this analysis is that it was an imagining of Protestant and British community raised above the sense of a wider corruption. The expansion of space Anderson identifies with the newspapers inscription of its readers into the imperial nation extended to Eternity. *The Task* explicitly situates itself in the context of national degeneration after the American Revolution, including a loss of traditional male virtues, but Cowper's response is not to seek out a 'heroic' (or even prophetic) bulwark against this perceived decline in manly talk.[29] In his correspondence of the time, Cowper places himself as someone looking out towards the world from a distinctively feminized environment. 'Though we Live in a Nook', he told William Unwin in December 1781 (I: 568) 'yet we are not unconcerned about what passes in it. The present awfull Crisis, Big with the Fate of England, engages much of our Attention.' *The Task* describes a domestic situation oriented towards what circulates in the world outside and uses conversation 'to sift' (as Fielding put it) its goods into a more sanctified form.[30]

Book IV of *The Task* in particular rewrites the daily news into what is presented as a coherent form of domestic conversation. This conversation

---

[27] Kevis Goodman, *Georgic Modernity and British Romanticism: Poetry and the Mediation of History* (Cambridge: Cambridge University Press, 2004), 67–105.

[28] See Benedict Anderson, *Imagined Communities: Reflections on the Origin and Spread of Nationalism*, rev. edn (London: Verso, 1991), 35, quoted in Goodman, *Georgic Modernity*, 69.

[29] Cowper was much exercised by events in America. Sympathetic to the colonies, he wrote to John Newton on 17 December 1781 wondering if divine retribution would be visited on London: 'Her distress is infinite, her destruction appears inevitable, and her heart as hard as the nether millstone' (I: 563).

[30] See above, p. 17 on Fielding's essay, and also Goodman's discussion of 'sift' (*Georgic Modernity*, 86).

is imagined as shaping the poetry that is returned along the 'two-way paper-channel' between Olney and London.[31] Offering this scene of reading encourages its own readers to perform similar acts of salvation in their own domestic conversations, not least by reading *The Task* together. Various passages in *The Task* pick up and rework material from the columns of the *Morning Chronicle* and *General Evening Post*, the main London newspapers to which Cowper subscribed.[32] Cowper versifies accounts of the parliamentary debates, a point I'll return to later, but also rewrites advertising copy from September 1783 issues of both newspapers:

> Roses for the cheeks
> And lilies for the brows of faded age,
> Teeth for the toothless, ringlets for the bald,
> Heav'n, earth, and ocean plunder'd of their sweets,
> Nectareous essences, Olympian dews,
> Sermons and city feasts and fav'rite airs,
> Aetherial journies, submarine exploits,
> And Katerfelto with his hair on end
> At his own wonders, wond'ring for his bread. (iv.79–87)[33]

Goodman rightly notes the particularly dissociated organization of eighteenth-century newspapers and their lack of the demarcated sections usually found in papers today. The *London Magazine*, for instance, noted 'the abrupt transitions from article to article, without the smallest connection between one paragraph and another'. The same periodical in 1780—a year when the anxieties at the proliferation of opinion were particularly acute—observed 'there is not so inconsistent, so incoherent, so heterogeneous, although so useful and agreeable a thing, as a publick Newspaper.'[34] Rather than mourn the loss of heroic virtue in the small change of the commercial world, Cowper set his poetry the alchemical task of producing a coherent form of poetic conversation out of the everyday circulation of information. In this regard, Cowper's poetry suggests a continuing role for the technology of conversation in turning the chaos of London talk into a more regulated national culture, but one that has abandoned the possibility of working *within* urban spaces. Cowper *is* a newspaper politician, but one explicitly situated *beyond* the coffee house. 'Divine illumination' ('Argument', Book iii) is the ultimate end looked to

---

[31] Goodman, *Georgic Modernity*, 71.
[32] See Ellison, 'Cowper's Busy World', 225, and Goodman, *Georgic Modernity*, 68.
[33] For details, see Ellison, 'Cowper's Busy World', 230.
[34] Both quoted in Goodman, *Georgic Modernity*, 74–5. Goodman's definition of conversation overlooks the extent it had long been identified with the newspapers.

in Cowper's poetry, but it is given an earthly correlative in a very specific kind of social setting in domestic retirement, where the monitory male mediates news from the world outside to his female listeners. The scenario is reminiscent of Richardson's reading to his female senate from the manuscript of *Sir Charles Grandison*, the novel Cowper had defended much earlier in his career against the criticism of those who thought it too religious to be polite.

The terms of the *London Magazine*'s account of the random heterogeneity of newspapers in 1780 also underpins Cowper's ambivalent position towards the 'flow' of information. It was the lifeblood of the nation, but also an 'incoherent' and 'heterogenous' raw material than needed to be worked upon and made 'agreeable' if it was not to inundate and drown out what it was meant to be sustaining. Olney as a scene of retirement is carefully created as the scene of composition in *The Task*, but Cowper makes it clear he is no solitary. Although he lived like 'A Recluse', he told William Unwin in October 1781, he didn't have 'the temper of one, nor am I the least an Enemy to cheerfullness and good humour' (I: 527). Cowper's poem makes the domestic space the crucial transitional space between the decadence of London talk and the divine communion that he regards as the ultimate form of discourse. *The Task* gives a detailed account of the joys of domesticity in terms of affective family relations. The fact that Cowper was not married to either Mrs Unwin or Lady Austen (the sister-in-law of a local curate), the two women he entertained at Olney, was a potential source of scandal, but the need to airbrush the facts only points up the extent of *The Task*'s investment in creating an idea of family domesticity and what Julie Ellison calls 'sociable sensibility':[35]

> His warm but simple home, where he enjoys
> With her who shares his pleasures and his heart,
> Sweet converse (iii.389–91).

The conversable reading circle reproduces the monitory male interacting with female participants of the Richardsonian senate:

> Then to his book
> Well chosen, and not sullenly perused
> In selfish silence, but imparted oft
> As aught occurs that she may smile to hear,
> Or turn to nourishment digested well (iii.392–6)

If this scenario is a very controlled laboratory, then mediating the news from the outside world—rather than the solid reading of Book iii—is the

---

[35] Ellison, 'Cowper's Busy World', 226.

more difficult test Cowper sets himself in Book iv. The potential for discord is announced with 'the twanging horn' (iv.1) of the post boy, 'herald of a noisy world' (iv.5). With the newspapers, the content—but not, it turns out, the manner—of coffee shop conversation possesses Cowper's cosy circle. The most obvious controversial topic is the parliamentary news of 1783, specifically the furore surrounding Fox's India Bill:[36]

> The grand debate,
> The popular harangue, the tart reply,
> The logic and the wisdom and the wit
> And the loud laugh—I long to know them all;
> I burn to set th'imprison'd wranglers free,
> And give them voice, and utt'rance once again. (iv.30–5)

The last line goes beyond the implication that Cowper and his little circle retain a curiosity about the outside world to suggest that they wish to give its news proper articulation in the double sense scouted by Goodman's discussion, that is, to render it into a coherent form of language, but also make it part of a larger unity. Instead of the kinds of partisan argument that were increasingly taken to vitiate London talk, Cowper domesticates and gentrifies the news into the idea of a national conversation. *The Task* attempts to give the public as a coherent concept 'voice and ut'rance once again'. The distance from the metropolitan world is what now guarantees this talk as a genuinely inclusive form of circulation.[37]

What follows in Book iv more seriously questions how these scattered forms of broken talk might be integrated into a healthy flow. Although modestly cast in mock-heroic terms, the process begins with the arrangement of a properly conversable space:

> Now stir the fire, and close the shutters fast,
> Let fall the curtains, wheel the sofa round,
> And while the bubbling and loud-hissing urn
> Throws up a steamy column, and the cups
> That cheer but not inebriate, wait on each,
> So let us welcome peaceful evening in. (iv.36–41)

'Wheel the sofa round' has the air of staking out a defensive position on a field of battle, and, of course, Cowper is implying the importance of the home front in the struggle for the nation's manners and morals, but one very different from his hero Milton's 'wars of Truth'. If the space is being very precisely arranged for the task ahead, so is the time very definitely

---

[36] Ibid. 231. Fox was eventually dismissed by George III and defeated by Pitt in the April 1784 general election.
[37] See ibid. 228.

evening. An air of things naturally coming together at the end of the day is created, reinforced by a cinematic crosscut to the routs going on in London at the same time. Again the monitory circle forms in Olney;

> Fast bound in chains of silence, which the fair
> Though eloquent themselves, yet fear to break. (iv.53–4)

Women are a necessary presence in Cowper's conversable world, but their prerogative is limited. Fascinating though the newspapers may be, they are defined by their dissonance, if comically rendered, which Cowper's companions are careful not to precipitate. Leaving 'comprehension...lost' (iv.75), the newspapers offer 'a wilderness of strange | But gay confusion' (iv.78–9). Ellison presciently draws a parallel with this situation and Addison's tears of joy at the Royal Exchange. Addison's position implies that 'urban, commercial variety is susceptible to elevation'. Digesting the newspapers 'defines a pleasurable image of nation and the world for the newspaper-reading citizen, who is at once seduced and resistant'.[38] The ambivalence of Cowper's 'gay confusion' is well caught by Ellison's analysis, but the formulation understates the differences in location between Addison and Cowper. Addison may be a spectator, but he is there *in* the metropolis, looking at the Royal Exchange. Cowper's position is much more definitely outside the 'busy world' in the feminized domestic-affective space of his pseudo-family. The defensive position of the sofa creates 'loop-holes of retreat' from which to 'peep at such a world' (iv.88–9). Then, in a movement that looks forward to the trajectory of Coleridge's 'Frost at Midnight', the specificities of this earthly domestic situation give way to a more transcendent point of view:

> Thus sitting and surveying thus at ease
> The globe and its concerns, I seem advanced
> To some secure and more than mortal height,
> That lib'rates and exempts me from them all. (iv.94–7)

The expansion to this universal point of stillness is then followed by the kind of return—a device Coleridge exploited for the same diastolic and systolic pattern in his conversation poems—to its origins in 'social converse and instructive ease' (iv.135). Importantly, this converse is the kind where praise of God is not dismissed as 'a jarring note' (iv.181), as it might have been by those for whom evangelical enthusiasm offended against the laws of polite conversation. Compared to the 'pent-up breath of an unsav'ry throng' (iv.196), the poem again cutting to the world of London theatrical amusements, Cowper's domesticity aims to blend mortal speech

---

[38] Ibid. 236.

with the holy word, but it does so in the form of a flexible blank verse aiming to insulate its religious warmth from any charge of fanaticism.

There are other passages in *The Task* that offer moments of visionary insight into 'animated Nature' (i.198). Take the passage that Coleridge directly reworked in 'Frost at Midnight':

> In the red cinders, while with poring eye
> I gazed, myself creating what I saw.
> Nor less amused have I quiescent watch'd
> The sooty films that play upon the bars
> Pendulous, and foreboding in the view
> Of superstition prophesying still
> Though still deceived, some stranger's near approach.
> 'Tis thus the understanding takes repose
> In indolent vacuity of thought,
> And sleeps and is refresh'd. (iv.289–98)

Cowper renders such moments within domestic space and presents them as a natural prelude to the reintegration into its 'sweet converse'. The ebb and flow of the conversational situation is imagined as capable of recreating a kind of paradisal situation in socialized retirement.

Lack of unity has long been a critical complaint about *The Task*.[39] Cowper's advertisement to the poem explicitly presented it as centred on the play of his own subjective responses, 'the train of thought to which his situation and turn of mind led him'. The freedom to follow its various episodes are not rendered into unified organic form, but allowed to follow the contingent zigzag associated with conversation. The poem hangs on the idea of the poet interacting with his circle of friends and with the reader. These conversations implicitly organize the world of fallen conversation that circulates around them. Where does this process leave poetry as a medium? Is it continuous with or somehow distinct from conversation as a form of verbal exchange? Goodman thinks *The Task* at least entertains the idea of poetry as 'a distinctive *medium*—one bearing a superior relation to the sound of "proper" intercourse than other print forms'.[40] Presumably this superiority also applies to the everyday mediations of conversation. Important to Goodman's analysis in this regard are those moments of 'indolent vacuity' (iv.297) wherein the mind suspends itself

---

[39] See Joseph F. Musser Jr., 'William Cowper's Rhetoric: The Picturesque and the Personal', *Studies in English Literature*, 19 (1979), 515–31. Musser identifies the 'picturesque' with an author–reader relationship that 'moves from perspective to perspective without being treated to a view of the whole' (523). Conversation as a speech genre was and is usually perceived as open in precisely this kind of way.

[40] Goodman, *Georgic Modernity*, 72.

beyond the exchanges of conversation, at best talking to itself. Cowper
was widely admired by his contemporaries as 'a master of melody'.[41] In its
disavowal of the chiming effects he identified with Pope's couplets, the
melody of Cowper's blank verse may be attuned towards a higher harmony, but these moments are nearly always presented as a prelude to
reintegration in the 'sweet converse' of the domestic circle. Nor, as we
have seen, do they simply stand free from the circulating news of the day
and the wider world of talk.[42] In the 1790s Coleridge developed a form of
blank verse now identified as 'the conversation poem' because of its ease
and flexibility of address. No less than Cowper, too, he developed a 'scene
of reading' centred on the intimate often domestic conversable circle in
these poems. Cowper's moments of deeper intimation appear as preludes
to a reintegration into the domestic circle. Coleridge's poetry registers a
much stronger pull towards a 'sentient language' transcending both the
domestic and the wider world of circulation it draws upon.

COLERIDGE'S COMMUNION

On or around 10 March 1798, Samuel Taylor Coleridge wrote a letter to
his brother George that has often been read as a staging post on his mazy
retreat from radical politics:

I collect from your letter, that our opinions and feelings on political subjects are
more nearly alike, than you imagine them to be. Equally with you (& perhaps
with deeper conviction, for my belief is founded on actual experience) equally
with you I deprecate the moral & intellectual habits of those men both in England
& France, who have modestly assumed to themselves the exclusive title of
Philosophers & Friends of Freedom. I think them at least *as* distant from greatness
as from goodness (*CL*, I: 395)[43]

Against the degeneration of 'the morals & domestic habits of the people',
Coleridge hoped that 'Individuals will see the necessity of individual
effort; that they will act as kind neighbours & good Christians, rather
than as citizens & electors.' Unsurprisingly, given his opposition between
domestic morality and the degeneracy of the times, he also quoted from
Cowper's *The Task* (v.496–508):

---

[41] The phrase is used in a dialogue in More's *Coelebs in Search of a Wife*, 2 vols (1808),
II: 200, that moves on to the problem of Cowper's imitators.

[42] See Goodman, *Georgic Modernity*, 104.

[43] See Nicholas Roe, *Wordsworth and Coleridge: The Radical Years* (Oxford: Oxford
University Press, 1988) for an account of this retreat.

>   He that takes
>   Deep in his soft credulity the stamp
>   Designed by loud Declaimers on the part
>   Of Liberty, themselves the slaves of Lust,
>   Incurs derision for his easy faith
>   And lack of Knowledge (*CL*, I: 396)

Poetry has an important function now 'to destroy the bad passions not by combating them, but by keeping them in inaction' (I: 397). 'In general conversation & general company' also, he has turned away from the collision of mind with mind: 'I endeavour to find out the opinions common to us—or at least the subjects on which difference of opinion creates no uneasiness' (I: 398).

The attack on 'loud Declaimers' quoted from Cowper hints at an anxiety about the appeal to the passions in oratory that I have suggested was not uncommon in late-eighteenth-century thought. Coleridge had been a vigorous participant in the collision of mind with mind in Bristol and London earlier in the 1790s, but now turns away from these circles in favour of Cowper's domesticity. This turn may not be an abjuration of politics in any simple sense. After all, Book v of *The Task* is largely taken up with the representation of George III as a threat to the settlement of 1688–9 and the liberties of Englishmen, an irony perhaps intended in Coleridge's far from straightforward letter to his clergyman brother. The letter was written towards the end of a period when Coleridge had been experimenting with the extended lyrics in blank verse indebted to Cowper's 'divine Chit chat'.[44] Any account of these 'conversation poems' as simply a retreat from his Jacobin phase needs to consider the complex position of conversation in relation to political discourse more generally, especially in the 1790s. This requires thinking about longer term cultural trajectories of retrenchment and domestication as well as more local issues being negotiated by literary radicals like Godwin in the mid-1790s. Looming large among these circumstances was the fear shared by Godwin and Coleridge that the government was increasingly intruding into their private conversations and the countervailing intensification of the need to prove their domestic virtues as a foundation of their public spirit.

Invoking Cowper as one's poetic model was an obvious route to take in these circumstances, not least because his domestic poetry was still associated with political virtue. Coleridge's invocation of Cowper was signalled to John Thelwall as early as 1795 in their ongoing debate about the place of religious sentiments in poetry. His praise for Cowper's 'divine

---

[44] 'A Nightingale', written in April 1798 for *Lyrical Ballads*, is subtitled 'A Conversation Poem'.

Chit chat' may be a conciliatory gesture, stepping away from what Thelwall regarded as the religious enthusiasm of 'Religious Musings'. Whereas that poem adopts a prophetic register that presumes to range across history and (almost at least) offer a vision of the last days, in his conversation poems Coleridge adopts a quieter idiom 'belonging, rather, to common speech'.[45] These poems tend to include within their 'scene of reading' an addressee, whose presence opens up the idea of the poems as a dialogue. 'Reception renews the authenticity of representation,' as Rajan puts it, allowing Coleridge to imply his poetry has passed the test of an encounter with strangers, but in these poems dialogue usually tends towards univocity, not least because the addressee is figured as absent, silent, or unable to reply. In these circumstances, the incompletion of the conversational exchange in the domestic circumstance is in tension with visions of a higher communion. The 'scene of reading' usually represents an imagined sympathy in place of conversational exchange, 'preserving', in Rajan's terms, 'the "inspired" text from interpersonal difference'. Ultimately the poems imagine an interpretative interaction with its readers as a form of completion beyond social discourse, whether oral or written.[46]

Conversation as a continuous and ongoing 'supplement of reading', to use Rajan's phrase, is represented in the text but transformed into a form of communion that is imagined as transcending reception as a scene of differences. Coleridge's conversation poems attempt to mitigate the tendency towards visionary excess in 'Religious Musings', as Thelwall saw it, by imagining a countervailing tendency towards retirement. The domestic circle of Cowper's poetry opened up a more regulated scene of reading, but to Coleridge this retrenchment potentially endangered his sense of the heroic calling of poetry. 'I can *at times* feel strongly the beauties, you describe, in themselves, & for themselves—but more frequently *all things* appear little…an immense heap of *little* things,' he told John Thelwall in October 1797 (*CL*, I: 349). 'My mind feels as if it ached to behold & know something *great*—something *one & indivisible*.' From the purview of this order of visionary experience, any understanding of literature as a form of conversation, domestic or otherwise, was liable to seem small change indeed. Cowper's example also came to appear less 'divine' and more 'Chit chat', soon to be displaced by a sense of the heroic status of Wordsworth in Coleridge's poetic pantheon. For the decade from 1797, their 'conversation'

---

[45] The phrase is J. C. C. Mays's translation of Coleridge's Latin epigraph to 'Reflections on having left a Place of Retirement': see *Poetical Works I (Poems (Reading Text)): Part 1*, ed. Mays (Princeton: Princeton University Press, 2001), 260. Unless otherwise stated, all quotations are from this edition with line numbers given in the body of my text.

[46] Rajan, *The Supplement of Reading*, 103 and 4.

became increasingly intimate and allusive—implying 'a private bond...with the initiated'—a very specific idea of select company that increasingly defined itself against any more pragmatic perception of the republic of letters as a nexus of exchange.[47]

In the conversation poems of 1796–8, these tendencies play out in a complex manner. Among the earliest was 'Reflections on Having Left a Place of Retirement', probably written some time in spring 1796. The 'place of retirement' is the cottage in Clevedon, to which Coleridge had withdrawn after the political activism of 1794–5. In fact, as originally published in the *Monthly Magazine* in October 1796, a significant venue, to which I will return, the title was 'Reflections on Entering into Active Life'.[48] The original title places the poem, probably written while he was completing 'Religious Musings', on the turn in the nexus whereby conversation in retirement—with nature or a closed circuit of friends—provides a prelude to civic involvement.[49] Coleridge was considering the Unitarian ministry, journalism, or tutoring, before he finally decided to retire more deeply into the country. Increasingly, the feeling that 'the best of us are liable to be shaped & coloured by surrounding Objects' predisposed him to conclude that 'Man was not made to live in Great Cities!' (*CL*, I: 154). He rejected the advice John Thelwall gave in May 1796 that 'London is your proper sphere.'[50] For Thewall participation in the urban republic of letters would have provided a prophylactic against what he considered Coleridge's tendency towards withdrawal into himself. Although they had not met in any of the popular political associations in which Thelwall participated, Coleridge had been no stranger to the convivial sociability of London. He published political sonnets in the *Morning Chronicle*, lectured on politics, and was meeting with Godwin, Holcroft, and other radicals in this period. In December 1794, the backroom of a London tavern, the 'Salutation and Cat', provided a space where Coleridge and his friends could gather 'to read, write and talk of reform, both in poetry and politics'.[51] Charles Lamb, who features

---

[47] See Lucy Newlyn, *Coleridge, Wordsworth, and the Language of Allusion* (Oxford: Oxford University Press, 1986), vii. Newlyn's book provides a detailed account of their relationship, alert to their 'conversation', as she puts it several times, and its many underlying tensions.

[48] *Monthly Magazine*, 2 (Oct 1796), 732.

[49] For an account of this nexus, see Jon Mee, *Romanticism, Enthusiasm, and Regulation: Poetics and the Policing of Culture in the Romantic Period* (Oxford: Oxford University Press, 2003), 155–9.

[50] See Warren E. Gibbs, 'An Unpublished Letter from John Thelwall to S. T. Coleridge', *Modern Language Review*, 25 (1930), 85–90 (89).

[51] See Felicity James, *Charles Lamb, Coleridge and Wordsworth: Reading Friendship in the 1790s* (Basingstoke: Palgrave Macmillan, 2008), 13.

as addressee of 'This Lime Tree Bower my Prison', never forgot these meetings, as Felicity James has demonstrated, and to a certain extent after 1800 reoriented himself back towards 'low Urban Taste'.[52] In December 1796, he wrote to Coleridge:

That Sonnet [on Mrs Siddons]…brings afresh to my mind the time when you wrote those on Bowles, Priestly, Burke—'twas 2 Christmas[e]s ago—& in that nice little smoky room at the 'Salutation', which is even now continually presenting itself to my recollection, with all its associated train of pipes, tobacco, Egghot, welch Rabbits, metaphysics & Poetry—Are we *never* to meet again?

When Southey came to rescue Coleridge from the 'most foul stye', he found to his disgust that he had left with Lamb for the Unitarian Chapel.[53]

Coleridge may have left behind the smoky tavern sociability of London and the networks of Rational Dissent, but the rising importance of the retirement trope in his writing from the mid-1790s is not in itself the sign of an abandonment of politics. In 'Reflections on Having Left a Place of Retirement', for instance, the temptation to 'pamp'ring the coward Heart' (l. 47) in 'delicious solitude' is put aside in the name of 'the bloodless fight | Of Science, Freedom, and the Truth in CHRIST' (ll. 61–2). The poem's revised title, however, may suggest an adjustment to the centre of gravity of the poem. The poem begins with a kind of 'ascent' from which a wider perspective on universal harmony can be seen (a moment of transport that becomes a familiar trope in the conversation poems). In the form of retirement literature associated with Shaftesbury, for instance, such a moment could provide the prelude to social re-engagement. So just where Coleridge's 'overwhelmed Heart' (l. 41) seems as if it might burst from its sense of plenitude, it is brought into harmony with the kind of practical benevolence associated with Rational Dissent:

> I therefore go, and join head, heart, and hand,
> Active and firm, to fight the bloodless fight
> Of Science, Freedom, and the Truth in CHRIST (ll. 60–2)

This linear narrative of the poem is complicated by the experience in it of the continual pullback to the joy of simply dwelling in solitude with a

---

[52] See 'Lamb to Robert Lloyd, 7 February, 1801', in *The Letters of Charles and Mary Anne Lamb*, ed. Edwin W. Marrs, Jr, 3 vols (Ithaca and London: Cornell University Press, 1975), I: 271.

[53] See ibid. I: 65, and 'Southey to Edith Fricker, January 12 1795', *New Letters of Robert Southey*, ed. Kenneth Curry, 2 vols (New York/London: Columbia University Press, 1965), I: 91. See the excellent discussions of Lamb's continuing nostalgia for this scene in James, *Charles Lamb*.

vision of the divine. The poem ends with a regretful look back towards the cottage that he has been 'constrain'd' (l. 44) to quit for the active life:

> My Spirit shall revisit thee, dear Cot!
> Thy Jasmin and thy window-peeping Rose,
> And Myrtles fearless of the mild sea-air. (ll. 65–7)

The trope of the 'embowering refuge' is a familiar feature of Coleridge's writing.[54] Here the cottage is a form of delicious solitude rather than the kind of sociable domestic scene found in Cowper's *The Task*.

In what might be regarded as the earliest of the conversation poems, 'The Eolian Harp', published in *Poems on Various Subjects* (1796), the 'more serious eye' (l. 49) of his wife 'Sara', named as his addressee in the poem's first line, pulls Coleridge back from his abstruse musings. The scenario is a reminder that in circles associated with the *Monthly Magazine*, including John Aikin's (who edited it), the domestic virtues in retirement were often represented as the foundation of civic duty, not its antithesis. Where Sara 'biddest me walk humbly with my God' (l. 52), she is not simply calling Coleridge back to domestic as against civic duty, but potentially at least to both of these things as opposed to 'Philosophy's aye-babbling spring' (l. 57). The overflowings of this spring are what take up most of the poem and, again, the regulating inclusion of Sara's admonitory eye might be considered to validate Coleridge's imagination as recognizing proper limits rather than cancelling it out. Only present in the text as Coleridge's voice, his imagination effectively incorporates and levels off difference. As with Godwin's incorporation of Mary Wollstonecraft in his *Memoirs*, Coleridge acknowledges other—feminized—points of view to imply his own perspective participates in a transcendent converse with the whole created universe. Coleridge had written in his preface to the *Poems on Various Subjects* (1796): 'There is one species of egotism that is truly disgusting; not that which leads us to communicate our feelings to others, but that which would reduce the feelings of others to an identity with our own.'[55] Given that Lamb did not enjoy the experience of having his poetry rewritten by his friend for the volume, Coleridge may be acknowledging his own tendency to sublate even mutual converse to his own abstruse musings.

Coleridge did not abandon the idea of the literary sphere as a conversable circle when he returned to Somerset. He embarked on an overlapping

---

[54] See Mary Jacobus, *Romanticism, Writing, and Sexual Difference: Essays on the Prelude* (Oxford: Oxford University Press, 1989), 147. Jacobus is discussing Lamb's essay 'The Genteel Style in Writing'.

[55] *Poems on Various Subjects* (1796), viii. See James, *Charles Lamb*, 56–62.

sequence of relationships (Charles Lamb and Charles Lloyd, John Thelwall, William and Dorothy Wordsworth, for instance) dedicated more or less to social authorship.[56] These relationships offered their participants what Nicholas Roe calls 'a compelling prospect of social renovation'.[57] The principle was carried across to Coleridge's book making. His 1797 edition of *Poems* was a collaboration with Charles Lamb and Charles Lloyd. The privately printed anthology *Sonnets from Different Authors* (1796), assembled in Bristol as he prepared to decamp for Nether Stowey, might be read as 'bringing together such an ideal, literary circle'.[58] Lamb, of course, appears as the absent addressee of 'This Lime Tree Bower my Prison', written in July 1797, a poem that takes off from a moment when the social circle is broken:

> Well, they are gone, and here I must remain,
> This Lime-Tree Bower my Prison! I have lost
> Beauties and Feelings, such as would have been
> Most sweet to my remembrance (ll. 1–4)

The importance of these interpersonal relationships is the accepted starting point of the poem, but they also serve to affirm the authority of the poet as he hymns the power of his imagination to reproduce them:

> A delight
> Comes sudden on my heart, and I am glad
> As I myself were there! (ll. 44–6)

In his 'prison' and 'bereft of promised good' (l. 66), Coleridge creates a paradise within himself from the imagined community of his friends. In the process, of course, any resistance from others is also short-circuited by an inclusivity that avoids the collision of difference.

As it happens, Lamb later protested at being co-opted as 'gentle-hearted Charles' (l. 28).[59] More generally, he was suspicious of the tendency in Coleridge's yearning to transcend the mundane exchanges of life and complained at 'a certain air of mysticism, more consonant to the conceits

---

[56] The analysis of this series of relations provides the structure of David Fairer's *Organising Poetry: The Coleridge Circle, 1790–1798* (Oxford: Oxford University Press, 2009).

[57] Nicholas Roe, *The Politics of Nature*, 2nd edn (Basingstoke: Palgrave Macmillan, 2002), 27.

[58] Richard Holmes, *Coleridge: Early Visions* (London: Hodder and Stoughton, 1989), 126. For useful discussions of the anthology, see Fairer, *The Coleridge Circle*, 192–4, and James, *Charles Lamb*, 98–9.

[59] In August 1800, after the poem first appeared in *The Annual Anthology* (1800), Lamb begged Coleridge not to 'make me ridiculous any more by terming me gentle-hearted in print' (Marrs, *Letters of Charles and Mary Lamb*, I: 217). Denise Gigante, *Taste: A Literary History* (New Haven/London: Yale University Press, 2005), 91, sees this letter as 'a foundational gesture of his literary personality'.

of pagan philosophy, than consistent with the humility of genuine piety'.[60] 'Piety' here opposed to 'mysticism' implies the practical Christianity of Rational Dissent rather than any form of quietism. Barbauld reiterated the point in her poem 'To Mr. S. T. Coleridge', published in the *Monthly Magazine*.[61] Her references to 'fairy bowers entranced' (l. 28) and the dangers of indolent solitude reply to Coleridge's 'Reflections', originally published in the same journal. Typically combining the domestic affections ('a Parent's love!', l. 43) with a sense of civic responsibility, Barbauld's poem urges Coleridge back to 'Active scenes' (l. 38), in the process reaffirming the *Monthly Magazine* as 'a medium of conversation and exchange'.[62] Coleridge's conversation poems never turn away decisively from the idea of the literary as sociable discourse in the 1790s. The redefinition of the conversable as the distinctively Coleridgean version of Kantian free play waited in the future. I do not want to suggest its presence in the conversation poems as any kind of prior intention, but the poems do register a strong pressure towards converting conversation into monologue, recognized by friends like Barbauld, Lamb, and Thelwall. Coleridge's desire for 'something great—something *one & indivisible*' oriented him towards the idea of a reader with whom he could find a form of sympathetic exchange, but this impulse was itself continually haunted by the fear that the other would turn out to be the stranger who was not the same and would not reciprocate.[63] No wonder, perhaps, the circles of collaborators and readers he formed around himself in the 1790s ended up as a sequence of broken relationships. Each ended up in the heap of Coleridge's 'little things' that refused to be 'sympathetically subordinate'.[64] If it does not define the poetry of the 1790s, then Coleridge's writing from the decade does at least contain a reflex that would 'efface' both the network of interpersonal relationships and his own divided subjectivity 'before a larger collective belief'.[65]

[60] 'Lamb to Coleridge, 24 [23] October 1796', *Letters of Charles and Mary Lamb*, I: 53, and see the discussion in James, *Charles Lamb*, 85–91.

[61] *The Poems of Anna Letitia Barbauld*, ed. William McCarthy and Elizabeth Kraft (Athens/London: University of Georgia Press, 1994), 132–3. The editors note that Coleridge first met Barbauld on a visit to their mutual friend J. P. Estlin in Bristol in 1797 (296), although Godwin's diary suggests they were moving in similar circles from at least 1794. The poem was originally published in the *Monthly Magazine*, 7 (April 1799), 231–2.

[62] James, *Charles Lamb*, 78.

[63] To an extent Coleridge invented Wordsworth as an ideal audience, but their conversation became increasingly strained. See Newlyn, *Language of Allusion*, vii. Thompson, 'Coleridge's Conversation with Thelwall', 439, contrasts 'the unnatural isolation and silence of Coleridge's midnight landscape' in the poem with 'the emphatically social and audible landscape' of Thelwall's 'On Leaving the Bottoms of Gloucestershire'.

[64] Rajan, *Supplement of Reading*, 102.

[65] Ibid. 103.

Literature for Coleridge became increasingly identified with this religious impulse as against the small change of the republic of letters. Reading as conversation in Coleridge's hands tended towards reading as 'conversion', to continue using Rajan's terms, whereby the properly passive reader could receive the benediction granted by 'the secret ministry' (l. 72) at the end of 'Frost at Midnight'.[66] By 1812, Coleridge seems to have abandoned any earlier understanding of literary culture as a form of conversation. Whereas the 'Salutation and Cat' had provided a scene for convivial authorship in December 1794, after the assassination of Spencer Percival a tavern could only be a place that harboured a form of radical sociability so debased it could not be considered in any way related to Coleridge's former Jacobin self.[67] Even the feminized locus of the domestic becomes belittled, as women writers like Barbauld are either erased from literary history or slighted in the lectures he gave in the same year.[68] The irony is that Coleridge retained a reputation as a great talker, whose conversation was worth collecting by his son-in-law Henry Nelson Coleridge into *Specimens of the Table Talk of the Late Samuel Taylor Coleridge* (1835) the year after his death.[69] The conversation of authors was a sought-after commodity in the 1820s and 1830s, but this talk was often being recorded as the *ana* of celebrities rather than a relay of exchanges in the republic of letters. Coleridge became 'the Sage of Highgate', a curiosity to visiting tourists who expected verbal fireworks.[70] Even his admirers recognized a tendency towards monologue in this regard, 'leaving colloquy out of the question entirely'.[71] In an earlier chapter, I suggested that this idea of the professional writer as genius was prepared by the heroic Samuel

---

[66] On the 'benediction' of the 'secret ministry', see Rajan, *Supplement of Reading*, 103. Thompson, 'Coleridge's Conversation with Thelwall', 437, sees the line as defensively directed at Thelwall because of the choice of a poetic ministry over the actual ministry of the Unitarian congregation at Shrewsbury. In 1796, Thelwall had thought even the Unitarian ministry a 'miserable speculation' compared to coming to London and joining the wider conversation of the republic of letters there. See Gibbs, 'Unpublished Letter', 89.

[67] See Kevin Gilmartin, 'The "Sinking Down" of Jacobinism and the Rise of the Counter-revolutionary Man of Letters', in Philip Connell and Nigel Leask (eds), *Romanticism and Popular Culture in Britain and Ireland* (Cambridge: Cambridge University Press, 2009), 128–47.

[68] See *Lectures 1808–1819 on Literature*, ed. R. A. Foakes, 2 vols (Princeton: Princeton University Press, 1987), I: 406–8. In April 1796, Coleridge believed Barbauld one of the best stylists in the language (*CL*, I: 197).

[69] See *Table Talk recorded by Henry Nelson Coleridge (and John Taylor Coleridge)*, ed. Carl Woodring, 2 vols; *Complete Works*, Vol. 14 (Princeton: Princeton University Press, 1990). Woodring describes *Table Talk* as 'a work of commercial success such as Coleridge's prose had never known', I: xcviii.

[70] See Seamus Perry, 'The Talker', in Lucy Newlyn (ed.), *The Cambridge Companion to Coleridge* (Cambridge: Cambridge University Press, 2002), 103–25.

[71] David Scott, the illustrator, quoted in Perry, 'The Talker', 109.

Johnson of Boswell's *Life* (even if Coleridge would have hated the comparison), except that for all his violence, Boswell's Johnson is continually
captured in processes of exchange, usually represented as bruising and
victorious perhaps, but nothing if not interactive.[72] Coleridge, on the
other hand, continually strained to write his readers into a scene of reading
as a higher communion rather than a querulous republic of letters.

WORDSWORTH AND PROBLEMS WITH STRANGERS

Although Coleridge's friendship with Wordsworth might be seen as the
culmination of the conversable circles he formed in the 1790s, Wordsworth never really had his friend's reputation as a talker, but his poetry
from this period does consistently take its readers to scenes of verbal
exchange. Where Coleridge's conversation poems nearly always configure
the scene of conversation as a circle of friends or family—if often absent or
unable to speak—with Wordsworth it is the encounter with strangers that
becomes central. In the Wordsworthian encounter poem, there is often
dialogue in formal terms, at least two speakers are often represented in the
text, but mutual comprehension is rarely its outcome. Interiorities resist
disclosure. The overwhelming implication is that 'the motives of every
moral agent are special to that agent, and we can never enter into them
sufficiently to judge them.'[73] Against this scepticism about verbal mediation, another strain appears that implies interiorities can only be grasped at
a level of intuition. From this perspective, the imperfections of verbal
exchange come to be fundamentally disabling, but neither perspective has
the last word, at least not in the poetic experiments Wordsworth carried
out in the name of conversation in the 1790s.

Wordsworth's encounter poems develop a well-worn trope of late-
eighteenth-century magazine poetry. They are predicated on a meeting
between the poet's persona and an object of sensibility, a victim of suffering,
frequently a casualty of war, especially after 1793 when hostilities with
the French began.[74] Often in this genre of poetry the thoughts and feelings
of a wounded soldier or his widow are transparent to the figure of
the poet, sometimes to the extent that they need not be put into words,
their sufferings vocalized as social protest or an occasion for a display of

---

[72] Coleridge preferred Burke's conversation to Johnson's 'bow-wow manner' (*Table
Talk* I: 405).

[73] See David Bromwich, *Disowned by Memory: Wordsworth's Poetry of the 1790s*
(Chicago/London: University of Chicago Press, 1998), 65.

[74] See Heather Glen, *Vision and Disenchantment: Blake's Songs and Wordsworth's Lyrical
Ballads* (Cambridge: Cambridge University Press, 1983), 33–56.

feeling by the poet. Developing scepticism about the power of sympathy and the question of inequality could bring with it a more self-conscious approach to scenarios of this kind. John Thelwall's aspirations to join the republic of letters expressed itself in the magazine poetry he published in the 1780s and early 1790s.[75] Some of this poetry also appears in the remarkable Shandean prose miscellany *The Peripatetic; or, Sketches of the Heart* (1793). These 'politico-sentimental journals', as Thelwall's title page calls them, are organized around the excursions of the narrator Sylvanus Theophrastus across England, interspersed with political commentary on the state of the nation, including the presence of a government informer, 'the *betrayer of private conversation*'.[76] To some extent *The Peripatetic* is a travel book like Wollstonecraft's *A short residence in Sweden, Norway, and Denmark* centred on the affective responses of its narrator. Sylvanus is the man of sentiment oriented towards openhearted discourse, often travelling with a circle of sympathetic companions. Judith Thompson has noted the importance of '*friendly Converse*' to *The Peripatetic* 'as [a] means of testing and balancing opinions, forging and maintaining social bonds, unsettling fixed or pre-conceived ideas, expanding the mind and amending the heart'.[77] These are the same values Thelwall expounded at his speech at Coachmakers' Hall in 1792. *The Peripatetic* continuously links them to a classical precedent of 'high converse' (as his title implies).[78]

Although many of Sylvanus's views are close to what we know of Thelwall's, they are not unchallenged by his friends, nor does the narrator only encounter people of his own social class. Not free of a sense of literary superiority, a trait not uncommon in Thelwall himself, Sylvanus is nevertheless willing to act as participant-observer in 'some cottage, or little ale-house, by the way side, where the conversation and manners of an order of society, whose habits, sentiments, and opinions are so widely different from what the usual intercourses of life present me, may pass in entertaining review before me'.[79] Thelwall consistently develops these sentimental responses into an explicitly political critique, but retains an awareness of problems of social mediation. One key passage in this regard is his encounter with an old sailor, spoiled by the 'little paltry vanity of arbitrary

---

[75] See *Poems upon Various Subjects* (1787). Thelwall had also edited and published his poetry in the *Biographical and Imperial Magazine*.

[76] John Thelwall, *The Peripatetic*, ed. Judith Thompson (Detroit: Wayne State University Press, 2001), 63 and 346.

[77] See ibid. 116 and 38–9. Thompson relates some of these dialogues to discussions Thelwall had at the Physical Society (14), from which he was expelled for expounding his materialist beliefs, and others to the metropolitan debating societies. The Philomathian Society might be added to these (see my previous chapter, p. 152).

[78] *Peripatetic*, 79.

[79] Ibid. 226.

and ideal distinctions'. The result is a stalling of what Sylvanus calls 'that freedom of conversation from which alone the human heart can be revealed; and those shades and distinctions of character that constitute the vast and entertaining variety of human nature can be developed'.[80] Even so, for Thelwall, these differences can be bartered across if not transcended. Sylvanus praises the old sailor's 'evident benevolence of mind', despite his disappointment at his desire for war to recommence. Thelwall's writing allows for at least provisional and imperfect comprehension between the speakers without suggesting they need be transparent or identical to each other for communication to take place.

Wordsworth probably read *The Peripatetic* some time in 1797–8, possibly at Coleridge's recommendation.[81] Encounters like Sylvanus's with the old sailor appear in many of the poems Wordsworth developed as his contributions to the collaboration with Coleridge on *Lyrical Ballads*. Wordsworth's experiment with a language of the lower and middle classes looks to transcend the barriers Thelwall experiences with the sailor, but many of the individual poems pivot on moments of incomprehension. In 'Simon Lee', 'We are Seven', and 'Old Man Travelling', for instance, Wordsworth's poetic persona takes on the role of participant-observer. I'll be returning to these experimental encounter poems later, but there are others more obviously akin to the 'friendly converse' between social equals found in Coleridge's conversation poems (and much of *The Peripatetic*). These include the 'Matthew' poems 'Expostulation and Reply' and 'The Tables Turned'. The 'Advertisement' (I: 117) tells the reader these poems 'arose out of conversation with a friend who was somewhat unreasonably attached to modern books of moral philosophy' (another 'Matthew' poem, 'The Fountain', added to the 1800 edition, is subtitled 'A Conversation'). As a description of the origins of these poems, this might almost be a parody of the earnest discussions of philosophical benevolence and sympathy Coleridge and his friends (including Wordsworth) enjoyed. Books of 'moral philosophy', Godwin's *Political Justice* among them, were central to the print war being waged over the status of universal benevolence after the French Revolution. In 'Expostulation and Reply', Matthew calls on 'William' to return to his books and 'drink the spirit breath'd | From dead men to their kind' (ll. 7–8).[82] For many eighteenth-century writers, reading was imagined as a kind of conversation between

---

[80] Ibid. 97. See also Thompson's own commentary on the encounter with the old sailor (26).

[81] See Wu, *Wordsworth's Reading 1770–1799*, 135–6.

[82] All quotations from the collection are taken from *Lyrical Ballads, and Other Poems, 1797–1800*, ed. James Butler and Karen Green (Ithaca/London: Cornell University Press, 1992) with lines numbers given in the text.

those who were living and those who were dead, but one often less fulfilling than the spark of social talk. William's response to the expostulation is exactly to invoke the superiority of 'converse', but not as a form of vivifying social talk:

> Then ask not wherefore, here, alone,
> Conversing as I may,
> I sit upon this old grey stone,
> And dream my time away. (ll. 29–32)

'The Tables Turned', subtitled 'An Evening Scene, on the Same Subject', invites its readers to imagine the poems as the natural outcomes ('arose out of') of an ongoing friendly converse on philosophical matters, but the paratextual invocation of this scene of reading only invokes what is again put aside for conversation with nature:

> One impulse from a vernal wood
> May teach you more of man;
> Of moral evil and of good,
> Than all the sages can. (ll. 21–4)

Like many other eighteenth-century texts, Thelwall's *Peripatetic* had also imagined the relationship with nature as a form of conversation, but as one among many more or less equivalent forms of sympathetic exchange. Coleridge's poems operate with an even more 'inclusive and integrating' drive, even if they seek to transcend the scene of difference in the process.[83] Wordsworth's poems almost parody this impulse in his collaborator's poetry by insisting on the gap between encoding and decoding, even in conversation. Where 'tender-hearted Charles' is folded into a kind of monologue in 'This Lime Tree Bower my Prison', Wordsworth's poems often present themselves as formal dialogues, as do the 'Matthew' poems, but ones where difference is left starkly unresolved.

To return to the more experimental poems of encounter, Coleridge's later objection was that they dwelt rather too much on the heteroglossic diversity of language, right down to the 'burr, burr, burr' of 'The Idiot Boy'.[84] Many of these poems register precisely the kind of social difference

---

[83] Bromwich, *Disowned by Memory*, 70. A poem like 'Nutting' with the destructive violence unleashed on the bower might be read as a parody of the 'embowering' motif in Coleridge.

[84] Coleridge criticized the line for failing to 'preclude from the reader's fancy the disgusting images of *ordinary, morbid idiocy*'. In terms of Wordsworth's theories more generally, Coleridge insisted even 'prose itself, at least, in all argumentative and consecutive works, differs, and ought to differ, from the language of conversation; even as reading ought to differ from talking.' Coleridge thought 'the best part of human language, properly so called, is derived from reflection on the acts of the mind itself...the greater part of which

Thelwall acknowledged in his encounter with the old sailor in *The Peripatetic*, but with little hope for the interlocutors to barter their way forward. The starkest example is perhaps 'Old Man Travelling', whose scenario is close to Thelwall's episode of the old sailor. Wounded soldiers and sailors were a staple of the political poetry of the 1790s, like Robert Merry's *The Wounded Soldier* (1795), often providing parables of the folly of the English crusade against revolutionary France. Wordsworth began the Salisbury Plain poems with the aim of exposing 'the vices of the penal law and the calamities of war as they affect individuals', but a different emphasis came to emerge.[85] Increasingly protest at social dislocation comes to focus on the dissolution of any 'knowable community of discourse'.[86] Much more than most of the protest poetry of the period, the participant-observer in 'Old Man Travelling' seems to have failed to understand what he sees or create a dialogue of any kind with the old man. The old man's simple prosaic response to the narrator's moralizing about his relation to nature is left by Wordsworth as the kind of stark collision between incommensurate points of view that can stop any conversation dead. Wordsworth 'does not presume, or aim to produce, a reading of an inward state of mind'.[87] Even in poems that take up dialogue formally, as in 'We Are Seven,' a chasm opens up between two voices. There the certainty of the rustic girl's sense of community clashes with the sceptical observations of an outsider figure. ''Twas throwing words away' (l. 67) is the final comment of the participant-observer as he turns away from the conversation. On the other hand, 'The Brothers' punctures any reading of 'We are Seven' as a glib affirmation of the girl's rustic community of discourse as simply superior to the urban observer's perspective. 'The pleasure which the mind derives from the perception of similitude in dissimilitude' that the 1800 preface was to claim as 'the life of our ordinary conversation' (I: 148) is thwarted in both poems. The priest in 'The Brothers' offers a complacent version of the idea that rural communities speak a purer language closer to nature than the taxonomies of written culture:

have no place in the consciousness of uneducated man.' See *Biographia Literaria, or Biographical Sketches of My Literary Life and Opinions*, ed. James Engell and W. Jackson Bate, 2 vols, *Complete Works*, Vol. VII (Princeton: Princeton University Press, 1983), II: 48, 60–1, and 54.

[85] To Francis Wrangham, 20 November 1795, *The Letters of William and Dorothy Wordsworth: The Early Years 1787–1805*, ed. Chester L. Shaver, 2nd edn (Oxford: Clarendon Press, 1967), 156.

[86] Jon P. Klancher, *The Making of English Reading Audiences, 1790–1832* (Madison: University of Wisconsin Press, 1987), 20.

[87] Bromwich, *Disowned by Memory*, 19.

> We have no need of names and epitaphs,
> We talk about the dead by our fire-sides. (ll. 176–7)

In the event, he neither recognizes Leonard nor the importance to him of
the story he complacently passes on. Leonard leaves the priest without
hope of explaining to him what has happened, but writes to him later:

> with a hope to be forgiven,
> That it was from the weakness of his heart
> He had not dared to tell him who he was. (ll. 427–9)

These poems of encounter imply that 'feelings may not be shareable',
maybe not even in a provisional sense of negotiation between different
forms of speech.[88]

For Rajan, the sense that languages 'can never quite connect' in *Lyrical
Ballads* is offset by other poems that explore 'the sense that the hermeneutic stories we construct to bridge such distances do sometimes produce
insights'.[89] Wordsworth often reveals a law of unintended consequences
in this regard: his narrator figures suggesting they have gained unexpected
and barely iterable insight from the encounters in these poems. So in
'Anecdote for Fathers' the strained 'intermitted talk' (l. 7) between father
and son may have produced a productive inversion of the normal hierarchies of learning:

> Oh dearest, dearest boy! my heart
> For better lore would seldom yearn,
> Could I but teach the hundredth part
> Of what from thee I learn. (ll. 57–60)

The conversation is on the relative merits of Kilve and Liswyn Farm
(Llyswen, Brecknockshire), the place Thelwall finally retired to after
Coleridge got cold feet about him joining the Somerset circle.[90] David
Simpson has also noted an allusion to contemporary debates on education;
especially Godwin's discussion in *The Enquirer* of the way the predisposition of the pedagogue can influence responses of students. Certainly, the
child in Wordsworth's poem picks up the hint that the father prefers Kilve

---

[88] See Rajan, *The Supplement of Reading*, 157.
[89] Ibid. 154.
[90] See Roe, *Radical Years*, 234–62. Dorothy and William Wordsworth visited Thelwall
with Coleridge at Llyswen in August 1798, just after the composition of 'Tintern Abbey'.
'Anecdote for Fathers' was composed a few months earlier, probably April 1798. Wordsworth acknowledged the reference to Thelwall in the Fenwick note of 1843. See the
transcription from Dove Cottage manuscript in *The Poetical Works of William Wordsworth*,
ed. Ernest de Selincourt, 5 vols (Oxford: Clarendon Press, 1940), I: 363.

to Liswyn Farm.[91] Godwin's preference for public education was focused
on his belief that 'Society is the true awakener of man' (*PPW*, V: 107), a
tenet that reveals the influence of his own education in Rational Dissent
on his thinking, including its sensitivity to the operations of power within
pedagogic relations.[92] Given Thelwall's shadowy presence in 'Anecdote
for Fathers', his voice could be added to the debate on education described
by Simpson. In *The Peripatetic*, Thelwall celebrated the pedagogic possibilities of 'amicable *Conversatione*' against the hierarchies of 'the timid
circle that usually surrounds the desk of a pedagogue'. For Thelwall the
lack of a more open pedagogy is 'a principle reason why so few of the
English excel in the talent of conversation'.[93] Wordsworth's poem over-
turns the hierarchies of the didactic relationship, but in a way that puts the
whole question of communication under a question mark ('*Could I but
teach*' [my italics]). If the poem from one perspective affirms that conversational collision may be unexpectedly productive, it also implies that
difference may be more discomforting than Thelwall imagines. After all,
in literal terms, the son's choice of Kilve rather than Liswyn Farm leaves
Thelwall potentially isolated, as indeed he was when his desire to share in
the 'philosophic amity' of the Coleridge–Wordsworth circle was
thwarted.[94] Part of the decision had to do with fears that his presence
would attract government interest in its private conversation (as it did).[95]
Whatever unintended products of the exchange are offered to the reader,
the emphasis of Wordsworth's poem is on the distance between the
participants and the obstacles to the pedagogy of candour that Godwin
and Thelwall encouraged.

Wordsworth's admission of other voices and the often stark registration
of their difference is in tension with another tendency in *Lyrical Ballads*
perhaps more usually thought of as Romantic. A series of poems in *Lyrical
Ballads* invokes a version of conversation with nature that aspires to the
condition of music or forms of sound not socialized into language. Take
the 'the sweet inland murmur' (l. 4) opposed to 'the din | Of towns and

---

[91] See David Simpson, 'Public Virtues, Private Vices: Reading between the Lines of
Wordsworth's "Anecdote for Fathers" ', in *idem* (ed.), *Subject to History: Ideology, Class,
Gender* (Ithaca/London: Cornell University Press, 1991), 163–90 (169–70).
[92] All references to Godwin's prose are to the *Political and Philosophical Writings of
William Godwin*, 7 vols, gen. ed. Mark Philp (London: William Pickering, 1993) and cited
cited as *PPW* with volume and page numbers in the main text.
[93] Thelwall, *Peripatetic*, 300 and ibid.
[94] See Thelwall, 'Lines Written at Bridgewater', in *Poems written chiefly in Retirement*,
129.
[95] Simpson notes ('Public Virtues, Private Vices', 177) that the interest in Thelwall's
conversation was quite public. Thomas Mathias, for instance, published a dialogue describing 'his *Schools of Reason* in country towns' in his *Pursuits of Literature*.

cities' (ll. 26–7) in 'Tintern Abbey'. Julie Ellison relates these lines to 'the roar' of 'the crowd' in 'the great Babel' softened to 'a murmur on th'uninjur'd ear' in *The Task* (iv.90–3).[96] Ellison's point is that for both the sound of the city's noisy coffee shop conversations is refined into a musicality ('still, sad music of humanity' (l. 92), 'sweet sounds and harmonies' (l. 143)). For Cowper this harmony can still be found in the social converse of the domestic circle. In Wordsworth too the quasi-familial circle matters, but governed by much more intuitive forms of relationship than Cowper's tea-table chatter suggests. David Bromwich makes a case for seeing 'Tintern Abbey' as a conversation poem more like 'This Lime Tree Bower my Prison' in so far as both 'are meditations on a landscape that need to address a second person apart from the reader, a particular listener to the poet's hopes and fears'.[97] In 'Tintern Abbey', it is the poet's 'dear, dear Sister' for whom he seeks benediction from nature, much like Coleridge in 'Frost at Midnight'. What Wordsworth adds is virtually an admonition to 'remember me, | And these my exhortations!' (ll. 146–7). These closing lines claim a moral credit drawn upon the poet's converse with nature in ways presented as not reducible to mere moral maxims or any form of socialized language. In certain respects, the poem offers a distinctively new form of the 'culture' of tact Cowper had suggested could be the only true guide to genuine converse, but lending even more credence to nature as guiding spirit of the intuition. The implicitly pre-social relationship between siblings is privileged over any more open and negotiable form of the republic of letters.

In the 1800 preface to *Lyrical Ballads*, Wordsworth offered his readers the prospect of overcoming the barriers of social mediation if they attended to the poems in the collection. The understanding of the reader 'must necessarily be in some degree enlightened, his taste exalted, and his affections ameliorated' (I: 126). For Hume, such habits were inculcated by participation in the conversable world of the republic of letters. For Wordsworth, poetry opens up an ameliorative conversation with its readers, but they must already be properly cultured (to twist Cowper's term) by habits of meditation on general nature, strengthened by reflections on

---

[96] See Ellison, 'Cowper's Busy World', 232.

[97] See Bromwich, *Disowned by Memory*, 70. Bromwich notes the increased exclusivity of Wordsworth's situation: 'Wordsworth's nature in "Tintern Abbey" is a seclusion that belongs to the poet alone…the reader of "Tintern Abbey" is an eavesdropper, or at most a passerby.' Bromwich describes the address to Dorothy as 'sometimes officious, sometimes severe'. Newlyn, *Language of Allusion*, reads the poem as the culmination of the year in Somerset and 'the origin of a private myth' (52). Within its mythos, she also sees uncertainties about Coleridge's 'One Life', wherein Wordsworth's 'personal association supplants religious dogma' (56).

Wordsworth's poetry. These habits of reflection seem to turn away from the diversity of language that the earlier 'Advertisement' had celebrated. Instead they articulate the idea of 'a more permanent and a far more philosophical language' (I: 124) that Wordsworth at least imagines (to Coleridge's disappointment) somehow persisting in the language of 'low and rustic life' (I: 124). This internalization and narrowing of the conversational process is no sudden break. No doubt Coleridge and Wordsworth, no less than many others writing after the Two Acts, were feeling the vulnerability even of private conversation to various forms of invasion and wilful misunderstanding, but they were also responding to a longer term cultural logic among the middling sort. For all its recurrent emphasis on the power of the feeling 'heart', the evacuation of social space and incorporation of verbal exchange into a dialogue with the self appear in their conversation poetry of the 1790s, as they did in many other forms of writing. A democratic sphere beyond the mediations of social difference may be glimpsed in these imaginings, but often at the cost of elevating literary culture beyond the diversity of talk. If David Bromwich is right to see in Wordsworth's poetry 'a new sense of the way a person may be joined to humanity', its newness ought not to be mistaken for simple progress, in this regard at least.[98]

[98] Bromwich, *Disowned by Memory*, 19.

5

Jane Austen and the Hazard
of Conversation

Jane Austen is often regarded as the doyenne of conversation in the
English novel. This judgment is the product of her technical command
of dialogue, the distinctive speech patterns of her characters, and the way
that distinctiveness so brilliantly plays into the labile economy of free
indirect speech. So much depends on conversation in Austen's novels that
philosophers like Alasdair MacIntyre have seen its tactful maintenance as a
moral imperative.[1] More concerned with the textual complexity of the
novels, Kathryn Sutherland has suggested that Austen's commitment to
'the exchange of conversation, whether as dialogue or reported speech' has
been submerged by an editorial desire to render the texts as literary classics
beyond the turbulence of everyday speech.[2] My discussion of Austen in
this chapter focuses mainly on *Emma* (1816), perhaps her most concentrated account of a conversable world. Its action, such as it is, never strays
far from the tight circle of Highbury, or even within that world, far from
the Woodhouse family's domestic space at Hartfield, where the novel's
various plot lines come to rest, if perhaps not to any resolution. Even in
such select circles, conversation is far from being presented as a stable
medium. Values of easy circulation and frank exchange are continually put
under pressure. The question of conversation's role in forging any larger
community is much more sceptically treated than it is among novelists
contemporary with Austen, like Maria Edgeworth and Hannah More.
Conversation in Austen turns out to be a painful pleasure, difficult to
maintain, and often unable to deliver the rewards it promises.

---

[1] See Alasdair MacIntyre, *After Virtue: A Study in Moral Theory*, 3rd edn (London:
Duckworth, 2007), 181–7 and 239–43.
[2] Kathryn Sutherland, *Jane Austen's Textual Lives: From Aeschylus to Bollywood* (Oxford:
Oxford University Press, 2005), 274.

CONVERSABLE AUSTEN

Austen doesn't really do much description. Conversations make up much of the matter of the novels, including reflections on past ones, often in representations of other dialogues. Take Emma's judgement of her earliest (re-)encounter with Jane Fairfax:

> She was, besides, which the worst of all, so cold, so cautious! There was no getting at her real opinion. Wrapt up in a cloak of politeness, she seemed so determined to hazard nothing. She was disgustingly, was suspiciously reserved. (*Emma* 169)[3]

Rendered in free indirect speech, blurring Emma's point of view with the narrator's, the judgement might reveal Jane Austen's opinion that proper conversation requires some risking of the self, some 'hazard' of engagement with the other. The word 'hazard' echoes around the novels, especially *Emma*, usually in the context of judgements about when reserve ought to be put aside, particularly by women, but so too does a prior sense of relish at the free flow of conversation. Catherine Morland in *Northanger Abbey*, for instance, is full of delight for the 'fluency and spirit' (*NA* 25) of Henry Tilney's talk and, for a while at least, the 'unreserved conversation' (35) of Isabella Thorpe. Most famously, in *Pride and Prejudice*, Elizabeth Bennet's attractions both for Darcy and generations of readers are to do precisely with the spontaneity and zest of her conversation. If Lizzie's conversation goes beyond the reserve and restraint recommended for ladies in the conduct books of the period, the more reserved heroines of *Mansfield Park* and *Persuasion* still have their own delight in the flow of conversation. Even so, the example of Isabella Thorpe in *Northanger*, among others, reminds us that the flow comes with risk. Isabella is not to be trusted to speak her true feelings, a question of deceit perhaps, but also of her lack of self-awareness. Isabella's talk may exceed and obscure her true feelings, even to herself, but for other characters conversation is a necessary means to self-knowledge. If there is a hazard of self-revelation and exposure in conversation, so too is there a risk in a silence that keeps others from knowing one's feelings or even making those feelings known to one's self. Faced with the genial but intimidating opposition of Sir Thomas Bertram, for instance, Fanny Price's inability 'to hazard another word' (*MP* 275) forces her further towards an unwanted intimacy with Henry Crawford.

---

[3] All references to Austen's fiction are to *The Novels of Jane Austen*, ed. by R. W. Chapman, 3rd edn (London/New York: Oxford University Press, 1933) with the page reference given in the text after abbreviated (except *Emma*) forms of the titles.

Typically of the recursive structure of Austen's novels, Emma's judgement of Jane Fairfax's reserve, initially made as interior monologue, becomes the subject of a conversation (with Mr. Knightley) at the beginning of the next chapter. There it is revealed that 'neither provocation nor resentment were discerned by Mr. Knightley' (*Emma* 170). Austen's labile narration leaves the reader never quite sure whether the third-person narrative voice does share Emma's judgement. Is her desire for sincerity naïve? Is it only naïve in its relative disregard for Jane's circumstances? Austen's awareness of Jane's state of dependency complicates the flow of conversation in *Emma*. If Knightley's response in the next chapter suggests Emma's judgement of this particular instance of Jane Fairfax's behaviour is amiss, we soon discover that he too thinks Jane lacks an 'open temper' (288), at least of the kind he would want in a wife. Moreover, it also appears that Knightley's own opinion is being influenced if not formed by his conversation with Emma. Far from producing 'transparent minds', as Dorrit Cohn famously put it, Austen's narration offers an endless awareness of the warping effects of social and gender inequality on freedom of speech, but also of the complicated nature of the individual subject, whose ideas and aspirations may not be fully known to itself before it speaks.[4]

Judgements such as Emma's of Jane Fairfax are regularly submitted to explicit discussion within the text, sometimes by the narrator outside the fiction, sometimes within the diegesis, often, as we've already seen, between the heroine and Mr Knightley, but not always. Perhaps the most famous opening gambit from among Austen's novels is the first sentence of *Pride and Prejudice*: 'It is a truth universally acknowledged, that a single man in possession of a good fortune, must be in want of a wife' (*P&P* 3). In fact, this universal truth is immediately revealed to be in something like free indirect speech, the expression of the hopes and wishes of local families, soon embodied in the person of Mrs Bennet, and then contested with her husband in the conversation that swiftly follows. This recursive method puts most judgements up for debate. 'Seldom, very seldom,' the narrator of *Emma* (431) tells the reader, 'does complete truth belong to any human disclosure; seldom can it happen that something is not a little disguised, or a little mistaken.' Austen's novels make her readers aware of the emergence of truth between different and even contested points of view, however restricted the social spectrum may be.[5] Although Emma

---

[4] See Dorrit Cohn, *Transparent Minds: Narrative Modes for Presenting Consciousness in Fiction* (Princeton: Princeton University Press, 1978), on *Emma*, 34–7. Cohn's emphasis on translating 'consciousness' somewhat takes the focus away from inter-subjective relations.

[5] Sutherland, *Austen's Textual Lives*, 309, identifies a shift towards this more complicated layering of voices with *Mansfield Park*. In *Pride and Prejudice*, in contrast, she suggests,

wishes Jane Fairfax to 'hazard' a little more, the word implies the more general sense of their being an element of risk in conversation. To start out on a conversation is a gamble, as the phrase (post-dating Austen in this sense, according to OED) 'opening gambit' recognizes. Nor, once a conversation gets started, is conversational implicature bound to work. Even if a conversation carries on in Austen, it often only proves that 'identity of words cannot guarantee identity of intention'.[6] Examples are almost too numerous to catalogue, but the cross purposes of Mr Elton and Emma are obvious instances, as too, if more consciously in their deceit on one side at least, are the conversations between Emma and Frank Churchill. The damage caused by the latter culminates in Emma's minor eruption to Miss Bates and its breakdown in the code of deference to inferiors largely observed by Emma. Austen's technical mastery of free indirect speech constantly opens up this awareness of the uncertain terrain of conversation, often counterpointing dialogue with a subtle shift into the thought processes of the participants.

Incomers in the novels, like Henry and Mary Crawford in *Mansfield Park*, bring with them different ways of speaking and different ideas of conversation, increasing the risk involved in any opening gambit before any terms of exchange are established. Sometimes a situation develops where silence is the only possible reply. *Emma* affords a wonderful example of the riskiness of conversation in this regard with the frostily formal exchanges between Emma and the new Mrs Elton, Miss Hawkins that was, the one confident of her family's pre-eminence in Highbury, the other keen to assert her own dignity by comparing her brother's house at Maple Grove to Hartfield. After some initial polite sparring, Emma tries modesty:

'When you have seen more of this country, I am afraid you will think you have over-rated Hartfield. Surry is full of beauties.'

'Oh! yes, I am quite aware of that. It is the garden of England, you know. Surry is the garden of England.'

'Yes; but we must not rest our claims on that distinction. Many counties, I believe, are called the garden of England, as well as Surry.'

'No, I fancy not,' replied Mrs. Elton, with a most satisfied smile. 'I never heard any county but Surry called so.'

Emma was silenced. (*Emma* 273–4)

'conversation is as formal an affair as dancing, with the various players taking their turn with a considerable degree of ceremony and choreographed direction.'

[6] Bharat Tandon, *Jane Austen and the Morality of Conversation* (London/New York: Anthem Press, 2003), 155.

Here are two new acquaintances that have heard quite a bit about each other before they meet. Differences in social station rankle in each direction, exacerbated by the fact Emma has been courted by the man who is now Mrs Elton's husband. There is a scarcely hidden competition for authority. Emma's irritation is bounded by a stronger sense of polite restraint, although Austen manages to convey a palpable sense of her grinding her teeth. Eager to assume an important place in Highgate society, Mrs. Elton is gauche enough to contradict her host (and social superior). Few conversations occur in Austen without some exploration of this kind into what is going on beyond the words spoken, a constant awareness of the currents beneath the flow that may ultimately silt up the channels of communication.

Despite all the undertow, conversation matters in Austen. *Emma* begins with the horrible prospect of the heroine having no one to talk to after the departure of her former governess:

How was she to bear the change?—It was true that her friend was going only half a mile from them; but Emma was aware that great must be the difference between a Mrs. Weston only half a mile from them, and a Miss Taylor in the house; and with all her advantages, natural and domestic, she was now in great danger of suffering from intellectual solitude. She dearly loved her father, but he was no companion for her. He could not meet her in conversation, rational or playful. (*Emma* 6–7)[7]

Emma's desire to be with those who can 'meet her in conversation, rational or playful' is at the heart of the novel, driven by the sense that the best conversation depends on equality. Her interest in Frank Churchill revolves initially around the question of whether he is conversable (the word's second appearance in the novel): she tells Knightley, 'If I find him conversible, I shall be glad of his acquaintance; but if he is only a chattering coxcomb, he will not occupy much of my time or thoughts' (*Emma* 150). Emma glosses the word 'conversible' in terms of a version of Addisonian agreeableness:

'My idea of him is, that he can adapt his conversation to the taste of every body, and has the power as well as the wish of being universally agreeable. To you, he will talk of farming; to me, of drawing or music; and so on to every body, having that general information on all subjects which will enable him to follow the lead, or take the lead, just as propriety may require, and to speak extremely well on each.' (ibid.)

Knightley's response, motivated, the reader may begin to suspect, by an unconscious jealousy, is that such protean politeness would sacrifice too much sincerity:

---

[7] See Tandon, *Morality of Conversation*, 157, following the argument of Tony Tanner's *Jane Austen* (Basingstoke/London: Macmillan, 1986).

'And mine,' said Mr. Knightley warmly, 'is, that if he turn out any thing like it, he will be the most insufferable fellow breathing! What! at three-and-twenty to be the king of his company—the great man—the practised politician, who is to read every body's character, and make every body's talents conduce to the display of his own superiority; to be dispensing his flatteries around, that he may make all appear like fools compared with himself! My dear Emma, your own good sense could not endure such a puppy when it came to the point.' (ibid.)

Knightley may be suspicious of social performance and display, but conversability still matters to him. Later, in the novel's third use of the word, he admits to Emma that he has found Harriet more 'conversable than I expected' (*Emma* 331). His own manner may be 'downright' (*Emma* 34), as Emma puts it, but he has a very strong sense of what is owed to others, especially social inferiors, as his later animadversions on Emma's behaviour to Miss Bates make clear.

Tact becomes an important quality for characters in judging these matters. Significantly the word 'tact' was probably imported into English from the French in the 1790s, a chronology that itself indicates the importance of properly managing conversation at the time. Austen seems never to have used the word in her fiction, but her novels are deeply aware of the difficulties recognized by its appearance in the language. Dugald Stewart's lectures on moral philosophy had recognized the word's usefulness for describing a fraught conversational world.[8] Lecturing as he was in Edinburgh, Stewart was putting into perspective Hume's mid-century hopes for a league between the learned and the conversable worlds. Even in the most conversable of eighteenth-century cities, acquiring the skills of conversation is now a difficult matter, 'the slow result of experience'. Of course, Stewart's French import does not discount the continuing importance of conversation in polished society; it only acknowledges the difficulty of negotiating through. For all the anxieties about politeness and candour that I have outlined in this opening discussion of Austen's fiction, the pervasive relish for conversation, for its sparkle and fluidity, for its ability to create relations between people, for the possibility of creating community out of dispersal, can scarcely be overestimated in the novels. In this regard, Austen was self-consciously developing an important strand that already existed in the history of the novel she inherited.

---

[8] Dugald Stewart, *Outlines of Moral Philosophy* (1801), 66. Austen does not use the word in her novels, but she would have come across it, for instance, in Edgeworth's. See below, pp. 212–15.

A CONVERSABLE HISTORY OF THE NOVEL

The world of literary relations, including those between writers and their readers, and between readers and texts, was broadly construed in terms of a conversation of culture when Austen was writing, and continued to be so. She inherited at least one tradition of the novel that was committed to the Humean idea of the conversable world, reproducing it in print, exploring varieties of social life, including ways of speaking, and enjoining its values onto its readers. Nancy S. Struever understands Austen's novels as 'the literary fulfilment, the fleshing out, of [Hume's] programme'.[9] This bold assertion perhaps underestimates the way that Richardson and others had already been at work on this project in the novel, as many contemporaries recognized. Writing in 1783, James Beattie, a fellow Scotsman, but no friend of Hume's irreligion, recognized novelists had increasingly oriented their work 'to the level of common life, conversed with man as his equal, and as a polite and chearful companion'.[10] Beattie was another Scotsman intent on bringing philosophy out of the cloisters and fiction out of the wilds of romance into the conversable world. Like Sir Charles Grandison, Beattie recommended conversation as a restorative for those involved 'in laborious speculation': 'Nor with our friends only should we associate: the company of strangers may be of singular use, in sweetening our tempers, and refining our manners.'[11] Placing his emphasis on cherishing cheerfulness and benevolence, he warned his readers against the dangers of 'romances' unless they are such that 'paint the pursuits and fortunes of mankind with simplicity and truth, and have no tendency to inflame appetites, or encourage wild expectation' (a contrast between romance and more conversable fictions that partially anticipates Austen's critique of Gothic in *Northanger Abbey*).[12] Although Beattie acknowledges *Clarissa* 'does honour to literature', he warns against its succession of horrors and sorrows as liable to 'wear out the spirits', just the kind of sympathetic criticism that had set Richardson off on writing *Sir Charles Grandison* to provide a model of the genuinely conversable man.[13] These sentiments

---

[9] Nancy S. Struever, 'The Conversable World: Eighteenth-Century Transformations of the Relation of Rhetoric and Truth', in Brian Vickers and Struever (eds), *Rhetoric and the Pursuit of Truth: Language Change in the Seventeenth and Eighteenth Centuries* (Los Angeles: William Andrews Clark Memorial Library, 1985), 79–119 (94).

[10] James Beattie, *Dissertations Moral and Critical* (London/Edinburgh, 1783), 564.

[11] Ibid. 204 and 200.

[12] Ibid. 195.

[13] Ibid. 202–3. Beattie notes that Grandison is too perfect 'to invite imitation' (568), but praises Richardson's 'moral sentiments' as 'profound and judicious' and notes that if 'his

from Beattie were transcribed by Katherine Plymley into her study notebooks (*KPN* 152), probably soon after 1800. Even though she appears to have been no great novel reader, they form part of her more general affirmation of the importance of conversation as a medium of knowledge about the world.[14]

Jane Austen's position as an unmarried woman, dependent to a large extent for entertainment and information on family-oriented sociability, contained some parallels with Plymley's, but perhaps with a greater emphasis on the literary traditions of eighteenth-century poetry and the novel, especially Cowper and Richardson's.[15] *Sir Charles Grandison* held an important place in the Austen family's sociable reading and writing. Austen owned a set of the novel with her name carefully inscribed on the title-page of each volume. She seems to have written a burlesque *History of Sir Charles Grandison* for a family performance some time after 1800, a parody dependent for its effect on just how well known the novel was to those involved.[16] Her nephew, James Edward Austen-Leigh, claimed that she knew by heart 'all that was ever done or said in the cedar parlour [of Selby House, Harriet Byron's favourite place in *Grandison*]'.[17] Satirized in her juvenilia, Austen probably gave Richardson more serious reconsideration after Barbauld's edition of his correspondence.[18] It would have made her aware that the novel was itself the product of a feminized sociability ('He lived in a kind of flower-garden of ladies'), including the circles of women who wrote to

dialogue is sometimes formal…many of his conversation-pieces are executed with elegance and vivacity'.

[14] The previous notebook quotes from Smellie's *Life of Hume* on the ease of access to the conversation of literary men in Edinburgh. (See Plymley's notebooks at the Shropshire Archives, Shrewsbury, MS 1066/1–197. All in-text references are to the relevant notebook number preceded by *KPN*.) Aspects of Plymley's situation offer interesting parallels with Austen's, not least the family-centred intellectual sociability. When her father died, she was very much dependent on the good graces of her brother, Joseph, who changed his surname after inheriting the estates of his mother's side of the family. She and her sister, Anne, remained unmarried, but were closely involved in the upbringing of her brother's children, living in the original family home nearby after her brother moved to the grander Corbett house.

[15] Anna Laetitia Barbauld's 'The Life of Mr. Richardson', in *The Correspondence of Samuel Richardson*, ed. Barbauld, 6 vols (London, 1804), I: cxcii, compares Cowper with the novelist as men who 'felt their hearts opened by the caressing manners and delicate attentions of female friendship'.

[16] *Jane Austen's 'Sir Charles Grandison'*, ed. Brian Southam (Oxford: Clarendon Press, 1980). Southam shows the family tradition that the play was written by Austen's niece Anna to be almost certainly inaccurate. On Austen's copy of Richardson's novel, see D. J. Gilson's 'Jane Austen's Books', *The Book Collector*, 23 (Spring 1974), 27–39 (36–7).

[17] James Edward Austen-Leigh, *Memoir of Jane Austen*, 2nd edn, ed. R. W. Chapman (1926), 89.

[18] For a full discussion of Austen's engagement with Richardson's novel, see Jocelyn Harris, *Jane Austen's Art of Memory* (Cambridge: Cambridge University Press, 1989), 34–47.

him about the novel as it progressed.[19] Austen's own novels were themselves products of a domestic circle, originally with a patriarchal monitor in the shape of her father, until his death in 1805, but with a more distinctively family complexion than Richardson's literary gatherings.[20] Kathryn Sutherland believes 'habits of confidential collaborative writing and circulation persisted throughout Austen's career even after conventional print publication became her dominant method,' but sees the novels from *Mansfield Park* onwards as the products of a tightening of the conversational circle. 'So close', Sutherland continues, 'that what functions in the early work to collapse the boundary between storyteller and audience, inviting them to conspire in imagining and rioting within a shared textual space, becomes in the indirect style of the mature fiction a device for dissolving the perspectives of narrator/narration and character.'[21] Dispensing with epistolary style in her more mature novels, Austen more fully incorporated dialogue into the fabric of her text, making the novels 'an ongoing experiment to test conversation's limits'.[22]

Compared with the intensifying complexities of point of view in Austen's novels, conversation is a relatively untroubled activity in Grandison's world. For all its aristocratic setting, the Christian family values of the middling sort are firmly articulated, often in what struck some of Richardson's social superiors as too common a style.[23] Sir Charles is loyal to his dissipated father, a point to which 'the female senate' objected, and Harriet dutifully reports everything back to her family in Northamptonshire (the English county of Austen's *Mansfield Park*) as well as being virtually adopted into the Grandison family before she marries. Sir Charles repeatedly makes it clear that he would rather be home than out in the world ('to fix my happiness within my own little circle', II: 80). Public amusements that take women beyond the domestic sphere are places to be distrusted. Wherever he is, Sir Charles cultivates his own version of Addison's 'unconstrained Carriage and...Openness of Behaviour' (*S* 119, I: 487), notwithstanding the 'stiffness', as Barbauld put it, of

---

[19] Barbauld, 'Life of Richardson', I: clxi.

[20] See Carol Shields, *Jane Austen* (London: Weidenfeld and Nicolson, 2001), 31, on the way 'all of the work appears to have been shared openly with family and friends'.

[21] Sutherland, *Austen's Textual Lives*, 231–2.

[22] Ibid. 174.

[23] Lady Mary Wortley Montagu believed that Richardson had 'no Idea of the manners of high Life' and 'never had (probably) money enough to purchase any, or even a Ticket for a masquerade, which gives him such an aversion to them'. See Lady Mary Wortley Montagu to Lady Bute, 20 October 1755, in *The Complete Letters of Lady Mary Wortley Montagu*, ed. Robert Halsband, 3 vols (Oxford: Clarendon Press, 1967), III: 97. Montagu was smarting at the novel's representation of her; see *Letters*, III: 94–5. Unsurprisingly, Barbauld bridled at Montagu's aristocratic condescension in 'Life of Samuel Richardson', I: clxxiv-v.

Richardson's dialogue.[24] In general, the novel is in favour of freedom and easiness in conversation and against too much reserve, even in young ladies. Harriet describes 'DELICACY' as 'often a misleader; an idol, at whose shrine we sometimes offer up our Sincerity' (II: 1). She confesses her love for Sir Charles early in the novel, although not to him directly. For readers like Lady Mary Wortley Montagu, representative of an older courtly code, Harriet was a blabbermouth, who says 'all she thinks to all the people she sees, without reflecting that in this Mortal state of Imperfection Fig leaves are as necessary for our Minds as our Bodies, and tis as indecent to shew all we think as all we have.'[25] In Richardson's novel there is a relative privileging of sincerity against courtly artifice in manners, even if it is in a continual negotiation with questions of modesty.

One of the earliest entries in Fanny Burney's journals records a discussion about *Sir Charles Grandison* in tête-à-tête with her sister's beau, Alexander Seton. After they have discussed the relative 'politeness, sense & conversation' of English and Scottish ladies, Burney records her disappointment at Seton's opinion that 'Sir Charles Grandison is all perfection, & consequently, the last Character we find in real Life'.[26] Whatever Seton's reservations, Grandison probably provided a model for Lord Orville in *Evelina*:

His conversation was sensible and spirited; his air and address were open and noble; his manners gentle, attentive, and infinitely engaging; his person is all elegance, and his countenance the most animated and expressive I have ever seen. (30)

In practice, Burney struggled to convey this idea of easiness in Orville's dialogue, as did Richardson with Grandison's. Jane Austen used Orville as an example of conversational stiffness when criticizing her niece's efforts at novelistic dialogue: 'it is too much like the formal part of Lord Orville, & I think is not natural.'[27] Orville apart, Burney's novel shows a greater facility than Richardson's in its variety of distinctive speech patterns, reflecting the fact it takes its heroine much more out into the world than *Sir Charles Grandison*. Both heroines venture to a masquerade, but Harriet is extremely reluctant, and her fears are confirmed when she is abducted. After Sir Charles saves her, Harriet remains safe within various family spaces until Sir Charles marries her and they create their own.

---

[24] 'Life of Richardson', I: cxxix. All references to *The Spectator* are to Donald F. Bond's edition, 5 vols (Oxford: Clarendon Press, 1987) as *S* followed by original issue number and then volume and page number.

[25] To Lady Bute, 20 October 1755; *Letters*, III: 97.

[26] 17 November 1768, *The Early Journals and Letters of Fanny Burney*, ed. Lars E. Troide and Stewart J. Cooke, 3 vols (Oxford: Clarendon Press, 1988–94), I: 47.

[27] See Jane to Anna Austen, mid [?] July 1814 in *Jane Austen's Letters*, 3rd edn, ed. Deirdre Le Faye (Oxford: Oxford University Press, 1995), 267.

Although she experiences trepidations similar to Harriet's, Evelina is more fully immersed into the proliferating worlds of eighteenth-century sociability, even if she finds conversation extremely difficult to read there. Austen may be closer to Richardson in the circumscribed nature of the social world she describes, but her labile rendition of dialogue makes the reader even more aware of the difficulties of negotiating one's way through conversation than Burney. Abandoning the epistolary style of *Sir Charles Grandison* and *Evelina*, Austen developed a narrative method that gave intense expression to the fraught nature of the conversable world, while continuing their valorization of the flow of talk.

In 1814, Austen observed to her niece Anna 'I have made up my mind to like no Novels really, but Miss Edgeworth's, Yours & my own.'[28] Critical comparisons of their novels usually stall around Edgeworth's overt didacticism, but when her reputation was at its height her facility with dialogue was routinely praised.[29] The *Edinburgh Review* thought she excelled nearly all other novelists in her 'faithful but flattering representation of the spoken language of persons of wit and politeness of the present day'.[30] Even an ideological opponent like the *Quarterly Review*, discussing one of her least successful novels, *Patronage* (1814), put Edgeworth with Burney at the head of those novelists who had excelled in representing 'probable events in private life'.[31] Edgeworth is praised as an *'anti-sentimental novelist'* teaching 'practical morality', not through dry maxims but 'reasons put into the mouths of the actors themselves'. Generally speaking the *Quarterly* has no objection to the morality of the novels as such, but thinks they display 'too unfavourable an estimate of London manners and society'. For all its praise of her practical morality and facility at handling sketches of society and conversation, it was critical of her tendency to give 'all her virtuous characters a tincture of science, and to make them fond of chemistry and mechanics.' Hannah More thought such topics ought to be excluded from the conversation of ladies, as we will see, but Edgeworth had grown up in a culture of improvement more welcoming to scientific talk, even in mixed company.

Interest in Edgeworth has undergone a revival of late, especially in relation to her Irish novels, but her interest in social talk was cosmopolitan.[32] She was a keen satirist of the manners of the English elite. She saw a lot of intellectual

---

[28] Jane to Anna Austen, 28 September 1814, ibid. 278.
[29] See Marilyn Butler, *Jane Austen and the War of Ideas*, 2nd edn (Oxford: Clarendon Press, 1987), 145.
[30] *Edinburgh Review*, 20 (July 1812), 100–26 (103).
[31] *Quarterly Review*, 11 (January 1814), 301–21 (302).
[32] The most important landmark is this revival was Marilyn Butler's *Maria Edgeworth: A Literary Biography* (Oxford: Clarendon Press, 1972).

society in Edinburgh, London, and Paris after 1800 and wrote for and about it. James Chandler defines her novels in terms of a 'scientific method' based on 'observation, comparison, principled selection of objects to be examined, hypotheses about casual relations, and so on'.[33] The list might be extended to include conversation as both an ethnographical object and pedagogical method. Her novels comprise a careful attempt to reproduce the idioms of speech—across several classes—and a willingness to expand the subjects permissible in everyday talk, even among polite circles. Edgeworth was the product of a family circle that participated in the networks of the Midlands enlightenment, including the Lunar Society.[34] In this world, conversation was regarded as a medium capable of the discovery and dissemination of truth, including scientific knowledge.[35] There is a kinship between Edgeworth and the radical novelists of the 1790s around 'an ideal of perfect sincerity', to use Jenny Davidson's phrasing, although it is overstating the case to say that she implies 'tact is moral weakness'.[36] Edgeworth was not, after all, Harriet Freke, the anti-heroine of *Belinda* (1801). Despite its relatively recent importation into English, the cosmopolitan Edgeworth, who had toured the Continent in 1802–3, actually makes positive use of 'tact' in her novels from at least as early as *Ennui*, published in the first volume of *Tales of Fashionable Life* (1809).[37] In *Patronage*, a novel Austen read and admired, the word is used in praise of the character of the Lord Chief Justice in a passage that particularly irritated the *Quarterly* reviewers:

---

[33] See James Chandler, 'Why we need Irish Studies', *Field Day Review*, 2 (2006), 18–39 (36).

[34] See Butler, *Maria Edgeworth*, 32–5, 59–61, and 114–20, and *Jane Austen and the War of Ideas*, 125–6.

[35] Edgeworth's first publication, *Letters to Literary Ladies* (London, 1795), exploited the techniques of the epistolary novel for an educational tract (a common use of the 'conversation' form that had developed into a distinct educational subgenre). The barely novelized first section is a debate about female education, where R. L. Edgeworth's friend Thomas Day tries to argue him out of educating his daughter. The second section is a dialogue between two women friends about the values of a life of aristocratic display and feeling as against a more rational home life. To some extent this opposition is between the fashionable and domestic values, but the latter are strongly encoded in terms of rational enquiry rather than the retrenchment of female experience to household and family matters. See the discussion in Butler, *Jane Austen and the War of Ideas*, 126–7.

[36] See Jenny Davidson, *Hypocrisy and the Politics of Politeness: Manners and Morals from Locke to Austen* (Cambridge: Cambridge University Press, 2004), 154. She refers to Edgeworth's attack on 'address' in *Manoeuvring* (1809).

[37] Among the faults ascribed to Lady Geraldine by the narrator, Lord Glenthorn, are 'want of polish, elegance, and tact'. See *Ennui* in *The Novels and Selected Works of Maria Edgeworth*, 12 vols, Vol I, ed. Jane Desmarais, Tim McLoughlin, and Marilyn Butler (London: Pickering and Chatto, 1999), 214. The word is used in a more unequivocally positive context in *Patronage*.

He possessed perfect conversational *tact*, with great powers of wit, humor, and all that felicity of allusion, which an uncommonly recollective memory, acting on stores of various knowledge, can alone command. He really conversed; he did not merely tell stories, or make bon-mots, or confine himself to the single combat of close argument, or the flourish of declamation; but he alternately followed and led, threw out and received ideas, knowing how to listen full as well as how to talk, remembering always Lord Chesterfield's experienced maxim, 'That it is easier to hear, than to talk yourself into the good opinion of your auditors.'—It was not, however, from policy, but from benevolence, that the Chief Justice made so good a hearer.[38]

The *Quarterly* took it for granted that this liberal lawyer was 'a distinguished friend of the liberty of the press, or he would hardly have obtained so much valuable praise from Miss Edgeworth, who as appears from several passages in her writing, is animated by a more than ordinary zeal on that subject'.[39] Certainly Edgeworth distinguished the Chief Justice's tactful liberality from the cynical formality of Chesterfield, opening up an idea of politeness that was not simply taken to be the prescribed forms of upper class civility, but combined knowledge with pleasurable discourse.

The *Quarterly* identified such talk with dangerously progressive opinion, including the opening up of questions of 'knowledge' to polite conversation in mixed company. There was a general preconception that the Edgeworths suffered from a predisposition to discussing such matters even in domestic circumstances. When Frances Beaufort—Maria's future sister-in-law—visited the family estate in Edgeworthstown in 1797, she was relieved to find these accounts exaggerated:

The family are all you know chymists and mechanics, & lovers of literature & a more united more happy more accommodating more affectionate family never yet came under my observation. How enormous are the lies, how confounded the reports that have [been] told concerning them.[40]

Edgeworth's scientific interests continued in her later life as part of a practise of feminized sociability, which included women such as Mary Somerville and Elizabeth Fry.[41] Evening parties of this circle quite happily

---

[38] *Patronage*, in *The Novels and Selected Works of Maria Edgeworth*, 12 vols, Vol. VI, ed. Connor Carville and Marilyn Butler (London: Pickering and Chatto, 1999), 223–4.

[39] *Quarterly Review* (January 1814), 313.

[40] Frances Beaufort to her brother William, 2 July 1797, quoted in Butler, *Maria Edgeworth*, 131.

[41] See James Secord, 'How Scientific Conversation Became Shop Talk', in Aileen Fyfe and Barnard Lightman (eds), *Science in the Marketplace: Nineteenth-Century Sites and Experiences* (University of Chicago Press: Chicago and London, 2007), 23–59, and for the earlier eighteenth-century context, Alice N. Walters, 'Conversation Pieces: Science and Politeness in Eighteenth-Century England', *History of Science*, 35 (1997), 121–54. Walters'

discussed the kind of agricultural improvements found in Katherine Plymley's records of Shropshire conversation. One letter home from Edgeworth to her stepmother from 1822 records an evening with the agricultural improver Sir John Sebright:

Mrs Somerville and I were sitting on the opposite sofa all night and Dr Wollaston sitting before us talking most agreeably and giving us a clear account of the improvement of refining sugar.[42]

Talking about such technical matters in mixed company was neither tactless nor disagreeable from Edgeworth's point of view. Her interest in rational improvements extended to society itself, which her novels suggest is both knowable in the aggregate and susceptible of amelioration. *Belinda* (1801) and both series of *Tales of Fashionable Life* (1st series 1809, 2nd series 1812) have a commitment to reforming the upper classes into usefulness, but their ethnographic concerns only intensified the obvious relish for dialogue.

When in *Belinda* Clarence Hervey first encounters the Percival family, he finds a contrast between a rational domesticity and the aristocratic parade at Lady Delacour's:

The unconstrained cheerfulness of lady Anne Percival spoke a mind at ease, and immediately imparted happiness by exciting sympathy; but in Lady Delacour's wit and gayety there was an appearance of art and effort, which often destroyed the pleasure that she wished to communicate.—Some people may admire, but none can sympathise with affectation.[43]

For Edgeworth, this 'ease' does not simply smooth social relations, it facilitates the fungibility of knowledge, as Hervey discovers:

The children at lady Anne Percival's happened to be looking at some gold fish, which were in a glass globe, and Dr. X—, who was a general favourite with the younger, as well as with the elder part of the family, was seized upon the moment he entered the room: a pretty little girl of five years old took him prisoner by the flap of the coat, whilst two of her brothers assailed him with questions about the ears, eyes, and fins of fishes. One of the little boys fillipped the glass globe, and observed, that the fish immediately came to the surface of the water, and seemed to hear the noise very quickly; but his brother doubted, whether the fish heard the

---

analysis of 'polite science' suggests it was 'limited to the enrichment of social interactions' (129). Edgeworth and her circle were more committed to the transmission of knowledge than the world Walters describes.

[42] To Mrs. Edgeworth, 16 January 1822, in Maria Edgeworth, *Letters from England 1813–1844*, ed. Christina Colvin (Oxford: Clarendon Press, 1971), 322.

[43] Maria Edgeworth, *Belinda*, in *Novels and Selected Works*, vol. II, ed. Siobhan Kilfeather (London: Pickering and Chatto, 2003), 77.

noise, and remarked, that they might be disturbed by seeing or feeling the motion of the water, when the glass was struck.

Dr. X— observed, that this was a very learned dispute, and that the question had been discussed by no less a person than the abbé Nollet; and he related some of the ingenious experiments tried by that gentleman to decide, whether fishes can or cannot hear.[44]

Significantly, the science in question is concerned with communication in the natural world.[45] Conversation for Edgeworth ought to be in an extension of communication conceived of as a universal quality of nature. Throughout the novel, she explores what constitutes natural communication in a complicated commercial society dominated by a fashionable elite.

If *Belinda* and Edgeworth's later tales of fashionable life represent aristocratic sociability as a form of hypocrisy in Davidson's terms, where no one ever says what they mean, then they also scout an alternative form of conversational enquiry, where truth can be got at through the relatively free exchange of opinions on a relatively broad range of topics (certainly broader than those that appear in Austen's novels). Tact remains more important to Edgeworth in this process than Davidson allows. Harriet Freke in *Belinda* represents a 'limit case' in this regard where the sacrifice of modesty to sincerity goes too far. The same kind of case was explored by Hays in *Emma Courtney*, but where her novel is in sympathy with someone whose excesses are shown to be the product of the gendered restrictions of polite society, Edgeworth's emphasis is on Harriet Freke's lack of rational judgement and failure to negotiate the conditions of her society. The dream of a sentient language in Hays is replaced in Edgeworth by a scientific but worldly confidence that conversation can function as a rational form of communication. The great critical success of the fashionable tales made Edgeworth the premier novelist writing as Austen was publishing her first novels.[46] Edgeworth's fiction focused on conversational women from the upper classes with an interest in the natural rhythms and idioms of drawing-room talk. Little wonder Austen sent Edgeworth a presentation copy of *Emma*, although the recipient disliked its lack of plot and purpose.[47] Austen's satires of fashionable conversation are not as overtly didactic as Edgeworth's, whose reader is more often placed with the narrator outside the dialogue, looking in at the experiment

[44] Ibid. 77–8.

[45] Dr. X follows Joseph Priestley's belief that the 'ease and freedom of conversation' were particularly adapted to educating young minds, but the idea was a commonplace of educational writers by 1800. See Joseph Priestley, *A Catechism for Children, and Young persons*, 5th edn (Birmingham, 1787), A2.

[46] Butler, *Maria Edgeworth*, 347.

[47] Ibid. 445.

going on. If Austen's 'differential' narrative method does not expose the reader to such a range of kinds of conversation, nor does it provide such a stable ethnographic vantage point outside the exchange. From this perspective, Austen's conversable world might be judged at once both more conservative and more sceptical than Edgeworth's.

The scepticism becomes clearer when Austen's novels are compared to Hannah More's *Coelebs in Search of a Wife*. When her sister urged her to read this hugely popular novel, Austen replied: 'My disinclination for it before was affected, but now it is real: I do not like the Evangelicals.'[48] More's novel obviously did not fill Austen with enthusiasm, despite its explicit interest in conversation and female learning. 'Always the Paladin of the reading ladies' (II: 194), Charles—the hero and first-person narrator—has no problem with learned women as such, but he expects them to have a modest default setting of silence.[49] He defends them against the 'illiberal sarcasms of men' (II: 194), but there are limits to what constitutes appropriate forms of female knowledge to be brought forward in conversation:

I confess that what is sneeringly called a learned lady, is to me far preferable to a scientific one, such as I encountered one evening, who talked of the fulcrum, and the lever, and the statera, which she took care to tell us was the Roman steel-yard, with all the sang-froid of philosophical conceit. (II: 194)

What was agreeable in conversation to Edgeworth was to offend against the conversational proprieties in More's novel. Charles greatly prefers a wife who 'could modestly discriminate between the beauties of Virgil and Milton, to one who was always dabbling in chemistry, and who came to dinner with dirty hands from the laboratory' (II: 194–5). Miss Sparkes is this sort of woman, full of pretensions to practical knowledge, liable to exchange opinions with her groom, and grab the leg of her horse to examine the causes of its lameness. Scientific knowledge is the sort of diversion from practical morality likely to seduce women like Miss Sparkes into a 'sovereign contempt' for 'domestic economy' (II: 209). More's heroine, Lucilla, is well read, but not prone to display, and her non-scientific learning does not distract at all from her charity work or her ability to manage a household.

More's novel professes a delight in 'the pleasures of conversation' (I: 21) and her preface locates its origins in an excursion she had taken to the home of a modest Christian family and the 'familiar conversations of this

---

[48] Jane to Cassandra Austen, 24 January 1809, *Letters*, 170.
[49] All references to More's novel are to *Coelebs in Search of a Wife*, 2 vols (London, 1808) and given in the text with volume and page number.

little society' (I: vii). The plot begins with Charles journeying to London, his anticipation whetted by 'Dr. Johnson's remark, that there is no pleasure on earth comparable to the *fine full flow of London talk'* (I: 37, More's italics).[50] What he finds there disappoints him and underpins More's own critique of fashionable life. London is full of 'desultory chat' (I: 44) rather than discussion. 'The ever restless, rolling tide of new intelligence' (II: 184) overwhelms conversation. Charles searches for the familiar 'feast of reason and the flow of soul' (I: 38) in London, but gives 'reason' and 'soul' definitions far from universally agreed upon. More's object in her novel is to insist that 'religion may be brought to mix with the concerns of ordinary life' (I: ix). The novel distances itself from theological controversy. Lucilla's father insists 'he never contended for words or trifling distinctions' (I: 171), and argues 'bad taste could never advance the interests of Christianity' (170), but men like Sydney Smith could only see her writing as too severe upon 'the ordinary amusements of mankind'.[51] Smith's review of *Coelebs* gives an account of conversation that owes much to his Edinburgh education in the principles of Hume:

Conversation must and ought to grow out of materials on which men can agree, not upon subjects which try the passions. But this good lady wants to see men chatting together upon the Pelagian heresy—to hear, in the afternoon, the theological rumours of the day—and to glean polemical tittle-tattle at a tea-table rout.[52]

Religious zeal will only stop the agreeable flow and set everyone at each other's throats on matters of doctrine (as Hume had argued in the context of Scottish church in the 1750s). Tact from Smith's point of view meant putting religious faith to one side. For More, this kind of judgement sacrificed truth to politeness, anticipated in the character of Mr Flam, who would prefer 'an ounce of morality' to a 'ton of religion' (II: 396–7). In this regard, at least, More thinks of conversation as something more than a question of the polite reproduction of society. She is even willing to countenance 'collision' in conversation when it comes in the defence of the truth of Christian values.

More's idea of the rational pursuit of truth was very different from someone like Edgeworth's or even Plymley's, but she shared with them a suspicion of an agreeableness that sacrifices too much to politeness. Lucilla's father, Mr Stanley, insists on absolute truthfulness, even in

---

[50] See my discussion of Johnson's opinion p. 84 above.
[51] *Edinburgh Review*, 14 (April 1809), 145–51 (148). Smith had attended Dugald Stewart's lectures on philosophy in Edinburgh.
[52] Ibid. 150.

everyday conversation. More praised Richardson for providing 'living models' in *Sir Charles Grandison*, of the 'triumph of religion and reason over the passions' (II: 211), but for all his pious stiffness his moralizing is rarely as explicitly religious as More's. Even Cowper, as we have seen, is criticized in *Coelebs*.[53] More's stringency made her unpalatable even to many churchmen. In his review of *Persuasion*, Richard Whately, Archbishop of Dublin, contrasted the unobtrusive morality of Austen's novels with *Coelebs*. His contrast is preceded by a lengthier discussion of Edgeworth, praised for drawing characters and conversations 'such as they occur in real life', but her plots are improbable and she is too obtrusive for Whately, especially, again, with scientific knowledge.[54] Whately begins his review by suggesting novelists have now supplanted the function of essayists like Addison and Johnson, but makes the principle of agreeableness central to their role as a moral force. Religion in Austen 'is rather alluded to, and that incidentally, than studiously brought forward and dwelt upon'. The burden is put upon 'private conversations and uncommunicated feelings', with Austen 'saying as little as possible in her own person'.[55]

Austen's own distaste for More's evangelical directness is hinted at by the unflattering reference to *Coelebs* in her revision of the early manuscript *Catharine* (of which more in my next section). Mary Waldron sees *Mansfield Park* as a full-blown critique of *Coelebs*, examining weaknesses More ignores, especially 'the way Christianity operated among the rich and powerful'.[56] This judgement rather ignores More's own critique of upper class manners and morals. In this regard, More and Austen might be seen to differ primarily in approach, as Whately indicated. *Coelebs* complains at the tendency for novels to treat clerical characters as objects of derision, something Austen does with Mr Collins in *Pride and Prejudice*. In *Mansfield Park*, Austen takes up the challenge of a serious approach to the clergy, but implies even a clergyman may depend on tactful interaction with others to discover what he really believes. Charles in *Coelebs* has nearly all his prior beliefs confirmed by his experiences at Stanley Park. Very little space appears between speaking and thinking in those characters not manifestly dishonest. More looks to introduce some dramatic tension to *Coelebs* by introducing an aristocratic suitor for Lucilla

[53] See the discussion in my previous chapter, pp. 176–7.
[54] See *Quarterly Review*, 24 (January 1821), 352–76 (358). Whately also notes the lack of a religious framework in Edgeworth's novels. A similar hit was made in the *Quarterly's* review of *Patronage* discussed earlier.
[55] Ibid. 359 and 362.
[56] Mary Waldron, *Jane Austen and the Fiction of Her Time* (Cambridge: Cambridge University Press, 1999), 90.

in the guise of Lord Staunton, but he is no Henry Crawford. Lucilla and her family soon unite to send him on his way in an affirmation of their Christian beliefs, while also making it clear they are in general 'a little aristocratic in our political principles' (I: 283). Edmund and Fanny in *Mansfield Park* lead an active religious life, bringing belief into their everyday conversations, as recommended by More, but the challenge brought to their conversation by the incursion of the Crawfords requires rather more than the affirmation of prior principles.

DOMESTICATING ANTI-JACOBINISM

In my previous chapters, I have tracked the relationship between ideas of conversation and the uneven development of a domestic ideology that saw 'the great community', in Sir Charles Grandison's words, as constituted from 'so many miniatures'. By the 1790s, these more general pressures were being sharply reinforced by magistrates and legislation like the Two Acts of 1795. The Two Acts did not directly target conversation as such, although debating societies and benefit clubs now had to be registered with magistrates, but many of those committed to freedom of speech perceived them as threatening the civic foundations of British liberty. Katherine Plymley feared their effects 'even in private conversation' (*KPN* 38). For others the legislation was to be understood as only a necessary interregnum in the more general tradition of British liberty, at least partly justified by exceptional circumstances. Just such an account appeared in *The Microcosm of London* (1808–10), invoking 'circumstances' that made it 'expedient, if not absolutely necessary, to restrain that freedom of discussion, which generating into licentiousness, had nearly involved this country in a scene of murder and desolation, similar to that by which France had been afflicted.'[57]

The Microcosm was a strange place for such a commentary to appear in many ways. One of a series of lavishly illustrated books published by Rudolph Ackermann, it was ostensibly a celebration of early-nineteenth-century London. Its 104 hand-coloured aquatints of London life by Auguste Pugin and Thomas Rowlandson came with a commentary in the first two volumes by W. H. Pyne. His comments on the Two Acts appear with an aquatint of the Athenian Lyceum debating society, towards the end of the first volume (see Fig. 6). Somewhat oddly, the subject is picked up again at the beginning of the second volume. Nothing is said

---

[57] *The Microcosm of London*, 3 vols (London, 1808–10), II: 3.

Fig. 6. Thomas Rowlandson, and Joseph Constantine Stadler, after Augustus Charles Pugin, 'Debating Society, Piccadilly' (1808). Courtesy of the Yale Center for British Art, Paul Mellon Collection.

about the Athenian Lyceum, which met off Piccadilly, in either part of the commentary. In the aquatint, it looks a respectable gathering, attended by both men and women, but the commentary presents a jeremiad on the

disposition to convert that spirit of freedom so interesting to the feelings of an Englishman, and that liberty of canvassing political subjects which the laws allow to be done with decency, into a theatre of licentious discussion, and a means of disseminating principles injurious, not only to the true interests of society, but ultimately to the safety of the individuals who venture to utter them.[58]

The whole project of *The Microcosm* is haunted by a more general uncertainty about the relationship between particular spaces of conversation and the larger idea of the public: 'Among the numerous inhabitants of this great city, there are some whose particular pursuits have so much engrossed their time and thoughts, that they know little more of the scenery which surrounds

---

[58] Ibid. I: 223–4.

them than barely the names.' The book is designed to 'induce them to notice and contemplate objects so worthy of their attention'.[59] Rowlandson's participation was meant to ensure the project was attentive not just to architecture, but to 'the general air and peculiar carriage, habits, &c of such characters as are likely to make up the majority in particular places'.[60] The ambition was to present particular characters and their conversable worlds as microcosms of a larger sense of community.

The panoramic perspective of *Microcosm of London* moves alphabetically from the Royal Academy to a final picture of the Thames, the great conduit for the circulation of people and goods, at the end of volume III. Several pictures, including 'The Corn Exchange' (see Fig. 7), show knots of conversation in a commercial context. Addison's famous essay on the felicity of trade—that 'knit[s] mankind together in a mutual intercourse'—is quoted in the commentary on the Royal Exchange in the third volume.[61] The question remains how these conversations integrate into any coherent sense of a larger society. In what sense are they a microcosm? Discussing Rowlandson's 'spirited drawing' of the Exhibition Room, Somerset House (see Fig. 8), the commentary praises the 'infinite variety of small figures, contrasted with each other in a way so peculiarly happy, and marked with appropriate character'. It goes on to reassure the reader that the figures are all serious art viewers: 'The peculiar mode by which different persons shew the earnestness with which they contemplate what they are inspecting, and display an absorbed attention to the objects before them…forms an admirable little picture of that busy scene.'[62] The insistence seems to register a concern as to whether the chatting groups who stand before the paintings, not very obviously absorbed by what they see, really do constitute a public, a constant issue for exhibitions in the period.[63] The question of the relationship between conversation in these particular groups and the larger idea of 'the public' recurs, predictably enough, with the picture of crowds at Bartholomew Fair (see Fig. 9): 'To be pleased in their own way, is the object of all. Some hugging, some fighting, others dancing: while many are enjoying the felicity of being borne along with the full stream of one mob, others are encountering all the dangers and vicissitudes of forcing their passage through another.'[64] The description descends from the relative complacency about each being 'pleased in their own way' into the anarchy of different kinds of

[59] Ibid. I: i-ii.   [60] Ibid. I: iii.
[61] Ibid. III: 25–6.   [62] Ibid. I: 10.
[63] See David H. Solkin, ' "This Great Mart of Genius": The Royal Academy Exhibitions at Somerset House, 1780–1836', in *idem* (ed.), *Art on the Line: The Royal Academy Exhibitions at Somerset House 1780–1836* (New Haven, CT/London: Yale University Press, 2001), 1–8.
[64] *Microcosm*, I: 52.

degenerate sociability. Faced with making sense of this diversity, the essay soon turns from the present to the historical origins of the Fair. 'Our warlike and gallant ancestors' provide a more comforting prospect than the contentious present.[65] The question this digression begs is whether all these different kinds of social interaction are included in the larger flow emblematized by the Thames. Within the larger picture of the commercial nation as a home to a diversity of social talk lurked the question of articulation in its other sense. How are these different scenes of social talk brought together into a larger whole? Could the nation be construed as a community forged out of conversations between private citizens as Addison had hoped at the beginning of the previous century?

Fig. 7. John Bluck, and Thomas Rowlandson, after Augustus Charles Pugin, and after Thomas Rowlandson, 'Corn Exchange' (1808). Courtesy of the Yale Center for British Art, Paul Mellon Collection.

[65] Ibid. 54.

EXHIBITION ROOM, SOMERSET HOUSE.

Fig. 8. John Hill, after Augustus Pugin and Thomas Rowlandson, 'Exhibition Room, Somerset House'. Plate 2 from vol. I of *The Microcosm of London*. Courtesy of the Yale Centre for British Art, Paul Mellon Collection.

In these trying circumstances, conversation within the domestic circle became overdetermined as the privileged forum for the airing of political discussion, but one continually haunted by the larger question of how these local communities could be articulated—if at all—into the idea of a broader public conversation. Kevin Gilmartin has provided an arresting account of the treatment of conversation in the wave of anti-Jacobin novels that emerged after 1795, a chronology that implies that the struggle against radicalism on a directly political level had shifted to the policing of culture with a new focus—as Plymley and others feared—on managing the private sphere.[66] Although these novels do contain (often highly

---

[66] See Kevin Gilmartin, *Writing against Revolution: Literary Conservatism in Britain, 1790–1832* (Cambridge: Cambridge University Press, 2007), esp. 150–206.

BARTHOLOMEW FAIR.

Fig. 9. John Bluck and Thomas Rowlandson, after Augustus Charles Pugin, 'Bartholomew Fair' (1808). Courtesy of the Yale Center for British Art, Paul Mellon Collection.

stereotyped) descriptions of the radical debating societies discussed in *The Microcosm of London*, they are not scenes where radicals are confronted by loyalist counter-arguments. Even when, as in, for instance, Thomas Haral's *Scenes of Life* (1805), such places are visited by the respectable heroes of the novels, polite breakfast-table conversation in mixed company more often provides the forum for countering radical ideas.[67] Usually the state acts as a *deus ex machina* in the plot when it comes to actually breaking up radical meetings, the equivalent to Eleanor Tilney's confidence that 'proper measures will undoubtedly be taken by government'

---

[67] See Thomas Harral, *Scenes of Life*, 3 vols, (London, 1805), I: 156–7 and 173–88, discussed in Gilmartin, *Writing against Revolution*, 182–3. The novel's hero, Sir Frederick Stanley, and his worldly friend Henry Mailtland attend a radical assembly as part of a tour of the London underworld. Maitland prevents Stanley from intervening in the debate. The next morning they give an account of their adventure at the breakfast table, including an explanation of why they did not intervene.

(*NA* 112). Partly this anxiety about interventions by private citizens expresses the reticence on behalf of some of these novelists in taking it upon themselves to act for the state, but the contrast also suggests the fear that the freedoms of eighteenth-century civil society had been its undoing.[68] The same concern might be present even as early as those notices for the Association for Preserving Liberty and Property against Republicans and Levellers that insisted their meetings were not for 'talk and debate' but to expedite legal measures against radicals in 'subordination to the Magistrate'.[69] Political talk of whatever complexion starts to look suspect from this perspective. For much of the eighteenth century and afterwards, the encounter with strangers on a stagecoach provides a key trope for the problem of finding a common language of conversation.[70] In Henry Pye's anti-Jacobin novel *The Democrat* (1796), the French agent Jean Le Noir imagines he has come to a country ripe for revolution after hearing the disaffection of the passengers on a stagecoach. In fact, not only do the complaints really stem from inconsequential grumbling rather than political disaffection, but their origins originate in the failure of conversation to cohere: 'it often happens, even while a conversation is going on, that a person struck by any particular part of it, instead of attending to what afterwards passed, forms a chain of ideas from that which particularly struck him.' Only the intervention of another traveller, a grave American Quaker, manages to secure the company from the insinuations of Le Noir and recall to them their real blessings, a fact that suggests the novel's own deep-seated anxieties about the efficacy of the flow of opinion within British society.[71]

Coelebs in Search of a Wife can be seen as attempting its own navigation of these difficulties. More's novel is not explicitly oriented against any Jacobin threat, unlike her Cheap Repository Tracts of the 1790s, but it is aimed at an internal enemy in the shape of moral complacency and religious laxity among the elite. It adopts the strategies of the anti-Jacobin novelists, using conversations within the domestic space to meet and

---

[68] For a discussion of this point, see Gilmartin, *Writing against Revolution*, 183–8.

[69] See the report of the meeting on 24 November 1792 in the *Public Advertizer* of November 28.

[70] The trope appears several times in *The Spectator*, for instance, where Steele prints a letter complaining about indecent conversation in mixed company on a stagecoach (*S* 242; II: 439). See also *S* 132, II: 22–5. In Harum Skarum's account of the debating society at Coachmakers' Hall, he comments 'our introductory sixpences, like *death* and *stage-coaches*, had levelled all distinctions, and jostled wits, lawyers, politicians, and mechanics, into the confusion of the last day.' See Chap 2, 99.

[71] *The Democrat*, 2nd edn, in *Anti-Jacobin Novels*, Vol I, ed. W. M. Verhoeven (London: Pickering and Chatto, 2005), 64. See the illuminating discussion in Gilmartin, *Writing against Revolution*, 162–7.

overcome these dangers, but, like them, she is also acutely aware of presuming too much, especially of making her evangelical opinions into tactless enthusiasm. The hero's disgust at London talk, for instance, is swiftly followed by a careful set piece in praise of the capital as the seat of the institutions of state:

The advantages too which it possesses, in being the seat of the court, the parliament, and the courts of law, as well as the common centre of arts and talents of every kind, all these raise it above every other scene of intellectual improvement, or colloquial pleasure, perhaps in the whole world. (I: 22)

With similar care, the rejection of Lord Staunton's suit of the evangelical Lucilla Stanley is glossed by the affirmation of her family's aristocratic principles. More's problem was how to blend her evangelical commitment to domestic ideology with principles of good taste and an affirmation of social hierarchy. Dr. Barlowe (the local clergyman, and equivalent of Grandison's Dr Bartlett) summarizes the key principle as '*Zeal without Innovation*' (I: 197), but the medium More develops is uncomfortable even with its own idea of conversation. It also leaves open the question of how the pious conversations that make up *Coelebs* relate to any broader idea of a public. More, like Cowper, was looking for a different kind of communion based on the word of God, perhaps, but she was reluctant to have her tessellation of evangelical conversations understood as either challenging the institutions of the state or turning away from 'public' welfare entirely.

ARTICULATED AUSTEN

Those critics who emphasize the importance of the tactful maintenance of conversation in Austen's novels often assume she saw it as the answer to these larger questions, but even private conversation works only fitfully in her fiction, quite apart from the question of its aggregation into any larger unity. Like many others families, the Austens did enjoy the sense of connection provided by Cowper's poetry. A letter to Cassandra from 1798 records how Austen strained to listen when her father read to the family circle.[72] When the shrubbery was being put in order for the family's new home at Castle Square in Southampton, it was Austen herself who asked for the garden to memorialize Cowper: 'I could not do without a

---

[72] Jane to Cassandra Austen, 19 December 1798, *Letters*, 26. In an earlier letter, 25 November 1798, 22, she reports that a sum of money 'is to be laid out in the purchase of Cowper's works'.

Syringa, for the sake of Cowper's line.—We also talk of a Laburnam.'[73] The letter implies that the sisters shared a detailed knowledge of *The Task* and its 'Laburnum, rich | In streaming gold; syringa, iv'ry pure' (*The Task*, vi.149–50). Hannah More had quoted from the same passage in *Coelebs* (II: 155) and her hero goes on to praise Cowper's ability to animate nature with a moral spirit:

The scenery of Cowper is perpetually animated with sketches of character, enlivened with portraits from real life, and the exhibition of human manners and passions. His most exquisite descriptions owe their vividness to moral illustration.—Loyalty, liberty, patriotism, charity, piety, benevolence, every generous feeling, every glowing sentiment, every ennobling passion, grows out of his descriptive powers.—His matter always bursts into mind. (II: 197–8)

If Austen and her family enjoyed their own version of the retired sociability described in *The Task*, in her novels Cowper is strongly identified with this kind of communion with nature.[74] Discussing the allusions to Cowper in *Mansfield Park*, Clara Tuite discerns 'a specifically English Protestant version of georgic…emblematized by the English oak'.[75] Whereas Book iv of *The Task* included the reprocessing of the newspapers into the georgic, Austen's version of Cowper is more focused on those moments of communion with nature now translated into a landscape inspirited with English history, perhaps even more distanced from 'opulent, enlarged and still | increasing London' than is *The Task*. There is something in common here with the positive aspect of More's view of Cowper. By the time she was writing *Mansfield Park*, Austen may have been more patient with her species of patriotic evangelism: 'I am by no means convinced that we ought not all to be Evangelicals, & am at least persuaded that they who are so from Reason & Feeling, must be happiest & safest.'[76] Fanny Price, sometimes seen as an evangelical heroine, quotes from Cowper on hearing that the avenue of trees is to be cut down.[77] Her response merges the poet into a distinctively English and Protestant heritage threatened by the thoughtless improvers of the present: 'Cut down an avenue! What a

---

[73] Jane to Cassandra Austen, 8–9 February 1807, ibid. 119.

[74] More quotes, 'These naked shoots, | Barren as lances' (iv.141–2). The hero's praise of Cowper's nature poetry is followed up by the criticism of his 'ease', as discussed above (Chap 2, pp. 176–7). Austen showed herself to share a sense of similar dangers when she made Willoughby's skill at reading Cowper part of the attraction for Marianne in *Sense and Sensibility*.

[75] See Clara Tuite, *Romantic Austen: Sexual Politics and the Literary Canon* (Cambridge: Cambridge University Press, 2002), 119–20.

[76] Jane Austen to Fanny Knight, 18 November 1814; *Letters*, 280. See the discussion in Butler, *Jane Austen and the War of Ideas*, 162–3.

[77] See Butler, *Jane Austen and the War of Ideas*, 242–5, on Fanny as evangelical heroine.

pity! Does it not make you think of Cowper?' (*MP* 56). Later, in response
to Fanny's rhapsody on the shrubbery at the Parsonage, Mary Crawford—
representative of the world of London fashionable talk—can only say:
'I see no wonder in this shrubbery equal to seeing myself in it' (*MP* 209–10).
A sense of religious wonder in the winter shrubbery was precisely what
both Austen's letter to her sister and More's novel had praised in Cowper.
The historical continuities prized in their perspectives mean nothing from
the purview of fashionable life, Austen implies, but speaks to something
far more deeply interfused for Fanny. Mary and Fanny are scarcely able
to communicate across their different life-worlds in this regard. Fanny's
tactful intimations inhabit a different language from the wit and sparkle of
Mary, whose conversation demonstrates Austen's ear for the fashionable talk
celebrated in silver fork novels like Caroline Lamb's *Glenarvon* (1816),
published the same year as *Emma*.[78]

   Something of the difference between these conversable worlds is captured in the illustration to the chapter 'Of Interiors' in Humphry Repton's
Fragments on the Theory and Practice of Landscape Gardening (1816), one
section of which has been used as an illustration in recent volumes of
Austen criticism (see Fig. 10).[79] The en suite arrangement that Repton
identifies with fashionable modernity—the portion most used in books
about Austen—is contrasted with the empty circle of chairs in the other
part of the print. Repton describes its purpose as 'to shew the contrast
betwixt the ancient cedar parlour and the modern living room'. A poem
'A MODERN LIVING-ROOM' is also included to 'describe those
comforts enjoyed in the latter, [and] the silent gloom of the former':

A MODERN LIVING-ROOM

No more the *Cedar Parlour's* formal gloom
With dulness chills, 'tis now the *Living Room*;
Where Guests, to whim, or taste, or fancy true,

---

[78] The critical obsession with the Byronic aspect of Lamb's novel rather obscures the ear
for witty dialogue she shared with Austen. See John Clubbe, '*Glenarvon* Revised—and
Revisited', *Wordsworth Circle*, 10 (1979), 205–17. There was a great deal of interest in
Byron's conversation, as the content and titles of the biographies published soon after his
death imply. See, for instance, Marguerite Blessington's *Conversations of Lord Byron*
(London, 1834).

[79] Humphry Repton assisted by J. Adey Repton, *Fragments on the Theory and Practice of
Landscape Gardening. Including some Remarks on Grecian and Gothic Architecture* (London,
1816). For uses of Repton's plate, see Janet Todd's *The Cambridge Introduction to Jane
Austen* (Cambridge: Cambridge University Press, 2006) and the cover of Claudia Johnson
and Clara Tuite's (eds), *A Companion to Jane Austen* (Chichester: Wiley-Blackwell, 2009).
In her discussion of *Emma*, Todd associates Knightley with conservative values against
improvers like Repton (107).

Fig. 10. Henry Repton, 'Interiors', from *Fragments on the Theory and Practice of Landscape Gardening* (London: Printed by T. Bensley and Son, 1816). Courtesy of the Yale Center for British Art, Paul Mellon Collection.

> Scatter'd in groups, their different plans pursue.
> Here Politicians eagerly relate
> The last day's news, or the last night's debate,
> And there a Lover's conquer'd by Check-mate.
> Here books of poetry and books of prints
> Furnish aspiring Artists with new hints;
> Flow'rs, landscapes, figures, cram'd in one portfolio,
> There blend discordant tints to form an olio.
> While discords twanging from the half-tun'd harp,
> Make dulness cheerful, changing flat to sharp.
> Here, 'midst exotic plants, the curious maid
> Of Greek and Latin seems no more afraid.
> There lounging Beaux and Belles enjoy their folly,
> Nor less enjoying learned melancholy.
> Silent midst crowds the Doctor here looks big,
> Wrap'd in his own importance and his wig.[80]

The 'ancient cedar parlour' refers to the room Austen's nephew claimed she knew so well from *Sir Charles Grandison*. Richardson's 'cedar parlour' is in Northamptonshire, where *Mansfield Park* is set.[81] Repton's empty chairs offer a confident narrative of 'changes or improvements' suggesting Richardson's world has naturally passed away in favour of a more vital '*Living Room*' [Repton's italics].[82] Social life is now 'scattered in groups', but this is a sign of improvement rather than dispersal for Repton. Austen's novels are more regretful, even painfully aware of this loss. They seek to create a relationship with ancestors like Richardson and Cowper that look to deeper continuities beyond the interactions of 'modern' conversation.

'Scattered in groups' is a phrase that catches something of the sense of the breakdown in relations—even in provincial Northamptonshire—described in *Mansfield Park*, exaggerated by the absence of Sir Thomas Bertram, whose presence has at least maintained a veneer of order. Austen has the news of Sir Thomas's imminent return received in the kind of scattered scenario represented in Repton's modern living room: everyone there also has their different plans to pursue, most of which have not been fully expressed, some not even owned to themselves by those who harbour them say.[83] Mary Crawford hints at what everyone suspects by bringing up the impending marriage of Mr Rushworth and Miss Bertram:

---

[80] Repton, *Fragments*, 57–8.

[81] For a detailed account of the novel's debts to *Sir Charles Grandison*, see Harris, *Art of Memory*, 130–68.

[82] Repton, *Fragments*, 57.

[83] See the discussion of the scene in Tandon, *Morality of Conversation*, 209–10.

'Edmund looked round at Mr. Rushworth too', Austen tells us, 'but had nothing to say' (*MP* 108). His silence confirms the breakdown in the orderly progress of Sir Thomas's expectations in his absence, which is not to say there had been a perfect congruity between words and deeds before he left Mansfield Park. In general terms, Austen deals with the incomprehension and misprision intensified by society's dispersal into scattered groups by drawing back into a smaller domestic space where individuals may meet in conversation: the situation created for Edmund and Fanny at the end of *Mansfield Park* as for Knightley and the heroine in *Emma*. The contraction of what is included in the process of articulation shares some things in common, as I've been hinting, with the anti-Jacobin fictions to which Marilyn Butler linked Austen long ago, but the intense sense of the difficulties of creating understanding even within such a contracted circle also marks an important difference.[84] Unlike Harrel's *Scenes of Life*, no news from out there is ever really brought to the breakfast table for discussion. In Austen's fiction, there are certainly no direct encounters with the Jacobin threat on the stagecoach or other spaces where very different verbal codes collide. The rights of man and women are reduced to a passing joke in *Emma*. Talk of politics in *Northanger Abbey* inevitably leads to 'silence' (*NA* 111). Scientific topics of the kind broached in Edgeworth's conversations are avoided. Katherine Plymley began her journal to record the earnest conversations of her brother with Thomas Clarkson and William Wilberforce on the question of abolition. Plymley's domestic world sustained such conversations, her diary shows, but they never make it into the conversation of Austen's novels. Nor do we get any direct discussion of questions of religious observance or the probity of the aristocracy found in More's *Coelebs*.

Austen may have subscribed to Hannah More's estimation of the disastrous effect of 'collision with the world at large' and the 'barbarous project of assembling *en masse*', but she also avoided bringing questions of moral reformation directly into private conversation in her novels.[85] Where public issues are hinted at, as with the slave trade in *Emma* and *Mansfield Park*, they are quickly closed down as topics for conversation. In *Northanger Abbey,* the possibility of political trouble is scouted only to be mocked as a misunderstanding of news of the latest Gothic novel. Later in the novel, when Catherine herself has imagined if not political than domestic misdeeds in Northanger, Henry Tilney offers what seems to be an authoritative account of the flow of information across his modern society:

[84] Butler, *Jane Austen and the War of Ideas*, 88–123.
[85] Hannah More, *Strictures on the Modern System of Female Education*, 2 vols (London, 1799), II: 135.

'Does our education prepare us for such atrocities? Do our laws connive at them? Could they be perpetrated without being known, in a country like this, where social and literary intercourse is on such a footing; where every man is surrounded by a neighbourhood of voluntary spies, and where roads and newspapers lay every thing open?' (*NA*, 197–8)

Unlike Pye's *The Democrat*, here newspapers and stagecoaches only guarantee the proper kind of circulation, but is Henry's complacency entirely vindicated in Austen's novel? Does conversation flow as smoothly as Tilney's narrative of modernizing improvement suggests from the local to the larger community? Austen was sceptical of putting too much emphasis on the exertions of domestic morality in the maintenance of the larger community.

The early fragment *Catharine*, probably first drafted around 1792, questions the presumptions of those who make too much of the importance of the home front in the struggle for public morality. Mrs Percival's harangues at the heroine appear disproportionate and pompous:

You are Mistaken Child, replied she; the welfare of every Nation depends on the virtue of it's individuals, and any one who offends in so gross a manner against decorum & propriety is certainly hastening it's ruin. (*C*, 232–3)

Significantly returning to her draft some time after the publication of *Coelebs in Search of a Wife*, Austen took the trouble to add More's novel to the improving texts gifted to the heroine in the preceding passage. More's evangelism (literal and metaphorical) is too dogmatic and pretentious to be properly conversable in Austen's terms. The exchange in *Catharine* also suggests a deep scepticism about the possibility of articulating small talk into any sense of a larger conversation of culture. Even in the novel with perhaps the most tightly circumscribed speech community, the little platoon of Highbury in *Emma*, all kinds of differences conspire to make conversation a hazardous game. Even though the openhearted discourse between equals remains a positive goal, the problems faced creating such conditions appear almost insuperable. Mr Knightley informs Emma in their discussion of why Jane Fairfax bears with Mrs Elton:

'Another thing must be taken into consideration too—Mrs. Elton does not talk *to* Miss Fairfax as she speaks *of* her. We all know the difference between the pronouns he or she and thou, the plainest-spoken amongst us; we all feel the influence of a something beyond common civility in our personal intercourse with each other—a something more early implanted. We cannot give any body the disagreeable hints that we may have been very full of the hour before. We feel things differently.' (*Emma* 286)

Far from cementing a metaphysics of presence, face-to-face communication in Knightley's view ensures that one does not say exactly what one feels, because of the unavoidable fact of social difference, even Mrs Elton's behaviour acknowledges that much, sometimes at least.

Knightley might be right about Mrs Elton in this case, but typically of Austen's conversational method, he does not have a Grandisonian equally wide survey over these matters, even if critics often compare him to Richardson's hero.[86] Earlier in the novel when discussing Frank Churchill's failure to visit his father, it is Emma who makes a palpable hit on the question of the social constraints on openhearted discourse:

'That's easily said, and easily felt by you, who have always been your own master. You are the worst judge in the world, Mr. Knightley, of the difficulties of dependence. You do not know what it is to have tempers to manage.' (*Emma* 145–6)

Emma's consciousness of such issues, and the novel's general awareness that these constraints weigh most heavily on women, only makes her behaviour to Miss Bates at the picnic all the more glaring an affront. She fails to orient herself properly to the perspectives of another, and, rather than negotiating a tactful *via media*, which the reader knows Emma has frequently found exhausting, she simply shuts Miss Bates up. Emma imagines marriage to Mr. Knightley as transcending all these difficulties: he is someone who can 'meet her in conversation, playful or rational'. Of course, it is significant that it is only the discovery of something that has always been close at hand, as if confirming that conversation is safest in a familial context. Emma anticipates 'all necessity of concealment from Mr. Knightley would soon be over. The disguise, equivocation, mystery, so hateful to her to practise, might soon be over. She could now look forward to giving him that full and perfect confidence which her disposition was most ready to welcome as a duty' (*Emma* 475). Here conversation has full flow, but only in the tight circle of pre-selected company at Hartfield, and even then the newlyweds will not be able to speak freely in front of Mr. Woodhouse. The situation is a marked retreat from Richardson's idea of the place of domestic conversation within the larger aggregation of the community, or even from the more expanded conversations in Highfield that make up the central portions of the novel.

Austen's mastery of free indirect discourse, especially after *Mansfield Park*, might be taken as a pointer in this direction in so far as it brings about an intensely close relationship between narrator and reader. If, as some critics suggests, the device covertly interpolates the reader into an

---

[86] On the tendency to identify Knightley and Grandison, see Waldron, *Fiction of her Time*, 114.

authorized perspective, then her narrative technique might be seen as privileging reading as a form of communion rather than as a species of verbal exchange.[87] The notion of 'transparent minds' is not one that foregrounds social mediation, but describes ways of bringing the reader over to the perspectives of a character almost without noticing. Furthermore, free indirect discourse can also work to bring the reader over to the point of view of a broader community. Casey Finch and Peter Bowen see this device as Austen's 'articulation of the mechanisms by which gossip binds communities together under a mild system of surveillance and self-control'.[88] One thinks immediately of Henry Tilney's idea of the binding force of the national 'system' of communication, but Finch and Bowen, like Henry, may underestimate the fragility of the process as Austen represents it. *Emma* constantly returns to the issue of interference in the channels of communication.

Free indirect style depends upon a continual negotiation for the reader with the other two forms of narration, reported speech and straight third-person narration. The end result scarcely affirms any unified perspective beyond conversational exchange and its local imperfections. Knowledge of the effects of dependence, for instance, belongs absolutely neither to Emma as a woman nor to Mr. Knightley as a Grandisonian agreeable man. In this regard, the reader is in a situation not unlike Catherine in *Northanger Abbey*, faced with the problem of conversational implicature when one does not know the rules of the particular speech community. Even when one learns the verbal cues to see when the narration is being blurred with a particular character's point of view, the relation between that viewpoint and others is never entirely resolved. Finch and Bowen's model may be present in many anti-Jacobin novels, although usually without the subtleties of free indirect speech they identify with Austen, but in *Emma* and the other novels it meets a form of sceptical resistance that complicates any inclusive build-up of community. This places Austen's novels in a difficult relationship to the kind of participatory nationalism identified by Gilmartin as the central paradox of conservative writing in the period.[89] Whereas there may be signs of anxiety about this process in many anti-Jacobin novels, in Austen it is hardly even entertained as a possible outcome of her many local conversations. Instead, a sense of hope entangled with regret imbues places like the avenue of trees in *Mansfield Park* with an *aura* of Englishness. Rather than national identity being

---

[87] See Casey Finch and Peter Bowen, ' "The Tittle-Tattle of Highbury": Gossip and the Free Indirect Style in *Emma*', *Representations*, 31 (1990), 1–18, discussed below.
[88] Ibid. 1.
[89] See Gilmartin, *Writing against Revolution*, 13.

constructed out of ongoing exchanges within and between the private and public spheres, Austen appeals to a powerful sense of it depending upon more customary associations, difficult to translate into forms of conversation and very much in jeopardy from improvement. Even if one takes the final utopia of Emma and Knightley at face value, then the novel's sociability has followed a pattern of retrenchment *back* to Hartfield into a narrower domestic space after expanding out at least into Highbury, including its influx of relative strangers (Frank Churchill, Jane Fairfax, Mrs Elton, etc). Mr Knightley must quit his residence in Donwell to make this retrenchment possible, but Mr. Woodhouse's presence means that, even in Hartwell, they will never quite be able to speak their minds to each other freely.

The further from home one gets in *Emma*, the more conversation proliferates and degrades into a kind of Babel. London is barely imaginable in the novel, it seems, but even when Mr Weston takes the microcosm of Highbury out into the very slightly wider world of Box Hill, he quickly discovers 'a want of union' and tries 'in vain, to make them harmonize better' (*Emma* 367). The dangerous interplay between Frank and Emma—which has 'such an appearance as no English word but flirtation could very well describe' (368)—has a centrifugal effect. The language of the novel itself breaks down into staccato exchanges. Conversation literally degenerates on the page when it gets too far from home. Looking beyond *Emma*, one character that does have some sense of the interconnectedness of domestic life and the fate of the nation is Lady Russell in *Persuasion*. She is the main voice calling for Sir Walter Elliot to 'retrench' his domestic arrangements. She—like a coffee house politician—also 'gets all the new publications' (*P* 146). Later Elizabeth is bored with her 'new poems and states of the nation' (*P* 215). Lady Russell persuades Anne Elliot to listen to advice based on general precepts rather than the particularities of her situation. She is deaf to any engagement that would constitute a really open and frank expression of opinion with Anne. For all her knowledge of 'manners', or perhaps because of it, she is taken in by Mr. Elliott's 'general politeness and suavity' (*P* 249). What Lady Russell lacks is tact, the ability to feel her way in conversation, the 'quickness of perception...nicety in the discernment of character, a natural penetration' (ibid.), that would have given her a better idea of the characters of Anne and Wentworth.

More limited though her circle of information may be, Anne, in contrast, learns from the ebb and flow of conversation, even if she is not always an active participant. The same holds true for Wentworth, whose feelings are clarified by the debate between Harville and Anne on female constancy, a conversation in which he is a silent participant. In this complex exchange, Wentworth is an addressee as much as an eavesdropper, not least because Anne suspects he can hear what she says. Anne's ability to get beyond Lady Russell's precepts could be understood as the product of the widening of the female experience of the conversable world. Jacobin novels of the 1790s, such as Eliza Fenwick's *Secresy*, often aimed at this kind of issue, subjecting codes of politeness to a stringent form of the hypocrisy critique described by Jenny Davidson in the process, except that these Jacobin novels tend to enjoin a stronger idea of self-expression and a wholesale rejection of the social hierarchy. For Austen, as Davidson points out, more emphasis is given to the struggle for women to find a form of expression *within* the obtaining system of social relations (critique without innovation, Hannah More's Dr Barlowe might say).[90] Opportunities for expression often pass Anne by in a flash in a world thick with forms of social mediation and difference, brilliantly conveyed by Austen flicking her narrative into the stream of Anne's consciousness as the flow of conversation washes over her on Wentworth's first appearance:

And it was soon over. In two minutes after Charles's preparation, the others appeared; they were in the drawing-room. Her eye half met Captain Wentworth's; a bow, a curtsey passed; she heard his voice—he talked to Mary, said all that was right; said something to the Miss Musgroves, enough to mark an easy footing: the room seemed full—full of persons and voices—but a few minutes ended it. (*P* 59)

Anne's struggle to find a place from which to articulate her thoughts is much more like Fanny Price's situation than either Elizabeth Bennet or Emma Woodhouse's, who do often have their say with some wit and sparkle.

Anne is finally only really able to talk to Wentworth in 'the comparatively quiet and retired gravel-walk', where 'the power of conversation would make the present hour a blessing indeed' (*P* 240). In this bubble, Anne and Wentworth are 'heedless of every group, around them, seeing neither sauntering politicians, bustling house-keepers, flirting girls, nor nursery maids and children' (*P* 241). The social mix of Bath is acknowledged, but put aside. The communion between the lovers is markedly contrasted with the chatter of politicians and the lower classes. Ironically, then, it is this novel that makes the most obvious linkage between domestic life and public matters:

She gloried in being a sailor's wife, but she must pay the tax of quick alarm for belonging to that profession which is, if possible, more distinguished in domestic virtues than in its national importance. (*P* 252)

---

[90] Davidson, *Hypocrisy and the Politics of Politeness*, 168–9.

The mention of 'domestic virtues' in relation to questions of 'national importance' brings us close to the territory of Mrs Percival in *Catharine* and even the anti-Jacobin novelists, except that the disjunction between 'domestic virtues' and 'national importance' is as much to the fore as their interdependence. The syntax resists any easy articulation of the domestic and military into the public sphere.

Austen's novels more generally do not provide an orchestration of conversation into a larger sense of community.[91] Conversation does play an important part in revealing truth, such as it is, *between* different points of view. In this regard, at least, in her hands, the novel may have taken over something of the function of the philosophical dialogue (a perception also hinted at in Whately's defence of novelists with Austen's skills).[92] The novel's development of the representation of everyday life made the older genre unsatisfyingly abstract in comparison. In Austen's hands, the sense of thickly mediated space between people tends to resist any opening out into the larger social perspectives found, for instance, in Edgeworth's ethnographic novels of high life. More mundanely, Emma may be saved from the fate of having no one to talk to, but the ambit of her conversation looks to be much more circumscribed than it has been even for much of the novel itself. By the time of the Regency, especially after the disillusion of the 1790s, conversation had perhaps become not so much a trope of a community of culture as a reminder of linguistic dispersal and potentially of social disintegration. Austen's novels are sharply conscious of the different kinds of speech communities inscribed even on the few inches of ivory at Highbury and Hartfield and painfully aware of the problem of managing a flow of openhearted discourse even between two individuals.

Nancy Struever sees this sense of difficulty as proof of Austen's 'tough-minded precision' as against Hume's 'pictures of domestic peace'.[93] She credits Austen with revealing that 'domestic discourse improves on [Hume's] general conversation'. In this chapter, I've suggested the shift

---

[91] Possibly the limiting horizon of Austen's sense of hazard in conversation is her veneration for old settled families, like Knightley's, an implicit repudiation of the Addisonian discourse of 'commerce'. Knightley is agreeable in Addisonian terms, but also chivalric in more Burkean ones. The potential contrast can be found in Wollstonecraft's attack on Burke's politeness as 'Gothic affability' rather than 'the civility of a liberal man'. Against the diverse interchanges going on around her, Austen seems to transform the idea of politeness into a more organic sense of English culture. Knightley has a patience with Miss Bates's prattling that Emma sometimes lacks, but he often has a 'downright' manner, suggesting an idea of old English bluntness, which Emma finds attractive.

[92] See Michael Prince, *Philosophical Dialogue in the British Enlightenment: Theology, Aesthetics and the Novel* (Cambridge: Cambridge University Press, 1996), 237–50, and Whately's review in the *Quarterly*, 357.

[93] See Struever, 'The Conversable World', 100.

had already been taking place in novels such as Richardson's soon after Hume's essays. Whether Austen's novels present the confident picture of 'ruled liberty' Struever paints is also open to question. In Struever's reading, 'discursive sensitivity is the source of oral sensitivity for author, reader, and protagonist.' To be sure, but I think this process is uneven and faltering. Often what the reader is sensitized to is the difficulty of conversation working at all. Perhaps this is why, at times, the narrative in *Emma*, exhausted perhaps by shuttling between different points of view, abandons the interplay of perspectives and simply insists 'it really was so' (*Emma* 129). Austen's conversable aspirations involve her characters in a risky business, best undertaken in the insulated circumstances of the domestic space. Even in these restricted circles the discovery of those capable of meeting one in conversation is no easy task in itself. No less than finding out what one thinks one's self, finding someone to talk to 'out there' seems impossible without hazarding conversation in Austen's novels. To have a chance of success the circle seems to need to contract as tightly as possible and even then yearns to be underpinned by a sense of organic connection to a distinctively English past.

6

Hazlitt, Hunt, and Cockney
Conversability

Recent work on the 'Cockney' phenomenon of the 1810s and 1820s has emphasized the importance of urban sociability as part of a distinctive 'group' identity within Regency culture.[1] These welcome analyses may sometimes obscure the exclusions involved in 'coterie dynamics', but they do enable us to see at least one place where a conversable paradigm remained alive in the first decades of the nineteenth century. 'Cockney' culture defined itself against the hierarchies of the patrician elite, the atomism of commercial society, and the defensively introverted aesthetics that it associated with the Lake School.[2] This chapter pays particular attention to William Hazlitt's position within this cultural formation. Often read as a strong defining presence in Romanticism, theorist of 'gusto', and defender of 'genius', Hazlitt was nevertheless a writer for whom the theory and practice of conversation were part of his affiliation to an inclusive idea of the republic of letters as a species of open and ongoing exchange.

Even allowing for these aspects of his writing, choosing Hazlitt as the focus of this chapter may appear odd because of his reputation for abstruse reasoning, shyness, as well as misanthropy, and even misogyny. Parts of this charge sheet approximate to the portrait put about by his opponents before and after his death. Early on, Coleridge described him to Thomas Wedgwood as 'brow-hanging, shoe contemplative *strange*' (*CL*, I: 990). De Quincey gave a very hostile posthumous account of Hazlitt's constitutional 'misanthropy', exacerbated, he believed, by 'accidents of life, by disappointments, by mortifications, by insults, and still more by having

---

[1] See, especially, Jeffrey N. Cox, *Poetry and Politics in the Cockney School: Keats, Shelley, Hunt and their Circle* (Cambridge: Cambridge University Press, 1998). Cox offers an interesting discussion of the category of the 'group' as 'an intersubjective collectivity always in the process of being imagined' (5).

[2] Greg Kucich, '"The Wit in the Dungeon": Leigh Hunt and the Insolent Politics of Cockney Coteries', *Romanticism on the Net*, 14 (May 1999). Accessed 17 July 2009.

wilfully placed himself in collision from the first with all the interests that were in the sunshine of the world, and with all the persons that were then powerful in England'.[3] In some essays, including 'On the Shyness of Scholars', Hazlitt joined in by painting himself as a moody introvert, unable to 'come off with applause in the retailing of anecdote or the interchange of repartee' (XVII: 255). Even so, plenty of contemporary accounts emphasized his sociability, including his great powers of conversation, and many of his greatest essays retail anecdote, and even transcribe repartee.[4] Henry Crabb Robinson was often outraged by Hazlitt and his indiscretions, not least his use of personal knowledge in his printed attacks on Coleridge and Wordsworth, but after a meeting in December 1815 admitted: 'Hazlitt was sober, argumentative, acute, and interesting: I had no conversation with him, but I enjoyed his conversations with others.'[5] A year later, Charles Lamb told Wordsworth he couldn't drop Hazlitt because 'I get no conversation in London that is absolutely worth attending to but his.'[6] Lamb suffered at Hazlitt's hands himself, but his 'Letter of Elia to Robert Southey' provides a moving defence of his friend's conversation:

I wish [Hazlitt] would not quarrel with the world at the rate he does; but the reconciliation must be effected by himself, and I despair of living to see that day. But, protesting against much that he has written, and some things which he chooses to do; judging him by his conversation, which I enjoyed so long, and relished so deeply; or by his books, in those places where no clouding passion intervenes— I should belie my own conscience, if I said less, than that I think W. H. to be, in his natural and healthy state, one of the wisest and finest spirits breathing.[7]

---

[3] See Thomas De Quincey's 'Notes on Gilfillian's Gallery of Literary Portraits: Godwin, Foster, Hazlitt, Shelley, Keats', in *Tait's Edinburgh Magazine*, 12 (ns), 756–61. De Quincey begins by noting Hazlitt's origins in Dissent, but then goes on to the description quoted (756).

[4] 'Of Persons One Would Wish to Have Seen', for instance, first published in the *New Monthly Magazine* in 1826, presents itself as a transcription of the imperfectly remembered conversation at Charles and Mary Lambs' 'Wednesday' club. See also Thomas Noon Talfourd, *Final Memorials of Charles Lamb*, 2 vols (London, 1848), II: 116–35, and Catherine M. Maclean, *Born under Saturn: A Biography of William Hazlitt* (London: Collins, 1943), 217–18. All in-text references to Hazlitt's writing are to *The Complete Works of William Hazlitt*, ed. P. P. Howe, 21 vols (London: Dent, 1930–4).

[5] *Henry Crabb Robinson on Books and Their Writers*, ed. Edith Morley, 3 vols (London: J. M. Dent, 1938), I: 178. Coleridge told Robinson that Lamb 'ought not to admit a man into his house who abuses the confidence of private intercourse so scandalously'. Robinson met Hazlitt the next day, upbraided him for his treatment of Wordsworth in *The Examiner*, and refused to shake his hand on parting (I: 201–2).

[6] Lamb to Wordsworth, [23 September] 1816, in *The Letters of Charles and Mary Anne Lamb*, ed. Edwin W. Marrs, Jr, 3 vols (Ithaca/London: Cornell University Press, 1975), III: 225.

[7] 'Letter of Elia to Robert Southey', in *Works of Charles and Mary Lamb*, ed. E. V. Lucas, 8 vols (London: Methuen, 1912), I: 274. The essay first appeared in the *London Magazine* of October 1823, and was a reply to Southey's comments in the *Quarterly* on Elia's religious opinions.

Hazlitt's conversation was very highly valued in the circles who gathered at the weekly club held by Charles and Mary Lamb between 1806 and 1814; those associated with *The Examiner* after 1814; and then the *London Magazine* in the 1820s, to identify but three of the overlapping literary groups in which he participated. Even his staunchest defenders acknowledged the tendency towards quarrelling with the world, but the proclivity was not just temperamental. Hazlitt was self-consciously committed to the version of conversation as the collision of mind with mind that has been a major theme of this book.[8] In this regard, his conversation was rather different from both the amiability associated with Lamb's 'Elia' persona and the agreeable 'sociality' of his close friend Leigh Hunt.[9]

No less than either Hunt's or Lamb's, Hazlitt's writing was predicated on a conversational persona, the figure of an essayist known on the scene of urban culture, but their 'group' aesthetic was far from stable or unitary.[10] Conversation for Hazlitt was associated with an open-ended idea of literary form, developing, especially, its long-standing identification with the familiar essay. Hunt and Lamb made the same associations, but for Hazlitt they came combined with a much fiercer and often deliberately paradoxical desire to strike flint with flint in the cause of truth.[11] Hazlitt was often explicit about the genealogy of this idea of conversation in English Dissent, but one area where he departed from his inheritance was in the hardening of the gendered aspects of this metaphor into a more literal and even misogynistic hostility towards the perceived softening influence of women. Unlike many of his forebears in Rational Dissent, Hazlitt identified the feminization of culture with mannered forms of social propriety and the commodity culture of the fashionable world. Like Byron, Hazlitt tended to identify the feminization of culture with 'cant'. To this extent, he anticipates Habermas's melancholy account of the decline of the classical public sphere into the

---

[8] P. G. Patmore, *My Friends and Acquaintance*, 3 vols (London, 1854), I: 81, for instance, admitted that Hazlitt 'could not abstain from speaking the truth even of his best friends'. As a result, according to Patmore, only he, Hazlitt's son, and Lamb attended his funeral (see I: 80).

[9] B. W. Procter [Barry Cornwell], a friend of all three men, compared Hazlitt, Hunt, and Lamb as 'accomplished talkers' in his *Autobiographical Fragment and Biographical Notes* (London, 1877). Hazlitt he described as 'attached…to abstract subjects', but he 'was the best talker of the three. Lamb said the most pithy and brilliant things. Hunt displayed the most ingenuity' (125).

[10] For a discussion of this kind of persona in the maintenance of the idea of literary culture as a conversable world, see Clifford Siskin, *The Work of Writing: Literature and Social Change in Britain 1700–1830* (Baltimore/London: Johns Hopkins University Press, 1998), 164.

[11] For recent readings of Lamb in the context of his 'low-Urban Taste', see Denise Gigante, *Taste: A Literary History* (New Haven/London: Yale University Press, 2005), 89–116, and Felicity James, *Charles Lamb, Coleridge and Wordsworth: Reading Friendship in the 1790s* (Basingstoke: Palgrave Macmillan, 2008), 185–214.

marketplace of a feminized consumerism, except he often seeks to translate nostalgia into a subject for new forms of urban conversation.[12]

Despite his hostility to the feminization of culture, to which I'll return, Hazlitt looks like a committed participant in the Humean project of bringing metaphysics into the conversable world. He may have regarded Hume as the last 'metaphysician in this country worth the name' (VIII: 65), but his career followed the Scotsman's abandonment of the philosophical treatise in favour of an approachable and familiar medium.[13] Appropriately enough, in neither case was the shift a straightforward matter of principled choice, but rather a negotiation with the circumstance of failing to find an audience.[14] For both Hazlitt and Hume, the essay is associated with informal and everyday modes, bringing matters of social and cultural importance out of the cloisters of learning to lay them before a broader readership in a familiar style 'as any one would speak in common conversation, who had a thorough command and choice of words, or who could discourse with ease, force, and perspicuity, setting aside all pedantic and oratorical flourishes' (VIII: 242).[15]

Quite apart from these democratizing aspects of his medium, Hazlitt frequently discusses and explores the uses and pleasures of conversation directly in the essays. His career was made in the give and take of periodical publication. His essays are papers to be put on the table for further talk and response.[16] He was aided in this last regard by what Lamb described as 'his singular ability in retaining all conversations at which he has ever been present'.[17] Hazlitt's essays addressed many of the topics

---

[12] Jürgen Habermas, *The Structural Transformation of the Public Sphere: An Inquiry into a Category of Bourgeois Society*, trans. Thomas Burger with the assistance of Frederick Lawrence (Cambridge, MA: MIT Press, 1989), 161, argues that by 1830 'rational-critical debate had a tendency to be replaced by consumption, and the web of public communication unravelled into acts of individual reception, however uniform in mode.'

[13] For a contrast between Habermas and Hazlitt in this and others regards, see David Panagia, 'The Force of Political Argument', *Political Theory*, 32 (2004), 825–48. Panagia draws upon Adorno's contrast between the essay and 'discursive logic characterized by theoretical continuity and coherence' (828). See Theodor W. Adorno, 'The Essay as Form', in *Notes to Literature*, vol I, ed. Rolf Tiedemann, trans. Shierry Weber Nicholsen (New York: Columbia University Press, 1991), 3–23.

[14] Hazlitt implicitly acknowledged the parallel when he used Hume's phrasing (see above, p. 61) to claim his own philosophical treatise 'fell still-born from the press' in 'On the Causes of Popular Opinion' (XVII: 312).

[15] Interestingly enough, Hazlitt insists on the importance of 'tact' (VIII: 243) as 'adhering to those [words] which are perfectly common, and yet never falling into any expressions which are debased by disgusting circumstances, or which owe their signification and point to technical or professional allusions'.

[16] See Jon Cook, 'Hazlitt, Speech, and Writing', in Kate Campbell (ed.), *Journalism, Literature and Modernity: From Hazlitt to Modernism* (Edinburgh: Edinburgh University Press, 2000), 15–37.

[17] Lamb to J. D. Collier, 4[?] October 1812, *Letters*, II: 85–6.

familiar from earlier chapters of this book as key to the period's thinking about conversation: 'On the Difference of Writing and Speaking', 'On Familiar Style', 'On Public Opinion', 'On the Conversation of Authors', and 'On Coffee-House Politicians'. His mature style was announced in a collaboration with Hunt called *The Round Table* (1817), originally intended to recreate the conversation of the *Examiner* group, including Lamb, after the manner of *The Tatler The Spectator*. The titles of Hazlitt's great collections of familiar essays, *Table Talk* (1821, 1822) and *The Plain Speaker* (1826), identify two of the key aspects of his conversable style: a relaxed familiarity that could modulate into a blunt directness. Even the painful *Liber Amoris* (1823) was presented as '*Conversations*' (IX: 97) in its first part. The last book he published was *Conversations with Northcote* (1830), a self-consciously Boswellian enterprise.[18]

Hazlitt may often appear in his own essays as a shy and introverted metaphysician, but he also frequently promotes 'the genial expansion of the moral sentiments and social affections' (IV: 117). Conviviality and conversation—usually defined against the mechanical or dogmatic—are linked as key concepts in his late essay 'On Disagreeable People':

> To make conversation interesting or agreeable, there is required either the habitual tone of good company, which gives a favourable colouring to everything—or the warmth and enthusiasm of genius, which, though it may occasionally offend or be thrown off its guard, makes amends by its rapturous flights, and flings a glancing light upon all things. The literal and *dogged* style of conversation resembles that of a French picture, or its mechanical fidelity is like evidence given in a court of justice, or a police report. (XVII: 229)

Hazlitt's familiar style does not aim at being agreeable in the way that Addison and Hume imagined when inaugurating their conversable worlds. The first passage from one of his greatest pieces of writing, his *Letter to William Gifford* (1819), provides a good example of one of his more abrasive opening gambits:

> You have an ugly trick of saying what is not true of any one you do not like; and it will be the object of this letter to cure you of it. You say what you please of others: it is time you were told what you are. In doing this, give me leave to borrow the familiarity of your style—for the fidelity of the picture I shall be answerable.
> You are a little person, but a considerable cat's paw; and so far worthy of notice. Your clandestine connexion with persons high in office constantly influences your opinions, and alone gives importance to them. You are the *Government Critic*, a

---

[18] Initially published from August 1826 as a series in the *New Monthly Magazine* over the signature 'Boswell Redivivus', but Hazlitt did not repeat the claims to accuracy of his 'great original and predecessor': 'All that can be relied upon for certain is a striking anecdote or a sterling remark or two on each page' (XI: 350).

character nicely differing from that of a government spy—the invisible link, that connects literature with the police. (IX: 13)

For this kind of disregard of polite forms, its colloquial vigour of address, Hazlitt was regularly 'accused of revelling in vulgarisms and broken English' (VIII: 244). Rebutting these charges, Hazlitt explained he aimed to convey 'ordinary life and colloquial speaking', but insisted 'it is not easy to write a familiar style' (VIII: 242). With the *Letter to Gifford*, we may be at the extreme pole of Hazlitt's colloquial willingness to 'offend or throw off guard', at a point where the conversational turn acknowledges the pleasure of hating (a pleasure that may make exchange precarious, but scarcely rules it out). 'The mind', Hazlitt wrote in 'The Aristocracy of Letters', 'strikes out truth by collision, as steel strikes fire from the flint' (VIII: 208). 'Collision' is the thing for Hazlitt, as it was for Godwin, with whom he shared an intellectual genealogy in the pedagogy of Dissent, but for Hazlitt collision is frequently presented in terms of relationships between bodies in physical space rather than a Godwinian exchange of deliberated reasoning. 'To remain conversational', for Hazlitt, was 'to be open to the unexpected and unanticipated'.[19] One card evening at Lamb's house dissolved into violence when John Lamb—brother of Charles—punched him for his impertinence. Hazlitt is reported to have forgiven him with the comment: 'I am a metaphysician, and do not mind a blow; nothing but an *idea* hurts *me*.'[20] The anecdote illustrates both the risks Hazlitt took in conversation and the curiously physical view he took of ideas, which he believed always participated in the complexity of our 'limited, imperfect, and mixed being' (VI: 132). In *Political Justice*, Godwin had warned that the conviviality of the table could break up into the depredations of violence.[21] To indemnify conversation too fully against this risk for Hazlitt was to endanger what might be most productive about it.

HAZLITT, HUNT, AND 'SOCIALITY'

'Sociality', in the OED's sense of *'friendly* social interaction' (my italics), was privileged in Hunt's idea of the conversable world over Hazlitt's investment in combative exchange. To be sure, Hunt was quite capable of producing a direct and challenging manner in his political writing, and

---

[19] Cook, 'Hazlitt, Speech, and Writing', 28.
[20] See the account given in Duncan Wu, *William Hazlitt: The First Modern Man* (Oxford: Oxford University Press, 2008), 199. I quote from the account given in Thomas Moore's journal. See *Memoirs, Journal, and Correspondence of Thomas Moore*, 8 vols (London, 1753–6), III: 146. I am grateful to Kevin Gilmartin for pointing this source out to me.
[21] See above, p. 151.

the two men remained in a 'continuing dialogue' through most of their writing lives.[22] Their Saturday Night Club was apparently more boisterous and informal than the kind of gatherings associated with John Murray's literary conversazione or Lord Holland's aristocratic salon. The American tourist George Ticknor visited all these literary gatherings. Writing home in 1819, he defined the Hunt circle in terms of [its] common hatred of everything that has been more successful than their own works...the most curious and amusing *olla podrida* I ever met.' Their peppery stew of opinion was too spicy for a palate used to the smoother coherence and consistency of more elevated circles.[23]

Predictably enough, Hunt shared Hazlitt's identification of conversation with the medium of the essay, if not exactly its conceptualization in terms of collision. In his *Classic Tales, Serious and Lively* (1806–8), Hunt had claimed 'the most perfect style seems to be that which avoids the negligence while it preserves the spirit of conversation.'[24] Not surprisingly, then, the 'Prospectus' for *The Examiner* framed the enterprise in terms of 'literary conversation'. Hunt characterized the press more generally by its 'subserviency to the follies of the day, very miserably merry in it's [*sic*] puns and it's [*sic*] stories, extremely furious in politics, and quite as feeble in criticism'.[25] An Addisonian assumption that situates the conversable world beyond party is integral to Hunt's address.[26] He offers his readers participation in an exchange beyond 'the disturbers of coffee-houses'. The familiar spectatorial position within society but beyond its excesses is put agreeably but firmly in place as the locale of *The Examiner*. Its commerce will be above the market, advertisements even for the publisher's own books will be avoided, and quacks will have no place in its pages, but Hunt's prospectus also suggests a position outside the crowd for its politics, 'escaped from the throng and bustle', rehearsing a trajectory, like Godwin's in the 1790s, that aims to guarantee what he later called 'spirited and independent discussion' (*E*, 11 March 1810, 115: 145) by insulating it from a wider world of talk.[27]

---

[22] See Payson G. Gates, *William Hazlitt and Leigh Hunt: The Continuing Dialogue*, ed. Eleanor M. Gates (Essex, CT: Falls River, 2000).

[23] See Ticknor, *Life, Letters, and Journals of George Ticknor*, 2 vols (London, 1876), I: 294. Talfourd, *Memorials of Charles Lamb*, II: 116–35, contrasts the sociability at Holland House with Lamb's Wednesday night club.

[24] Leigh Hunt, *Classic Tales, Serious and Lively*, 5 vols (1806–8), I: 55.

[25] Leigh Hunt, 'Prospectus', *The Examiner* (3 January 1808), 1: 6–8. All future references to *The Examiner* will be given in the text with date and issue and page number after the abbreviation *E*.

[26] More generally, Hunt's version of literary sociability was far from averse to puns.

[27] See the discussion in Kevin Gilmartin, *Print Politics: The Press and Radical Opposition in Early Nineteenth-Century England* (Cambridge: Cambridge University Press, 1996), 208.

'On Periodical Essays' in the second number further refined the position of the new journal (*E*, 10 January 1808, 2: 26). He will claim 'a peculiar intimacy with the public', an intimacy defined against the more formal commitments he associates with reading books. The periodical essayist offers a relationship that grows with acquaintance, returning to the home at regular intervals, a relationship more likely to last 'because it is more gradual and because you see him in a greater variety of subject and opinion'. Because of its contingency, because it builds up through a process of exchange, the relationship may be easily broken off, 'if you do not like him at first you may give up his conversation.' Hunt delights in imagining the ways the periodical essay may be returned to the everyday world from which it came:

It may assist your meditation by lighting your pipe, it may give steadiness to your candle, it may curl the tresses of your daughter of your sister, or lastly, if you are not rich enough to possess an urn or a cloth-holder, it may save you a world of opodeldoc by wrapping the handle of your tea-kettle.

The paper returns not to the everyday world of the streets exactly, but instead to a quasi-domestic environment. The different departments of the paper, the 'Political Examiner', the 'Theatrical Examiner', and the 'Literary Examiner', are all imagined as 'children of the same family'.[28]

This *mise en scène* perpetuates the orientation of conversational freedom towards the domestic sphere that has been one of the key narrative threads of this book, but Hunt also explicitly relates the persona of *The Examiner* to the early-eighteenth-century essay tradition. Swift, Addison, and Steele, especially the last two, are to be the presiding deities of the paper. 'On Periodical Essays' commits Hunt to the 'ease and gentility', the 'graceful familiarity' of Addison (*E*, 10 January 1808, 2: 26). Not that Addison entirely escapes censure: 'I must not forget his occasional incorrectness of language and his want of depth, when he attempted to display the critic.' Hunt had a developed sense of the higher calling of his writing, which sometimes created a tension, for instance, when it came to reconciling *The Examiner*'s political and poetic aspirations. As a periodical essayist, Hunt distanced himself from the didactic heaviness of Johnson, 'who claimed rather than entreated notice'. Hunt's desire is to create a more informal style of address to his reader: 'I wish to make an acquaintance with him, and I know that it is not customary on your first introduction to a person to tell him how you mean to enchant him in your future connexion.' The

---

[28] *The Examiner* was a Hunt family business. One brother, Robert, originally acted as fine arts critic, and John Hunt was *The Examiner*'s printer and publisher. The whole enterprise was framed in 'the reassuring terms of domestic relationship'. See Gilmartin, *Print Politics*, 200.

imagined scene of reading in 'On Periodical Essays' is framed by national character, 'my new acquaintance and I therefore will sit still a little and reconnoitre each other with true English civility,' but it also imagines the relationship between writer and reader in terms of co-dependence rather than authority, an elective affinity rather than necessary hierarchy. In his political writing, Hunt liked to present himself as loftily above faction, including even most species of extra-parliamentary radicalism. As he pointed out in his 'Newspaper Principle' series, he saw in the model of the early-eighteenth-century essayists *a reference to dignified principle scarcely discernible in the present times*' (*E*, 6 August 1809, 84: 497). Such principled writing had been lost in a systemic break, ushering in an age of corruption, Hunt implied.[29] Elsewhere, his chatty familiarity was used to show that corruption had not divided him from his own opinions. His vaunted intimacy with his readers, explicitly affiliated to an Addisonian frankness of exchange, is represented as a continuation of a peculiarly English civic ideal. Personality in *The Examiner* is supposed to act as an index of sincerity with the reader.

Similar principles also influenced Hunt's poetry. Obvious examples of what Hazlitt called Hunt's 'gay and conversational style' (XI: 177) are the epistles published in *The Examiner* in 1816 under the pseudonym 'Harry Brown'. Four of the poems address his cousin Tom Brown, that is, Thomas Moore, himself no mean practitioner of flexible chatty verse.[30] The other three epistles hale his friends Hazlitt, Barron Field, and Charles Lamb.[31] The results are 'personal, unhurried, chattily expansive' in a way that recalls Cowper's development of the conversation poem, but maintain an engagement with urban spaces like his Harry Honeycomb essays.[32] Even Hunt's more florid Italianate poetry with its tendency towards Spenserian luxury still aspires to an easy flow of talk. Shelley recognized Hunt's commitment to this aesthetic when he sent him the fair copy of his dialogue poem 'Julian and Maddalo' from Italy:

> You will find the little piece, I think, in some degree consistent with your own ideas of the manner in which Poetry ought to be written. I have employed a certain familiar style of language to express the actual way in which people talk with each other whom education and a certain refinement of sentiment have placed above the use of vulgar idioms. I use the word *vulgar* in its most extensive

---

[29] Ibid. 201.
[30] See *E*, 30 June 1816, 444: 409–10; 7 July, 445: 424; 21 July, 447: 456; 28 July, 448: 472.
[31] See *E*, 14 July 1816, 446: 440–1; 11 August, 450: 504; 25 August, 452: 536–7.
[32] Nicholas Roe describes these poems as 'breakthrough' in their move away from 'jacked-up claims for visionary insight' (*Fiery Heart: The First Life of Leigh Hunt* (London: Pimlico, 2005), 261).

way; the vulgarity of rank and fashion is as gross in its way as that of Poverty, and its cant terms equally expressive of bare conceptions, and therefore equally unfit for Poetry. Not that the familiar style is to be admitted in the treatment of a subject wholly ideal, or in that part of any subject which related to common life, where the passion exceeding a certain limit touches the boundaries of that which is ideal.[33]

The conflict between Shelley's idealizing tendencies and 'familiar style' was to be often pointed out by Hazlitt, causing problems for his friendship with Hunt, who continually defended Shelley over the next few years.[34] In its dialogic form and familiar style, 'Julian and Maddalo' reproduces something of the sense of intellectual exchange so important to the world Hunt created around himself. When Hunt sent Shelley his portrait, the poet felt he could recreate at least a trace of their communicative sympathy: 'What a delightful present!', came the reply, 'It is almost yourself, & we sate talking with it & of it all the evening. There wants nothing but that deepest & most earnest look with which you sometimes draw aside the inner veil of your nature when you talk with us, & the liquid lustre of the eyes.'[35]

Hunt had a great facility for attracting writers and forming them into loose and often shifting groups, usually with a centre of gravity in his own chaotic domestic arrangements. Hazlitt, Lamb, Keats, Shelley, and Byron are the most famous of those involved, but others came and went as the scene mutated across the 1810s and 1820s. What remained across the different participants—except perhaps for the years he spent in Italy with Shelley and Byron—was the ability to reproduce the idea of culture as a form of amiable exchange in which readers could easily join. Several readers of *The Examiner*, including Keats, became collaborators after they had been keen followers of the paper. This relatively porous and easy-going sociability infuriated many elite reviewers, who saw it as a debasement of what the republic of letters should represent. If hostile reviewers associated Hazlitt with the tavern, Hunt's idea of the literary was nearly always represented as a feminized one, centred on the family. Even in prison from 1813 to 1815, Hunt managed to entertain his literary friends in quasi-domestic circumstances, producing his own version of the civility under pressure that the inmates of Newgate created in the 1790s.[36] Hunt occupied two rooms, one covered with wallpaper painted with a trellis of roses, which opened into a small garden. A stream of visitors,

[33] To Leigh Hunt, 15 August 1819, in *The Letters of Percy Bysshe Shelley*, ed. Frederick L. Jones, 2 vols (Oxford: Oxford University Press, 1964), II: 108.

[34] See Gates, *Continuing Dialogue*, 80–9 on the series of letters between Hunt and Hazlitt provoked by 'On Paradox and Commonplace' in *Table Talk*. Hazlitt described Shelley as a 'philosophic fanatic' who lacked the checks of 'sympathy and habit' (VIII: 148–9).

[35] Shelley to Hunt, Livorno, *c.* 20 August 1819, *Letters*, II: 111.

[36] See Chap 3, pp. 149–51.

many of whom decamped to the home of the journalist Thomas Alsager when the prison closed, constantly interrupts his letters to his wife, Marianne.[37] Among these visitors was Hazlitt, at this stage not an intimate, who typically found difficulties with making himself agreeable:

> Even William Hazlitt, who there first did me the honour of a visit, would stand interchanging amenities at the threshold, which I had great difficulty in making him pass. I know not which kept his hat off with the greater pertinacity of deference, I to the diffident cutter-up of Tory dukes and kings, or he to the amazing prisoner and invalid who issued out of a bower of roses.[38]

Hunt tried quite literally to turn his prison into a bower of bliss, one of his favourite tropes, drawn from a favourite author in Spenser.[39] In certain respects, the trope papers over a tension within Hunt's conversational mode. The bower was a version of the desire for 'select' company, as it was, for instance, in Coleridge's conversation poems, a closed circle of like minded spirits, transported to a richly imagined timeless zone. As an avid reader of *The Examiner*, Keats was familiar enough with Hunt's predilections before he had ever met him to imagine his imprisonment in precisely this way in his sonnet 'Written on the Day that Mr. Leigh Hunt left Prison':

> In Spenser's halls he strayed, and bowers fair,
> Culling enchanted flowers.[40]

In his own writing, Hunt's resistance to the commercial spirit is often tied to the chivalric values of the Round Table. For Hazlitt, who effectively took over the 'round table' metaphor from Hunt, its primary implication, in contrast, was contemporary table talk between friends and equals, but in Hunt's hands it hovered ambivalently between chivalric past and communicative present. 'The Round Table' project was first announced in *The Examiner* for New Year's Day 1815 (*E*, 366: 11–12).[41] The date was appropriate for a project Hunt defined in terms of fireside joviality between a group of companions, 'letting the stream of conversation wander through any ground it pleases', but it also implied a nostalgic remembrance of times passed, reawakening the spirit of 'our good old

---

[37] See Kucich, '"The Wit in the Dungeon"'.

[38] *The Autobiography of Leigh Hunt*, ed. and intro. J. E. Morpurgo (London: Cresset Press, 1948), 246.

[39] On Hunt and Spenser more generally, see Greg Kucich, *Keats, Shelley, and Romantic Spenserianism* (University Park, PA: Penn. State University Press, 1991).

[40] See *The Poems of John Keats*, ed. Jack Stillinger (London: Heineman, 1978), 32.

[41] Originally the collection culled from the 'Round Table' essays in *The Examiner* was to have included ten by Hunt. The published two-volume book contained only five, the rest supplied by Hazlitt, some of them newly written. See the account in Stanley Jones, *Hazlitt: A Life: From Winterslow to Frith Street* (Oxford: Clarendon Press, 1989), 185–6, 208–11, and 279.

periodical works'. Where it differs from those precursors, Hunt claims, is in putting aside the disguises adopted by Addison and Steele to bring it before the public in their own personalities:

We have avoided the trouble of adding assumed characters to our real ones; and shall talk, just as we think, walk, and take dinner, in our own proper persons.

The 'solitary and dictatorial manner of the later Essayists', presumably another hit at the Johnsonian style, is to be discarded in favour of the easiness of 'a small party of friends, who meet once a week at a Round Table'.[42] The circle is not entirely closed. Readers can become writers, 'all persons not actually admitted to the said Table, must write to us in the form of a letter'. Even so, an understanding of the field of literary production in terms of conversation is being redefined towards the personalities of the participants, just as the attraction of Byron's way of chat was developed around the suggestion that he was constantly offering his readers a glimpse of his own magnetic personality.[43] The table talk of authors was a marketable commodity in the 1820s and 1830s, but, as with the example of Coleridge's celebrity conversation, not always as open to its readers as Hunt's *Examiner* at least aspired to be.

Hunt's next essay in the 'Round Table' series continued to define the project in terms of conversation (*E*, 8 January 1815, 367: 26–7), but now in relation to the style of the essays themselves. Conversational ease allows room for digression and a variety of tone that can move between the 'facetious' and the 'profound'. The topics will similarly vary between 'Manners, or the surface of society' and 'Morals, metaphysically considered, or it's [*sic*] utmost causes of action.' Mediating between them and implicitly identifying the position of *The Examiner* is 'Taste'. Hunt imagines himself as an ambassador in the manner of Addison and Hume between polite society and the abstruse learning of the cloisters, but explicitly strikes out against the narcissistic aspects of the Addisonian inheritance. For the progress of politeness, society is 'indebted to Steele

[42] *Blackwood's* later declared itself 'sick of the *personalities* of this man'. See 'On the Cockney School of Poetry, no. V', *Blackwood's Edinburgh Magazine*, 5 (1819), 97–100 (98).

[43] For Byron's development of this flirtatious, chatty persona, exploiting public knowledge of his personal life, see Tom Mole, *Byron's Romantic Celebrity: Industrial Culture and the Hermeneutic of Intimacy* (Basingstoke: Palgrave Macmillan, 2007), esp. 44–59. See also Corin Throsby, 'Flirting with Fame: Byron's Anonymous Female Fans', *Byron Journal*, 32 (2004), 115–23, and 'Byron, Commonplacing and Early Fan Culture', in Tom Mole (ed.), *Romanticism and Celebrity Culture, 1750–1850* (Cambridge: Cambridge University Press, 2009), 227–44. For Hazlitt's own fascination with Byron's conversation, see *Conversations with Northcote*, where he reports telling Mary Shelley that he 'could not conceive him [Byron] to be in conversation, or in any other way, a flat and *common-place* person' (XI: 187, 188).

and his associates', a point he returned to in the Harry Honeycomb essays. Their success has provided a 'freedom from grossness' and a 'tincture of literature' to 'high life or in middle'. The problem had become the constricting hegemony of politeness: 'the levelling spirit in manners' has produced a 'coxcombical sort of exclusiveness'. *The Examiner* intends 'to set men, not upon disliking smoothness, but avoiding insipidity not starting into roughness, but avoiding a flimsy sameness'.

Hunt distinguished his principle of sociality from the regulated flow of commerce. People passing 'smoothly with each other' like 'so much worn-out coin' may have been Addison's goal, but it was not quite to be *The Examiner*'s. Where Hazlitt differed from Hunt was in his comparative unconcern about falling into 'roughness' at the other extreme. His contributions to the series made his reservations about the small change of polite culture abrasively clear. His rant against the feminization of culture in his essay 'On Classical Education' (*E*, 12 February 1815, 372: 107–8) provides an example I'll return to later, but for now I just want to note the nature of Hunt's response (*E*, 19 February 1815, 373: 121–4). Hunt's reply brings to the fore the Arthurian aspects of his conception of the 'round table' trope. Hunt's doesn't simply rebut Hazlitt's ideas, but brings to the exchange a more playful tone, teasing Hazlitt, posing as a gallant defender of female talents, orienting the 'round table' metaphor back towards its chivalric Arthurian connotations. From the very beginning of his political writing, Hunt had presented himself as a man dragged from his proper sphere as a poet by public necessity. If the trope of the 'round table' can be understood as an aspect of 'the radical effort to resist specialization in periodical discourse, and recuperate a utopian sphere of unalienated labour', then it is equally a remodelling of the eighteenth-century idea of the 'select' circle into something both more cosily domestic and nostalgic for a fairyland past.[44]

After setting up his new journal *The Indicator* in 1819, Hunt claimed to have been asked about the differences between it and *The Examiner*. He distinguished them as different kinds of conversational space:

The fact is, that as far as the Editor is concerned, the Examiner is to be regarded as the reflection of his public literature, and the Indicator of his private. In the one he has a sort of public meeting with his friends: in the other, a more retired one. The Examiner is his tavern-room for politics, for political pleasantry, for criticism upon the theatres and living writers. The Indicator is his private room, his study, his retreat from public care and criticism, with the reader who chuses [*sic*] to accompany him.[45]

---

[44] Gilmartin, *Print Politics*, 205.
[45] *The Indicator*, 20 October 1819, 2: 9.

He goes on immediately to invite his readers to join the domestic *mise en scène*:

Here we are then again, with our fire before us, and our books on each side. What shall we do? Shall we take out a Life of somebody, or a Theocritus, or Dante, or Ariosto, or Montaigne, or Marcus Aurelius, or Horace or Shakespeare who includes them all? Or shall we read an engraving from Poussin or Raphael? Or shall we sit with tilted chairs, planting our wrists upon our knees, and toasting the up-turned palms of our hands, while we discourse of manners and of man's hearts and hopes, with at least a sincerity, a good intention, and good nature, that shall warrant what we say with the sincere, the good-intentioned, and the good-natured?

Notwithstanding the distinction drawn in the first *Indicator*, many of Hunt's contributions to *The Examiner* have more of the cosy fireside about them than the theatre and the tavern: certainly when compared to Hazlitt's more generally pugnacious contributions. Sometimes Hunt's essays were presented as playfully emollient responses to Hazlitt's more combative style. For his part, Hazlitt often provocatively interrogated some of Hunt's most treasured maxims, even in his essays for *The Examiner*. There were aspects of the culture associated with the Cockney circle often oriented more to a boozy homosociality than the domestic scenes Hunt liked to construct for himself.

Keats's letters provide a frank insight into this world, often repressed in Victorian memoirs of the group.[46] Writing to his brothers, George and Tom, Keats recounted an evening at a dance with other aspiring literati:

there was a younger Brother of the Squibs made him self very conspicuous after the Ladies had retired from the supper table by giving Mater Omnium—Mr Redhall said he did not understand anything but plain English—where at Rice egged the young fool on to say the World plainly out. After which there was an enquirey [*sic*] about the derivation of the word C—t when while the two parsons and Grammarians were setting together and settling the matter Wm Squibs interrupting them said a very good thing—'Gentlemen says he I have always understood it to be a Root and not a Derivitive [*sic*]'. On proceeding to the Pot in the Cupboard it soon became full on which the Court door was opened Frank Floodgate bawls out. Hoollo! Here's an opposition pot—Ay, says Rice in one you have a Yard for your pot, and in the other a pot for your Yard.[47]

The dance was in a private home, but a masculine space had been created by the retirement of the women. In this liminal place, drunkenness and obscene punning, the old vices of libertine conversation, could flourish.

[46] See Gillian Russell, 'Keats, Popular Culture, and the Sociability of Theatre', in Philip Connell and Nigel Leask (eds), *Romanticism and Popular Culture in Britain and Ireland* (Cambridge: Cambridge University Press, 2009), 194–213.
[47] Keats to George and Tom Keats, 5 January 1818, *The Letters of John Keats 1814–1821*, ed. Hyder Edward Rollins, 2 vols (Cambridge, MA: Harvard University Press, 1958), I: 200–1. Cancelled words omitted.

Gatherings in Hunt's home, even in mixed company, also sometimes developed into boozy events, as Hazlitt hinted when *The Spirit of the Age* praised Hunt's 'natural gaiety and sprightliness of manner, his high animal spirits, and the *vinous* [Hazlitt's italics] quality of his mind, [which] produce an immediate fascination and intoxication in those who come into contact with him' (XI: 176). Lamb's facility with punning and pleasure in a drink made him a particularly popular participant at bibulous evenings.[48] Bryan Waller Procter remembered that at Hunt's suppers 'the cheerfulness (after a "wassail bowl") soared into noisy merriment. I remember one Christmas or New Year's evening, when we sat there till two or three o'clock in the morning, and when the jokes and stories and imitations so overcame me that I was nearly falling off my chair with laughter.'[49] Conservative reviewers were keen to represent Hunt's household as too prone to intoxication, morally dubious, and ridiculous in its social pretensions at the best of times.

Hostile reviewers rarely attended very closely to the differences between Hunt and Hazlitt I have sketched out: both men were more likely to be viewed as part of the same low urban formation of 'aspiring apprentices and critical clerks'.[50] If Hunt believed this chatty manner to be an updated version of Addison's 'agreeableness', reviewers in the *Quarterly* and *Blackwood's* represented it as grubby over-familiarity, not least in presuming to reduce great authors to mere objects of domestic discourse. Their attacks on the Cockneys raised a new version of the old spectre of learning reduced to chitchat. Of the five essays by Hunt included in *The Round Table*, two were the early ones from *The Examiner* setting out the affiliation with the *The Tatler* and *The Spectator*. One of the others, to the vengeful glee of the reviewers, was his long essay 'On Washerwomen'. Nowhere is the democratizing aspect of *The Examiner* more evident than here. Turning aside from 'polished life', Hunt offered an account of the conversation between washerwomen in a London street: 'we go farther than

---

[48] Perhaps Lamb's most famous performance in his cups was at the so-called 'Immortal Dinner'. See Penelope Hughes-Hallett, *The Immortal Dinner: A Famous Evening of Genius and Laughter in Literary London, 1817* (London: Viking, 2000). Haydon, Keats, and Wordsworth were also present. The 'bad and repeated puns' (*Letters* II: 8 and 11) in Hunt's circle began to tire Keats, who also grew weary of affected literary conversation in London more generally. See his letter to B. R. Haydon, 8 March, 1819: 'Conversation' has become 'not a search after knowledge, but an endeavour at effect. In this respect, two most opposite men, Wordsworth and Hunt are the same' (*Letters*, II: 43).

[49] See Procter's *Autobiographical Fragment*, 196. Later, Procter insists Hunt 'himself led a very domestic and correct life' (197), but beyond defending Hunt against the aspersions in *Blackwood's* and elsewhere it is hard to know exactly what this means.

[50] See 'Cockney School of Poets, no. V', *Blackwood's*, 5 (1819), 97. The review begins by contrasting Wordsworth's reclusive 'genius' with the Cockney's perpetual 'chatter about themselves'.

Mr. Wordsworth, for, though as fond, perhaps of the country as he, we can manage to please ourselves in the very thick of cities, and even find there as much reason to do justice to Providence.'[51] To the reviewer in the *Quarterly*, it was proof of just how ludicrous was the claim to be carrying on 'the manner of the early periodical Essayists, the Spectator and Tatler'.[52] Where Addison was a master of 'urbanity', 'ease and softness', and 'cheerful benevolence', the *Quarterly* saw in *The Round Table* only an uneasy blend of 'vulgar descriptions, silly paradoxes, flat truisms, misty sophistry, broken English, ill humour and rancorous abuse'. Despite the reviewer's failure to distinguish between the authors until his final paragraph, the sarcastic criticism of the author as 'a very eminent creator of words and phrases' turns on examples drawn from Hunt's contributions. The complaint at words like 'firesider' and 'kitcheny', phrases such as 'to tiptoe down', and the description of Spenser as 'dipt in poetic luxury' point to the kind of chattiness long blamed by traditional critics as an unfortunate feminizing influence on Keats. The complaints at 'foul and vulgar invective' are aimed at Hazlitt's contributions; only at the very end does the review recall Hunt authored some of the essays. In his prefatory remarks to the published edition, Hazlitt pointed out that it had fallen 'somewhat short of its original intention'. Mentioning the original design of bringing together 'various persons on a variety of subjects', he describes the title of *The Round Table* as most descriptive of its 'nature and design'. Hunt was to have taken 'the characteristic or dramatic part of the work upon himself', but the project broke up with the re-appearance of Napoleon: 'our little congress was broken up as well as the great one': 'Politics called off the attention of the Editor from the Belles Lettres; and the task of continuing the work fell chiefly upon the person who was least able to give life and spirit to the original design.' The implication is that the fireside drollery disappears (as does any Arthurian connotation in the title) in favour of the political urgency of Hazlitt's plain speaking.[53]

HAZLITT AND OPPOSITION

Hazlitt was more strongly associated in the public imagination of the 1810s and 1820s with the worlds of the tavern and the theatre than the

---

[51] *The Round Table*, 2 vols (Edinburgh, 1817), II: 182.
[52] See *Quarterly Review*, 17 (April 1817), 154–9. The claim about following the manner of Addison et al. was made in Hazlitt, 'Advertisement', *Round Table*, I: v, as it had been in Hunt's *Examiner* essays.
[53] 'Advertisement', v–vi.

parlour. When he started as a parliamentary reporter at the *Morning Chronicle* in 1812, his hard-drinking colleague Peter Finnerty, recently released from prison, would take him to the 'Cider Cellars' in Maiden Lane.[54] 'On the Difference between Writing and Speaking' described Finnerty as a man with a 'lively flow of animal spirits, a good deal of confidence, a communicative turn, and a tolerably tenacious memory with respect to floating opinions and current phrases' (XII: 264). A decade later, when Hazlitt frequented the Southampton Coffee House in Chancery Lane, the proprietor reserved a table for him in the corner, where he sometimes met with William Hone and George Cruikshank, who would dip his finger in ale and draw his latest idea for a squib on the table.[55] Patmore recalled Hazlitt as 'always more or less ready to take part in that sort of desultory "talk"…in which he excelled every man I ever met with'.[56] Charles Wells, also a friend of Keats, described a period when he would stay up all night getting drunk with Hazlitt at the Southampton.[57] The theatre played an important part in the roistering urban sociability of 'Cockney' circles. Originally theatre critic for *The Examiner*, Hunt celebrated the playhouses as places that 'scatter egotism, and collect sociality' (*E*, 20 July 1817, 499: 456). The topic was a favourite of Hazlitt's: 'Whoever sees a play ought to be better and more sociable for it: for he has something to talk about, some ideas and feelings in common with his neighbours,' as he wrote in his late essay 'Our National Theatres' (XX: 288). The theatre represented a rare place that brought different kinds of talk and different kinds of people into 'a splendid confusion' (XX: 287), including vigorous disagreement. 'The invidious distinction of the *private boxes*' he regarded as an abrogation of its spirit of democratic mixing, and the affirmation of the sad truth bluntly stated at the opening of the essay: 'The motto of the English nation is "exclusion".'

Hazlitt's very popular lectures at the Surrey Institution, begun early in 1818, created an atmosphere that threatened to disrupt the venue's

---

[54] See Wu, *William Hazlitt*, 145. Hazlitt is sometimes reported as abstaining from drink in the 1820s, but there is no evidence he became tee-total. See ibid. 181 and 476, n 73, and Jones, *Hazlitt*, 179–80.

[55] Frederick W. Hackwood, *William Hone: His Life and Times* (London: T. Fisher Unwin, 1912), 236. On Hazlitt's unofficial office at the Southampton and the 'coffee-house politicians' he met there, see Patmore's description of the 'evening levee' that met 'till a very *un*certain hour in the morning' (*Friends and Acquaintance*, II: 316), and Wu, *William Hazlitt*, 289–90. Patmore also claimed that Hazlitt was more comfortable with Hone than any other of his friends (III: 74).

[56] Patmore, *Friends and Acquaintance*, II: 316.

[57] See Wu, *William Hazlitt*, 217. A solicitor with literary aspirations, Wells was the dedicatee of the Keats sonnet 'To a Friend who Sent me some Roses'. See Cox, *Cockney School*, 93.

respectable intentions with the values he identified with the theatre. Rowlandson and Pugin's drawing of the Institution for *The Microcosm of London* (see Fig. 11) is supported by a commentary that celebrates the improving marriage of commerce and literature in the modern metropolis. 'General communication' is encouraged as 'an incentive to mutual improvement'. Hazlitt certainly gave his audience an interactive event, but not perhaps in the fashion projected by the Institution's founders.[58] Even if many in his audience disapproved of his sentiments, Hazlitt delighted in playing off them. 'The comparative insensibility of the bulk of his audience', remembered Thomas Noon Talfoud, 'sometimes provoked him to awaken their attention by points which broke the train of his discourse; after which, he could make himself amends by some abrupt paradox which might set their prejudices on edge, and make them fancy they were shocked.' Many in the audience were respectable non-conformists, whom Hazlitt relished baiting: 'Mrs. Hannah More is another celebrated modern poetess, and I believe still living. She has written a great deal which I never read' (V: 107). 'More pity for you!' someone called out, but Hazlitt would have known Keats and his other friends in the audience enjoyed the barb.[59] Hazlitt later described his lecturing technique as 'merely to read over a set of authors with the audience, as I would do with a friend' (VI: 301). Mary Mitford delighted in his 'genius for malice'. She believed him 'more delightful viva voce than in a printed book'.[60] The Surrey Institution's 'conversation-rooms' were intended to encourage talk about its lectures, but not in the provoking manner Hazlitt brought to the place.[61]

[58] *The Microcosm of London*, 3 vols (London, 1808–10), III: 155. Hazlitt had been recommended by Alsager, who was a committee member. Hazlitt's friendship with P. G. Patmore, also a committee member, stemmed from this period. See *Friends and Acquaintance*, I: 249–50. For further details, see Frederick Kurzer, 'A History of the Surrey Institution', *Annals of Science*, 57 (2000), 109–41.

[59] Talfourd, *Memorials of Charles Lamb*, II: 175. *Blackwood*'s 'Cockney School, no. V', 97, took a rather different view: 'Mr. Hazlitt cannot look around him at the Surrey, without resting his smart eye on the idiot admiring grin of several dozens of aspiring apprentices and critical clerks.' Keats attended the lectures regularly: 'I went last Tuesday, an hour too late, to Hazlitt's Lecture on poetry, got there just as they were coming out, when all these pounced upon me. Hazlitt, John Hunt & son, Wells, Bewick, all the Landseers, Bob Harris Rox of the Burrough Aye & more' (To George and Tom Keats, 23 January 1818, *Letters*, I: 214). Keats thought Hazlitt's decision to repeat the lectures again at the 'Crown and Anchor' was 'letting his talents down a little' (To J. H. Reynolds, 25 March 1818, *Letters*, I: 259). On Hazlitt's lecturing more generally, see Peter J. Manning, 'Manufacturing the Romantic Image: Hazlitt and Coleridge Lecturing', in James Chandler and Kevin Gilmartin (eds), *Romantic Metropolis: The Urban Scene of British Culture, 1780–1840* (Cambridge: Cambridge University Press, 2005), 227–45.

[60] See Mary Mitford to Sir William Elford, 1 November 1818. Mitford's MSS correspondence, 6 vols, Reading Central Library, III: 350.

[61] See the discussion in Gillian Russell, 'Spouters or Washerwomen: The Sociability of Romantic Lecturing', in Gillian Russell and Clara Tuite (eds), *Romantic Sociability: Social*

Fig. 11. Joseph Constantine Stadler, and Thomas Rowlandson, after Augustus Charles Pugin, 'Surrey Institution' (1809). Courtesy of the Yale Center for British Art, Paul Mellon Collection.

Pierce Egan's *Life in London* (1822) painted a picture of Hazlitt—sharing his ideas for a lecture in the less improving environs of a tavern—as one of the sights of the metropolis:

Mr. HAZLITT, in the evening lolling at his ease upon one of *Ben Medley*'s elegant couches, enjoying the reviving comforts of a *good tinney*, [fire] smacking *his cha*ffer [tongue] over a glass of old hock, and topping his *glim* [candle] *to a cla*ssic nicety, in order to thro*w a new l*ight upon the elegant leaves of ROSCOE's Life of Lorenzo de' Medic*i, as a com*position for a NEW LECTURE at the Surrey Institution.[62]

Networks and Literary Culture in Britain, 1770–1849 (Cambridge: Cambridge University Press, 2002), 126–7. Russell contrasts the layout of the Institution with 'the "open theatre of the world" that was [Thelwall's] Beaufort Buildings'. I am suggesting that Hazlitt's lectures may have been more disruptive than the Institution's intended fare.

[62] Pierce Egan, *Life in London; or, the Day and Night Scenes of Jerry Hawthorn, Esq. and his Elegant Friend Corinthian Tom* (London, 1822), 31–2.

Egan's book is more complacent about the mixed cultural marketplace than the Institution's respectable idea of 'commerce'. Visiting the Royal Academy exhibition, for instance, unashamedly represents to Egan 'a *bob* [shilling] well laid out'.[63] Without turning away from the life of London around him, Hazlitt's disposition was rather more oppositional than Egan's, but at least one contemporary blamed him for bringing the 'uproar of a one-shilling gallery' to the Surrey Institution.[64] The criticism echoes those of the crowds who were thought to ruin the equal wide survey of the true connoisseur at the Academy exhibitions.[65] This aspect of Hazlitt's lecturing was not merely showmanship, but a feature of the provocative idea of opposition that was a structuring principle in his writing.

The pugnacity of Hazlitt's political journalism has often brought apologetic commentary from literary critics mainly interested in his writing on the arts, but more recent accounts by Phillip Harling and Kevin Gilmartin have sought to place his work in careful dialogue with the rise of popular radicalism after 1815.[66] Hazlitt was often explicitly hostile to the culture of patrician politeness in ways that directly play off its insidious violence as a more grievous form of injury than any political insurrection:

I can endure the brutality (as it is termed) of mobs better than the inhumanity of courts. The violence of the one rages like a fire; the insidious policy of the other strikes like a pestilence, and is more fatal and inevitable. The slow poison of despotism is worse than the convulsive struggles of anarchy. (VIII: 164)

He also clearly differentiated himself from the Addisonian model of polite conversation when he quotes Horne Tooke in 'The Prose Style of Poets' on the defects of the *Spectator* style:

Its smooth, equable uniformity, and want of sharpness and spirit, arose from his not having familiarized his ear to the sound of his own voice, or at least only among friends and admirers, where there was but little collision, dramatic fluctuation, or sudden contrariety of opinion to provoke animated discussion, and give birth to different intonations and lively transitions of speech. (XII: 6)

---

[63] Ibid. 339.

[64] See the letter from 'A Friend to Order' in *The Times*, 12 November 1818, 3.

[65] See David H. Solkin, ' "This Great Mart of Genius": The Royal Academy Exhibitions at Somerset House, 1780–1836', in *idem* (ed.), *Art on the Line: The Royal Academy Exhibitions at Somerset House 1780–1836* (New Haven: Yale University Press, 2001), 1–8, esp. 3, and also C. S. Matheson, ' "A Shilling Well Laid Out": The Royal Academy's Early Public', ibid. 39–53.

[66] See, Phillip Harling, 'William Hazlitt and Radical Journalism', *Romanticism*, 3 (1997), 53–65, and Kevin Gilmartin, 'Hazlitt's Visionary London', in Heather Glen and Paul Hamilton (eds), *Repossessing the Romantic Past* (Cambridge: Cambridge University Press, 2006), 40–62.

'Lively transitions of speech' define Hazlitt's ideal of conversation, often based on sudden reversals and sparks of wit, frequently practised in the mixed language and sharp changes of direction found in his essays. The importance of the conversational idea of the essay for Hazlitt was made very clear in his lecture 'On the Periodical Essayists,' but his model is nominated as Montaigne not the early-eighteenth-century British essayists. For Hazlitt, Montaigne—praised for the enlivening virtues of 'dramatic contrast and ironical point of view'—is celebrated as 'the first author who was not a bookmaker' (VI: 93). 'Book-making' here implies a form of writing that abjures the power of colloquial language, associated by Hazlitt with the desiccated learning of the cloisters rather than the attempt to capture the familiarity of speech associated with the essay. When it comes to Montaigne's English imitators, Hazlitt prefers Steele to Addison. His essays 'are more like the remarks which occur in sensible conversation, and less like a lecture' (VI: 97). Given the accounts of Hazlitt's own lecturing style—with its conversational, often provocative nods and winks to the audience—one imagines the knowing delight he took in delivering this distinction to an audience. Samuel Johnson is even more to blame than Addison for steering the essay towards the style of 'scholastic theses' (VI: 100). Johnson as a writer lacked the 'spark of genius' that will 'disturb the ordinary march of our thoughts' (VI: 101) in Hazlitt's eyes. The contrast may appear a familiar Romantic preference for 'genius' against neo-classical values, but Hazlitt's taste for such *bouleversement* is not a rejection of the conversational paradigm as such. Rather, Hazlitt affirms an alternative strain within it. Johnson 'the complete balance-master' (VI: 102) in his prose is praised at the end of the lecture for his combative conversation: 'the life and dramatic play of his conversation forms a contrast to his written works. His natural powers and undisguised opinions were called out in convivial intercourse. In public, he practised with the foils on: in private, he unsheathed the sword of controversy' (VI: 103). The alignment of 'conversation', 'convivial intercourse', and 'controversy' here is in striking contrast with the insistence by so many eighteenth-century essayists that controversy was always inimical to conversation.

Where genius fails to reach outside of itself and submit to conversation, when it is too averse to contention with its readers, then for Hazlitt it represents a pathology of sensibility. The key to Hazlitt's valorization of conversation is the resistance it offers to tendencies that abstract from mixed imperfect being (even as he acknowledged the tendency within himself).[67] His attacks on Wordsworth centred precisely on the

---

[67] On abstraction in Hazlitt, see David Bromwich, *Hazlitt: The Mind of a Critic* (New York/Oxford: Oxford University Press, 1983), 75–7.

fact that the poet seemed able only to converse with either himself or a
generalized nature:

All accidental varieties and individual contrasts are lost in an endless continuity of
feeling; like drops of water in the ocean-stream! An intense intellectual egotism
swallows up every thing. Even the dialogues introduced in the present volume are
soliloquies of the same character, taking different views of the subject. (IV: 113)

Demonstrating his own startling ability to stage *bouleversement* in his
essays, Hazlitt concedes the attraction of Wordsworth's power even as
he disavows its egotism. Wordsworth's genius, as Hazlitt sees it, withdraws
itself from conversation with its world to the position of spectator *ab extra*.
Always replete with their own 'accidental varieties and individual contrasts', Hazlitt's essays, in contrast, wrestle with their subjects. For Talfourd, sounding a very Coleridgean note, Hazlitt lacked 'that imagination
which brings all things into one'. From this point of view, the effect
resulted from the strong sense 'of the *personal* on Hazlitt's abstract spec-
ulations', but personality in Hazlitt is not a flattening egotism but a
constant reassessment of his own responses. Talfourd, who thought 'no
one's conversation was ever more delightful', recognized in Hazlitt a
'penetrating spirit of human dealing'. Much of Hazlitt's writing on poetry
is explicitly or implicitly a conversation with Wordsworth's example,
frequently turning around and interrogating his own admiration of his
subject's writing as he expected all 'human dealing' to do.[68]

For all their plain speaking, this facility permeates even the greatest of
Hazlitt's political essays. 'What is the People?' is at the same time inter-
rogative, continually questioning the terms of political debate, including
its own, and fiercely committed to the cause of radical change.[69] In certain
respects, Hazlitt develops the style Paine's *Rights of Man* (1791–2) be-
queathed to the radical press, encouraging his readers to think through
traditional political vocabularies, while presenting a powerful argument
for the renovation of politics, but it is the directness of Hazlitt's second-
person address that makes the essay's opening so memorable. The result
has the air of a spirited rejoinder in a taproom discussion:

And who are you that ask the question? One of the people. And yet you would be
something! Then you would not have the People nothing. For what is the People?

---

[68] Thomas Noon Talfourd, 'Thoughts upon the Intellectual Character of the Late
William Hazlitt', in W. C. Hazlitt (ed.), *Literary Remains of William Hazlitt* (1836),
cii, xcv, cxxv, and cviii–cix.

[69] Not intended for a narrowly literary audience, the essay first appeared in *The
Champion* on 12, 19, and 16, October 1817, then took its final two-part format in *The
Yellow Dwarf* 7 and 14 March 1818, before being collected in *Political Essays* (1819).

Millions of men, like you, with hearts beating in their bosoms, with thoughts stirring in their minds, with the blood circulating in their veins, with wants and appetites, and passions and anxious cares, and busy purposes and affections for others and a respect for themselves, and a desire of happiness, and a right to freedom, and a will to be free. (VII: 259)

If the parallel clauses of the opening rise towards rhapsody, they are shaped also by the sense of an excited argument going on. Moreover, the opposition between the writer and the anonymous other who poses the title question is soon incorporated into a first-person plural: 'that detestable fiction, which would make you and me and all mankind its slaves or victims…and makes us turn our eyes from the light of heaven…exentrates us of our affections, blinds our understandings, debases our imaginations' (VII: 259–60). Joined together as victims of 'Legitimacy', Hazlitt does not simply assume a unity of position and purpose between writer and reader, but builds it up through the two parts of the essay, admitting doubts and uncertainties, while insisting 'the cause of the people' can only be judged by 'common feeling and public opinion' (VII: 267). This cause is not taken to be infallible in its operations: 'A certain degree of folly, or rashness, or indecision, or even violence in attaining an object, is surely less to be dreaded than a malignant, deliberate, mercenary intention in others to deprive us of it' (VII: 267). 'Popular feeling, as arising out of the immediate wants and wishes of the great mass of the people' will guide it in dialogue with 'public opinion, as arising out of the impartial reason and enlightened intellect of the community' (VII: 267–8). 'Impartial reason and enlightened intellect' are phrases that allow for a certain kind of rational conversation in a Godwinian mode, but it soon emerges that it must be the product of and continually resubmitted to 'incessant, and incredible struggles' (VII: 270). Against those who 'fear the progress of knowledge and a *Reading Public*' (a swipe at Coleridge's *Statesman's Manual*) (VII: 273), Hazlitt sees the extension of the conversation as crucial to any culture worth having.

Perhaps unconsciously adverting to Paine's 'open theatre of the world', a remarkable passage towards the end of the second part of the essay offers the playhouses as a microcosm of the cultural forms of democracy: 'the present system of universal suffrage and open competition among the candidates, the frequency of rows in the pit, the noise in the gallery, the whispers in the boxes, and the lashings in the newspapers the next day!' (VII: 274).[70] Aspects of the theatre that encouraged the polite to withdraw

---

[70] For Paine's phrase, see *Rights of Man*, ed. Eric Foner (Harmondsworth: Penguin, 1984), 182.

from the collisions of mixed social spaces are those that affirm the theatre's importance for Hazlitt. In their colloquial form and imagining of a scene of democratic interaction, passages such as these seem far from Habermas's rational deliberation. Hazlitt accepts unexpected collisions and divided purposes as part of the political process. His version of democratic life as a conversation of culture engages the imagination of his readers 'so they may appraise their own modes of attachment and detachment and experience the limits of representation characteristic of democratic life'.[71] 'I am not for "a collusion",' Hazlitt put it in 'On People's with One Idea', 'but "an exchange of ideas"' (VIII: 67). 'Life would turn to a stagnant pool', he wrote in 'The Pleasure of Hating', 'were it not ruffled by the jarring interests, the unruly passions of men' (XII: 128). His development of the association between the form of the essay and conversation was not predicated on polite exchange or rational convergence, but neither were they entirely original and peculiar to Hazlitt. They owed a lot to an alternative idea of conversation as a riskier and even explosive form of exchange found in Rational Dissent.

HAZLITT AND DISSENT

Earlier chapters of this book have placed eighteenth-century ideas of politeness and rational improvement in the context of others that explored creative collision as the mainspring of conversation. Although far from uniformly abjuring politeness, the culture of Dissent placed great store in the sparking flints of inter-subjective exchange. Hazlitt's intellectual heritage lay in this culture: 'I am by education and conviction inclined to republicanism and puritanism' (XX: 283).[72] The ideal type of the Dissenter 'speaks his mind bluntly and honestly, therefore he is a secret disturber of the peace, a dark Conspirator against the State' (VII: 239). While Hazlitt could be frank about the decline of Dissent as a force in public life, he continually drew upon its values of plain speaking as a corrective contrast to what he saw as the fawning conformity of contemporaries such as the Poet Laureate Robert Southey. 'On Court Influence' ends with a powerful eulogy to its values: 'Nothing else can sufficiently inure and steel a man against the prevailing prejudices of the world, but that habit of mind which arises from non-conformity to its decisions in

---

[71] Panagia, 'The Force of Political Argument', 838.
[72] For critical responses to Hazlitt and Dissent, see John Kinnaird, *William Hazlitt: Critic of Power* (New York: Columbia University Press, 1978), 32–4; Bromwich, *The Mind of a Critic*, 59; Gilmartin, 'Hazlitt's Visionary London', 42.

matters of religion' (VII: 240). He insisted on the relevance of those values to a period that seemed to be reinventing government by Divine Right: 'It is a pity that this character has worn itself out; that that pulse of thought and feeling has ceased almost to beat in the heart of a nation, who, if not remarkable for sincerity and plain downright well-meaning, are remarkable for nothing.' Comparing what he perceives as the principled rectitude of Dissent with the 'whirligig court poet' Southey, he concludes: 'The Dissenting Minister is a character not so easily to be dispensed with, and whose place cannot well be supplied' (VII: 241).

Gilmartin succinctly defines Hazlitt's attitude to Dissent as combining 'regret for a passing legacy with a vivid sense of achieved community'.[73] Hazlitt had experienced at least something of the latter as a student at the New College, Hackney from 1793 to 1795.[74] Watts's *Improvement of the Mind* would have been a familiar text there. Hackney gave him direct experience of the pedagogical practice derived from its ideas on conversation. Joseph Priestley's discourse on *The Proper Objects of Education in the Present State of the World*, addressed to the supporters of Hackney College in April 1791, had emphasized the importance of 'continual discussion', especially of religious and political matters.[75] Looking back on the mid-1790s, as he so often did, Hazlitt fondly remembered the Unitarian preacher Joseph Fawcett: 'the conversations I had with him on subjects of taste and philosophy…gave me a delight, such as I can never feel again' (III: 171 n). In his essay on 'The Aristocracy of Letters', he invokes the Unitarian principles of open discussion expounded by men like Fawcett and Priestley:

There can be no true superiority but what arises out of the presupposed ground of equality: there can be no improvement but from the free communication and comparing of ideas. Kings and nobles, for this reason, receive little benefit from society—where all is submission on one side, and condescension on the other. The mind strikes out truth by collision, as steel strikes fire from the flint! (VIII: 208)

The final sentence, especially, sounds a direct echo of Watts on conversation.[76] The other obvious influence on this aspect of Hazlitt's thinking was Godwin's *Political Justice*, itself indebted to Watts. Although he was out of

---

[73] Gilmartin, 'Hazlitt's visionary London', 42.

[74] See Stephen Burley's *New College, Hackney (1786–96): A Selection of Printed and Archival Sources* on the Dr Williams's Centre website at http://www.english.qmul.ac.uk/drwilliams/pubs/nc%20hackney.html (accessed May 26, 2010). Hazlitt was funded at Hackney by the Presbyterian Fund thanks to the help of his father's friend Andrew Kippis, who had been Godwin's teacher.

[75] Joseph Priestley, *The Proper Objects of Education in the Present State of the World* (London, 1791), 20.

[76] See my discussion of the relevant passage above, pp. 69–70.

sympathy with many aspects of the personality and philosophy of Godwin, Hazlitt nominated 1793—the year *Political Justice* was published—as a kind of *annus mirabilis* against which everything else had to be judged.[77] Take, for instance, his review of Robert Owen's *New View of Society* (1813):

Does not Mr. Owen know that the same scheme, the same principles, the same philosophy of motives and actions, of causes and consequences, of knowledge and virtue, of virtue and happiness, were rife in the year 1793, were noised abroad then, were spoken on the house-tops, were whispered in secret, were published in quarto and duodecimo, in political treatises, in plays, poems, songs, and romances—made their way to the bar, crept into the church, ascended the rostrum, thinned the classes of the universities, and robbed 'Durham's golden stalls' of their hoped-for ornaments, by sending our aspiring youth up to town to learn philosophy of the new teachers of philosophy; that these 'New Views of Society' got into the hearts of poets and the brains of metaphysicians, took possession of the fancies of boys and women, and turned the heads of almost the whole kingdom. (VII: 99)

The 'philosophy of motives and actions, of causes and consequences, of knowledge and virtue, of virtue and happiness' refers to *Political Justice*. Hazlitt begins his review by hailing Godwin's book as one of the originals for Owen's ideas on the 'doctrine of Universal Benevolence'. In his larger career, Hazlitt had followed Godwin in turning from the rigours of writing a philosophical treatise to a more familiar style, better adapted to exploit 'the vivacity...and richness', as Godwin put it in his *Enquirer* preface, of 'hints struck out in conversation'. Some of the phrasing from Godwin's preface may even have made its way to the introduction Hazlitt wrote for the Paris edition of *Table Talk* (1826):

I had remarked that when I had written or thought upon a particular topic, and afterwards had occasion to speak of it with a friend, the conversation generally took a much wider range, and branched off into a number of indirect and collateral questions, which were not strictly connected with the original view of the subject, but which threw a curious and striking light upon it, or upon human life in general.

This method, Hazlitt continued, allowed for a 'greater variety and richness' and perhaps 'greater sincerity' than could be obtained by 'a more precise and scholastic method' (VIII: 333).

---

[77] Reference to the Hazlitt family first appears in Godwin's diary from 1794, when Godwin had tea with the 'Hazlitts'—the editors of the online edition of the diary take this to refer to William and his older brother John Hazlitt. The relationship between Godwin and Hazlitt only finally foundered after Godwin read in the newspapers that *The Plain Speaker* (1826) would contain anecdotes about him. 'On the Qualifications Necessary to Success in Life' claimed that Godwin 'in conversation has not a word to throw at a dog'. The essay had actually been in print since 1820, when it appeared in the *London Magazine*. See Wu, *William Hazlitt*, 383–4.

What Hazlitt does *not* follow Godwin in doing when he takes up the essay form is moderating the collision of mind with mind into something less vigorous. Hazlitt's pugnacious emphasis on lively transitions keeps alive the contrarian traditions of Rational Dissent apparent in *Political Justice*. On the other hand, his distinctive emphasis on 'our limited, imperfect, and mixed being' was indebted to the sentimental philosophy of Hume and Adam Smith that Godwin claimed had influenced his turn to sentiment in *The Enquirer* and other later works.[78] Hazlitt agreed with Hume and Smith at least that the imagination was the faculty that could power our sympathetic identification with others, but his version of the process is uneasy at the merging of perspectives into social consensus. Hazlitt's essay on Godwin in *The Spirit of the Age* is typically complex in its judgements in relation to these issues. The primary focus is on the author of *Political Justice* and *Caleb Williams* (the *Enquirer* isn't mentioned bar the brief description of Godwin as an 'essayist' among his other attainments). The problem Hazlitt identifies is Godwin's rationalist abrogation of the mediations of everyday sociability: 'He absolves man from the gross and narrow ties of sense, custom, authority, private and local attachment, in order that he may devote himself to the boundless pursuit of universal benevolence' (XI: 18–19). The dismissive references in several other Hazlitt essays to Samuel Parr's critique of Godwin in his influential *Spital Sermon* (1801) help illuminate the point. Parr continually ranged against *Political Justice* the authority of the British moralists, including Hume and Smith, presenting himself as speaking for the private and domestic affections against utopian and impracticable notions of universal benevolence.[79] In his scattered references to Parr, Hazlitt consistently presents the clergyman as doing the servile work of the Burkean counter-revolution in this critique of Godwin.[80] Hazlitt, unlike Parr, constantly insists on the necessity of challenging rather than simply accepting the 'narrow ties', as he terms them, of a Burkean second nature:

We may not be able to launch the bark of our affections on the ocean-tide of humanity, we may be forced to paddle along its shores, or shelter in its creeks and rivulets: but we have no right to reproach the bold and adventurous pilot, who dared us to tempt the uncertain abyss, with our own want of courage or of skill, or

---

[78] The phrase occurs in his discussion of Godwin's fiction. Hazlitt's *Essay on the Principles of Human Action* twice acknowledges the influence of Smith on his own thinking (I: 24 and 80).

[79] Samuel Parr, *A Spital Sermon, preached at Christ Church, upon Easter Tuesday, April 15, 1800* (London, 1801).

[80] In the review of Owen's *New View of Society*, for instance, Hazlitt imagines 'Dr. Parr will preach a Spital sermon against him' if the book becomes popular (VII: 102).

with the jealousies and impatience, which deter us from undertaking, or might prevent us from accomplishing the voyage! (XI: 19)

From Hazlitt's perspective, *Political Justice* had served the contrarian logic of Dissent even if it does not in itself embody truth. Popular radicals such as Thelwall had effectively used it in this way in the 1790s, debating its principles in popular discussion clubs and London Corresponding Society meetings, without necessarily signing up to all its tenets. In his lectures on the English comic writers, Hazlitt described *Political Justice* as a vitally important '*experimentum crucis*' (VI: 132). Compared with the usefulness of his book, Godwin himself seemed the classic man with only one idea, with no perspective on his own beliefs: 'In private, the author of *Political Justice* at one time reminded those who knew him of the Metaphysician engrafted on the Dissenting Minister. There was a dictatorial, captious, quibbling pettiness of manner' (XI: 27). The criticism both acknowledges Godwin's indebtedness to the culture of Dissent, and also raises what for Hazlitt remained one of its potential problems, its inflexible sense of its own peculiar virtue in opposition. As he told his son:

It was my misfortune (perhaps) to be bred up among Dissenters, who look with too jaundiced an eye at others, and set too high a value on their own peculiar pretensions. From being proscribed themselves, they learn to proscribe others; and come in the end to reduce all integrity of principle and soundness of opinion within the pale of their own little communion. (XVII: 88)

The opinion demonstrates Hazlitt's own ability to turn around on and reflect upon his own dearest principles, without—as the 'perhaps' hints—repudiating what he values about them. At the end of *The Spirit of the Age* essay, Godwin is remembered as the custodian at least—if not its best practitioner—of the memory of the vivid conversational culture of the 1790s:

Mr. Godwin has kept the best company of his time, but he has survived most of the celebrated persons with whom he lived in habits of intimacy. He speaks of them with enthusiasm and with discrimination; and sometimes dwells with peculiar delight on a day passed at John Kemble's in company with Mr. Sheridan, Mr. Curran, Mrs. Wolstonecraft and Mrs. Inchbald, when the conversation took a most animated turn, and the subject was of Love. Of all these our author is the only one remaining. Frail tenure, on which human life and genius are lent us for a while to improve or to enjoy! (XI: 28)[81]

---

[81] Although there is no extended discussion of Wollstonecraft in any of Hazlitt's published works, his references to her are nearly all positive, and usually focus on her powers of conversation. See, for instance, the account of meeting her with Godwin in 'My First Acquaintance with Poets': '[Coleridge] asked me if I had ever seen Mary Wolstonecraft [*sic*], and I said, I had once for a few moments, and that she seemed to me to turn off

Other custodians of this vivacious conversational culture besides Godwin appear in Hazlitt's essays. Hazlitt's father, a Unitarian clergyman, for instance, often features as an embodiment of the conversable world of Dissent. In 'My First Acquaintance with Poets', the elder Hazlitt's visits with neighbouring clergymen establish 'a line of communication..., by which the flame of civil and religious liberty is kept alive' (XVII: 107). Crucial to Hazlitt's continuing animus against Wordsworth and, especially, Coleridge, whom the same essay introduces as the trainee dissenting minister of the 1790s, is their betrayal of this potentiality. The conversable world represented by Dissent remains central to Hazlitt's controversial interest in the diffusion of knowledge. So, for instance, Hazlitt's account of the dispersing congregation of Richard Baxter in 'The Spirit of Controversy' gives us a glimpse of texts issuing out of and feeding back into a culture of vigorous discussion, but here tinctured perhaps by an eighteenth-century idea of openhearted exchange:

See that group collected after service-time and pouring over the gravestones in the churchyard, from whence, to the eye of faith, a light issues that points to the skies! See them disperse; and as they take different paths homeward while the evening closes in, still discoursing of the true doctrine and the glad tidings they have heard, how 'their hearts burn within them by the way!' (XX: 308)

If there is nostalgia here, a culture represented at its twilight, with a tone of wistfulness and regret, then with the kind of sudden gear change typical of Hazlitt's conversational style, it is brought sharply to bear on the question of 'the way we live now': 'Such is the business of human life; and we, who fancy ourselves above it, are only so the much more taken up with follies of our own' (XX: 308). The value of 'the Spirit of Controversy' manifested in Dissent is to do with the structural utility of their 'incessant wrangling and collision' independent of 'their results when discovered'. What matters is 'their affording continual scope and employment to the mind in its endeavours to reach the fancied goal, without its being ever (or but seldom) able to attain it' (XX: 307).[82]

Godwin's objections to something she advanced with quite a playful, easy air' (XVII: 111). See Chapter 3, p. 142.

[82] Compare James Chandler's account of *The Spirit of the Age* as a collection of essays effectively in conversation within and across individual essays. Chandler understands Hazlitt's view of history as defined by 'catachresis' (which might include the idea of 'collision'); its resistance to 'epitome' and 'resolution'; and its commitment to 'the chronologically coded domestic manners of uneven social development': see Chandler, *England in 1819* (Chicago/London: Chicago University Press, 1998), 184–5. See also Elizabeth Fay, 'Portrait Galleries, Representative History, and Hazlitt's *Spirit of the Age*', *Nineteenth-Century Contexts*, 24 (2002), 151–75.

Hazlitt's 'method of 'inhabit[ing] a perspective and then mov[ing] beyond it' can be seen plainly at work in 'Coffee-House Politicians', a topic central to eighteenth-century anxieties about the ambit of the conversable world.[83] The title of the essay invites an expectation of a standard diatribe against the vulgarization of culture. With an early nod and a wink to Swift, the essay does set out the familiar complaint against 'the mechanical operations of the spirit of newsmongering':

> It is not conversation, but rehearsing a part. Men of education and men of the world order this matter better. They know what they have to say on a subject, and come to the point at once. Your coffee-house politician balances between what he heard last and what he shall say next; and not seeing his way clearly, puts you off with circumstantial phrases, and tries to gain time for fear of making a false step. (VIII: 194)

Compared to this modern-day debasement, the Elizabethan past is invoked in the early part of the essay as a golden age—as it often is in Lamb's *Elia* essays—when London throbbed with genuine conversation, but as the essay develops so the company at the Southampton Coffee House starts to display its own modern attractions. Hume's word 'conversible' even appears, restamped, and put back into circulation by Hazlitt:

> M[ounsey] without being the most communicative, is the most conversible man I know. The social principle is inseparable from his person. If he has nothing to say, he drinks your health; and when you cannot from the rapidity and carelessness of his utterance catch what he says, you assent to it with equal confidence: you know his meaning is good. (VIII: 199)

From this point onwards, the essay digresses into a consideration of what makes for good conversation—'sympathy', 'real fellowship', 'freedom from affectation and constraint'—before modulating into a remarkable visionary account of London as 'the only place in which each individual in company is treated according to his value in company, and to that only' (VIII: 202–3).

Hazlitt's critical responses to Wordsworth often turn on this kind of reimagining of the urban experience, most explicitly, perhaps, in 'On Londoners and Country People'. Where *The Excursion* offers a vision of 'men in cities as so many wild beasts or evil spirits, shut up in the cells of ignorance, without natural affections', echoing the responses of travellers like Goede, Hazlitt's metropolis is a scene of fertile exchange:

> In London there is a *public*; and each man is part of it. We are gregarious, and affect the kind. We have a sort of abstract existence; and a community of ideas and knowledge (rather than local proximity) is the bond of society and good-fellowship. This is one great cause of the tone of political feeling in large and populous cities.

---

[83] Cook, 'Hazlitt, Speech and Writing', 25.

There is here a visible body-politic, a type and image of that huge Leviathan the State. We comprehend that vast denomination, *the People*, of which we see a tenth part daily moving before us; and by having our imaginations emancipated from petty interests and personal dependence, we learn to venerate ourselves as men, and to respect the rights of human nature. Therefore it is that the citizens and freemen of London and Westminster are patriots by prescription, philosophers and politicians by the right of their birth-place. (XII: 76–7)

Notice that in this vision the Londoner is not simply the passive consumer of spectacle, but part of a community involved in turning things around together: 'He lives in the eye of the world, and the world in his'. Nor are '*the People*' simply confirmed at the end of the essay as an object of discourse. The political concept needs corroboration against 'the tenth part' that is 'daily moving before us'. Implicitly, Hazlitt's essay opens the concept of 'the people' up to debate in coffee houses and taverns beyond the text.[84]

Jon Klancher understands Hazlitt's position much more pessimistically as articulating the melancholy experience of a world from which community has been erased.[85] Most immediately, in terms of Klancher's assessment, what had been destroyed for Hazlitt personally were the networks of the 1790s. 'Of all the members of the *Examiner* circle', according to Klancher, 'Hazlitt struggled the most comprehensively to preserve a strong enough conception of the political nation within a spacious enough sense of cosmopolitan knowledge and justice.' By 1823, according to Klancher, when 'On Londoners and Country People' first appeared, Hazlitt had come to focus on the role of the professional writer, who 'comprehends the cockney condition without being subject to it'.[86] I'm not entirely convinced by the writerly version of Hazlitt this implies. Cockney 'group' ethics did often betray an exclusive faith in the power of the pen. Hazlitt's writing after 1823 is often marked by a melancholy experience of defeat as the post-1815 surge of popular radicalism subsided, but generally his articulation of the conversation of culture is not insulated by a tightly bound idea of an autonomous literary sphere. Hazlitt certainly did struggle against this retrenchment of the republic of letters. Most of those at the Southampton Coffee House celebrated in 'Londoners and Country People' were not professional writers, although many were aspirants. *Conversations with Northcote* records his dislike of talk with literary men:

---

[84] See Gregory Dart, 'Romantic Cockneyism: Hazlitt and the Periodical Press', *Romanticism* 6 (2000), 143–62 (153, 157–9).

[85] See Jon Klancher, 'Discriminations, or Romantic Cosmopolitanisms in London', in James Chandler and Kevin Gilmartin (eds), *Romantic Metropolis: The Urban Scene of British Culture, 1780–1840* (Cambridge: Cambridge University Press, 2005), 65–82 (70).

[86] Ibid. 78.

they poured the same ideas and phrases and cant of knowledge out of books into my ears, as apothecaries' apprentices made prescriptions out of the same bottles…go to a linen-draper in the city, without education but with common sense and shrewdness, and you pick up something new, because nature is inexhaustible, and he sees it from his own point of view, when not cramped and hood-winked by pedantic prejudices. (XI: 209)

The sudden switch to a different social perspective ('go to a linen-draper in the city') is a device typical of Hazlitt, and hints at his awareness of the exclusions of the older idea of the republic of letters as conversation among the polite. He insisted to his son that 'though you are a master of Cicero's *Orations*, think it possible for a cobbler at a stall to be more eloquent than you' (XVII: 92). If *Blackwood*'s mocked the shallow egotism of Cockney self-advertisement, Hazlitt constantly opened it up to the circulation of talk as a larger and more diverse metropolitan social arena. In 'The Fight', to give just one instance, Hazlitt gives the full flavour of this colloquial banquet by inviting his readers to enjoy the feast: 'this fellow's conversation was *sauce piquante*. It did one's heart good to see him brandish his oaken towel and to hear him talk. He made mince-meat of a drunken, stupid, red-faced, quarrelsome, *frowsy* farmer, whose nose "he moralised into a thousand similes," making it out a firebrand like Bardolph's' (XVII: 77–8). The allusion to Shakespeare may seem exclusively literary, but 'The Fight' puts it in the mix with the heteroglossia of popular speech, reanimating the authority of the common reader by putting it into contact with the diversity of London life.[87] Not everyone thought the same way in the professionalizing literary culture of the metropolis of the early nineteenth century. Patmore recalls that Henry Colburn, publisher of the essay in the *New Monthly Magazine*, thought the 'title and subject […] unsuitable to the "ears polite" of [his] book customers, and only to be tolerated in the ephemeral pages of a periodical miscellany'.[88]

HAZLITT AND THE FEMINIZATION OF CULTURE

For Hazlitt conversation was not a medium of elegant commerce. Controversy and conversation for Hazlitt was not polar opposites, but motors capable of driving social change, as they had been for Godwin in the 1790s. By the same token, but on a darker note, Hazlitt also understood

---

[87] See Bromwich's account of the differences between Coleridge and Hazlitt. These include Hazlitt's continuing commitment to 'the common reader' and his refusal to see 'why opposites should be reconciled' (Bromwich, *The Mind of a Critic*, 231–6 (233)).

[88] Patmore, *Friends and Acquaintance*, III: 59.

inter-subjectivity as capable of stalling, open to working at cross-purposes, and blocking the 'flow' of inter-subjective relations. If there is a desire for openhearted discourse at work in his writing, plenty of submerged boulders are discerned in the rapids upon which the bark of progress may founder and sink. Perhaps the most intractable example is *Liber Amoris, or, The New Pygmalion* (1823), a book presented in part as a record of conversation, but one wherein the exigencies of desire continually disturb rather than replenish the flow of sentiment.[89] *Liber Amoris* is a self-conscious account of the problems caused when an assumption of sympathy leads to a demand for like with like. In *Liber Amoris*, to use Maurice Blanchot phraseology, 'the "I" wants to annex the other'. Interestingly, given my earlier comments about Hazlitt and his regret for Dissent, Blanchot's discussion of this situation is part of a longer consideration of the nostalgic longing for unity as 'the movement of return toward true Being'.[90] Blanchot's discussion of this longing for unity intimates what is distinctive about Hazlitt's resistance to utopian ideas of perfect being. Nostalgia there may be in Hazlitt's writing, but it often operates to propel the present forward. *Liber Amoris* explores a different personality, perhaps from the other side of the same coin; the personality unable to accept difference in its pursuit of a perfect union with the other.

Reading *Liber Amoris* in this way relates it to more general features of Hazlitt's writing rather than just its immediate autobiographical context alone. Possibly, its exploration of the deformations of sympathy owed something to Mary Hays's *Memoirs of Emma Courtney*, a text Hazlitt must have known from the 1790s.[91] Radical-liberal writers wrote both books in

---

[89] Many of Hazlitt's friends, like Haydon, writing in August 1822, noted the compulsive aspect to his 'wilful moral degradation'. See *The Diary of Benjamin Robert Haydon*, ed. W. B. Pope, 5 vols (Cambridge, MA: Harvard University Press, 1960), II: 374. Later, his diary mentions Hazlitt calling on him late at night 'in a state of absolute insanity about the girl who has jilted him. Poor Hazlitt, his candour is great, & his unaffected frankness is interesting' (375–6).

[90] Maurice Blanchot, *The Infinite Conversation*, trans with foreword by Susan Hanson (Minneapolis/London: University of Minnesota Press, 1993), 53 and 77.

[91] Although he mentions it nowhere in his extant writings, Hays and Hazlitt were moving in similar circles by 1797. Hazlitt called on Godwin on 2 August 1797, for instance, and again on 21 August. Hays and Godwin saw each other frequently during this month, although never with Hazlitt as far as the diary records. Given the amount of controversy surrounding *Emma Courtney*, it is hard to believe the book didn't come up or that Hazlitt never read it. Hays may coincide with Hazlitt in Godwin's diary at least once later. The entry for 28 March 1818 reads: 'Dine at Aldis's, w. Hazlit, Adams, Spencer & Powys; adv. Hayes'. There is one anecdote in Hazlitt's writing that may have been furnished by Hays around this time. In 'On the Conversation of Authors' appears a variant of the anecdote from 'My First Acquaintance with Poets' (see p. 266 above): '[Curran] and Sheridan once dined at John Kemble's with Mrs Inchbald and Mary Woolstonecroft, when the discourse almost wholly turned on Love "from noon to dewy eve, a summer's

a period of counter-revolution. Each of them more generally placed their faith in the possibility of improvement via the extension of human relations outward, but in *Memoirs of Emma Courtney* and *Liber Amoris* they both explore the pathology of the liberal imagination seeking reciprocation from the love object. Nicola Watson reads Hazlitt's book in terms of the narrator H's attempts to incorporate his beloved 'within a properly sentimental correspondence via a series of appropriate objects and texts'.[92] Where *Liber Amoris* displaces these demands on to the small bust of Napoleon that passes between the lovers (and is eventually broken), a similar role is played in *Emma Courtney* by the portrait of Harley, a man its heroine has—at this stage—never met.[93] Both books represent the flow of conversation as disrupted by the unexpected reversals of our mixed, imperfect beings, an aspect of human nature Hays continually insisted upon in the conversations with Godwin that went directly into *Emma Courtney*. 'How is it', Hays wrote to Godwin in February 1796, 'my friend, that after so many conversations & so many letters, we do not seem thoroughly to comprehend each other?'[94] Central to their differences was the question of what Hazlitt saw as Godwin's commitment to 'abstract reason and general utility' (VI: 132). Hays always insisted that the mind must have an object to focus its benevolence upon against Godwin's emphasis on disinterested reason, as in Hazlitt's critique of Godwinian thinking two decades later, but her novel is a study of the power of such objects (principally Harley's portrait) to muddy the flow of feeling. Like Hazlitt's book, *Emma Courtney* soon came to be regarded in the press as a scandalous act of self-revelation. What may be radical about Hazlitt's book is its rendering up for examination behaviour stereotypically regarded as a pathology of female sensibility. *Liber Amoris* is a study of what Hazlitt called 'the prevalence of the sensibility over the will' (VIII: 248). The 'Advertisement' introduces the character H as a study in 'disappointment preying on a sickly frame and morbid state of mind' (IX: 97). The main character fails precisely to show fortitude in the political and

---

day!' What a subject! What speakers, and what hearers! What would I not give to have been there, had I not learned it all from the bright eyes of Amaryllis, and may one day make a Table-Talk of it!' (XII: 41). In a letter that mentions the relationship between Hays and Charles Lloyd, Lamb referred to Hays as 'Amaryllis'. See Lamb to Thomas Manning, 13 February 1800, *Letters*, I: 185. I'm grateful to Mary Addyman for bringing the 1818 entry in Godwin's diary to my attention.

[92] Nicola Watson, *Revolution and the Form of the British Novel 1790–1825: Intercepted Letters, Interrupted Seductions* (Oxford: Oxford University Press, 1994), 167.

[93] See Andrea Henderson, *Romanticism and the Painful Pleasures of Modern Life* (Cambridge: Cambridge University Press, 2008), 178, on 'fetishistic displacement' in *Liber Amoris*.

[94] Mary Hays, *The Correspondence of Mary Hays (1779–1843), British Novelist*, ed. Marilyn L. Brooks (Lewiston/Queenston/Lampeter: Edwin Mellen Press, 2004), 433.

emotional misfortunes that mimic Hazlitt's own. That character is 'a native of North Britain, who left his own country early in life, in consequence of political animosities and an ill-advised connection in marriage'. 'Disappointment in politics' hints at a mindset that crumbles when its utopian hopes are not met in full. Resistance in the world and from the other produces anger and resentment, as it does in the love story of the book itself. Moreover the key role played by the bust of Napoleon suggests a painful self-consciousness about Hazlitt's own political affiliations and the tendency towards despondency and disappointment that he and many commentators traced to the disappointment of his hopes for the French Revolution.[95]

Liber Amoris is not usually read in this way now. For those involved in the hagiography of the recent Hazlitt revival, it is an embarrassment. For many feminist critics, it represents at best the masculine Romantic fascination with the gloomy and involuted spectacle of its own genius, at worst an endemic misogyny.[96] Sonia Hofkosh has given an influential reading of the book, emphasizing the autobiographical background.[97] Hofkosh gives a very convincing account of the way the voices of women have been effaced in the name of a master narrative of Romanticism concerned with a defining struggle between Hazlitt and Wordsworth. Mary Hays is excised in just this way from Hazlitt's extant accounts of literary history. If *Liber Amoris* is indebted to *Memoirs of Emma Courtney*, then Hazlitt represses all traces of what he had appropriated for his own discourse, both in *Liber Amoris* and in his critical essays and lectures.[98] I'm less convinced by Hofkosh's narrative of *Liber Amoris* in terms of a 'desire for (self) mastery and (self-) possession'.[99] Such an approach threatens to merge H with Hazlitt, disregarding the framing fiction of the disappointed 'North Briton', and assumes the text

---

[95] Patmore, for instance, who appears in *Liber Amoris* as P. G., claimed Hazlitt's primary fault was a 'morbid imagination' (*Friends and Acquaintance*, II: 295). Although 'no one could possess a more social turn of mind than Hazlitt did under ordinary circumstance', he was a 'disappointed man' because of the French Revolution, the 'pivot on which moves the whole character of Hazlitt's actual life and destiny' (II: 319, 325, and 322). Hazlitt often presented himself in this light. 'On the Pleasure of Hating', for instance, ends by asking 'mistaken as I have been in my public and private hopes, calculating others from myself, and calculating wrong; always disappointed where I placed most reliance; the dupe of friendship, and the fool of love; have I not reason to hate and to despise myself? Indeed I do; and chiefly for not having hated and despised the world enough' (XII: 136).

[96] However, Nicola Watson and Andrea Henderson offer readings that in different ways explore the resistance to resolution in *Liber Amoris* and influence my own approach; see footnotes 92 and 93 above and p. 274 below.

[97] Sonia Hofkosh, *Sexual Politics and the Romantic Author* (Cambridge: Cambridge University Press, 1998).

[98] Compare James Chandler's discussion of the subsumption of the feminine in Keats: see *England in 1819*, 398–402.

[99] Hofkosh, *Sexual Politics*, 111.

what does it mean to be human? to *suppress* our animal instinct to physical response?

274   *Hazlitt, Hunt, and Cockney Conversability*

affirms the obsessive demands of its protagonist.[100] Towards the end of the book, H tells one of his correspondents: 'I will make an end of this story; there is something in it discordant to honest ears' (IX: 154). The discordance running throughout, as in *Memoirs of Emma Courtney*, is at least partly to do with the question of how much credence the reader may give to the obsessive main character's point of view. Both texts exploit the epistolary tradition, supplemented in *Liber Amoris* by the conversational format of the opening section. As a result Hazlitt's book is 'mutilated and generically incoherent', as Watson's scrupulous analysis points out. Sarah's identity remains resistant to any 'appeal to outside authority'. Even the narrator's friend P. G. cannot provide corroboration for H's vilification of her character.[101]

The aim of my brief account of *Liber Amoris* is not to forgive Hazlitt for whatever he may have done or not done in real life with regard to Sarah Walker or the woman Coleridge and Wordsworth claimed he harassed in the Lake District. Nor is it to forgive him his erasure of women's involvement in the conversation of culture, which Hofkosh restores to some extent by her exemplary reading of Sarah Hazlitt's journal. Hazlitt's conflictual model of conversation might be understood as oriented against Hume's view that women were 'the sovereigns of the empire of conversation'. He often identified female conversation with a consensual model of social reproduction that obscured the examples, for instance, of Hays and Wollstonecraft's more pugnacious ideas of conversation, readily available to him from the 1790s. Such views were not uncommon in his circle. Take Keats's letter to J. H. Reynolds of 21 September 1817:

The world, and especially our England, has within the last thirty year's [*sic*] been vexed and teased by a set of Devils, whom I detest so much that I almost hunger after an acherontic promotion to a Torturer, purposely for their accomodation [*sic*]; These Devils are a set of Women, who having taken a snack or Luncheon of Literary scraps, set themselves up for towers of Babel in Languages Sapphos in Poetry—Euclids in Geometry—and everything in nothing. Among such the Name of Montague has been preeminent.[102]

To aim the blow at Montagu, whose pre-eminence was decidedly in the past by 1817, suggests how deep-seated the anxiety about the feminization

---

[100] Contrast Henderson's reading of the book in terms of 'a fully developed and self-conscious aesthetic of erotic submission': *Painful Pleasures of Modern Life*, 173.

[101] Watson, *Revolution and the Form of the English Novel*, 168. Although Watson does not mention *Emma Courtney*, she does see Hazlitt in the context of two other texts from the 1796–8 period: Wollstonecraft's *Short Residence* and Godwin's *Memoirs of the Author of a Vindication of the Rights of Woman* (165 and 169).

[102] Keats, *Letters*, I: 163. See also Russell, 'Keats, Popular Culture, and the Sociability of Theatre', 206, on his ambition to 'upset the drawling of the blue stocking literary world' as he put it in his letter to Benjamin Bailey of August 1819, *Letters*, II: 139.

of culture had become. Often Hazlitt identifies women's literary talk with consumerist gossip contrasted with the taste he shared with Lamb for old books: 'Women judge of books as they do of fashions or complexions, which are admired only "in their newest gloss" ' (XII: 220). Like Coleridge, for all their differences, Hazlitt and Keats participated in a narrative of literary history that gained in strength after 1800 and systematically figured women's writing as a form of mere chatter too trivial to be part of the conversation of culture. For Coleridge, the process involved the effective abandonment of the conversational model as such. For Hazlitt it comes more often with a reiteration of the alternative model of conversation as open to collision, but usually gendered in distinctly masculine terms, with women's writing identified as too weak or too affected to sustain mental fight.

In this context, it is no surprise, for instance, that Hazlitt was dismissive of Cowper's influence on English poetry. His 'finicalness' spoke of 'an effeminacy about him, which shrinks from and repels common and hearty sympathy' (V: 91). Importantly, the criticism does not simply contrast Cowper littleness with an idea of the power of the autonomous imagination, but weighs him against 'common and hearty sympathy'. Burns is an important contrast to both Cowper and Wordsworth's 'puritanical genius' (V: 129) in this regard. Gendering his preference, Hazlitt celebrates the 'firm manly grasp' of Burns. His 'pictures of good fellowship, of social glee, of quaint humour, are equal to any thing: they come up to nature, and they cannot go beyond it' (V: 126 and 128). The same gendered bias structures his account of the history of the novel. Sterne's style is praised 'as the most rapid, the most happy, the most idiomatic of any that is to be found. It is the pure essence of English conversational style' (VI: 121). In contrast, while he acknowledges Fanny Burney's abilities as a 'quick, lively, and accurate observer of persons and things', he argues that her sex prevents her translating these talents into anything more challenging:

she always looks at them with a consciousness of her sex, and in that point of view in which it is the particular business and interest of women to observe them. There is little in her works of passion or character, or even manners, in the most extended sense of the word, as implying the sum-total of our habits and pursuits; her *forte* is in describing the absurdities and affectations of external behaviour, or *the manners of people in company.* (VI: 123)[103]

---

[103] Inchbald's novels *Nature and Art* and *A Simple Story* he allows as partial exceptions, no doubt because they critique what he calls 'small punctillios of female behaviour'. The recognition of Inchbald only makes the omission of Hays from his critical writing all the more stark.

In the *Examiner* essay on classical education that provoked Hunt, Hazlitt described women as

> the creatures of the circumstances in which they are placed, of sense, of sympathy and habit. They are exquisitely susceptible of the passive impressions of things, but to form an idea of pure understanding or imagination, to feel an interest in *the true* and *the good* beyond themselves, requires an effort of which they are incapable. (XX: 41)[104]

This identification of women with the smooth flow of opinion effectively excluded them a priori from participation in the transformative collision he valued most, but sometimes Hazlitt showed an awareness of 'effeminacy' as a gendered construct. Complaining that the presence of women in conversation means 'you cannot differ openly and unreservedly,' he suddenly concedes that the qualities he is attacking may be culturally determined:

> It is not so in France. There the women talk of things in general, and reason better than men in this country. They are mistresses of the intellectual foils; They are adepts in all the topics. They know what is to be said for and against all sort of questions, and are lively and full of mischief into the bargain. (XII: 31)

'Effeminacy', here at least, has more to do with codes of English politeness than with any quality intrinsic to women's talk, but it was an insight Hazlitt was never really able to develop towards the feminist critique found in Wollstonecraft.

Hazlitt's various pronouncements against 'effeminacy' were complicated further by his frequent identification of it as trait within his own psychology, especially in his more melancholy essays. So in 'On Thought and Action', for instance, he identifies himself with 'the effeminacy of the speculative and philosophical temperament, compared with the promptness and vigour of the practical!' (VIII: 102). *Liber Amoris* also suggests a self-consciousness about the yearning within himself for reciprocation. More usually, Hazlitt was impatient of the morbid and melancholic tendencies he represented as effeminate aspects of the speculative mind. Uttara Natarajan sees the key difference between Hazlitt and thinkers of the Scottish Enlightenment as the fact that 'Hume's imagination perceives likeness, Hazlitt's conquers difference'.[105] His emphasis on collision certainly emphasizes difference, energy, and contention, but I am not so sure about 'conquest', at least not in Blanchot's sense of the desire to annex the

---

[104] The comments were omitted from *The Examiner*'s 'On Classical Education' as published in *The Round Table*.

[105] Uttara Natarajan, 'The Circle of Sympathy: Shelley's Hazlitt', in Uttara Natarajan et al. (eds), *Metaphysical Hazlitt: Bicentenary Essays* (London/New York: Routledge, 2005), 112–22 (116).

other to one's self.[106] The pleasure in conversation expressed throughout his writing privileges its resistance to the egotistical reproduction of the self or the colonization of the other. *Liber Amoris* offers a case study of what may be the other side to the same coin, a psychology more like Rousseau and Wordsworth's as Hazlitt saw it, one that demands the fulfillment of the sentimental case, and turns nasty when it doesn't get it.[107] Writing *Liber Amoris*, Hazlitt may have made present to himself the fact just how much this pathology was also part of his own character. More characteristic, I would suggest, is his anti-utopian emphasis on mixed imperfect being and its insistence that human relations must be created in the hazardous conjunctions between subjects. Hazlitt preferred to risk 'the extremest violence or irritability' than submit to 'cavalier smooth simpering indifference' (VIII: 194). If this lazily reproduces a gendered opposition, the binary is not inherent to it, but it is a betrayal of the diversity he was more often willing to admit to his conversable world. Where so many others saw conversation best served by select company, Hazlitt insisted 'more *home* truths are to be learnt from listening to a noisy debate in an ale-house, than from attending to a formal one in the House of Commons'. (VIII: 75)

---

[106] But note that Procter's gendering of Hazlitt's conversation anticipates Natarajan's terms: 'He had a grand masculine intellect, which conquered details as well as entireties'. See *Autobiographical Fragment*, 169. Hunt's 'mind' he describes as 'feminine rather than manly', but goes on 'I do not intend to speak disrespectfully of his intellect, nor of the intellect of women, which by nature is perhaps generally equal to that of men' (200).

[107] Hazlitt admired Rousseau, and identified with him to an extent, including the fault of morbidity and 'excessive egotism, which filled all objects with himself, and would have occupied the universe with his smallest interest. Hence his jealousy and suspicion of others; for no attention, no respect or sympathy, could come up to the extravagant claims of his self-love' (IV: 89).

Epilogue

Hazlitt and Hunt in their different ways were often nostalgic for 'the humane openness of intercourse' identified with eighteenth-century coffee house culture. For Hazlitt, especially, the scenario was identified with Rational Dissent and the conversable world of the 1790s. He saw these worlds as sustaining the collision of mind with mind, open to the future and the risk of encounters with strangers. Ironically, then, these values often appear in his essays with a halo of regret. Especially in his more melancholy essays of the late 1820s, his perspective may seem to endorse Habermas's dreary vision of a public sphere newly dispersed into 'acts of individual reception, however uniform in mode'.[1] There is also a strain of visionary romanticism in Hazlitt that looks beyond a dismal world of fallen exchanges, but these moments in his writing are rarely left uncontested. Even in the later writing, Hazlitt tends to interrogate the grounds of his own judgments, as if he remains in restless and conflicted conversation with himself. Certainly in *The Spirit of the Age* (1825) collection, as James Chandler has shown, Hazlitt deliberately unsettles the idea of any representative 'spirit' animating the writing of his time, not least by making the claim from so many different grounds for so many different authors, a catachrestic sense of historical conjunction emphasized by the arrangement of the volume in terms of so many competing and cross-cutting contrasts.[2]

Hazlitt's nostalgia is rarely left focused on values left insulated in an unredeemable past. His writing bubbles, for instance, with his joy at the theatres as places of convivial social life. His writing was at least in dialogue with popular radicalism for some years after 1815. In the process, he frequently brought the values of Dissent to bear on a present that he

---

[1] Jürgen Habermas, *The Structural Transformation of the Public Sphere: An Inquiry into a Category of Bourgeois Society*, trans. Thomas Burger with the assistance of Frederick Lawrence (Cambridge, MA: MIT Press, 1989), 161.

[2] See James Chandler, *England in 1819* (Chicago/London: Chicago University Press, 1998), 178–85.

perceived as forging a traitorous hegemony between literature and the police. A prime target for Hazlitt in this regard was Coleridge's prose and its characteristic concern for 'the harmonious development of those qualities and faculties that characterise our *humanity*'.[3] If Hazlitt often made appeals to humane values persisting beyond the instrumentality of the commercial world, including his own version of a distinction between material and cultural prosperity, then he was less concerned than Coleridge to insist upon 'cultivation' as 'harmonious development'. Hazlitt's ideas on improvement were rarely led by what Coleridge called 'the *supernatural*'.[4] My point here is not about religion per se, but about a resistance to the elision of difference in order to cultivate some higher communion. In this regard, the familiar thematics of Romantic transcendence often appear to be as involved in avoiding trouble with strangers as with reaching beyond the selfhood.

Coleridge's ideas on cultivation and intellectual development, of course, are usually taken to have been much more influential on the modern university than Hazlitt's, although they have often been collapsed into each other in the name of the academic category of 'Romanticism'.[5] From an early-twenty-first-century perspective, when the universities are being increasingly squeezed by demands from government and business for a smooth flow of knowledge and information, Coleridge's version of an aesthetic education may seem a potential source of fruitful 'dissensus'.[6] My own emphasis is on the importance of conversation to criticism and pedagogy understood more in terms of the kind of collision explored, for instance, by the Dissenting Academies whose passing was mourned by Hazlitt. This form of conversation is not Michael Oakeshott's constrained and 'civilized' dialogue of the Oxbridge tutorial. Its cultivated maintenance of polite conversation flowing across a supposedly level plane has always been a myth, predicated on the pre-selection of like-minded or at least deferential interlocutors that echoes the narcissism of Addisonian agreeableness.[7] Similarly, Richard Rorty's desire to 'keep the conversation

[3] Samuel Taylor Coleridge, *On the Constitution of Church and State*, ed. John Colmer, *Complete Works*, Vol. X (Princeton: Princeton University Press, 1976), 43.

[4] Ibid. 44.

[5] See James Chandler's critique of the recruitment of Hazlitt to 'the Age of Romanticism' in *England in 1819*, 177–80. The classic discussion of Coleridge's influence is Raymond Williams, *Culture and Society 1780–1950* (Harmondsworth: Penguin, 1961), esp. 75–84.

[6] See Jacques Rancière, *Dissensus: On Politics and Aesthetics*, ed. and trans. Steven Corcoran (London: Continuum, 2010). The English 'aesthetic' tradition developed by Coleridge and Matthew Arnold is very different from the Franco-German one explored by thinkers like Rancière and Jean-Luc Nancy.

[7] See Michael Oakeshott, 'The Voice of Poetry in the Conversation of Mankind', in *Rationalism in Politics and Other Essays* (London: Methuen, 1962), 197–247.

going' is always likely to privilege 'polite' or 'rational' *via media* primed to
avoid the hazard of contention and dispute.[8] This kind of exchange tends
to allow minor modification, but disallows any fundamental questioning
of the basic assumptions at issue in any exchange of opinion.[9] The
eighteenth-century pedagogy that understood conversation as 'the collision of mind with mind' seems to me to have made much more room for
this kind of fundamental objection, as well as, sometimes at least, for a
diversity of linguistic codes. Alasdair MacIntyre's desire to make the
university 'a place of constrained disagreement, of imposed participation
in contention, in which a central responsibility of higher education would
be to initiate students into conflict' sounds much more in sympathy with
this idea, but his emphasis on 'constraint' opens up the question of limits
that also haunted Godwin's anxieties about popular assemblies.[10]

Thomas Docherty has traced in the work of both Habermas and
MacIntyre a displacement of 'the ethical regard for others within the
community' by 'an ethnic regard for self-identification'.[11] I have suggested
ways in which the 'rational-critical' in Habermas ends up foreclosing on
the possibilities of interventions that transgress his idea of communicative
competency. Docherty wants to promote a form of criticism focused on
the 'singularity of the aesthetic event', that is, the 'confrontation of a
subject of consciousness with what it is taking as its object'.[12] This
formulation might be extended to think beyond encounters between
autonomous 'subjects' and 'aesthetic' objects. The mediated relationships
between subjects in the classroom and elsewhere, for instance, are part of a
complex and uneven social process of making and revising judgments.
Encouraging productive collision in the structured environment of the
classroom is never going to be easy, especially given the pressures facing
the modern university I've just mentioned. Eighteenth-century explor-
ations of the pedagogy of conversation were well aware of a host of other
factors, including inequalities of power between student and tutor, that
made these conditions difficult to create and sustain. If these conditions

---

[8] See *Richard Rorty, Philosophy and the Mirror of Nature* (Princeton: Princeton University Press, 1979), 377. See David Simpson's reading of Rorty as the heir to Oakeshott
in *The Academic Postmodern and the Rule of Literature: A Report on Half-Knowledge*
(Chicago: University of Chicago Press, 1995), 43–4. He also develops (45–7) the debt to
Gadamer's emphasis on conversation noted in my Introduction.

[9] See Thomas Docherty, *Criticism and Modernity: Aesthetics, Literature, and Nations in
Europe and its Academies* (Oxford: Oxford University Press, 1999), 237. Docherty's analysis
also draws attention to a philosophy of education within the eighteenth-century Scottish
university and its 'intimate link between the intellectual life and the practical life' (214).

[10] Alasdair MacIntyre, *Three Rival Versions of Moral Enquiry: Encyclopaedia, Genealogy,
and Tradition* (London: Duckworth, 1990), 230–1.

[11] Docherty, *Criticism and Modernity*, 244.   [12] Ibid. 245.

make communication a fraught business, then, as Docherty points out, 'this risk is what makes the practice of criticism not only worthwhile, but possible.'[13] The alternative for universities, as for other places of discussion, is to suppress 'the resistances of a place and the opacities that belong to it,' as de Certeau puts it, 'for the sake of producing a system of transparence'.[14] Communication need not be conceived of in terms of either the conquest of alterity or the reciprocity of transparent minds.

Frequently, the conversable worlds of the eighteenth and early nineteenth centuries did shut down risk in the name of the reciprocal matching of minds with minds. In the process, they compromised another of the declared aims of the culture of improvement: to bring learning out of the cloisters and into the domain of the everyday. Against this dismal picture, this book has been an attempt to open literary history up to 'the daily murmur', the reformulation of 'situations and relations of interlocution' that persist in all their imperfections against both the atomization of daily life and the production of knowledge as the smooth flow of information. It understands the republic of letters not as the unfolding of consciousness but as the creation of manifold interactions that may never reach a common voice; a place of collision, misunderstanding, resistance, and silence as much as recognition or communion. By the same token, I accept that readers continue to think and talk about books in ways their authors cannot predict and may not enjoy. This book opened with a conversational gambit and ends by acknowledging the hazards of its dissemination. Over to you, then, readers, known and unknown.[15]

---

[13] Ibid.

[14] Michel de Certeau, *The Capture of Speech and Other Political Writings* (Minneapolis: University of Minnesota Press, 1997), 91.

[15] Michel de Certeau, *The Practice of Everyday Life*, trans. Steven Rendall (Berkeley: University of California Press, 1984), 102 and 96.

Bibliography

PRIMARY SOURCES

Manuscript Collections

MSS Abinger, Bodleian Library, Oxford

MSS Belsham, Harris Manchester College, Oxford

'George Drummond's Essay on Conversation' (Dc.4.54/17), Special Collections Department, Edinburgh University

'Mary Hays Correspondence', Pforzheimer Collection, New York Public Library

John Johnson Collection, Bodleian Library, Oxford

'Mary Mitford's MSS correspondence', Reading Central Library

'Elizabeth Montagu Correspondence', Huntington Library, San Marino, California

'Katherine Plymley's MSS', Corbett of Longnor Collection, Shropshire Archives, Shrewsbury

'Thrale-Piozzi MSS Collection', John Rylands Library, Manchester

Treasury Solicitors Papers, National Archives, Kew

Online Resources

Printed Sources

Newspapers and Journals

Analytical Review

Annual Register

Bee

Blackwood's Edinburgh Magazine

Censor

Champion

Edinburgh Magazine

Edinburgh Review

Examiner

Gazetteer

Gentleman's Magazine

Indicator

Ladies Magazine

London Magazine

Lounger

Memoirs of the Literary and Philosophical Society of Manchester

Mirror

Monthly Magazines

Monthly Repository of Theology and General Literature

Monthly Review

Morning Chronicle
Morning Herald
New Monthly Magazine,
Quarterly Review
Scots Magazine
Sentimental Magazine
Spectator
St. James's Magazine
Tait's Edinburgh Magazine
Tatler
Times
Universal Magazine of Knowledge and Pleasure
Weekly Miscellany
Wesleyan-Methodist Magazine
Yellow Dwarf

Burley, Stephen (ed.), *New College, Hackney (1786–96): A Selection of Printed and Archival Sources* at http://www.english.qmul.ac.uk/drwilliams/pubs/nc%20hackney.html.

Doddgridge, Philip, 'An Account of Mr. Jenning's Method' (1728), in *Dissenting Education and the Legacy of John Jennings, c.1720-c.1729,* ed. Tessa Whitehouse at http://www.english.qmul.ac.uk/drwilliams/pubs/jennings%20legacy.html.

Books and Essays

Place of publication London unless otherwise stated.

Aikin, John, and Anna Laetitia Barbauld, *Evenings at Home*, 6 vols (1792–6).

—— and ——, *Miscellaneous Pieces, in Prose* (1773).

Anderson, George, *An Estimate of the Profit and Loss of Religion, Personally and Publicly stated: Illustrated with references to Essays on Morality and Natural Religion* (Edinburgh, 1753).

Austen, Jane, *Jane Austen's Letters*, third edn, ed. Deirdre Le Faye (Oxford: Oxford University Press, 1995).

——, *Jane Austen's 'Sir Charles Grandison'*, ed. Brian Southam (Oxford: Clarendon Press, 1980).

——, *The Novels of Jane Austen*, ed. R. W. Chapman, 3rd edn (Oxford: Oxford University Press, 1933).

Austen-Leigh, James Edward, *Memoir of Jane Austen*, 2nd edn, ed. R. W. Chapman (1926).

Barbauld, Anna Laetitia, *An Address to the Opposers of the Repeal of the Corporation and Test Acts*, 4th edn (1790).

——, *Civic Sermons to the People*, no. 2 (1792).

——, *The Poems of Anna Letitia Barbauld*, ed. William McCarthy and Elizabeth Kraft (Athens/London: University of Georgia Press, 1994).

——, 'Thoughts on Devotional Taste on Sects, and on Establishments', in *Devotional Pieces, copied from the Psalms and the Book of Job* (1775), 1–50.

Barbauld, Anna Laetitia, *The Works of Anna Lætitia Barbauld, with a Memoir by Lucy Aikin.* 2 vols, ed. Lucy Aikin (1825).

—— (ed.), *Selections from the Spectator, Tatler, Guardian, and Freeholder, with a preliminary essay* (1804).

Barrell, John, and Jon Mee (eds), *Trials for Treason and Sedition 1792–1794*, 8 vols (Pickering and Chatto, 2006–7).

Beattie, James, *Dissertations Moral and Critical* (1783).

Bernard, John, *Retrospections of America 1797–1811*, ed. Mrs. Bayle Bernard (New York: Benjamin Blom, 1887).

——, *Retrospections of the Stage*, 2 vols (1830).

Bewick, Thomas, *A Memoir of Thomas Bewick, written by Himself*, ed. Iain Bain (Oxford: Oxford University Press, 1979).

Binns, John, *Recollections of the Life of John Binns: Twenty-Nine Years in Europe and Fifty-Three in the United States* (Philadelphia, 1854).

Blessington, Marguerite, *Conversations of Lord Byron with the Countess of Blessington* (1834).

Boswell, James, *Boswell: The English Experiment, 1785–1789*, ed. Irma S. Lustig and Frederick A. Pottle (Heinemann, 1986).

——, *Boswell in Extremes 1776–1778*, ed. Charles McC. Weis and Frederick A. Pottle (Heinemann, 1971).

——, *Boswell in Search of a Wife 1766–1769*, ed. Frank Brady and Frederick A. Pottle (Heinemann, 1956).

——, *Boswell: Laird of Auchinleck 1776–1782*, ed. Joseph W. Reed and Frederick A. Pottle (New York/London: McGraw-Hill, 1977).

——, *Boswell's Life of Johnson*, ed. G. B. Hill, rev. L. F. Powell, 6 vols (Oxford: Clarendon Press, 1934–50).

——, *Boswell's London Journal 1762–1763*, ed. Frederick A. Pottle (Heinemann, 1950).

Brightwell, Cecilia, *Memorials of the Life of Amelia Opie,* 2 vols (Norwich: 1854).

[Britannicus], 'Essay on Conversation', *Sentimental Magazine* (April 1775), 149–51.

Burney, Frances, *The Complete Plays of Frances Burney*, ed. Peter Sabor (Pickering and Chatto, 1995).

——, *The Early Journals and Letters of Fanny Burney*, ed. Lars E. Troide and Stewart J. Cooke, 3 vols (Oxford: Clarendon Press, 1988–94).

——, *Early Journals and Letters of Fanny Burney, IV.* ed. Betty Rizzo (Montreal/Kingston: McGill-Queen's University Press, 2003).

——, *Evelina*, ed. Edward A. Bloom (Oxford: Oxford University Press, 1982).

——, [Madame D'Arblay], *Memoirs of Doctor Burney*, 2 vols (1832).

Burns, Robert, *The Letters of Robert Burns*, vol. I: *1780–1789*, ed. G. Ross Roy, 2nd edn (Oxford: Oxford University Press, 1985).

Candid and Critical Remarks on the Dialogues of the Dead: in a Letter from A Gentleman in London to his Friend in the Country (1760).

Carter, Elizabeth, *Letters from Elizabeth Carter to Mrs Montagu between the Years 1755 and 1800*, 3 vols (1817).

Chesterfield, Lord, *Letters*, ed. David Roberts (Oxford: Oxford University Press, 1992).

Cicero, *On Duties*, ed. and trans. M. T. Griffin and E. M. Atkins (Cambridge: Cambridge University Press, 1991).

Coleridge, Samuel Taylor, *Collected Letters of Samuel Taylor Coleridge*, ed. E. L. Griggs, 6 vols (Oxford: Oxford University Press, 1956–71).

——, *The Collected Works of Samuel Taylor Coleridge*, ed. Kathleen Coburn, 16 vols (Princeton: Princeton University Press, 1969–2002).

——, *Poems on Various Subjects* (1796).

Cook[e], William, *Conversation: A Didactic Poem, in Three Parts* (1796).

——, *Conversation: A Didactic Poem*, new edn (London, 1807).

——, *The Pleasures of Conversation: A Poem*, new edn (1822).

——, *The Life of Samuel Johnson*, 2nd edn (1785).

Cowper, William, *The Letters and Prose Writings of William Cowper*, ed. James King and Charles Ryskamp, 5 vols (Oxford: Oxford University Press, 1979–86).

——, *The Poems of William Cowper*, ed. John D. Baird and Charles Ryskamp, 3 vols (Oxford: Oxford University Press, 1980–95).

De Quincey, Thomas, 'Notes on Gilfillian's Gallery of Literary Portraits: Godwin, Foster, Hazlitt, Shelley, Keats', *Tait's Edinburgh Magazine*, 12 (ns), 756–61.

D'Israeli, Isaac, *Curiosities of Literature*, 3 vols (1817).

Duncombe, John, *The Feminiad: A Poem* (1754).

Edgeworth, Maria, *Letters from England 1813–1844*, ed. Christina Colvin (Oxford: Clarendon Press, 1971).

——, *Letters to Literary Ladies* (1795).

——, *The Novels and Selected Works of Maria Edgeworth*, ed. Marilyn Butler and Mitzi Myers, 12 vols (London: Pickering and Chatto, 1999–2003).

Edgeworth, R. L., [and Maria Edgeworth], *Memoirs of Richard Lovell Edgeworth, Esq.*, 2 vols (1820).

Egan, Pierce, *Life in London; or, the Day and Night Scenes of Jerry Hawthorn, Esq. and his Elegant Friend Corinthian Tom* (1822).

'An Essay on Conversation', *Ladies Magazine*, 2 (2 November 1751), 405.

'An Essay on Conversation', *The Weekly Miscellany*, 13 (6 December 1779), 221–6.

Feltham, John, *The Picture of London for 1802* (1802).

Fenwick, Eliza, *Secresy*, 3 vols (1795).

Ferguson, Adam, *The Morality of stage-plays seriously considered* (Edinburgh, 1757).

Fielding, Henry, 'An Essay of Conversation', in *Miscellanies*, ed. Henry Knight Miller, 3 vols (Oxford: Clarendon Press, 1972): 119–62.

Fordyce, James, *The Character and Conduct of the Female Sex* (1776).

——, *Sermons to Young Women*, 2 vols (1766).

Godwin, William, *The Letters of William Godwin*, vol. 1: *1778–1797*, ed. Pamela Clemit (Oxford: Oxford University Press, 2011).

——, Memoirs of the Author of A Vindication of the Rights of Woman, ed. Pamela Clemit and Gina Luria Walker (Peterborough, ont.: Broadview, 2001).

Godwin, William, *Political and Philosophical Writings of William Godwin*, 7 vols., ed. Mark Philp (William Pickering, 1993).

Goede, C. A. G., *The Stranger in England; or Travels in Great Britain*, 3 vols (1807).

Goldsmith, Oliver, *The Citizen of the World*, 2 vols (1769).

John Gregory, *A Father's Legacy to his Daughters* (Edinburgh, 1774).

Grose, Francis, *The Olio, A Collection of Essays, Dialogues etc* (1792).

Harral, Thomas, *Scenes of Life*, 3vols, (London, 1805).

Hartley, David, *Observations on man, his frame, his duty, and his expectations*, 2 vols (1749).

Hawkins, Sir John, *The Life of Samuel Johnson, LL.D.* (1787).

Haydon, Benjamin Robert, *The Diary of Benjamin Robert Haydon*, ed. W. B. Pope, 5 vols (Cambridge, MA: Harvard University Press, 1960).

Hays, Mary, *The Correspondence of Mary Hays (1779–1843), British Novelist*, ed. Marilyn L. Brooks (Lampeter: Edwin Mellen Press, 2004).

——, *Cursory remarks on An enquiry into the expediency and propriety of public or social worship: inscribed to Gilbert Wakefield*, 2nd edn (1792).

——, *Letters and Essays, Moral and Miscellaneous* (1793).

——, *The Love Letters of Mary Hays (1779–1780)*, ed. A. F. Wedd (Methuen, 1925).

Hazlitt, William, *The Complete Works of William Hazlitt*, ed. P. P. Howe, 21 vols (Dent, 1930–4).

——, *Memoirs of Emma Courtney*, 2 vols (1796).

——, 'Memoirs of Mary Wollstonecraft', *Annual Necrology*, 1797–8 (1800), 411–60.

——, and Leigh Hunt, *The Round Table*, 2 vols (1817).

Hazlitt, William Carew (ed.), *Literary Remains of William Hazlitt* (1836).

Hill, John, *The Inspector*, 2 vols (1753).

Hume, David, *An Enquiry Concerning Human Understanding*, ed. Tom L. Beauchamp (Oxford: Oxford University Press, 1999).

——, *An Enquiry Concerning the Principle of Morals*, ed. Beauchamp (Oxford: Oxford University Press, 1998).

——, *Essays, Moral and Political*, 2 vols (Edinburgh, 1741–2).

——, *Essays and Treatises on Several Subjects*, 2nd edn (Edinburgh, 1758).

——, *Four Dissertations: I. The natural history of religion. II. Of the passions. III. Of tragedy. IV. Of the standard of taste.* (1757).

——, *The Letters of David Hume*, 2 vols, ed. J. Y. T. Greig (Oxford: Oxford University Press, 1932).

Hunt, Leigh, *The Autobiography of Leigh Hunt*, ed. J. E. Morpurgo (Cresset Press, 1948).

——, *Classic Tales, Serious and Lively*, 5 vols (1806–8).

—— [Harry Honeycomb], 'Coffee-Houses and Smoking', *New Monthly Magazine*, 16 (January 1826), 50–4.

Hutton, William, *Courts of Requests: Their Nature, Utility, and Powers described* (Birmingham, 1787).

Jackson, William, *The Four Ages; Together with Essays on Various Subjects* (1798).

Johnson, Samuel, *A Dictionary of the English Language: in which the Words are Deduced from their Originals, and illustrated in their different Significations*, 2 vols (1755–6).

——, *Johnsoniana; or A Collection of Bon Mots* (1776).

——, *Lives of the Most Eminent English Poets; with Critical Observations on their Works*, ed. Roger Lonsdale, 4 vols (Oxford: Oxford University Press, 2006).

——, *The Rambler*, ed. W. J. Bate and Albrecht B. Strauss, Vol. III of *The Yale Edition of the Works of Samuel Johnson*, 16 vols (New Haven: Yale University Press, 1969).

Kant, Immanuel, *A Critique of the Power of Aesthetic Judgment*, ed Paul Guyer, trans. Guyer and Eric Matthews (Cambridge: Cambridge University Press, 2000).

Keats, John, *The Letters of John Keats 1814–1821*, ed. Hyder Edward Rollins, 2 vols (Cambridge, MA: Harvard University Press, 1958).

——, *The Poems of John Keats*, ed. Jack Stillinger (Heinneman, 1978).

Lamb, Charles and Mary Lamb, *The Letters of Charles and Mary Anne Lamb*, ed. Edwin W. Marrs, Jr, 3 vols (Ithaca: Cornell University Press, 1975).

Lord Lyttelton, George [with Elizabeth Montagu], *Dialogues of the Dead* (1760). *The Microcosm of London*, 3 vols (London, 1808–10).

Milton, John, *Selected Prose*, ed. C. A. Patrides (Harmondsworth: Penguin, 1974).

Montagu, Elizabeth, *Bluestocking Feminism, Writings of the Bluestocking Circle, 1738–1785*, vol. 1: *Elizabeth Montagu*, ed. Elizabeth Eger (Pickering and Chatto, 1999).

——, *Mrs Montagu "Queen of the Blues": Her Letters and Friendships from 1762 to 1800*, ed. Reginald Blunt (Constable, 1923).

Montagu, Lady Mary Wortley, *The Complete Letters of Lady Mary Wortley Montagu*, ed. Robert Halsband, 3 vols (Oxford: Clarendon Press, 1967).

Moore, Thomas, *Memoirs, Journal, and Correspondence of Thomas Moore*, 8 vols (1853–6).

More, Hannah, *Coelebs in Search of a Wife*, 2 vols (1808).

——, *Essays on Various Subjects, principally designed for Young Ladies* (1777).

——, *Florio: A Tale for Fine Gentlemen and Fine Ladies and The Bas Bleu; or, Conversation: Two Poems* (1786).

——, *Sacred Dramas and Other Poems* (1827).

——, *Strictures on the Modern System of Female Education*, 2 vols (1799).

Morvan, Jean Baptiste, *Reflexions upon the Politeness of Manners; with Maxims for Civil Society*, trans. from the French (1707).

Muir, Thomas, *An Account of the Trial of Thomas Muir* (Edinburgh, 1793).

Paine, Thomas, *Rights of Man*, ed. Eric Foner (Harmondsworth: Penguin, 1984).

Parr, Samuel, *A Spital Sermon, preached at Christ Church* (1801).

Patmore, P. G., *My Friends and Acquaintance*, 3 vols (1854).

Pindar, Peter, *Bozzy and Piozzi, or, the British Biographers, A Town Eclogue* (1786).

——, *A Poetical and Congratulatory Epistle to James Boswell, Esq*, (1786).

Piozzi, Hester Lynch, *Anecdotes of the Late Samuel Johnson*, 4th edn (1786).

——, *British Synonymy, or, An Attempt at regulating the Choice of Words in Familiar Conversation*, 2 vols (1794).

——, *Thraliana: The Diary of Mrs. Hester Lynch Thrale (later Mrs. Piozzi) 1776–1809*, ed. Katherine C. Balderston, 2nd edn (Oxford: Clarendon Press, 1951).

Piozzi, Hester Lynch, *Letters to and from the Late Samuel Johnson, LL.D,*, 2 vols (London, 1788).

Pope, Alexander, *The Poems of Alexander Pope*, ed. John Butt (Routledge, 1989).

Priestley, Joseph, *A Catechism for Children, and Young persons*, 5th edn (Birmingham, 1787).

——, 'The Importance of Free Enquiry in Matters of Religion', in *Sermons by Richard Price and Joseph Priestley* (1791).

——, *The Proper Objects of Education in the Present State of the World* (1791).

——, *Reflections on Death, A Sermon, on occasion of the death of the Rev. Robert Robinson* (London/Birmingham, 1790).

Pye, Henry, *The Democrat*, 2nd edn, Vol. I of *Anti-Jacobin Novels*, 10 vols, ed. W. M. Verhoeven (Pickering and Chatto, 2005).

Repton, Humphry, *Fragments on the Theory and Practice of Landscape Gardening* (1816).

Reynolds, Joshua, *The Letters of Sir Joshua Reynolds*, ed. John Ingamells and John Edgcumbe (New Haven: Yale University Press, 2000).

Richardson, Samuel, *Correspondence of Samuel Richardson*, ed. Anna Laetitia Barbauld (1804).

——, *The History of Sir Charles Grandison*, 3 vols, ed. Jocelyn Harris (Oxford: Oxford University Press, 1972).

——, *Selected Letters of Samuel Richardson*, ed. John Carroll (Oxford: Clarendon Press, 1964).

Roberts, William, *Memoirs of the Life and Correspondence of Mrs. Hannah More*, 2nd edn, 4 vols (1835).

Robinson, Henry Crabb, *Henry Crabb Robinson on Books and Their Writers*, ed. Edith Morley, 3 vols (J. M. Dent, 1938).

Rousseau, Jean Jacques, *A letter from M. Rousseau, of Geneva, to M. d'Alembert, of Paris, concerning the effects of theatrical entertainments on the manners of mankind* (1759).

Seward, Anna, *Letters of Anna Seward: written between 1784 and 1807*, 6 vols (Edinburgh, 1811).

Seward, William, *Anecdotes of some Distinguished Persons*, 4 vols (1795–6).

Sewell, Sir John, *Critique on the late French Revolution, in a speech delivered at the Society for Free Debate* (1793).

Shaftesbury, Lord, *Characteristics of Men, Manners, Opinions, Times*, ed. Lawrence E. Klein (Cambridge: Cambridge University Press, 1999).

Shelley, Percy Bysshe, *The Letters of Percy Bysshe Shelley*, ed. Frederick L. Jones, 2 vols (Oxford: Oxford University Press, 1964).

'Skarum, Harum', *Account of a Debate in Coachmaker's Hall* (1780).

Smellie, William, *Literary and Characteristical Lives of Gregory, Kames, Hume, and Smith* (Edinburgh, 1800).

Smith, Adam, *Lectures on Rhetoric and Belles Lettres*, ed. J. C. Bryce (Indianapolis: Liberty Fund, 1985).

——, *The Theory of Moral Sentiments*, ed. D. D. Raphael and A. L. Macfie (Indianapolis: The Liberty Fund, 1984).

Smith, Charlotte, *Desmond. A Novel*, 3 vols (1792).

Smollett, Tobias, *The Expedition of Humphry Clinker*, ed. Lewis M. Knapp, rev. Paul-Gabriel Boucé (Oxford: Oxford University Press, 1984).

Southey, Robert, *The Life and Correspondence of the Late Robert Southey*, ed. C. C. Southey, 6 vols (1849).

——, *New Letters of Robert Southey*, ed. Kenneth Curry, 2 vols (New York: Columbia University Press, 1965).

The Spectator, ed. Donald F. Bond, 5 vols (Oxford: Clarendon Press, 1987).

Sterne, Laurence, *The Life and Opinions of Tristram Shandy*, 9 vols (1760–7).

——, *A Sentimental Journey through France and Italy,* 2 vols (1768).

Swift, Jonathan, *A Proposal for Correcting the ENGLISH TONGUE, Polite Conversation etc.* in *Prose Writings of Jonathan Swift*, Vol. IV, ed. Herbert Davis with Louis Landa (Oxford: Basil Blackwell, 1957).

Talfourd, Thomas Noon, *Final Memorials of Charles Lamb*, 2 vols (1848).

The Tatler, ed. Donald F. Bond, 3 vols (Oxford: Clarendon Press, 1987).

Taylor, John, *Records of My Life*, 2 vols (1832).

Thelwall, Cecil, *The Life of John Thelwall by his Widow* (1837).

Thelwall, John, *Ode to science. Recited at the anniversary meeting of the Philomathian Society, June 20, 1791* (1791).

——, *The Peripatetic*, ed. Judith Thompson (Detroit: Wayne State University Press, 2001).

——, *Poems on Various Subjects* (1787).

——, *Poems written Chiefly in Retirement*, 2nd edn (Hereford, 1802).

——, *Political Lectures (No. 1) on the Moral Tendency of a System of Spies and Informers* (1794).

——, *The Tribune*, 3 vols (1795–6).

Ticknor, George, *Life, Letters, and Journals of George Ticknor*, 2 vols (1876).

Tucker, Abraham, *The Light of Nature Pursued*, 7 vols (1768–77).

Turner, David, *A Short History of the Westminster Forum…wherein the Nature of such Societies is Examined*, 2 vols (1781).

V. F., 'Historical Account of the Warrington Academy', *Monthly Repository of Theology and General Literature*, 8 (1813), 161–72.

Verax, *Remarks on the Journal of a Tour to the Hebrides* (1785).

Walpole, Horace, *The Yale Edition of Horace Walpole's Correspondence*, ed. W. S. Lewis, 48 vols (New Haven: Yale University Press, 1937–83).

Watts, Isaac, *The Improvement of the Mind: or, a Supplement to the Art of Logick* (1741).

Wilberforce, Robert and Samuel Wilberforce, *The Life of William Wilberforce*, 5 vols (1838).

——, *Ecclesiastical Characteristics: Or, The Arcana of the Church Policy. Being an Humble Attempt to Open up the Mystery of Moderation*, 5th edn (Edinburgh, 1763).

Witherspoon, John, *A Serious Apology for the Ecclesiastical Characteristics* (Edinburgh, 1763).

Wollstonecraft, Mary, *The Collected Letters of Mary Wollstonecraft*, ed. Janet Todd (Penguin, 2005).

——, *Letters written during a short residence in Sweden, Norway, and Denmark* (1796).

——, *A Vindication of the Rights of Men, in a Letter to the Right Honourable Edmund Burke*, 2nd edn (1790).

——, *A Vindication of the Rights of Woman with Strictures on Moral and Political Subjects* (1792).

Wood, James, 'An Essay on Conversation', *Wesleyan-Methodist Magazine*, 4 (1825), 820–3.

Wordsworth, William, *Lyrical Ballads, and Other Poems, 1797–1800*, ed. James Butler and Karen Green (Ithaca/London: Cornell University Press, 1992).

——, *The Poetical Works of William Wordsworth*, ed. Ernest de Selincourt, 5 vols (Oxford: Clarendon Press, 1940).

——, *The Prose Works of William Wordsworth*, ed. W. J. B. Owen and Jane Worthington Smyser, 3 vols (Oxford: Oxford University Press, 1974).

Young, William, *The Spirit of Athens, Being a Political and Philosophical Investigation of the History of that Republic* (1777).

SECONDARY SOURCES

Unpublished PhD theses
Fairclough, Mary, '"The Sympathy of Popular Opinion": Representations of the Crowd in Britain, 1770–1849', University of York, 2008.

Green, Georgina, '"The Majesty of the People" and Radical Writing of the 1790s', University of Oxford, 2009.

McElroy, D. D., 'The Literary Clubs and Societies of Eighteenth Century Scotland, and their Influence on the Literary Productions of the Period from 1700 to 1800', University of Edinburgh, 1952.

Wallbank, Adrian J., 'Political, Religious, and Philosophical Mentoring of the Romantic Period: The Dialogue Genre, 1782–1829', University of Warwick, 2009.

Printed Books
Place of publication is London unless stated otherwise.
Anderson, Benedict, *Imagined Communities: Reflections on the Origin and Spread of Nationalism*, rev. edn (Verso, 1991).

Andrew, Donna T., *London Debating Societies, 1776–1799* (London Record Society, 1994).

Bakhtin, M. M., *The Dialogic Imagination: Four Essays*, ed. Michael Holquist, trans. Caryl Emerson and Holquist (Austin: University of Texas Press, 1981).

Barker-Benfield, G. J., *The Culture of Sensibility: Sex and Society in Eighteenth-century Britain* (Chicago: University of Chicago Press, 1992).

Barrell, John, *The Birth of Pandora and the Division of Knowledge* (Macmillan, 1992).

——, *Imagining the King's Death: Figurative Treason, Fantasies of Regicide 1793–1796* (Oxford: Oxford University Press, 2000).

——, *The Spirit of Despotism: Invasions of Privacy in the 1790s* (Oxford: Oxford University Press, 2006).

Benchimol, Alex, and Willy Maley (eds), *Spheres of Influence: Intellectual and Cultural Publics from Shakespeare to Habermas* (Oxford: Peter Lang, 2007).

Benjamin, Walter, *Charles Baudelaire: A Lyric Poet in the Era of High Capitalism*, trans. Harry Zohn (New Left Books, 1973).

Black, Scott, *Of Essays and Reading in Early Modern Britain* (Basingstoke: Macmillan, 2006).

Blanchot, Maurice, *The Infinite Conversation*, trans. with foreword by Susan Hanson (Minneapolis: University of Minnesota Press, 1993).

Borsay, Peter, *The English Urban Renaissance: Culture and Society in the Provincial Town 1660–1770* (Oxford: Oxford University Press, 1989).

Brewer, John, *The Pleasures of the Imagination: English Culture in the Eighteenth Century* (Harper Collins, 1997).

Bromwich, David, *Disowned by Memory: Wordsworth's Poetry of the 1790s* (Chicago: University of Chicago Press, 1998).

——, *Hazlitt: The Mind of a Critic* (Oxford: Oxford University Press, 1983).

Bryson, Gladys, *Man and Society: The Scottish Inquiry of the Eighteenth Century* (Princeton: Princeton University Press, 1945).

Bullard, Rebecca, *The Politics of Disclosure, 1674–1725: Secret History Narratives* (Pickering and Chatto, 2009).

Burke, Peter, *The Art of Conversation* (Cambridge: Polity Press, 1993).

——, *Popular Culture in Early Modern Europe* (Temple Smith, 1978).

Butler, Marilyn, *Jane Austen and the War of Ideas*, 2nd edn (Oxford: Clarendon Press, 1987).

——, *Maria Edgeworth: A Literary Biography* (Oxford: Oxford University Press, 1972).

Carlson, Julie, *England's First Family of Writers: Mary Wollstonecraft, William Godwin, Mary Shelley* (Baltimore: Johns Hopkins University Press, 2007).

Cash, Arthur, *Laurence Sterne, the Later Years* (Methuen, 1986).

de Certeau, Michel, *The Capture of Speech and Other Political Writings* (Minneapolis: University of Minnesota Press, 1997).

——, *The Practice of Everyday Life*, trans. Steven Rendall (Berkeley: University of California Press, 1984).

Chakrabarty, Dipesh, *Provincializing Europe: Postcolonial Thought and Historical Difference* (Princeton/Oxford: Princeton University Press, 2000).

Chandler, James, *England in 1819* (Chicago: Chicago University Press, 1998).

——, *Wordsworth's Second Nature: A Study of the Poetry and the Politics* (Chicago: University of Chicago Press, 1984).

——, and Kevin Gilmartin (eds), *Romantic Metropolis: The Urban Scene of British Culture, 1780–1840* (Cambridge: Cambridge University Press, 2005).

Chartier, Roger, *The Cultural Origins of the French Revolution*, trans. Lydia G. Cochrane (Durham, NC: Duke University Press, 1991).

Chase, Malcolm, *The People's Farm: English Radical Agrarianism 1775–1840* (Oxford: Oxford University Press, 1988).

Clark, Gregory, *Dialogue, Dialectic, and Conversation: A Social Perspective on the Function of Writing* (Carbondale/Edwardsville: Southern Illinois University Press, 1990).

Clark, Peter, *British Clubs and Societies, 1580–1800: The Origins of an Associational World* (Oxford: Oxford University Press, 2000).

Clarke, Linda, *Building Capitalism: Historical Change and the Labour Process in the Production of the Built Environment* (Routledge, 1992).

Clayden, P. W., *The Early Life of Samuel Rogers* (1887).

Clery, E. J., *The Feminization Debate in Eighteenth-Century England: Literature, Commerce and Luxury* (Basingstoke: Palgrave Macmillan, 2004).

Clifford, James L., *Hester Lynch Piozzi (Mrs. Thrale)*, 2nd edn (Oxford: Clarendon Press, 1952).

Cohn, Dorrit, *Transparent Minds: Narrative Modes for Presenting Consciousness in Fiction* (Princeton: Princeton University Press, 1978).

Connell, Philip, and Nigel Leask (eds), *Romanticism and Popular Culture in Britain and Ireland* (Cambridge: Cambridge University Press, 2009).

Corfield, Penelope J., and Chris Evans (eds), *Youth and Revolution in the 1790s: Letters of William Pattison, Thomas Amyot and Henry Crabb Robinson* (Stroud: Allan Sutton, 1996).

Cox, Jeffrey N., *Poetry and Politics in the Cockney School: Keats, Shelley, Hunt and their Circle* (Oxford: Oxford University Press, 1998).

Cust, Lionel Henry, *The History of the Society of Dilettanti*, ed. Sidney Colvin (Society of Dilettanti, 1914).

Davidoff, Leonore, and Catherine Hall, *Family Fortunes: Men and Women of the English Middle Class, 1780–1850*, rev. edn (Chicago: University of Chicago Press 2002).

Davidson, Jenny, *Hypocrisy and the Politics of Politeness: Manners and Morals from Locke to Austen* (Cambridge: Cambridge University Press, 2004).

Deutsch, Helen, *Loving Dr. Johnson* (Chicago: University of Chicago Press, 2005).

Docherty, Thomas, *Criticism and Modernity: Aesthetics, Literature, and Nations in Europe and its Academies* (Oxford: Oxford University Press, 1999).

Doody, Margaret Anne, *Frances Burney: The Life in the Works* (Cambridge: Cambridge University Press, 1988).

Duncan, Ian, *Scott's Shadow: The Novel in Romantic Edinburgh* (Princeton: Princeton University Press, 2007).

Dwyer, John, *Virtuous Discourse: Sensibility and Community in Late Eighteenth-Century Scotland* (Edinburgh: Donald, 1987).

Eagleton, Terry, *The Function of Criticism from the Spectator to Post-Structuralism* (Verso, 1984).

——, *Trouble with Strangers: A Study of Ethics* (Chichester: Wiley-Blackwell, 2009).

Eger, Elizabeth, *Bluestockings: Women of Reason from Enlightenment to Romanticism* (Basingstoke: Palgrave Macmillan, 2010).

——, and Lucy Peltz, *Brilliant Women: 18th-century Bluestockings* (National Portrait Gallery, 2008).

Ellis, Markman, *The Coffee-House: A Cultural History* (Phoenix, 2005).

Engell, James (ed.), *The Age of Johnson* (Harvard, MA: Harvard University Press, 1984).

Epstein, James A., *Radical Expression: Political Language, Ritual, and Symbol in England, 1790–1850* (Oxford: Oxford University Press, 1994).

Fairer, David, *Organising Poetry: The Coleridge Circle, 1790–1798* (Oxford: Oxford University Press, 2009).

Field, Ophelia, *The Kit-Cat Club* (Harper Collins, 2008).

Gadamer, Hans-Georg, *Truth and Method*, 2nd edn, trans. rev. Joel Weinsheimer and Donald G. Marshall (Continuum, 2004).

Gates, Payson G., *William Hazlitt and Leigh Hunt: The Continuing Dialogue*, ed. Eleanor M. Gates (Essex, CT: Falls River, 2000).

Gigante, Denise, *Taste: A Literary History* (New Haven: Yale University Press, 2005).

Gilmartin, Kevin, *Print Politics: The Press and Radical Opposition in Early Nineteenth-Century England* (Cambridge: Cambridge University Press, 1996).

——, *Writing against Revolution: Literary Conservatism in Britain, 1790–1832* (Cambridge: Cambridge University Press, 2007).

Glen, Heather, *Vision and Disenchantment: Blake's Songs and Wordsworth's Lyrical Ballads* (Cambridge: Cambridge University Press, 1983).

——, and Paul Hamilton (eds), *Repossessing the Romantic Past* (Cambridge: Cambridge University Press, 2006).

Goodman, Kevis, *Georgic Modernity and British Romanticism: Poetry and the Mediation of History* (Cambridge: Cambridge University Press, 2004).

Goodwin, Albert, *The Friends of Liberty: The English Democratic Movement in the Age of the French Revolution* (Cambridge, MA: Harvard University Press, 1979).

Grundy, Isobel, *Samuel Johnson and the Scale of Greatness* (Leicester: Leicester University Press, 1986).

Guest, Harriet, *Small Change: Women, Learning, Patriotism, 1750–1810* (Chicago: University of Chicago Press, 2000).

Habermas, Jürgen, *On the Pragmatics of Communication*, ed. Maeve Cooke (Cambridge: Polity Press, 1999).

——, *The Structural Transformation of the Public Sphere: An Inquiry into a Category of Bourgeois Society*, trans. Thomas Burger with Frederick Lawrence (Cambridge, MA: MIT Press, 1989).

Hackwood, Frederick W., *William Hone: His Life and Times* (Fisher Unwin, 1912).

Haggarty, Sarah, and Jon Mee (eds), *Blake and Conflict* (Basingstoke: Palgrave Macmillan, 2009).

Halsey, Katie, and Jane Slinn (eds), *The Concept and Practice of Conversation in the Long Eighteenth Century, 1688–1848* (Cambridge: Cambridge Scholars Press, 2008).

Hammond, Brean, *Professional Imaginative Writing in England 1670–1740: 'Hackney for Bread'* (Oxford: Oxford University Press, 1997).

Harris, Jocelyn, *Jane Austen's Art of Memory* (Cambridge, Cambridge University Press, 1989).

Henderson, Andrea K., *Romanticism and the Painful Pleasures of Modern Life* (Cambridge: Cambridge University Press, 2008).

Hitchcock, Tim, and Michèle Cohen (eds), *English Masculinities 1660–1800* (Longman, 1999).

Hofkosh, Sonia, *Sexual Politics and the Romantic Author* (Cambridge: Cambridge University Press, 1998).

Holmes, Richard, *Coleridge: Early Visions* (Hodder and Stoughton, 1989).

House, Humphrey, *Coleridge* (Rupert Hart-Davis, 1962).

Hughes-Hallett, Penelope, *The Immortal Dinner: A Famous Evening of Genius and Laughter in Literary London, 1817* (Viking, 2000).

Hyde, Mary, *The Impossible Friendship: Boswell and Mrs. Thrale* (Chatto and Windus, 1973).

Jacobus, Mary, *Romanticism, Writing, and Sexual Difference: Essays on the Prelude* (Oxford: Oxford University Press, 1989).

James, Felicity, *Charles Lamb, Coleridge and Wordsworth: Reading Friendship in the 1790s* (Basingstoke: Palgrave Macmillan, 2008).

Jewson, C. B., *The Jacobin City: A Portrait of Norwich in its Reaction to the French Revolution 1788–1802* (Glasgow: Blackie, 1975).

Johnson, Claudia, and Clara Tuite (eds), *A Companion to Jane Austen* (Chichester: Wiley-Blackwell, 2009).

Jones, Stanley, *Hazlitt: A Life: From Winterslow to Frith Stree*t (Oxford: Clarendon Press, 1989).

Kelly, Jason M., *The Society of Dilettanti: Archaeology and Identity in the British Enlightenment* (New Haven: Yale University Press, 2009).

Kinnaird, John, *William Hazlitt: Critic of Power* (New York: Columbia University Press, 1978).

Klancher, Jon P., *The Making of English Reading Audiences, 1790–1832* (Madison: University of Wisconsin Press, 1987).

Klein, Lawrence E., *Shaftesbury and the Culture of Politeness: Moral Discourse and Cultural Politics in Early Eighteenth-Century England* (Cambridge: Cambridge University Press, 1994).

Knott, Sarah, and Barbara Taylor (eds), *Women, Gender and Enlightenment: A Comparative History* (Basingstoke: Palgrave Macmillan, 2005).

Kucich, Greg, *Keats, Shelley, and Romantic Spenserianism* (University Park, PA: Penn. State University Press, 1991).

Langford, Paul, *A Polite and Commercial People: England 1727–1783* (Oxford: Oxford University Press, 1992).

Le Breton, Anna Letitia, *Memoir of Mrs. Barbauld* (1874).

Le Doueff, Michèle, *The Sex of Knowing*, trans. Kathryn Hamer and Lorraine Code (Routledge, 2003).

Leask, Nigel, *Curiosity and the Aesthetics of Travel Writing 1770–1840* (Oxford: Oxford University Press, 2002).

Leslie, Charles, and Tom Taylor, *The Life and Times of Sir Joshua Reynolds*, 2 vols (1865).

Levere, T. H., and G. L'Estrange Turner (eds), *Discussing Chemistry and Steam: The Minutes of a Coffee House Philosophical Society 1780–1787* (Oxford: Oxford University Press, 2002).

Lowes, John Livingston, *The Road to Xanadu: A Study in the Ways of the Imagination*, 2nd edn (Constable, 1951).

McCalman, Iain, *Radical Underworld: Prophets, Revolutionaries, and Pornographers in London, 1795–1840* (Cambridge: Cambridge University Press, 1988).

McIntosh, John R., *Church and Theology in Enlightenment Scotland: The Popular Party, 1740–1800* (East Linton: Tuckwell, 1998).

MacIntyre, Alasdair, *After Virtue: A Study in Moral Theory*, 3rd edn (Duckworth, 2007).

——, *Three Rival Versions of Moral Enquiry: Encyclopaedia, Genealogy, and Tradition* (Duckworth, 1990).

MacLean, Catherine M., *Born Under Saturn: A Biography of William Hazlitt* (Collins, 1943).

McVeigh, Simon, *Concert Life from Mozart to Haydn* (Cambridge: Cambridge University Press, 1989).

Major, Emma, *Madam Britannia: Women, Church, and Nation, 1712–1812* (Cambridge: Cambridge University Press, forthcoming).

Manaquis, Robert, and Victoria Myers (eds), *Godwinian Moments: From the Enlightenment to Romanticism (Toronto: Toronto University Press, forthcoming)*.

Mee, Jon, *Romanticism, Enthusiasm, and Regulation: Poetics and the Policing of Culture in the Romantic Period* (Oxford: Oxford University Press, 2003).

Miller, Stephen, *Conversation: A History of a Declining Art* (New Haven: Yale University Press, 2006).

Miller, Thomas P., *The Formation of College English: Rhetoric and Belles Lettres in the British Cultural Provinces* (Pittsburgh: University of Pittsburgh Press, 1997).

Mole, Tom, *Byron's Romantic Celebrity: Industrial Culture and the Hermeneutic of Intimacy* (Basingstoke: Palgrave Macmillan, 2007).

—— (ed.), *Romanticism and Celebrity Culture, 1750–1850* (Cambridge: Cambridge University Press, 2009).

Morton, Timothy, and Nigel Smith (eds), *Radicalism in British Literary Culture, 1650–1830* (Cambridge: Cambridge University Press, 2002).

Mossner, Ernest, *The Life of David Hume*, 2nd edn (Oxford: Oxford University Press, 1980).

Nancy, Jean-Luc, *The Inoperative Community*, ed. Peter Connor, trans. Connor, Lisa Garbus, Michael Holland, and Simona Sawhney (Minneapolis: University of Minnesota Press, 1991).

Nangle, Benjamin C., *The Monthly Review Second Series 1790–1815: Indexes of Contributors and Articles* (Oxford: Clarendon Press, 1955).

Newlyn, Lucy, *Coleridge, Wordsworth, and the Language of Allusion* (Oxford: Oxford University Press, 1986).

Nussbaum, Felicity A., *The Autobiographical Subject: Gender and Ideology in Eighteenth-Century England* (Baltimore: Johns Hopkins University Press, 1989).

——, *The Limits of the Human: Fictions of Anomaly, Race, and Gender in the Long Eighteenth Century* (Cambridge: Cambridge University Press, 2003).

Parker, Mark, *Literary Magazines and British Romanticism* (Cambridge: Cambridge University Press, 2000).

Paulson, Ronald, *Emblem and Expression: Meaning in English Art of the Eighteenth Century* (Thames and Hudson, 1975).

Peters, John Durham, *Speaking into the Air: A History of the Idea of Communication* (Chicago: University of Chicago Press, 2000).

Philp, Mark, *Godwin's Political Justice* (Duckworth, 1986).

Poole, Steve (ed.), *John Thelwall: Radical Romantic and Acquitted Felon* (Pickering and Chatto, 2009).

Postle, Martin et al., *Joshua Reynolds: The Creation of Celebrity* (Tate, 2005).

Potkay, Adam, *The Fate of Eloquence in the Age of Hume* (Ithaca: Cornell University Press, 1994).

Praz, Mario, *Conversation Pieces: A Survey of the Informal Group Portrait in Europe and America* (University Park, PA: Penn. State University Press, 1971).

Prince, Michael, *Philosophical Dialogue in the British Enlightenment: Theology, Aesthetics and the Novel* (Cambridge: Cambridge University Press, 1996).

Procter, B. W., *Autobiographical Fragment and Biographical Notes* (1877).

Rajan, Tilottama, *The Supplement of Reading: Figures of Understanding in Romantic Theory and Practice* (Ithaca: Cornell University Press, 1990).

Rancière, Jacques, *Dissensus: On Politics and Aesthetics*, ed. and trans. Steven Corcoran (Continuum, 2010).

Raven, James, *The Business of Books: Booksellers and the English Book Trade 1450–1850* (New Haven: Yale University Press, 2007).

Redford, Bruce, *Dilettanti: The Antic and the Antique in Eighteenth-century England* (Los Angeles: J. Paul Getty Museum, 2008).

Retford, Kate, *The Art of Domestic Life: Family Portraiture in Eighteenth-century England* (New Haven: Yale University Press, 2006).

Rivers, Isabel, *Reason, Grace and Sentiment: A Study of the Language of Religion and Ethics in England, 1660–1780*, 2 vols (Cambridge: Cambridge University Press, 1991–2000).

Rodgers, Betsy, *Georgian Chronicle: Mrs Barbauld and Her Family* (Methuen, 1958).

Roe, Nicholas, *Fiery Heart: The First Life of Leigh Hunt* (Pimlico, 2005).

——, *The Politics of Nature*, 2nd edn (Basingstoke: Palgrave Macmillan, 2002).

——, *Wordsworth and Coleridge: The Radical Years* (Oxford: Oxford University Press, 1988).

Rorty, Richard, *Philosophy and the Mirror of Nature* (Princeton: Princeton University Press, 1979).

Russell, Gillian, *The Theatres of War: Performance, Politics and Society 1793–1815* (Oxford: Clarendon Press, 1995).

——, *Women, Sociability, and Theatre in Georgian London* (Cambridge: Cambridge University Press, 2007).

——, and Clara Tuite (eds), *Romantic Sociability: Social Networks and Literary Culture in Britain, 1770–1849* (Cambridge: Cambridge University Press, 2002).

St. Clair, William, *The Godwins and the Shelleys* (Faber, 1989).

——, *The Reading Nation in the Romantic Period* (Cambridge: Cambridge University Press, 2004).

Schellenberg, Betty A., *The Conversational Circle: Rereading the English Novel, 1740–1775* (Lexington: University of Kentucky Press, 1996).

Schoenfield, Mark, *British Periodicals and Romantic Identity: The 'Literary Lower Empire'* (Basingstoke: Palgrave Macmillan, 2009).

Sennett, Richard, *Flesh and Stone: The Body and the City in Western Civilization* (New York: Norton, 1994).

Sher, Richard B., *Church and University in the Scottish Enlightenment: The Moderate Literati of Edinburgh* (Princeton: Princeton University Press, 1985).

——, *The Enlightenment and the Book: Scottish Authors and Their Publishers in Eighteenth-Century Britain, Ireland, and America* (Chicago: University of Chicago Press, 2006).

Shields, Carol, *Jane Austen* (Weidenfeld and Nicolson, 2001).

Simpson, David, *The Academic Postmodern and the Rule of Literature: A Report on Half-Knowledge* (Chicago: University of Chicago Press, 1995).

Siskin, Clifford, *The Work of Writing: Literature and Social Change in Britain 1700–1830* (Baltimore: Johns Hopkins University Press, 1998).

Solkin, David H, *Painting for Money: The Visual Arts and the Public Sphere in Eighteenth-Century England* (New Haven: Yale University Press, 1993).

——, (ed.), *Art on the Line: The Royal Academy Exhibitions at Somerset House 1780–1836* (New Haven: Yale University Press, 2001).

Stott, Anne, *Hannah More: The First Victorian* (Oxford: Oxford University Press, 2003).

Sunderland, John, *John Hamilton Mortimer: His Life and Works* (Walpole Society, 1988),

Sutherland, Kathryn, *Jane Austen's Textual Lives: From Aeschylus to Bollywood* (Oxford: Oxford University Press, 2005).

Tandon, Bharat, *Jane Austen and the Morality of Conversation* (New York: Anthem Press, 2003).

Thompson, E. P., *The Making of the English Working Class*, rev. edn (Harmondsworth: Penguin, 1980).

Todd, Janet, *The Cambridge Introduction to Jane Austen* (Cambridge: Cambridge University Press, 2006).

Tuite, Clara, *Romantic Austen: Sexual Politics and the Literary Canon* (Cambridge: Cambridge University Press, 2002).

Uglow, Jenny, *The Lunar Men: The Friends Who Made the Future* (Faber, 2003).

Valenza, Robin, *Literature, Language, and the Rise of the Intellectual Disciplines in Britain, 1680–1820* (Cambridge: Cambridge University Press, 2009).

Wahrman, Dror, *Imagining the Middle Class: the Political Representation of Class in Britain, c. 1780–1840* (Cambridge: Cambridge University Press, 1995).

Waldron, Mary, *Jane Austen and the Fiction of her Time* (Cambridge: Cambridge University Press, 1999).

Walker, Gina Luria, *Mary Hays (1759–1843): The Growth of a Woman's Mind* (Aldershot: Ashgate, 2006).

Watson, Nicola, *Revolution and the Form of the British Novel 1790–1825: Intercepted Letters, Interrupted Seductions* (Oxford: Oxford University Press, 1994).

Werkmeister, Lucyle, *Jemmie Boswell and the London Daily Press, 1785–1795* (New York: New York Public Library, 1963).

Wheatley, Kim (ed.), *Romantic Periodicals and Print Culture* (Frank Cass, 2003).

White, Daniel E., *Early Romanticism and Religious Dissent* (Cambridge: Cambridge University Press, 2006).

Williams, Raymond, *Culture and Society 1780–1950* (Harmondsworth: Penguin, 1961).

——, *Keywords: A Vocabulary of Culture and Society*, rev. edn (Fontana, 1983).

Worrall, David, *Radical Culture: Discourse, Resistance, and Surveillance, 1790–1820* (Detroit: Wayne State University Press, 1992).

Wu, Duncan, *William Hazlitt: The First Modern Man* (Oxford: Oxford University Press, 2008).

——, *Wordsworth's Reading 1770–1799* (Cambridge: Cambridge University Press, 1993).

Zeldin, Theodore, *Conversation: How Talk can Change your Life* (Harvill Press, 1998).

Essays and book chapters

Adorno, Theodor W., 'The Essay as Form', in *Notes to Literature, Volume One*, ed. Rolf Tiedemann, trans. Shierry Weber Nicholsen (New York: Columbia University Press, 1991).

Alderson, Simon, 'The Augustan Attack on the Pun', *Eighteenth-Century Life*, 20 (1996), 1–19.

Andrew, Donna, 'Popular Culture and Public Debate: London 1780', *Historical Journal*, 39 (1996), 405–23.

Barnard, John, 'First Fruits or "First Blights": A New Account of the Publishing History of Keats's *Poems* (1817)', *Romanticism*, 12 (2006), 71–101.

——, 'Charles Cowden Clarke and the Leigh Hunt Circle 1812–1818', *Romanticism*, 3 (1997), 66–90.

Benchimol, Alex, 'Cultural Historiography and the Scottish Enlightenment public sphere', in Alex Benchimol and Willy Maley (eds), *Spheres of Influence: Intellectual and Cultural Publics from Shakespeare to Habermas* (Oxford: Peter Lang, 2007), 105–50.

Bonnell, Thomas F., 'When Book History Neglects Bibliography: Trouble with the "Old Canon" in *The Reading Nation*', *Studies in Bibliography*, 57 (2005–6), 243–61.

Borsay, Peter, 'The Rise of the Promenade: the Social and Cultural Use of Space in the English Provincial Town *c.*1660–1800', *British Journal of Eighteenth-Century Studies*, 9 (1986), 125–40.

Carnochan, W. B., 'Gibbon's Silences', in James Engell (ed.), *The Age of Johnson* (Harvard, MA: Harvard University Press, 1984), 367–85.

Carter, Philip, 'James Boswell's Manliness', in Tim Hitchcock and Michèle Cohen (eds), *English Masculinities 1660–1800* (Longman, 1999), 111–30.

Chandler, James, 'The Languages of Sentiment', *Textual Practice*, 22 (2008), 21–39.

——, 'Why We Need Irish Studies', *Field Day Review*, 2 (2006), 18–39.

Claeys, Gregory, 'The Divine Creature and the Female Citizen: Manners, Religion, and the Two Rights Strategies in Mary Wollstonecraft's *Vindications*', in Glenn Burgess and Matthew Festenstein (eds), *English Radicalism, 1550–1850* (Cambridge: Cambridge University Press, 2007), 115–34.

Clemit, Pamela, 'Godwin, Women, and "The Collision of Mind with Mind" ', *Wordsworth Circle*, 35 (2004), 72–6.

Clubb, John, '*Glenarvon* Revised—and Revisited', *Wordsworth Circle* (1979), 205–17.

Cohen, Michèle, 'Manliness, Effeminacy and the French: Gender and the Construction of National Character in Eighteenth-century England', in Tim Hitchcock and Michèle Cohen (eds), *English Masculinities 1660–1800* (Longman, 1999), 44–61.

Colclough, Stephen, 'Recovering the Reader: Commonplace Books and Diaries as Sources of Reading Experience', *Publishing History*, 44 (1998), 5–37.

Coleman, Deirdre, 'Firebrands, Letters, and Flowers: Mrs. Barbauld and the Priestleys', in Gillian Russell and Clara Tuite (eds), *Romantic Sociability: Social Networks and Literary Culture in Britain, 1770–1849* (Cambridge: Cambridge University Press, 2002), 82–103.

Connell, Phillip, and Nigel Leask, 'What is the People?', in Phillip Connell and Nigel Leask (eds), *Romanticism and Popular Culture in Britain and Ireland* (Cambridge: Cambridge University Press, 2009), 3–48.

Cook, Jon, 'Hazlitt, Speech, and Writing', in Kate Campbell (ed.), *Journalism, Literature and Modernity: From Hazlitt to Modernism* (Edinburgh: Edinburgh University Press, 2000), 15–37.

Copley, Stephen, 'Commerce, Conversation and Politeness in the Early Eighteenth-Century Periodical', *British Journal for Eighteenth-Century Studies*, 18 (1995), 63–77.

Cowan, Brian, 'Mr Spectator and the Coffee House Public Sphere', *Eighteenth-Century Studies*, 37 (2004), 345–66.

Craciun, Adriana, 'Mary Robinson, the *Monthly Magazine*, and the Free Press', in Kim Wheatley (ed.), *Romantic Periodicals and Print Culture* (Frank Cass, 2003), 19–40.

Crane, Verner W., 'The Club of Honest Whigs: Friends of Science and Liberty', *William and Mary Quarterly*, 23 (1966), 210–33.

Dart, Gregory, 'Romantic Cockneyism: Hazlitt and the Periodical Press', *Romanticism*, 6 (2000), 143–62.

Ditchfield, G. M., 'Dr. Johnson and the Dissenters', *Journal of the John Rylands Library*, 68 (1986), 373–409.

Dwyer, John, '"A Peculiar Blessing": Social Converse in Scotland from Hutcheson to Burns', in John Dwyer and Richard Sher (eds), *Sociability and Society in Eighteenth-Century Edinburgh* (Edinburgh: Mercat Press, 1993), 1–22.

Eger, Elizabeth, '"The Noblest Commerce of Mankind": Conversation and Community in the Bluestocking Circle', in Sarah Knott and Barbara Taylor (eds), *Women, Gender and Enlightenment: A Comparative History* (Basingstoke: Palgrave Macmillan, 2005), 288–305.

Eley, Geoff, 'Nations, Publics, and Political Cultures: Placing Habermas in the Nineteenth Century', in Craig Calhoun (ed.), *Habermas and the Public Sphere* (Cambridge, MA: MIT Press, 1996), 289–339.

Ellison, Julie, 'News, Blues, and Cowper's Busy World', *Modern Language Quarterly*, 62 (2001), 219–37.

Emerson, Roger L., 'The Social Composition of Enlightened Scotland: The Select Society of Edinburgh, 1754–1764', *Studies on Voltaire and the Eighteenth Century*, 64 (1973), 291–329.

Epstein, James A., '"Equality and No King": Sociability and Sedition—The Case of John Frost', in Gillian Russell and Clara Tuite (eds), *Romantic Sociability: Social Networks and Literary Culture in Britain, 1770–1849* (Cambridge: Cambridge University Press, 2002), 43–61.

Fawcett, Trevor, 'Self-Improvement Societies: The Early "Lit. and Phils.",' in *Life in the Georgian Town: Papers given at the Georgian Group Symposium* (Georgian Group, 1985), 15–25.

Fay, Elizabeth, 'Portrait Galleries, Representative History, and Hazlitt's *Spirit of the Age*', *Nineteenth-Century Contexts*, 24 (2002), 151–75.

Fieser, James, 'The Eighteenth-Century British Reviews of Hume's Writing', *Journal of the History of Ideas*, 57 (1996), 645–57.

Finch, Casey, and Peter Bowen, '"The Tittle-Tattle of Highbury": Gossip and the Free Indirect Style in *Emma*', *Representations*, 31 (1990), 1–18.

Forman-Barzilai, Fonna, 'Sympathy in Space(s): Adam Smith on Proximity', *Political Theory* 33 (2) (2005), 189–217.

Fraser, Nancy, 'Politics, Culture, and the Public Sphere: Towards a Postmodern Conception', in Linda Nicholson and Steven Seidman (eds), *Social Postmodernism: Beyond Identity Politics* (Cambridge: Cambridge University Press, 1995), 287–312.

Gibbs, Warren E., 'An Unpublished Letter from John Thelwall to S. T. Coleridge', *Modern Language Review*, 25 (1930), 85–90.

Gilmartin, Kevin, 'Hazlitt's Visionary London', in Heather Glen and Paul Hamilton (eds), *Repossessing the Romantic Past* (Cambridge: Cambridge University Press, 2006), 40–62.

——, 'The "Sinking Down" of Jacobinism and the Rise of the Counter-revolutionary Man of Letters', in Phillip Connell and Nigel Leask (eds),

Romanticism and Popular Culture in Britain and Ireland (Cambridge: Cambridge University Press, 2009), 128–47.

Gilson D. J., 'Jane Austen's Books', *The Book Collector*, 23 (1974), 27–39.

Gleadle, Kathryn, '"Opinions Deliver'd in Conversation": Conversation, Politics, and Gender in the Late Eighteenth Century', in Josie Harris (ed.), *Civil Society in British History: Ideas, Identities, Institutions* (Oxford: Oxford University Press, 2003), 61–78.

Grice, H. P., 'Logic and Conversation', in Peter Cole and Jerry L. Morgan (eds), *Syntax and Semantics*, Vol. 3: *Speech Acts* (New York: Academic Press, 1975), 41–58.

Guest, Harriet, 'Bluestocking Feminism', *Huntington Library Quarterly*, 65 (2002), 59–80.

Harling, Phillip, 'William Hazlitt and Radical Journalism', *Romanticism*, 3 (1997), 53–65.

Hemlow, Joyce, 'Burney and the Courtesy Books', *PMLA*, 65 (1950), 732–61.

Hunter, J. Paul, 'Couplets and Conversation', in John Sitter (ed.), *The Cambridge Companion to Eighteenth-Century Poetry* (Cambridge: Cambridge University Press, 2001), 11–35.

Janowitz, Anne, 'Amiable and Radical Sociability: Anna Barbauld's "Free Familiar Conversation"', in Gillian Russell and Clara Tuite (eds), *Romantic Sociability: Social Networks and Literary Culture in Britain, 1770–1849* (Cambridge: Cambridge University Press, 2002), 62–81.

Jordan, Nicolle, 'The Promise and Frustration of Plebeian Public Opinion in *Caleb Williams*', *Eighteenth-Century Fiction*, 19 (2007), 243–66.

Klancher, Jon, 'Discriminations, or Romantic Cosmopolitanisms in London', in James Chandler and Kevin Gilmartin (eds), *Romantic Metropolis: The Urban Scene of British Culture, 1780–1840* (Cambridge: Cambridge University Press, 2005), 65–82.

Klein, Lawrence E., 'The Figure of France: The Politics of Sociability in England, 1660–1715', *Yale French Studies*, 92 (1997), 30–45.

——, 'Politeness and the Interpretation of the British Eighteenth Century', *Historical Journal*, 45 (4) (2002), 869–98.

——, 'Politeness for Plebes: Consumption and Social Identity in Early Eighteenth-Century England', in Ann Bermingham and John Brewer (eds), *The Consumption of Culture 1600–1800: Image, Object, Text* (Routledge, 1995), 362–82.

Kucich, Greg, '"The Wit in the Dungeon": Leigh Hunt and the Insolent Politics of Cockney Coteries', *Romanticism on the Net*, 14 (May 1999).

Kurzer, Frederick, 'A History of the Surrey Institution', *Annals of Science*, 57 (2000), 109–41.

Lau, Beth, 'William Godwin and the Joseph Johnson Circle: The Evidence of the Diaries', *Wordsworth Circle*, 33 (3) (2002), 104–8.

Leaver, Kristen, 'Pursuing Conversations: *Caleb Williams* and the Romantic Construction of the Reader', *Studies in Romanticism*, 33 (1994), 589–610.

Leland, Warren E., 'Turning Reality Round Together: Guides to Conversation in Eighteenth-Century England,' *Eighteenth-Century Life*, 8 (1983), 65–87.

Levinas, Emmanuel, 'The Other in Proust' (1947), in *The Levinas Reader*, ed. Séan Hand (Oxford: Blackwell, 1989), 161–5.

Levy, Michelle, 'The Radical Education of *Evenings at Home*', *Eighteenth-Century Fiction*, 19 (2006), 123–50.

Liddel, Peter, 'William Young and the *Spirit of Athens*', in James Moore et al. (eds), *Reinventing History: The Enlightenment Origins of Ancient History* (School of Advanced Study, University of London, 2003), 57–85.

McCalman, Iain, 'Newgate in Revolution: Radical Enthusiasm and Romantic Counterculture,' *Eighteenth Century Life*, 22 (1998), 95–110.

Major, Emma, 'The Politics of Sociability: Public Dimensions of the Bluestocking Millennium', in *Huntington Library Quarterly*, 65 (2002), 175–92.

Manning, Peter J., 'Manufacturing the Romantic Image: Hazlitt and Coleridge Lecturing', in James Chandler and Kevin Gilmartin (eds), *Romantic Metropolis: The Urban Scene of British Culture, 1780–1840* (Cambridge: Cambridge University Press, 2005), 227–45.

Marshall, David, 'Adam Smith and the Theatricality of Moral Sentiments', *Critical Inquiry*, 10 (1984), 592–613.

Matheson, C. S., '"A Shilling Well Laid Out": The Royal Academy's Early Public', in David H. Solkin (ed.), *Art on the Line: The Royal Academy Exhibitions at Somerset House 1780–1836* (New Haven: Yale University Press, 2001), 39–53.

Mee, Jon, '"The Press and Danger of the Crowd": Godwin, Thelwall, and the Counter-Public Sphere', in Robert Manaquis and Victoria Myers (eds), *The Godwinian Moments: From the Enlightenment to Romanticism* (Toronto: Toronto University Press, 2011), 83–102.

——, 'Morals, Manners, and Liberty: British Radicals and Perceptions of America in the 1790s', in Ella Dzelzainis and Ruth Livesey (eds), *The American Experiment and the Idea of Democracy in British Culture, 1776–1914* (Aldershot: Ashgate, 2011, forthcoming).

Money, John, 'The Masonic Moment: Or, Ritual, Replica, and Credit: John Wilkes, the Macaroni Parson, and the Making of the Middle-Class Mind', *Journal of British Studies* 32, (1993), 358–95.

Musser, Joseph F. Jr., 'William Cowper's Rhetoric: The Picturesque and the Personal', *Studies in English Literature*, 19 (1979), 515–31.

Myers, Victoria, 'William Godwin and the *Ars Rhetorica*', *Studies in Romanticism*, 41 (2002), 415–44.

Natarajan, Uttara, 'The Circle of Sympathy: Shelley's Hazlitt', in Uttara Natarajan et al. (eds), *Metaphysical Hazlitt: Bicentenary Essays* (Routledge, 2005), 112–22.

Nussbaum, Felicity A., 'Boswell's Treatment of Johnson's Temper: "A Warm West-Indian Climate"', *Studies in English Literature, 1500–1900*, 14 (1974), 421–33.

Oakeshott, Michael, 'The Voice of Poetry in the Conversation of Mankind', in *Rationalism in Politics and Other Essays* (Methuen, 1962), 197–247.

O'Shaughnessy, David, '*Caleb Williams* and the Philomaths: recalibrating political justice for the nineteenth century', *Nineteenth-Century Literature* (forthcoming).

Panagia, David, 'The Force of Political Argument', *Political Theory*, 32 (2004), 825–48.

Perry, Seamus, 'The Talker', in Lucy Newlyn (ed.), *The Cambridge Companion to Coleridge* (Cambridge: Cambridge University Press, 2002), 103–25.

Phillipson, Nicholas, 'Politics, Politeness and the Anglicisation of Early Eighteenth-Century Scottish Culture', in Roger A. Mason (ed.), *Scotland and England 1286–1815* (Edinburgh: John Donald, 1987), 226–46.

Remer, Gary, 'Political Oratory and Conversation: Cicero versus Deliberative Democracy', *Political Theory*, 27 (1999), 39–64.

Rumbold, Valerie, 'Locating Swift's Parody: The Title of *Polite Conversation*', in H. J. Real (ed.), *Reading Swift: Papers from the Fifth Münster Symposium on Jonathan Swift* (München: Wilhelm Fink, 2008), 255–72.

Russell, Gillian, 'Keats, Popular Culture, and the Sociability of Theatre', in Phillip Connell and Nigel Leask (eds), *Romanticism and Popular Culture in Britain and Ireland* (Cambridge: Cambridge University Press, 2009), 194–213.

——, 'Spouters or Washerwomen: The Sociability of Romantic Lecturing', in Gillian Russell and Clara Tuite (eds), *Romantic Sociability: Social Networks and Literary Culture in Britain, 1770–1849* (Cambridge: Cambridge University Press, 2002), 123–44.

——, and Clara Tuite, 'Introducing Romantic Sociability', in Gillian Russell and Clara Tuite (eds), *Romantic Sociability: Social Networks and Literary Culture in Britain, 1770–1849* (Cambridge: Cambridge University Press, 2002), 1–23.

Secord, James, 'How Scientific Conversation became Shop Talk', in Aileen Fyfe and Barnard Lightman (eds), *Science in the Marketplace: Nineteenth-Century Sites and Experiences* (Chiacgo: University of Chicago Press, 2007), 23–59.

Shapin, Steven, 'Property, Patronage, and the Politics of Science: The Founding of the Royal Society of Edinburgh', *British Journal of the History of Science*, 7 (1974), 1–41.

Sherbo, Arthur, 'Cowper's *Connoisseur* Essays', *Modern Language Notes*, 70 (1955), 340–2.

Simpson, David, 'Public Virtues, Private Vices: Reading between the Lines of Wordsworth's "Anecdote for Fathers"', in David Simpson (ed.), *Subject to History: Ideology, Class, Gender* (Ithaca: Cornell University Press, 1991), 163–90.

Solkin, David H., '"This Great Mart of Genius": The Royal Academy Exhibitions at Somerset House, 1780–1836', in David H. Solkin (ed.), *Art on the Line: The Royal Academy Exhibitions at Somerset House 1780–1836* (New Haven: Yale University Press, 2001), 1–8.

Solomonescu, Yasmin, 'Articulations of Community in *The Peripatetic*', in Steve Poole (ed.), *John Thelwall: Radical Romantic and Acquitted Felon* (Pickering and Chatto, 2009), 83–94.

Spencer, Jane, 'Narrative Technique: Austen and Her Contemporaries', in Claudia Johnson and Clara Tuite (eds), *A Companion to Jane Austen* (Chichester: Wiley-Blackwell, 2009), 185–94.

Struever, Nancy, 'The Conversable World: Eighteenth-Century Transformations of the Relation of Rhetoric and Truth', in Brian Vickers and Nancy Struever, *Rhetoric and the Pursuit of Truth: Language Change in the Seventeenth and Eighteenth Centuries* (Los Angeles: William Andrews Clark Memorial Library, 1986), 79–119.

Suarez, Michael F., S. J., 'Towards a Bibliometric Analysis of the Surviving Record, 1701–1800', in Michael Suarez and Michael L. Turner (eds), *The Cambridge History of the Book*, Vol. V: *1695–1830* (Cambridge: Cambridge University Press, 2009).

Thale, Mary, 'London Debating Societies in the 1790s', *Historical Journal*, 32 (1989), 57–86.

——, 'Women in London Debating Societies in 1780', *Gender and History*, 7 (1995), 5–24.

Thompson, Judith, '"An Autumnal Blast, a Killing Frost": Coleridge's Poetic Conversation with John Thelwall', *Studies in Romanticism*, 36 (1997), 427–56.

——, 'From Forum to Repository: A Case Study in Romantic Cultural Geography', *European Romantic Review*, 15 (2004), 177–91.

Throsby, Corin, 'Byron, Commonplacing and Early Fan Culture', in Tom Mole (ed.), *Romanticism and Celebrity Culture, 1750–1850* (Cambridge: Cambridge University Press, 2009), 227–44.

——, 'Flirting with Fame: Byron's Anonymous Female Fans', *Byron Journal*, 32 (2004), 115–23.

Towsey, Mark R. M., '"Patron of Infidelity": Scottish Readers Respond to David Hume c. 1750–c.1820', *Book History*, 11 (2008), 89–123.

Turnbull, Paul, 'Gibbon's Exchange with Joseph Priestley', *Journal for Eighteenth-Century Studies*, 14 (1991), 139–58.

Wagner, Corinna, 'Domestic Invasions: John Thelwall and the Exploitation of Privacy', in Steve Poole (ed.), *John Thelwall: Radical Romantic and Acquitted Felon* (Pickering and Chatto, 2009), 95–106.

Walker, Gina Luria, 'Mary Hays (1759–1843): An Enlightened Quest', in Sarah Knott and Barbara Taylor (eds), *Women, Gender and Enlightenment: A Comparative History* (Basingstoke: Palgrave Macmillan, 2005), 493–518.

Walters, Alice N., 'Conversation Pieces: Science and Politeness in Eighteenth-Century England', *History of Science*, 35 (1997), 121–54.

West, Shearer, 'Libertinism and the Ideology of Male Friendship in the Portraits of the Society of Dilettanti', *Eighteenth-century Life*, 16 (1992), 76–104.

Weston, Rowland, 'Politics, Passion and the "Puritan Temper": Godwin's Critique of Enlightened Modernity', *Studies in Romanticism*, 41 (2002), 445–71.

Whelan, Tim, '"For the Hand of a Woman, has Levell'd the Blow": Maria de Fleury's Pamphlet War with William Huntington, 1787–1791', *Women's Studies*, 36 (2007), 431–54.

Index